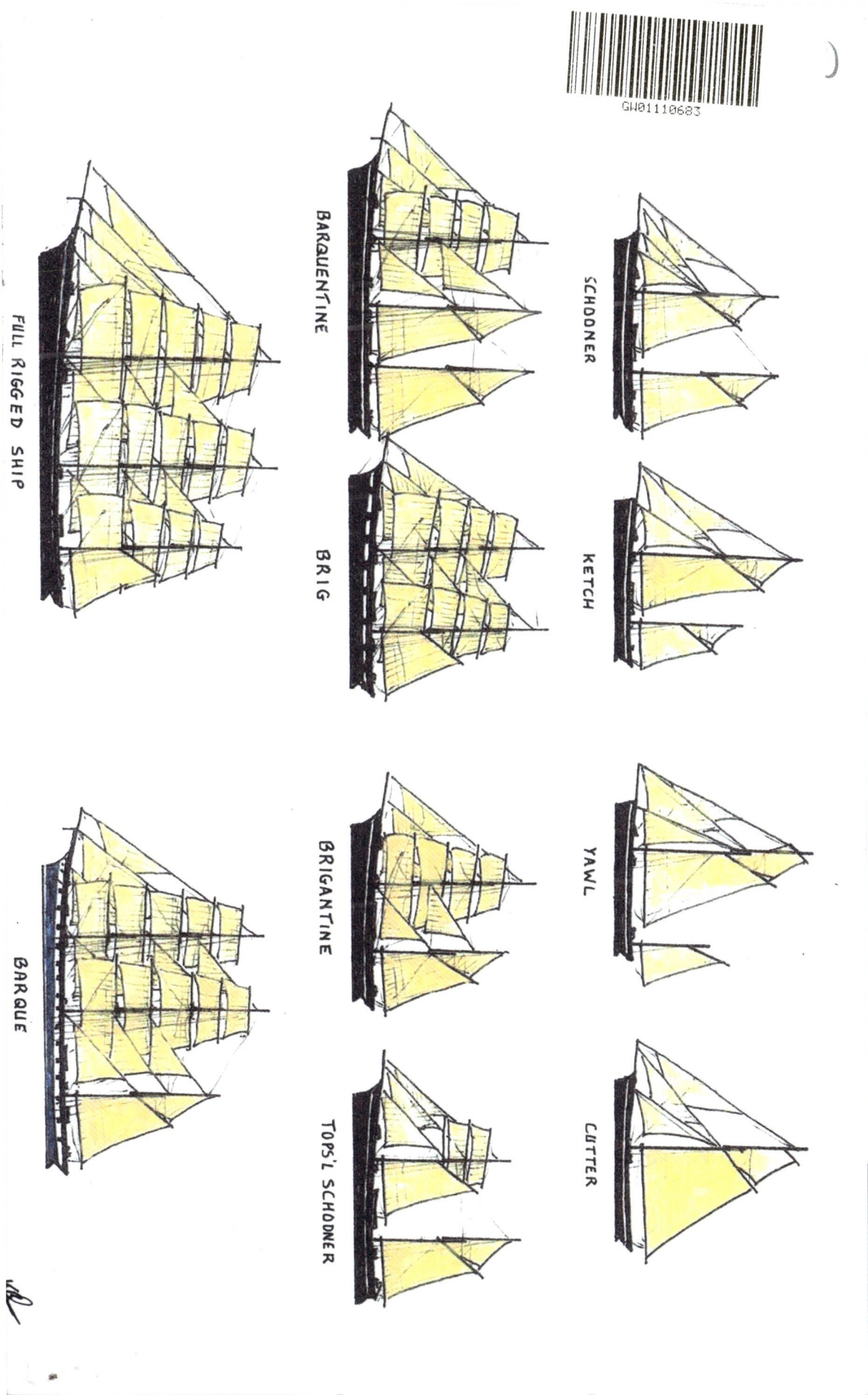

- FULL RIGGED SHIP
- BARQUENTINE
- BRIG
- SCHOONER
- KETCH
- BARQUE
- BRIGANTINE
- TOPS'L SCHOONER
- YAWL
- CUTTER

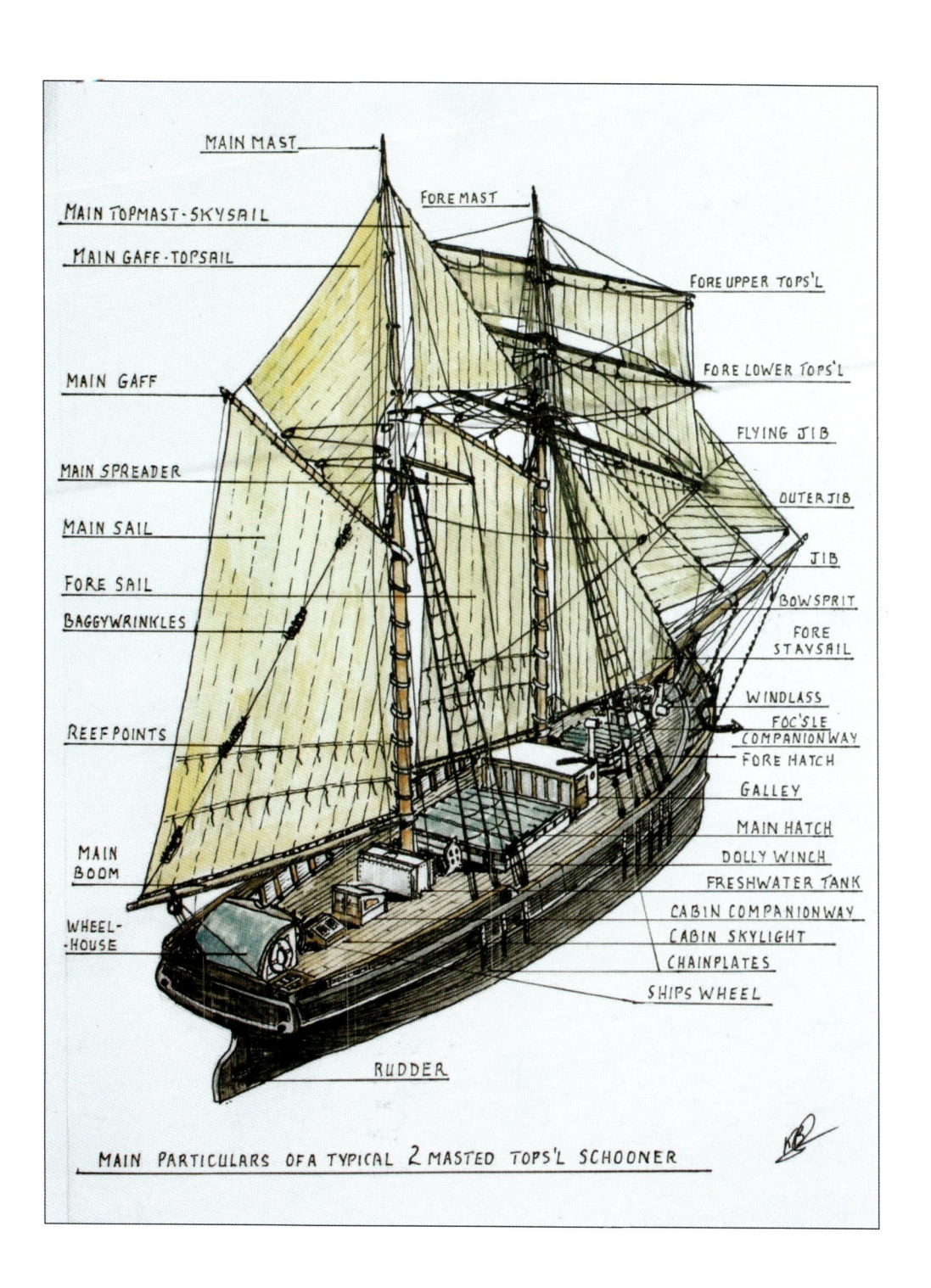

MAIN PARTICULARS OF A TYPICAL 2 MASTED TOPS'L SCHOONER

SAILING SHIPS OF WEXFORD

1840s to the 1940s

K. Brian Cleare and Jack O'Leary, Dip. Loc. Hist. (NUI Maynooth)

Gone is your glory – the day is long past
Since you held up to heaven the tracks of tall masts
Gone is your splendour – now grimy and grim
Once a fine lady, shipshape and trim.
With Golden grain from the port of Galatz
And emigrants for New Brunswick and fine timber back.
(After Capt. Eric Minett)

Saltee C Publications
2019

Published in 2019 by Saltee C Publications Suirway, The Quay, Passage East, Co. Waterford or 8 St. Magdalen's Terrace, Maudlintown, Wexford.

ISBN: 978-1-78972-503-2

© Saltee C Publications, 2019

All rights reserved. Without limiting the rights under copyright reserved alone, no part of this publication may be reproduced, stored in or introduced into a retrieval system or transmitted, in any form or by any means (electronic, mechanical, photocopying, recording or otherwise), without the prior written permission of both the copyright owners and the publishers of this book.

All pictures/paintings are from the authors collections unless otherwise stated. While every effort has been made to acknowledge copyright of illiustrations, apologies are made for any inadvertent ommissions.

Front cover designed by Aoifé Millea, Waterford
Front cover photo: Wexford barque **Saltee**

Back cover, Poem by 'Sahida' from Centenary Record of the twin churches, 1958, published by John English and Co., Wexford.

Printed by: C&R Print, Enniscorthy, Co. Wexford

Crescent Quay, Wexford.
Liam Gaul Collection.

Dedicated to the memory of the sailors from County Wexford who went to sea in the days of sail, many to find their final resting place in the ocean deep.

ACKNOWLEDGEMENTS

The authors wish to thank the following for their generous assistance while researching this volume: the staff of the County Wexford Library, Mallin St, Wexford, in particular Michael Dempsey, Grainne Doran, archivist, County Archives, Ardcavan, Wexford; Eamonn Doyle of Retreat Heights, Athlone, for the log of the **Alert**. Liam Gaul of Wexford Town for his advice and contribution; Desmond Kirwan of Rosbercon, New Ross, Co. Wexford, for his kindness and patience in allowing the authors to transcribe the log of the **Dispatch**; Ken Hemmingway, of Kiltealy. Co. Wexford; Captain Michael Murphy, The Faythe, Wexford, great grandson of Captain Murphy of the **Industry**. John Power, Olinda, Kilmore Quay, Co. Wexford, for allowing us access to his vast collection of newspaper cuttings concerning shipping on the Wexford coast, the Rosslare Harbour Maritime Enthusiasts; Pat Busher, John Boyce, Enda Murphy and in particular, Brian Boyce and Leo Coy for their technical assistance. Madeline Quirke of Rosslare Harbour whose administrative expertise proved invaluable. Joe Teesdale, Dunmore East, for access to his extensive maritime library. Myles Courtney of New Ross Street Focus. John Walker of Wexford. Historian Jim Rees and crew at Arklow Maritime Museum.

A very special thanks to the representatives of the late Robert Shortall, photographer of New Ross and to Andrew Kelly of Kilmacthomas, Co. Waterford for preserving this valuable historic collection of Irish maritime history.

A huge debt of gratitude is due to Celestine Murphy for the preparation and amendment of this manuscript.

Wexford County Council, in continuing to support communities across the County,

is delighted to support this wonderful tribute to the beautiful sailing ships that were either built locally or sailed in and out of Wexford Harbour over the centuries.

A significant piece of maritime history, embellished by exemplary illustrations, the work of Jack O'Leary and Brian Cleare is to be complimented.

SPONSORS:

We thank our sponsors;

Wexford County Council,
Dublin Port Company
Irish Rail, Rosslare Harbour.
The Port of Waterford.
Dr. David Dempsey, Wexford
The South End Resource Centre, Maudlintown, Wexford.

CONTENTS

Page

Foreword *by Capt. Phil Murphy, Harbourmaster, Wexford Harbour* viii

Introduction ix

Part 1: Sailing Ships of County Wexford 11

Part 2: Miscellaneous Other Ships Registered in Wexford 301

Part 3: Visitors to the Ports 353

Appendix 1: Extracts from Ships' Logs 407

Appendix 2: Traditional Local Craft 424

Appendix 3: Mariners Donations to Church Fund 433

Appendix 4: Emigrant Ships from New Ross 435

Appendix 5: Registered Masters and Mates from Wexford 437

Appendix 6: Prominent 19th Century Co. Wexford Shipowners 454

Glossary of Nautical Terms 457

Bibliography 462

FOREWORD

As the current Harbour Master of Wexford Harbour, I am deeply honoured to be requested to provide a few opening lines to this fantastic record of the ships that traded in this Harbour. I was enthralled when leafing through its pages. In today's world we rely on smart technology, broadband, connectivity etc. We are all busy going about our daily business, with sometimes little thought or chance to delve into the lives of those who have gone before us.

Wexford Harbour was for many centuries an integral cog in Ireland's economy, but looking seawards today, it's hard to envisage the hustle and bustle of what was once one of the busiest ports in Ireland. The ships that traded from here, the stories of foreign lands, the disasters, the board of trade enquires, etc. are all but forgotten.

Sailing Ships of Wexford brings us back to a time that is hard to imagine. Who would have known that one of the main trading routes was from Wexford to Galatz! The detailed research by our local renowned maritime historian Jack O' Leary, which has been painstakingly brought to life, with ship details, crew names and the cargoes they carried, is truly astonishing. *Sailing Ships of Wexford* commemorates the ships that called Wexford home and the men who 'went down to the sea' in them. Through this publication their lives will be forever remembered.

This book is both a valuable historical record of the Port and its ships, but also a testament to the lives of so many of our ancestors. I found it intriguing, hard to put down, as there is another tale from another ship on the very next page. It was fascinating to see that the family names of the crew are still replicated in the area, and are associated with seagoing men to this day. Once or twice I was somewhat unnerved to see even Christian names from centuries back that I would recognise on the streets of Wexford today!

Sailing Ships of Wexford is both a valuable record of the statistical data of the ships that traded from Wexford over the centuries, but it also dramatically brings to life the trials and tribulations of what it must have been like to serve in one of those vessels. Many never made it back home, or unfortunately met their demise within sight of the safety of the harbour. It must also be said that the glorious illustrations throughout the publication by the acclaimed maritime artist Brian Cleare really bring these stories to life.

The Port of Wexford has a rich maritime heritage which is probably little known by the people of the area today. Both Jack O'Leary and Brian Cleare must be commended on their dedication to ensuring that the lives of those who went before us, and the ships they toiled in, are forever recorded.

Capt. Phil Murphy
Harbourmaster
Ballast Office, Crescent Quay, Wexford Harbour

INTRODUCTION

Sailing Ships of Wexford is an extensive record of sailing ships both owned in County Wexford and registered in the ports of Wexford and New Ross. This information has been gleaned from years of research through local and national archives, newspapers and shipping records.

The majority of the ships featured in the book were small cross channel colliers. They plied their trade mainly to the Bristol Channel ports such as Newport, Swansea and Penarth. These small schooners usually carried a crew of Captain, Mate, Man and Boy. In the lists of crews for these coastal traders you will sometimes notice that, for a particular year, there are many more hands than four listed. The reason for this is that the crews of smaller coastal ships signed a six-month contract of employment with the owner of the vessel. These contracts were commonly known as 'ships articles' and they specified the pay, conditions and food to which each crew member was entitled.

After the six months expired, the ship changed the articles. The crew signed off and could, by mutual agreement with the master, sign back on again. Signing back on depended on the master's opinion of the seaman's conduct and ability to do his job and, of course, the seaman's willingness to stay on the ship. All seamen, deep sea or coastal carried a Discharge Book and before Discharge Books were developed they carried Certificates of Discharge, known as 'paper discharges'. A seaman's ability and conduct would be endorsed in his Discharge Book or on his paper discharge.

A Deep Sea Ship's articles were different: they specified which ports, if known, the vessel would call to and to where it would return. The ill-fated **Alert**, for example, signed articles on 6 January 1864 at *Wexford in Ireland to Galatz in Romania via Cardiff or any ports in the Mediterranean, Black Sea, Danube or Sea of Azof and back to a port of discharge in the United Kingdom or the Continent*. The food allowance for each member was specified, with substitutes at the master's discretion. The articles further state that: *Substitutes may be given at the master's option. Sweetening on Duff Days or for rice or barley*. In fact, everything was at the master's option including whether to allow the crew *money or spirits in a foreign port*.

It is safe to assume that most vessels under 100 tons were 'cross channel'; any over that mainly sailed deep sea. The larger barques, barquentines, and brigs left Wexford for ports all over the world. During the mid to late nineteenth century (1837-1882) the main port of call for the Wexford ships was Galatz, now called Galati, in Romania. This is situated some miles up the Danube and was a closed port until 1837.

When it was declared open in '37 the Wexford ships began the lucrative grain trade with Galatz, loading grain there and bringing it to Wexford. In 1882 Galatz was once again declared a closed port and that closure ended the Wexford/Galatz grain trade. This trade involved a long rigorous voyage that usually commenced leaving Wexford to cross to the Bristol Channel, often in ballast, to load coal for the coaling stations at Malta, Gibraltar or other ports. When the Galatz trade closed, some of the Wexford vessels were brought into dock and re-fitted for the timber trade to Canada's maritime provinces.

At the same period and for years before there was also another regular trade between Wexford and Savannah, Georgia in the USA. These ships left with emigrants and returned, usually to Liverpool, with cotton for the north of England cotton mills. Both these trading routes were successful but, as you will see throughout this book, were not without their casualties.

- Part 1: Sailing ships of County Wexford. Includes those vessels that were found to be well documented;
- Part 2: Miscellaneous Wexford vessels with little information other than their registration.
- Part 3: Visitors to the Port. Includes vessels that used Wexford on a regular basis but were not Wexford registered;

'Q' Ships
There are occasional references to 'Q' ships throughout this book. These ships were mainly old steel built schooners that were called up by the Admiralty during World War1 and converted into decoy ships. The ships had hidden guns mounted in false packing cases on deck, posing as deck cargo. They were crewed by Royal Navy personnel. It was not unknown for some of the crew to be dressed as women and to walk about the deck, furthering the appearance of a civilian vessel. Back then torpedoes were a scarce expensive commodity and, as submarines were not always near their home port, it was not easy to replace them. What the submarines often did was once they spied a merchant vessel in their periscope, they would come to the surface and order the crew of the merchantman to abandon ship. As soon as the crew of the ship were clear, they would sink the vessel either by shelling it or by putting a squad on board to lay explosives and blow her out of the water. To accomplish this the submarine had to come close in to the ship and this is when the gunners, who had been hiding around the decks of the 'Q' ships, sprang into action. The guns were uncovered and the submarine was attacked. Many of the 'Q' ships were very successful and sank the unsuspecting submarines. The **Cymric, Gaelic and Mary B. Mitchell** were all 'Q' ships and what's known of their careers will be related later in the book.

The title 'Q' ship, it has been suggested, came from the fact that many were converted to their tasks in the naval yards at Queenstown (Cobh). The effectiveness of the 'Q' ships has often been debated. It was argued that once the Germans knew that there were decoy ships out there luring them to their deaths, they stopped giving the crews the opportunity to abandon their ship and instead torpedoed them without warning, thus costing more British lives than the 'Q' ships ever saved.

Part 1: Sailing Ships of County Wexford

A

ABERFOYLE
1845 Built at Nova Scotia; a barque of 496 tons.

OWNERS
1848 Graves of New Ross. Her master was Captain Baldwin. She was an emigrant ship, serving Waterford to Quebec;
1851 Aman & Company, Liverpool;
1855 Getty of Liverpool;
1858 Out of register.

Although they were an international shipping company, little appears to have been written about Graves of New Ross. There are details of other Graves' ships throughout this book, not least the famous **Dunbrody**. It was only when researching Wexford owned and registered sailing ships that the extent of Graves' holdings in the shipping world became apparent. In the 1840s and 1850s Graves' ships sailed from New Ross and Waterford to Quebec and Savannah, Georgia. Initially in ballast, they later carried emigrants. On the return trip from Quebec, the cargo was usually timber or guano (Guano was bird droppings, much sought after for use as fertilizer). The Savannah-bound ships returned to Liverpool with cotton. The Savannah trip became the most popular due to the climate in the southern port. Unlike Quebec which froze in winter, Savannah was open all year round.

Graves' ships were often three times the tonnage of the ships of Wexford Port and were well regarded for their low mortality rate. This reputation and a possible reason for their low mortality rate is explained in this item from 1848:

> S.R. Graves, Esq. A very extensive ship owner, whom I had the pleasure of meeting in Canada, on renewing our acquaintance in England, assured me, that no vessel of his should ever again sail without a surgeon. Mr Graves cheerfully and approvingly goes to a very considerable expense to procure first-rate Medical men for his vessels. They are consigned to every port of North America (Sarah Mytton Maury, *An Englishwoman in America*).

From 1847 to 1858, New Ross-based ships, many owned by Graves', carried 19,913 people to the New World and declared just 85 deaths in that period; 33 of these were from cholera. Graves' also owned an impressive fleet of ships sailing out of Liverpool.

ALERT
Number 20249; Code MWHT.

1858 Built at St John, New Brunswick; a brig of 240 tons.
Dimensions   115.3x24.8x13.6ft.
1858 Registered at Wexford

OWNER Richard Devereux

Aberfoyle - A 496 ton barque. Built 1845 at Nova Scotia.

CREWS
1862
Master: Patrick Cogley, 36, New St (Parnell St.), Wexford.
Mate: Martin Dunne, 23.
ABs: Joseph Carberry, 42; Zacariah Guinton, 30; Myles Ennis, 25; James (surname unknown), 33; Bart Carty, 34; Nicholas Marshall, 28.
Apprentices: Laurence Murphy, 19; John Carr, 19, both from Wexford town.

1864
Master: Patrick Cogley, 38, New St. (Parnell St.), Wexford.
Mate: George Scallan, 26.
ABs: Joseph Carberry, 43; Zacariah Guinton, 29; Bart Carty, 30; Thomas Kean, 35; Edward Clancy, 21, and Patrick Brown, 22. All from Wexford town.

1864 7 July
The following crew signed on at Wexford Custom House for Galatz:
Master: Paddy Cogley;
Seamen: James Scallan, 22; Joseph Carberry, 44; Zacariah Guinton, 29; John FitzGerald, 21; James Devereux, 22; William Redmond, 22; Joseph Rossiter 21; John Murphy, 31.

Patrick Browne, a member of the crew of the **Alert** when she was lost with all hands in 1880.
Eamon Doyle Collection.

It was noted on the articles that John Murphy was a substitute for Carberry, who was Bosun, and who had been signed on the previous trip but had not turned up for this one. Owner Richard Devereux used the **Alert** almost exclusively in the booming Wexford/Galatz trade. These Black Sea voyages always began with the Wexford ships sailing, sometimes with pit props, other times in ballast, to the Bristol Channel ports to load coal for the coaling stations at Gibraltar and Valetta (Coaling Stations were used to supply 'bunkers' (fuel), to replenish the increasing steamer trade with coal to power the ships). Once the coal was unloaded at the coaling stations and their vessel cleaned out, they then set sail across the Mediterranean Sea, into the Aegean, through the Bosphorus and into the Black Sea, often to the port of Sulina.

From Sulina, they entered the mighty Danube for the rest of the trip up the river to Galatz (now Galati in Romania). The journey was not always as straightforward as it sounds. The normal procedure was to hire donkeys to tow their vessel through the insect infested Danube Delta. When these donkeys were not available, the unfortunate sailors had to get out and haul their ship through the swamps of the delta and up river themselves. Once they reached Galatz, they loaded grain for Wexford and set out for home.

Although there were reports of being attacked by pirates in the Bosphorus and close calls during wartime, the voyages home were usually – apart from fighting through bad weather – without incident. There is a log in existence that documents one voyage of

Captain Larry Murphy's 1st Mate's Ticket.

Alert- outward bound off Tuskar Rock, flying the Devereux house flag.

the **Alert** to the Black Sea in the period 12 June 1866 to 14 November 1866. The log is summarized in **Appendix 1**. Apart from a couple of incidents, it was a mostly uneventful trip. The master was Captain Paddy Cogley and the mate, who kept the log, was Laurence Murphy. Laurence was later lost when his vessel, the **Express** foundered on the Arklow Bank in 1897.

The **Alert** left Wexford on 22 May 1880, in ballast for Cardiff, where they loaded coal for some coaling stations. On this trip, their final destination was Odessa in the Black Sea. They arrived there in late July and began loading grain in early August. Once loading was completed she sailed to Constantinople (Istanbul). She left there on 26 August and came through the Mediterranean. She was last heard of when passing Gibraltar where she flew the signal URZ (report me well).

She was never heard of again. There were reports that, some weeks later, a broken ship's name plate bearing the letters 'ERT' was washed up on the coast between Carne and The Hook, but this was never verified. The crew, who were all lost, came from Wexford Town. They were: Captain Butler of Carrigeen, Wexford, Mate Kehoe of Maudlintown, Wexford, and crewmen, Brown, Connor, Boyle, Blake and Leary.

ALICE ELEANOR
Number 9828. Code KJWD.

1849 Built at Aberystwyth, Wales. Dimensions 52.5 x14.9 x 8.8 ft.
A schooner, of 57 tons, with a female figurehead and a square stern.

OWNERS
1865 Patrick Howlin, Wexford.
1867 John Radford, Ballyhealy, Kilmore.
1869 H. Jackman, Fishguard.
1897 John Way, Bideford.
1897 Registered as a ketch.
1900 Thomas Shorten, Roscarberry, Co. Cork.
1902 Michael Ahern, Youghal, Co. Cork.
1915 P. Donovan, Wexford.
1916 H. H. Bridge, Half Moon Lane, London.

CREWS
1864
Master: Patrick Howlin, 60.
Mate: William Atkinson, 50.
Seamen: Peter Warren, 28; Barthlomew Fortune, 20; Francis Wafer, 30.
Ordinary Seaman: Benjamin Smith, 20.
Boy: James Delaney,16; Boy: James Codd, 16.

Later that year:
Master: William Atkinson, 41.
Mate: Michael Doyle, 34; Mate: Michael Furlong, 42.
Seaman: William Atkinson, 21.

Alice Eleanor, trading as a ketch c1890.

Ordinary Seaman: Patrick Savage, 19.
Despite the remarkable discrepancy in the stated ages of William Atkinson, the Master and William Atkinson, the Mate, it is almost certainly the same person.

1890
Master: Richard Wafer, 44 (Wexford)
Mate: George Flaherty, 48 (Kilmore)
ABs: Thomas White, 29, (Kilmore); James Rankin, 26 (Kilmore).
Boy: Peter Wafer, 16 (Wexford)

Later that year:
Mate: Edward Flaherty, 52.
AB: William Murphy, 19.
Boy: James White, 16.

It was reported in October 1877 that three men from the schooner **Alice Eleanor** were going aboard their ship at Wexford in a small boat when it capsized. One of them, Nicholas Furlong, went under and but for the prompt action of Quay Watchman, Patrick Kelly, he would have drowned. Kelly caught Furlong with a boat hook and hauled him to the surface. He was taken, unconscious, to the home of Mr Somers in Common Quay St. Dr. Sheridan applied restoratives which brought him round.

Some years later, on 28 March 1894, the **Alice Eleanor** left Wexford, bound for Newport. She went ashore near Fishguard and was abandoned by her crew. Goodwick lifeboat came to their aid and two days later towed the ship safely to Fishguard Harbour. By 1896 she was owned by H.J. Jackman of Fishguard and had been re-rigged as a ketch and sold to B. Day of Appledore, Devon.

Alice Eleanor survived until July 1921, when Lloyd's reported from Sennen Cove that she had foundered one hundred miles northwest of Wolf. A lifeboat with four men on board had landed at Sennen Cove. At the time of her loss she was crewed by Arklow men and her master was Captain Tyrell.

ALICE & KATE
Number 70148. Code WLRJ.

1880 Built at Saundersfoot, Pembrokeshire, South Wales, 80 tons.

OWNERS
1882 Captain Laurence Murphy, Wexford.
1883 Elias Lewis, Newport, Monmouthshire, Wales.
1888-1891 Michael Flanagan, Skerries, Co. Dublin.
1893 W. Hartford, Skerries, Co. Dublin.

On 28 April 1882 the **Alice & Kate** struck the wreck of the steamer **Alert** near Penarth, South Wales and foundered. The following month she was successfully raised by the firm of Caple & Tucker of Cardiff and beached at Penarth for repairs.

Alice Latham, a two masted topsail schooner of 75 tons. Owned by John Monaghan of Kilmore Quay in 1911.

ALICE LATHAM
Number 54543/51088. Dimensions 76.4x19.5x8.2ft.

1865 Built at Barrow by Ashburners. A 75-ton schooner.
She was launched by Eliza, only daughter of Captain Henry Bond.

OWNERS
1870 Henry Bond of Barrow.
1872 William Ashburner of Barrow.
1880 James Postlethwaite of Ulverstone, Lancs.
1880 Thomas Ashburner of Barrow, Lancs.
1910 John Monaghan of Kilmore Quay, Co. Wexford.

In 1910, **Alice Latham** was in Robert Cock's shipyard, at Appledore for repair. Upon completion of the repairs she was then sold to Captain Monaghan for 430 pounds. However, it was later reported to have been sold to ship-breakers at Kilmore Quay in 1911. Perhaps this refers to the time in October 1911 when she broke free and ran ashore during a heavy gale at Kilmore Quay. Strenuous efforts were made to re-float her but she couldn't be shifted. Some local experts were of the opinion that the only way to get her back into deep water was to wait for the Spring Tides. However, she was eventually broken up.

THE BOARD OF TRADE INQUIRY AT CARDIFF.

The Board of Trade inquiry into the foundering of the Alice and Kate, schooner, of Wexford, on the 26th of April, in the Bristol Channel, was resumed on Saturday, before Mr. R. O. Jones, and Captains Kennedy and Rees, nautical assessors. Mr. Waldron appeared for the Board of Trade and Mr. Ingledew for the owner and master of the vessel. — The Court eventually expressed the opinion that the time during which the wreck of the Alert was allowed to remain in the roads was unnecessarily long. As regards the first question they found that the Alice and Kate struck the wreck of the Alert, whereby a hole was made in her bottom. 2. There was no evidence that any notices were posted at Dublin or anywhere. They were further told by the master that he had no occasion to go to the Custom-house before the voyage. 3. The lights exhibited by the vessel near the wreck were probably mistaken for those of a steam tug towing a ship. The use of lights one above the other where so many ships were at anchor was likely to lead to a mistake, but the captain ought to have been provided with night glasses. 4. The look-out probably was as efficient as could be kept by so small a crew. The master himself was probably on the look-out. 5. The vessel was navigated with proper and seamanlike care, but the use of night glasses might possibly have prevented the accident. The captain was not in default, but the Court recommended him to supply himself with all the necessary means of observation in the future.

Report of Board of Trade Inquiry into the foundering of the **Alice & Kate**, April 1882.

SCHOONER DAMAGED AT KILMORE QUAY.

During the heavy gale that prevailed on Friday night the schooner Alice Lathamer owned by Mr. Monaghan, Kilmore Quay, broke her moorings and was driven ashore at the slip. The schooner's stern was badly damaged through colliding with the pier wall, and on Saturday evening efforts were made to get her off, but were unsuccessful. The vessel, it is thought, will have to remain in her precarious position until the next spring tides, and it is doubtful if she will be got off even then, as on Saturday one of the highest tides seen for a long time was running, and every effort to float her proved futile. As the schooner stands, or rather lies, among the rocks and sand she presents a strange sight with her masts and spars overhanging the roadway. This is a sad memento of the inadequate state of our harbours, and one calculated to bring foreibly to the minds of shipowners and fishermen the insecurity of their craft. A similar disaster to that of a few years ago, when the whole fleet of fishing boats was destroyed, may happen at any time now that the winter is in, and many of the poorer people deprived of their sole means of making a livelihood.

Report to the damage to the **Alice Latham** at Kilmore Quay, October 1911.

ALICE T
Number 42664. Dimensions 81.5x23.7x8.7ft.

1861 Built at Dipper Harbour, St. John, New Brunswick by James Thompson, as a wooden schooner with two masts, 125 tons (Under Wexford registration, 71 tons).

OWNERS
1872 William Black, St John, New Brunswick.
1875 Richard Cuthbert, Bray, Co. Wicklow.
1894 M. Wickham and T. Harpur, Wexford; they went bankrupt in 1898. Administration was granted to J.F. Walsh.
1899 Thomas Morris of Carrigeen and Michael McDonald of Castle Hill Wexford. McDonald sold his shares to Morris for £150 in August 1900. Morris sold 32 shares to Catherine O'Connor, of Glena Terrace, Wexford for £150.
1916 In February, Catherine O'Connor sold her shares to James Billington.
1917 On 23 August, Morris and Billington sold her to Haigh Hall Steamship Co., Cardiff.
1918 On 25 May, Haigh Hall sold to Joseph Trott, Oatfield St., Cardiff. Trott sold to Hamilton McMath Hely of Truro, Cornwall.
1921 On 20 June the ship's certificate and registration were cancelled and the vessel was subsequently broken up.
1923 Out of register.

When Harpur and Wickham bought the **Alice T** in 1894, she was said to be a very suitable vessel for Wexford, carrying 150 to 160 tons deadweight on an easy draft of water and capable of sailing without ballast. This meant a great saving in running costs. The **Alice T** had been completely rebuilt only two years previously and was only sold because of the death of her owner.

In November 1905, when under the command of Captain Thomas Morris, the **Alice T** was in a collision with the steamer **Wexford** near the Gulbar. **Alice T** was outward bound for Newport with a cargo of pit props when the accident happened. The steamer was inward bound on her regular trip from Liverpool The schooner sustained damage to her starboard side and had to be brought back to the Dockyard for repairs. On 6 December Mr J. Maddock, Pilot Master wrote to the Wexford Harbour Commissioners regarding the recent collision between the steamer **Wexford** and the schooner **Alice T**:

*Sir, W. Breen reports that on the 17th of November, when piloting the ss **Wexford** up the harbor, he collided with the schooner **Alice T**, doing her considerable damage. He states the collision was unavoidable.*

Pilot Breen was brought before the Board to explain what occurred at the time and in his evidence told the Commissioners that on the morning in question he was bringing the **Wexford** up near the Gulbar and on nearing the red buoy he ordered the 'hooter' to be blown to signal to the vessel that they were going aport of her. Presently he saw the schooner alter its course and he made a remark to the captain drawing his attention to this. Immediately the steamer was put 'full astern' as the schooner came around their starboard bow. The chairman inquired as to the direction of the wind at the time and Breen told him that it was about northwest and that the schooner sailed down into them. Mr Armstrong, the chairman, asked how this was possible as the damage suffered by

Alice T under full sail off the Tuskar Rock Lighthouse.

the **Alice T** was all to her side and not to her bow which would have been the case if she had sailed directly into them.

After some more evidence Captain McGuire asked Breen if it was his evidence that the schooner drifted broadside on them so hard that it cut away her whole side. Breen said that was his evidence, to which Captain McGuire said: *I don't believe a word of it*.

Patrick Roche, who was piloting the **Alice T** on the day in question, stated that the wind was about north at the time and that he was steering north east by north in order to keep as close as possible to the wind. The yards of the vessel were 'braced up sharp' at the time and the schooner was doing about two knots whereas the steamer was under great way. He was of the opinion that, if the steamer had been put just a half point to starboard, the collision would have been avoided. Captain Morris, Master and owner of the **Alice T**, gave similar evidence and added that the steamer's engines had only been put astern after they had collided.

Captain Busher of the tug **Wexford** said that they were in the area but were not aware of any accident until he saw the side of the schooner. He noted that the schooner was broadside to the steamer. He said that the vessel's head was about east by north when he saw them, and that the steamer came around the Gulbar and went right for the

Captain Thomas Morris, Owner/Master of the **Alice T.**
Courtesy Mrs. Mary Roche.

Alice T at an unknown location, with her jolly boat tied astern.

schooner. Captain McGuire asked him if he thought that there was plenty of room for the steamer to go to the leeward steaming up and Captain Busher replied: *No doubt about it*. That concluded the evidence. Great sympathy was expressed about Captain Morris' situation and it was said that his only compensation would be the insurance. As the pilot of the steamer was found to be at fault in the collision, the decision on Breen's fate was deferred until the next meeting of the board.

Thomas O'Neill of Bride St., Wexford was severely injured when he fell from the mast of the **Alice T**. It was October 1908 and the **Alice T** was tied up in Wexford. O'Neill was scraping the mast and, when he looked around, his foot slipped and he fell 20 feet to the deck. He landed feet first and burst his left ankle. He was attended to immediately by his shipmates but had lost a lot of blood before the doctor arrived. He was brought to the County Infirmary in a very weak state.

In March 1918, while under the ownership of Trott of Cardiff, the **Alice T** once again made the newspapers in what *Sea Breezes* magazine of April 1964 referred to as the 'Bristol Channel's own **Marie Celeste**' (vessel referred to was actually named **Mary Celeste**). Apparently, on 1 March of that year some people in Quay St., Minehead were surprised to see a schooner passing close inshore. She drove on and went ashore on Warren Point, half a mile east of Minehead. There was a heavy sea running but despite that the people who had seen the ship going ashore set out, with some others, to see if they could be of any assistance to the crew. When they got aboard the **Alice T** they were nonplussed to discover that there was no one aboard. The cabin light was still lighting, the clock was still going and there was every indication that there had been a crew on board shortly before, but there was no one to be seen.

Eight days passed before what had happened to the crew of the **Alice T** was discovered. The ship had been on a voyage from Ireland to Cardiff with a cargo of pit props. A severe gale developed and she became unmanageable. They had to hove to and signal for help. It was during World War 1 and a patrol boat in the area answered the call. It took the men off and took the **Alice T** in tow. During the night the tow parted and aided by the winds and tides the **Alice T** rapidly drifted towards the Somerset coast. It was almost two weeks before she was re-floated and brought across the bay to Minehead to undergo repairs. The report referred to her as the **Alice T** of Youghal but research has confirmed that there was no vessel of that name registered in Youghal. It was definitely the former Wexford vessel. The likelihood is that the reporter confused the port she had sailed from with her original port of registry.

ALICIA
Number 21420. Code NGFW.

1831 Built at Lawrenny, Milford Haven. A schooner of 73 tons.

1834 Registered at Wexford. Master: Martin Walsh.
1853 Still registered in Wexford. Master: J. Morris.

OWNERS
1853 Denis Kenselah
1865 Nicholas Murphy, Wexford.
1868 Richard Devereux, Wexford.

Alicia- Two masted topsail schooner of 73 tons, sailing by Tuskar Rock c1870.

> AUCTION OF SCHOONER.—The *Alicia*, schooner, well known in this port for upwards of thirty-five years, as a most successful trader, has recently changed owners. Mr Hinton, Auctioneer, has sold her to Mr. Richard Devereux for £260. She has been placed on the Slip by her purchaser, and will undergo a thorough repair. She was built of oak, under the inspection of the late Captain Kenselah, of this town, for his own use; and we sincerely hope she may prove as successful in the employment of her present owner as she has ever been.

Notice of **Alicia** sale to R. Devereux of Wexford c1868.

1875 Mark Devereux, Wexford.
1887 Broken up at Ferrybank, Wexford.
1888 Out of register.

On 8 February 1838, the emigrant ship **Glasgow** left Liverpool for New York. She carried a crew of 17 and 95 passengers, mainly from the West of Ireland. After battling adverse winds and hazy weather, on 14 February Captain Robinson found himself in sight of Tuskar Lighthouse. At 5 am the following day, still in hazy weather, the captain found himself up on The Barrells Rocks. The **Glasgow** had been doing about 9 knots and the impact swung her around. The stern struck the rocks and she lost her rudder. Still with all sails set, she hit the rocks again and was holed and swept over the rocks into open water.

The **Alicia** of Wexford was bound from Dublin to Newport and was in the area. Hearing a bell tolling, Captain Martin Walsh headed his ship for the sound. When he saw the ship and the situation it was in, he attempted to bring his vessel alongside the **Glasgow's** lee side but was unable to do so. During the impact with the Barrells the **Glasgow** had lost all her oars so those onboard were unable to take to the boats. Captain Walsh dropped a boat with a crew and as many oars as he had and let them drift over to the stricken ship. They then attached a line to her and by this method managed to rescue a small number of people. By this time, the weather had worsened and Captain Walsh realised that he would not have time to save many more by this method. At great risk to himself and his crew, he ran the **Alicia** alongside the Glasgow. The ships collided twice and the **Alicia's** bulwarks were carried away and her mainsail was torn.

On the third attempt the flukes of the **Glasgow's** anchor went through the **Alicia's** bow. Undeterred, the brave Walsh – who was at the helm himself – went in again and again until he had taken eighty-two people aboard his vessel. Turning to make another run he saw the **Glasgow** give a lurch and sink beneath the waves. The **Alicia** remained in the area for some time afterwards and managed to rescue four more from the waters, but the others were never seen again. Captain Walsh brought the 86 survivors into Wexford where they were looked after and helped to return to their homes in the West.

A few years later Captain Walsh, then in command of another vessel, was homeward bound from Galatz and put into Falmouth for orders. While they were there the weather turned and they were weather-bound for a few days. When it cleared, they sailed but that night a terrible storm hit the area and neither the brave Captain Martin Walsh nor his crew were ever seen again.

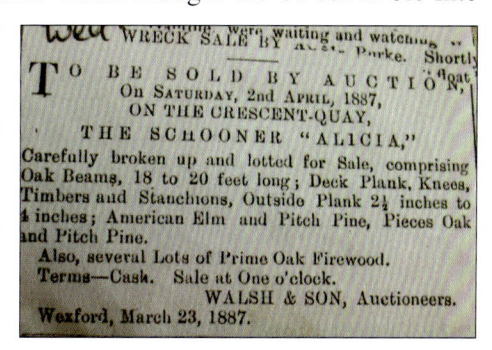

> WRECK SALE were waiting and watching by ... Purke. Shortly
> TO BE SOLD BY AUCTION,
> On SATURDAY, 2nd APRIL, 1887,
> ON THE CRESCENT-QUAY,
> THE SCHOONER "ALICIA,"
> Carefully broken up and lotted for Sale, comprising Oak Beams, 18 to 20 feet long; Deck Plank, Knees, Timbers and Stanchions, Outside Plank 2½ inches to 4 inches; American Elm and Pitch Pine, Pieces Oak and Pitch Pine.
> Also, several Lots of Prime Oak Firewood.
> Terms—Cash. Sale at One o'clock.
> WALSH & SON, Auctioneers.
> Wexford, March 23, 1887.

Alicia- Notice of sale by auction.

ANNIE
Number 62764.

1870 Built at Rothesay. A schooner of 89 tons.

OWNERS
1870 J. Whiteside, Wharton, Lancs.
1876 R.M. Rawstone, Freckleton.
1888 J. Whiteside, Wharton.
1891 R.W. Swyny, Liverpool.
1891 R. & R. Allen, Wexford.
1893 Mrs Mary Allen, Wexford.
1899 Register closed.

January 1891 saw the arrival of the **Annie**, formerly of Preston, a fine schooner, bought by R. &R. Allen. She arrived in Wexford with a cargo of 170 tons of coal for the Wexford Gas Company and discharged her cargo at the company's wharf. Described as a splendid model and well fitted throughout, the **Annie's** cabin and forecastle accommodation was far above the standard normally found on coastal vessels. It was said that she was destined to be one of the fastest vessels of her class in Wexford. Captain John O'Reilly, formerly of Allen's brigantine, **Rapid,** was appointed Master.

In February 1892, the schooner **Walter Ulric** of Caernarfon was towed into the river. In those days discharged ships were lined up, upriver from the present bridge, in preparation for being brought over the Bar. This was also to make room for incoming vessels to discharge their cargoes. For some unexplained reason, the schooner took off down river and, when she was almost opposite The Crescent, she ran into Allen's **Annie**. The damage to the **Annie** was considerable. The runaway ship was got under control and berthed safely. It seems that there was no crew aboard the **Annie** at the time, as they were all in their homes, having breakfast! In May 1899, **Annie** was sold to Spanish owners. Her register was closed and her certificate cancelled.

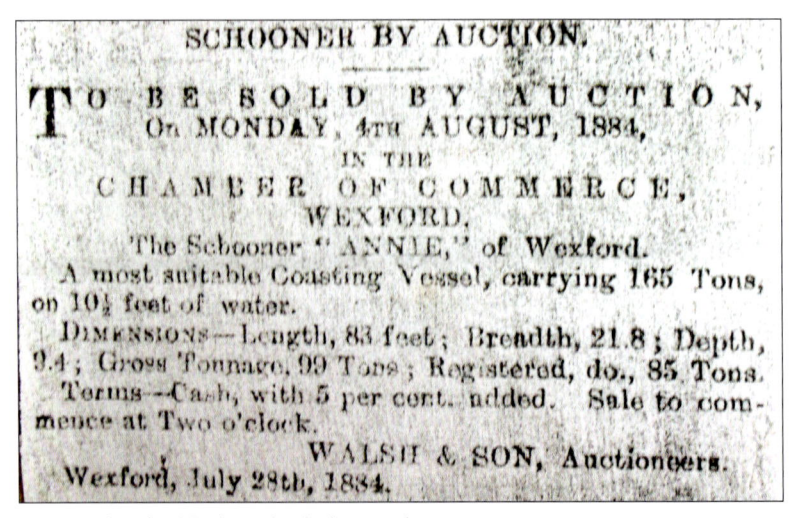

> **SCHOONER BY AUCTION.**
>
> TO BE SOLD BY AUCTION,
> On MONDAY, 4TH AUGUST, 1884,
> IN THE
> CHAMBER OF COMMERCE,
> WEXFORD.
> The Schooner "ANNIE," of Wexford.
> A most suitable Coasting Vessel, carrying 165 Tons, on 10½ feet of water.
> DIMENSIONS—Length, 83 feet; Breadth, 21.8; Depth, 9.4; Gross Tonnage, 99 Tons; Registered, do., 85 Tons.
> Terms—Cash, with 5 per cent. added. Sale to commence at Two o'clock.
> WALSH & SON, Auctioneers.
> Wexford, July 28th, 1884.

Annie- Notice of sale by auction. *Wexford People August 1884.*

ANGHARAD
Number 13267. Code (original LGHM) WTGN.

1853 Built at Porthmadog. A wooden schooner of 84 tons, with two masts. Dimensions 76.1x16.3x8.2ft.

OWNERS
1865 Morgan Jones, Porthmadog.
1874 William Vaughan, Penrhyndedraeth.
1885-1892 James Morris, Barrack St., Wexford.
1893 Out of registration.

In January 1892 the local schooner **Angharad** (Captain Morris, master and owner), was lost on the Bar of Wexford Harbour. She was inbound under the command of Pilot Moses Murphy. She 'took the ground' at Bull Bank and immediately began to take water. The **Angharad** became a total loss. Later that month, the Wexford Harbour Board held an inquiry at the request of the Board of Trade. The Harbour Board themselves had already decided on an inquiry because they thought *it was necessary for the credit of the pilot establishment*.

Several witnesses were called including Captain Morris, owner/master of the **Angharad**, Captain Cogley, the Pilot Master and Pilot Moses Murphy. After exhaustive examination, the inquiry exonerated the pilot of all blame and concluded that the loss was due to *a sudden change of wind, at a time and place where it was impossible to work the vessel, which was making water at the time*. It was remarked that *a pilot can do many things to safely navigate a vessel through local waters, but he can hardly be expected to control the elements*. No lives were lost but it was later reported by James Morris, the owner, that large portions of the wreckage were being *carried away surreptitiously by persons belonging to the coast where she lies*.

ANTELOPE
Number 70153 Code KLPT, later EIFB.

1886 Built at Wexford, a schooner, 120 tons. Dimensions 91.5x24.7x10.2ft. The **Antelope** has the distinction of being the last sailing vessel to be built by The Wexford Dockyard Company. Said to have been built from the timbers of an American vessel named **Antelope** which was wrecked on the Saltee Islands, she was launched in 1886 as a 129-ton schooner, with 1 deck and 3 masts. There was accommodation for four seamen in the fo'c'sle, with the master and the mate accommodated aft.

OWNERS
1886 J.W. Walsh and Patrick Lambert.
1896 Walsh died and his shares went to Lambert.
1896 Lambert died, too, and his ownership of the **Antelope**, went to his widow Margaret Lambert of Trinity Street, Wexford. Margaret Lambert sold her complete shareholding to J.F. Walsh and Francis James Walsh of the Wexford Dockyard Co, April 1896 (J. F. Walsh 16 shares and Francis James Walsh, 48 shares) The Dockyard Co. closed down in 1898.

Antelope- Departing Wexford under tow from the tug **Wexford**, with the schooner **Cymric** alongside the quay.
Courtesy of Mr Michael Cusack, Waterford.

1898 Sold to E. Fogarty of Arklow for 785 pounds.
1923 O' Toole of Arklow.
1923 Anthony Nolan, the Quay, Waterford.
1953 December 13, aground on Dollymount Strand, Dublin.

CREWS
1887
Master: Edward Clancy, 43.
Mate: M. Harwood, 55 (He was a Swansea man and signed off in Dunkirk).
Bosun: Peter Blake, 31.
ABs: William Murphy, 22; Thomas Marlow, 24.
Boy: William Murphy, 19.

1888 (March)
Master: Edward Clancy, Wexford, 43.
Mate: William Paul, 35.
ABs: Laurence Furlong, 34; Patrick Gaul, 24.
OS: William Murphy, 19.
Boy: Thomas Carr, 15.
Later that month:
Mate: Richard Bent, 45.
ABs: A. Sinnott, 55.
OS: Henry Ryan, 22.
Boy: Patrick Cogley, 17.

Antelope- Motoring out of Waterford Harbour, December 1942, note the cut down rig and the neutral markings displayed on her hull. *Photo: Theo Harris, Dublin.*

1888
Master: Edward Clancy, 46.
Mate: Richard Bent, 45.
Boy: Patrick Cogley, 17.
ABs: Andrew Sinnott, 35; Henry Ryan 22.
OS: Luke McGuire, 26.

On 6 January 1891, the **Antelope** grounded on the Dogger Bank, while in the charge of Pilot Laurence Duggan. A special meeting of the Harbour Board was held on 13 January to hear the evidence of Captain Paddy Cogley, Pilot Master; Captain Clancy of the **Antelope,** and Pilot Duggan.

Laurence Duggan told the board that he took charge of the **Antelope** in the South Bay on the Sunday afternoon at about 3 o'clock. Next morning the wind was ENE with a nice breeze. They got underway at about 6 am. High water was about 8 o'clock. They came down the Bay and made a track down the north end of the Trees. They tacked for about 30 minutes and he thought that they were well off the bank. It was a dark morning. Duggan remarked to the captain that she was going down pretty fast with the tide and the captain said that he would cast the lead. He proceeded to do this and the reading showed that they were in about 3 fathoms of water. They took further soundings 6 minutes later and found they still had 3 fathoms but then just as they were turning they touched the ground. The anchor was dropped and all sail was taken off, but the captain wasn't happy with the anchor out, so he took it up again. By this time the **Antelope** was

Antelope- Alongside at an unknown port with her boat swung out in order to work on the cargo at the main hatch.

Antelope- Aground on Dollymount Strand, Dublin early 1954. Later broken up where she lay.

broadside to the bank, not on it, and with a rising tide. Twenty minutes later they saw the tug boat coming up. After two attempts they attached a hawser to the **Antelope** and pulled her free. Duggan said it was so hazy that no lights could be seen, neither from the Lucifer Light vessel nor from the Fort.

Captain Clancy of the **Antelope** was called and he corroborated Duggan's evidence. In reply to the chairman as to the cause of the grounding, Captain Clancy said *I think it was about the vessel going faster than we expected*. The evidence of Captain Busher, Tug Master and Captain Cogley, Pilot Master also backed Pilot Duggan's statement. After some deliberation the Board considered the accident was caused by an error of judgement and ordered that in future, *the Pilot Master receive strict orders to inform staff to use the lead and use it frequently whilst bringing a vessel to Wexford Bar at all times when the buoys are not distinctly visible. Any neglect of the order will be treated by the Wexford Harbour Commissioners as a gross culpable neglect of duty, entailing severe punishment if not dismissal.*

A little over nine months later, on 18 October 1891, the **Antelope** arrived in Wexford Harbour after what was described as *a protracted passage*. She was bound home with coal from Ayr and had got as far as Wicklow Head when she met a south-westerly gale and had to run back into Kingstown (Dun Laoghaire). She was weather-bound there for a week and left around 14 October. When some distance on her homeward passage she met the full force of the storm yet again. This time her mainsail was split and a jib carried and she was driven back as far as Carlingford Lough. Captain Clancy, the master of the **Antelope**, said that he had never before experienced such weather. A tremendous sea was running and the deck was continuously being swept by the waves.

In May 1906, the **Antelope**, still with her Wexford registration, but since 1898 owned by Eugene Fogarty of Arklow and under the command of Captain James Brennan, went aground off Kilmore. She had sailed from Teignmouth, Devon on 27 April with a cargo of 214 tons of pipe clay for Runcorn. The winds were described as 'a light breeze'. However, on 1 May they were forced to put into Falmouth due to head winds. On 4 May the winds had moderated and she resumed her voyage. She passed the Longships Light on 5 May but the weather had deteriorated again. Very soon they were in thick fog and drizzle, but still maintaining her course.

Around 00.20 hours on 6 May, she was carrying a fair bit of sail with a single reef mainsail, gaff foresail, topsail and a topgallant sail plus standing jib, boom jib and fore stay sail 'out'. The master and mate were on deck when she struck ground off Bastardstown Strand. Captain Brennan had the topsail 'filled' in the hope of getting her to back off but the tide caught her head and swung her towards the land. Realising that there was no chance of getting her off the ground, he kept all sails on to hold her in the sand. He then sent a flare up for assistance.

The Coastguard arrived at about 4.30 am and set up their rocket apparatus. They successfully made contact on their first attempt. Half an hour later the Kilmore Quay Lifeboat, the **Sisters**, arrived alongside and the **Antelope's** crew decided to go with them, rather than risk getting off by the apparatus. All hands were landed safely at Kilmore Quay. The **Antelope** had stranded on a fine sandy bottom about half a mile east of Bastardstown Roads. How she came to be off Kilmore when she was bound from Teignmouth to Runcorn can probably be put down to the vagaries of wind and weather. She was successfully re-floated.

On 7 November 1923, it was reported that Captain Murray of the **Antelope** was missing at New Ross and was presumed drowned. Civic Guards on patrol near Bridge Street heard a splash and rushed down to the quayside but couldn't see anyone. When the captain did not turn up the next morning, it was presumed that it was he who had fallen into the water on the previous night. Boats dragged the river and the following day his body was found.

In 1923, the **Antelope** had a motor fitted by The Dan Motor Company of Copenhagen, and in 1932 she was converted to diesel. In April 1947, the coasts were lashed with severe gales and high seas. The **Antelope** was off the south-east coast, bound from Waterford to Dublin when she developed engine trouble and became difficult to control. The Irish Lights tender **Alexandra** was in the area and took her in tow to Rosslare Harbour. Later she struck Rosslare Pier and damaged her bulwarks and forced the windlass from its base. The Rosslare lifeboat, **Mabel Marion Thompson** took the crew off but they were able to return later and prevent the cargo of wheat that they were carrying from being damaged.

After a long career the **Antelope** ran aground near Dollymount Strand on 13 December 1953. Extensive attempts were made to salvage her or move her, all to no avail. The **Antelope** was subsequently bought for 15 pounds. After anything of use was removed from her, explosive charges were set on board and, following two abortive attempts, she was blown up where she lay. An ignominious end for the last Wexford built schooner. Her final owner was Robert Houston of Clontarf, Co. Dublin.

ATLANTA
Number 22799.
1846 Built at St John, New Brunswick. A barque of 286 tons.

OWNERS
1849-1853 July. Nicholas Sinnott of Enniscorthy (Master, Peter Sinnott).
1856 July. In a series of transactions, **Atlanta** was sold to William James Lamport and George Holt of Liverpool. They sold her to George Jordan, also of Liverpool. Then Jordan sold her to George Clifton Pocket of Cumberland. All of these transactions seem to have taken place on the same day, 31 July 1856. Registration was transferred to Cumberland.

As a Deep Sea vessel, on 3 February 1852 she signed on at Glasgow for Buenos Aires and Montevideo *… or wherever else freight or employment might offer in the Brazils or any other ports the master direct until the ship's return to a port of discharge in the UK for a period not to exceed 18 months'. The master has allowed that the crew be on board sober at the time stated or the master is at liberty to ship others in their place; signed Peter Sinnott, Master; 2 February 1852.*

CREW (signed on at Glasgow)
Master: Peter Sinnott.
Mate: Richard Wright, 42.
Carpenter: Nicholas McCormack, 27.
Cook: William Collit, 31.
Seamen: James Monk, 24; James Sinnott, 22; Hugh Young, 24; Robert Prince, 27; Peter Thompson, 29.

ATLAS
Number 21435. Code NGHW.

1839 Built at Wexford by Edward Hingston. A two masted schooner of 77 tons, with a figurehead and a square stern. Dimensions 68x19 x8ft.

OWNERS
1853-1865 Whitty & Company of Wexford; Master: L Sheil.
1876 Laurence Kirwan of Piercestown, Wexford.
1879 Nicholas Whitty of Wexford.
1882 John E. Barry of Wexford.
1888 J. Edmond Barry, Rocklands, Wexford.
1902 John Tregerthen, St. Ives, Cornwall.
1910 J.T. Short, St. Ives, Cornwall.
1912 31 May: vessel broken up.
1913 Out of register.

CREW 1888
Master: Thomas Bolger, 49.

Atlas - Up on the slip at Wexford Dockyard, possibly for repairs.

Atlas at St. Ives, Cornwall, early 1900s.

Mate: Edward Cleary, 40.
Abs: Bart Carty, 50; W. Kehoe, 18; F. Lambert.
Boys: Myles Furlong; Thomas Furlong, 21; P. Codd, 18.

On 19 February 1902, the Wexford schooner **Atlas** was in a serious accident off Cardiff Roads. She was going up the Bristol Channel when she met with a French barque, under tow by a tug. The **Atlas** got clear of the tug but the barque hit her midships. Her side was driven in, right down to the waterline and her mainmast broke. Captain Dempsey was at the wheel at the time and he was thrown hard against the bulwark. The rigging collapsed on top of him but the only injury he suffered was to his hip which was knocked out of joint. The rest of the men were unhurt. **Atlas** was towed into Cardiff for repairs.

Atlas. Another view of the schooner at St. Ives, Cornwall at low water.

B

BELLE
Number 63408.

1880 Built at Wexford. A smack of 23 tons.
OWNER: William Armstrong of Wexford.

The **Belle** was used by William Armstrong as a tender to the light vessels around the Wexford coast. On 2 April 1904, she was bound from the Lucifer Light Vessel, based off Wexford Harbour, with a crew of two and four lightship men. The lightshipmen were going home after being relieved from the vessel.

It had been normal practice for the **Belle** to cross the Bar at low tide, usually without mishap. However, on this occasion there was a heavy sea running and it hit her port bow and drove her onto the bank. Both the two crew and the four lightship men worked together to lighten the **Belle** by throwing any barrels of water or oil that were on board over the side. Despite this, the little smack remained fast. They then signalled for the lifeboat at the Fort which arrived promptly. The prompt arrival of the lifeboat proved lucky for the men on the **Belle** as, just as the lifeboat arrived alongside, the smack began to break up.

BOSTON PACKET
Number 25568. Code PGML.

1842 Built at Bridgetown, Nova Scotia. A schooner of 43 tons, carvel built, with a billet head.

1845 Registered at Wexford (Master: Barnaby Corish).

OWNERS
1845 Thomas Fortune, Ferrybank, Wexford 22 shares, and Robert Hughes, Ely Place, 42 shares.
1846 Edward Watson of Lacken, Wexford (Master: Walt. O' Brien). Watson died in October.

Auction notice of the **Boston Packet**.
Wexford People March 1862.

Report on the wreck of the **Boston Packet** at Ballygeary, Rosslare.
Wexford People, November 1880.

36

Boston Packet, a two masted schooner of 43 tons. Shown here beached on Duncannon Strand to discharge a cargo of coal c1870.

1852 Probate was granted to Andrew McCormack of New Ross, Wexford and Joshua Martin, of Coolbrook, Co. Wexford.
1852 Matthew Cullen and Nicholas Roche of Bannow, Co. Wexford
1870 Mrs Ellen Cullen and Nicholas Roche of Bannow.
1870 Nicholas Roche

CREW 1870
Master: Simon Roche, 38. This is the same Simon Roche who became a successful ship-owner and business man in the Wellingtonbridge/Bannow area, some years later.
Mate: Thomas Keane, age 46.
ABs, Patrick Shea, 23; Thomas Cullen, 18.
All came from Bannow.
On 13 November 1880, the **Boston Packet,** was moored at Ballygeary (Rosslare Pier), in a storm. She was secured by two hawsers but broke free and went aground near Rosslare. She was declared a wreck.

BRANDON

1847 Built at Quebec. A fully rigged ship of 956 tons.

OWNER: Hartrick of New Ross. The Hartricks were a Palatine family, prominent in the business life of New Ross.

The **Brandon** traded mainly carrying emigrants to Quebec/Newfoundland, returning to Wexford with timber.

BRITISH QUEEN

1851 Built at New Brunswick.

OWNERS
1853 T. Walters, Master; Captain G. Murphy.
1853 Captain Hutchinson.
1879 Captain Thomas Devereux, part owner

On 23 September 1879 the **British Queen** was at Ayr when her then master and part owner, Captain Thomas Devereux went ashore to post some letters home. The letters were delivered in due course but Captain Devereux was never seen alive again. His body was found in the river nine days later. It was assumed that Captain Devereux had fallen into the river and had been carried away by the fast running currents. He left a wife and one child. About nine months before his death he had joined the Mariners' Society which had been formed by Wexford shipowners and his wife had the dubious distinction of being the first person to receive a death benefit from it.
   In March 1882 the **British Queen** was driven ashore near Port Isaac on the coast of Cornwall. The crew were rescued by lifeboat but the ship was a total loss.

Brandon- A full rigged ship of 956 tons, owned by Hartrick of New Ross. Shown here at anchor off St. John's, Newfoundland c1860.

BROTHERS
Number 11625.

1849 Built at New Brunswick. A brigantine of 278 tons.

OWNERS: Allens of Wexford

> ARRIVAL OF EMIGRANTS.— The British Barque *Brothers*. Capt. ENGLISH, arrived yesterday from Wexford, Ireland, with 125 emigrants. It is rarely that we see a more respectable body of new comers from any portion of Europe, than those brought by the *Brothers*, and who we learn design settling in Savannah. May they realize their brightest anticipations of prosperity and happiness in their new home.

Brothers- Notice of arrival at Savannah, December 1850. *Courtesy, Peggy McHale and Kieron Cronin, Waterford Institute of Technology.*

The **Brothers** was one of three Wexford registered vessels to bear that name. The *Savannah Daily Morning News* of 6 December 1850, noted that: *The British barque, Brothers, Captain English, arrived yesterday from Wexford, Ireland, with 125 emigrants. It is rarely that we see a more respectable body of new comers from any portion of Europe, than those brought by the Brothers, and who we hear design settling in Savannah. May they realise their brightest anticipations of prosperity and happiness in their new home.*

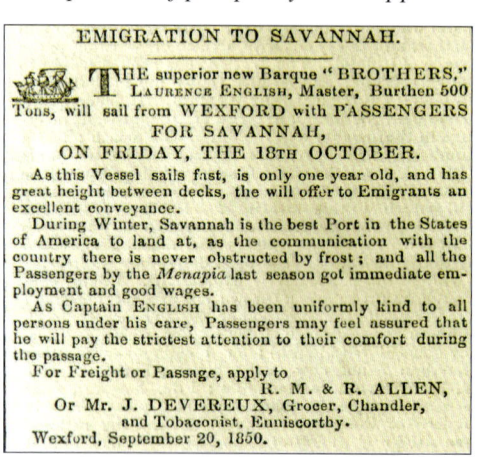

Brothers- Notice of forthcoming departure from Wexford to Savannah, September 1850. *County Wexford Archives.*

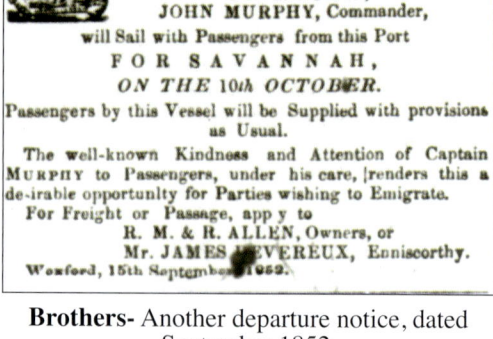

Brothers- Another departure notice, dated September 1852. *County Wexford Archives.*

Notice of sale by auction of the brigantine **Brothers**. *Wexford People June 1876.*

In 1853 she was on the Wexford to Savannah run with emigrants out and cotton back to Liverpool. Her captain was J. Murphy and she was classified as A1 by Lloyd's. Among the crew was a J. Hutchinson who signed on as clerk. On 3 August 1852, a crewman, Walter Busher jumped ship in New York.

On 3 January 1855, prospective customers were advised that Michael Ennis, Timber Merchant of Wexford, was now landing cargo from the barque the **Brothers,** from Miramichi. The cargo consisted of 6979 pine, spruce and deal of various lengths, 10 to 25 ft. Allens sold **Brothers** in 1876.

C

CALEDONIA
Number 49561.

1866 Built at Rothesay, by Robert Lea. 76 tons. Dimensions 82.1x19.4x9.9ft.
1880 Registered at Wexford.

OWNERS
1867 John Millar and Robert McVicar of Greenock.
1875 James Reney of Connah's Quay.
c. 1877 William Sloane of Guilden, Sutton, Cheshire.
c. 1881 William Gafney of Wexford.
1884 Miss Margaret Gafney.
1887 Miss A.C. Gafney.
1897 Charles M. Barry of Paul Quay, Wexford
1899 J.E Barry and Sons;
1899 Feb: Lost in Belfast Lough. Subsequently sold as she lay to McConchie of Donaghadee for 20 pounds

CREW 1891
Master: M. Dempsey, 54.
Mate: T. Carr, 52, Later that year, Mate: John Bourke.
ABs: J. Duggan 25; M. Redmond, 20;
Boy: L. Dempsey, 17.

The **Caledonia** was reported lost in Belfast Lough in February 1899. She was bound from Ayr to Wexford, with a cargo of coal. She went ashore at the entrance to Belfast Lough, in a dense fog, with a heavy gale blowing. All hands were rescued by lifeboat and were landed safely. On board were Captain Michael Dempsey of Michael St., Wexford, and crewmen, Martin Roche of Trinity St.; Nicholas Dempsey of Anne St.; Thomas Newport of William St. and a boy.

CARIOCA
Number 33328. Code RDTS.

1857 Built at Quebec. A barque of 315 tons. Dimensions 123x26.7 x12.6ft.

OWNERS
1865 J.P. Allen, Londonderry and registered in Liverpool.
1868 Jasper W. Walsh of Wexford.
1874 Out of register. Believed lost.

In early October 1868, Jasper Walsh's **Carioca** left Wexford for St John, New Brunswick. She battled fierce Atlantic gales for weeks and got as far as the Banks of Newfoundland with all her bulwarks and stanchions carried away. In the end she had to

Carioca- Three masted barque of 315 tons. Homeward bound passing the Rock of Gibraltar, c1870.

reverse course to run with the wind and eventually arrived at Ballyhack, after spending seven weeks at sea.

Throughout the 1860s and early 1870s, **Carioca** featured regularly in newspapers advertisements from her owner Jasper Walsh, informing prospective customers of her arrival from Savannah with various types of timber. These advertisements halted suddenly in 1873 and the **Carioca** was never mentioned in advertisements again.

In November 1892, the *Wexford People*, while reporting the death of Margaret Rossiter of the Faythe, notes that she was *the wife of seaman named Patrick Rossiter, who foundered in the ill-fated Carioca. Rossiter was first mate of the barque, which was captained on her last voyage by Mr Mark Connor.* The paper also notes that Mrs Rossiter was the daughter of Captain Rowe of the schooner **Forth** which had unknowingly brought cholera to Wexford town in 1867.

Stephen Sinnott, Sailor on board the **Carioca**.
Courtesy Eithne Agar-Sinnott.

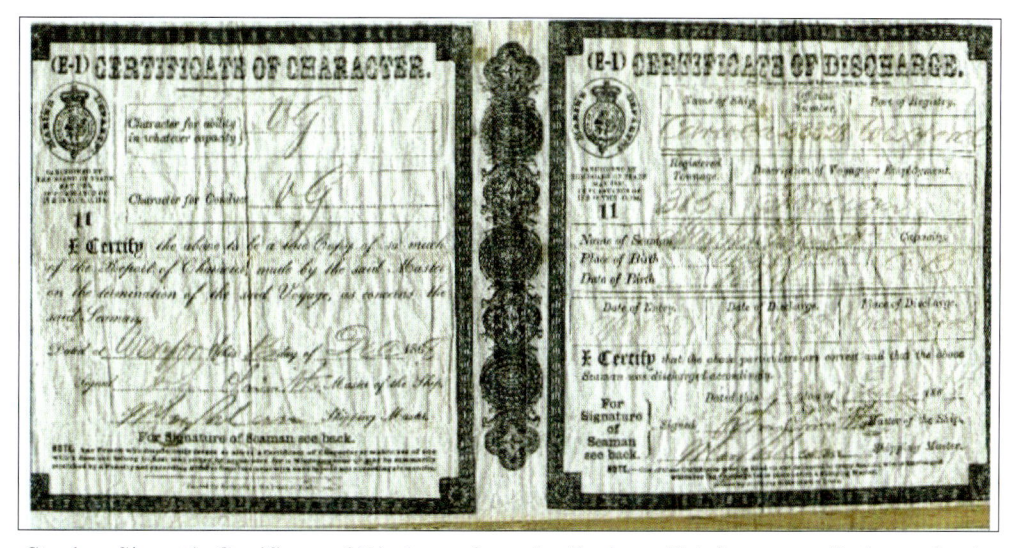

Stephen Sinnott's Certificate of Discharge from the **Carioca**. This is a paper discharge that in later years was superseded by the Discharge Book. *Courtesy, Diarmuid Sinnott.*

A busy day at Wexford Port with, at least thirteen sailing vessels and a steam ship alongside.
National Library of Ireland

CAROLINE

1851 Built at New Brunswick. A brigantine of 130 tons.

1855 Liverpool. **1858** Out of register

OWNER: T. Waters; Master: George Murphy.

On 28 September 1852, **Caroline** signed on a crew at Liverpool Sailors' Home, for Lisbon. Only one was from Wexford, James Keating, an Enniscorthy man. The rest came from Sweden, America, Wales and England.

CARRIG
Number 44125.

1861 Built at Nova Scotia. A barque of 291 tons. Dimensions 112.8x25.5x14.8ft.

OWNERS
1865 R. & R. Allen of Wexford.
1874 Out of register.

CREWS
1864
Captain: Joseph Codd, 35, of Henrietta St., Wexford. Certificate Number 37626.
Mate: John Breen, 45.
Carpente: Thomas Handrick, 24.
Bosun: Thomas Carberry, 41.
Cook: Nicholas Scully, 20 (deserted)
Assistant Cook: Gabriel English 23, St. John, New Brunswick.
Seamen: John Gallagher, 24, Donegal (deserted); William (last name unknown), 31, Plymouth (deserted); Philip Duff age 24; John Breen, 53; Michael Donovan 22; Henry Northcote, 40, Plymouth; William Go?, 28, Dublin; James Hamilton, 22,

1865
Captain: Joseph Codd, 35, of Henrietta St., Wexford.
Mate: John Breen aged 45.
Bosun: Thomas Carberry, 39.
Carpenter: John Gaddern, aged 23.
Seamen: James Byrne, 28; Patrick Rossiter, 24; Matthew Devereux, 22; Henry Leader, 30; Patrick Cullen, 33; Guiseppe Baldachino, 48, Malta.
Cook/Steward: William Murphy, 27.
All these were paid off at Liverpool with the exception of the Maltese who never showed up.

CHARLES
Number 36597. Code RWKQ.

1854 Built at Nova Scotia, by Jackson Cornwallis. Schooner, 94 tons. Dimensions 79.5x21.7 x9ft.

OWNERS
1865 A. Smith, Newport, Nova Scotia. Registered at Windsor, Nova Scotia.
1870 David Devereux of Wexford.
1872 Richard Devereux of Wexford.
1873 10 Jan. Wrecked, Arklow Bank. Captain Devereux and her crew of 6 were lost.

CREW 1870
Master: Devereux of Paradise Row, Wexford, 23.
Mate: Moses Murphy, age 24.
AB: William Blake, 32; John Cullen 25; Patrick Walsh, 19
Boy: James Sennes, 13.

In January 1873, the **Charles** was bound from Dundalk to Wexford with a cargo of barley. After being weather bound in Kingstown (Dun Laoghaire) for some days she left on a Sunday evening along with four other Wexford schooners. She carried a crew of six hands, including Captain James Devereux, who was eldest son of Captain Mark Devereux, Harbour Master of Wexford Port.

Charles- A two masted tops'l schooner at Bridgewater, Somerset at low tide.

New Ross, two schooners and a ketch at anchor in the river c1900.
National Library of Ireland.

According to accounts, all five vessels had to turn back and it appears that the **Charles** struck the Arklow Bank and became totally unmanageable. A steamer, the **Countess** came along but seems to have made little or no effort to rescue the men stranded on the **Charles**. In fact, one letter in a local paper stated that: *The master, Captain James Devereux, who held a certificate of competency. together with his mate, a Mr Rossiter, and crew were all young men, the latter being picked from amongst some hundred seamen in the employ of Messrs Devereux. I mention this to show that had these poor young fellows got any assistance from the steamer* **Countess** *of Dublin they would in all probability have succeeded in saving their lives.*

However, accounts given by people on the **Countess** state, that there was an attempt by her Master to get a boat into the water but it capsized, sending the volunteer crew tumbling into the sea. After a struggle, all of them were brought back on board their vessel. There was still another boat on the **Countess** and the captain called for more volunteers to man her but, after the close call of the first group of volunteers, this time there was no response to his request. Lost on the **Charles** were, Captain: James Devereux; Mate: Patrick Rossiter; Seamen: John Doyle; John Murphy; Apprentice: John Murphy; Boy: J. Roche.

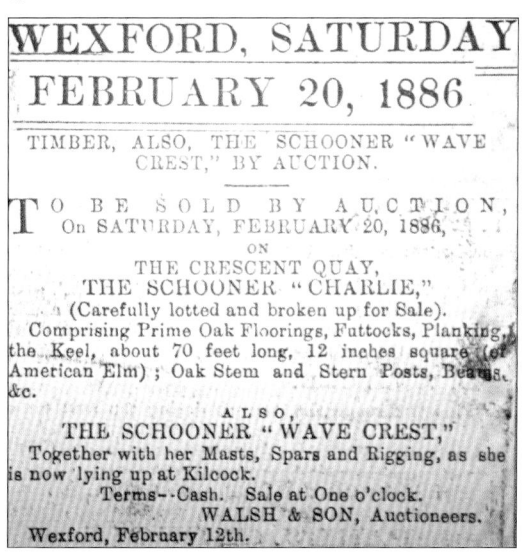

Charlie- A notice of sale by auction, February 1886. *Wexford People.*

Schooners at New Ross c1900.
National Library of Ireland.

CHARLES WALKER
Number 21402. Code NGDS.

1839 Built at Bideford. A schooner of 51 tons, carvel built, with a male figurehead. Dimensions 53.2x15.8x9ft.
1842 Registered at Wexford (Master: John Connolly).

OWNERS
1853 Captain John English.
1865-1889 Gafneys of Wexford.
1897 Wm. Hutchinson of Henrietta St., Wexford.
1904 Out of registration.

CREW 1864
Master: George Hatchell, 65.
Mate: Thomas Hatchell, 22.
Boys: Matthew Stafford; - Browne, 20.

In May 1902, Hutchinson's schooner, **Charles Walker**, was reported run down in the Bristol Channel, off St. Govan's Head. She was homeward bound with a cargo of coal when she ran into heavy weather. She was forced to run to Penarth Roads for shelter. She remained there for about two days until the weather abated and then proceeded on her way. They were off St. Govan's Head when they ran into thick fog, and the captain, James Connelly, sighted a steamer on a collision course with them.

Before any action to avoid the steamer could be taken, she hit them abaft the main rigging, sinking the schooner in a matter of minutes. The crew of the **Charles Walker** saved themselves by scrambling aboard the steamer that had hit them. This was the **Topic**, bound for Belfast. On arrival at Belfast, the shipwrecked crew were brought to the Sailors' Home in Corporation St., where their needs were looked after. The crew of the **Charles Walker** were: Captain James Connelly; Mate: Thomas Breen; Ordinary Seaman: Patrick Anderson; Boy: Patrick Roche.

CHARLIE
Number 21415. Code NGFQ.

1845 Built at Kelvindeck, Glasgow. A schooner of 76 tons. Registered at Wexford.
1875 27 Feb. Registered as a brig.

OWNERS
1846 Richard O' Connor, Wexford, merchant, 48 shares; Patrick Howlin, Wexford, M.M, 16 shares.
1856 Howlin sold his shares to O 'Connor.
1875 Miss Anna A. O'Connor, sole owner (Inherited all shares from Richard O'Connor)
1885 Vessel broken up

CREWS
1864
Master: John Hore, 41.
Mate: Nicholas Cullen, 52.
ABs: John Furlong, 34; Denis Devereux, 31.
Boy: John Smith, 18.

Later in 1864
Master: John Hore, 42.
Mate: John Dillon, 42.
ABs: Thomas Carberry, 42; Michael Byrne, 36.
OS: James Pender, 18.

On 14 July 1875 the **Charlie**, under P. French, master, got into difficulties near Rosslare and drove up and beached at Hayesland. On the same night the brigantine **New Zealand** also went ashore close by. They were both later re-floated. In 1885 the following was endorsed on the register: *Vessel out of repair and not likely to go to sea again, Signed Henry Carr, Registrar. Broken up, certificate cancelled.*

CLARA
Number 72460. Code JPQD.

1879 Built at Bridgewater. A wooden schooner of 69 tons with two masts, with a female figurehead and an eliptical stern. Dimensions 81 x21x8ft.

OWNERS
1879 J Ennor, Padstow
1880 James Bowerman, Bridgewater.
1882 Richard S. Arnold, Devon.
1887 J.H. Martinore, Mutley, Plymouth.
1889 W.G. Cricks, Plymouth.
1895 William Butt, Gloucester.
1895 John Rochford, Kilmore Quay, Co. Wexford.
1910 William Rochford, Kilmore Quay, Co. Wexford.
1923 Re-registered as a motor vessel.
1927 Wrecked at Kilmore Quay.

Remarkable as it seems for a vessel of such small tonnage, the **Clara** was originally engaged on the transatlantic run. On 28 January 1889, she lost her main boom and one crewman, in a force 9 gale. She was bound for Oporto from St. John's, Newfoundland, with a cargo of salt cod. She carried a crew of 5, under the command of Captain W. Maursen.

On 3 February 1912, the **Clara** was bound for her home port with a cargo of 120 tons of manure, in bags, from the Manure Co. of Wicklow, for her owner, William Rochford of Kilmore Quay, Co. Wexford. She was under the command of Captain Thomas Furlong. The weather was clear with snow squalls and a moderate ESE breeze. She arrived at Kilmore Quay on Wednesday the 7 February at 10.30 pm, in a Southerly

John Rochford of Kilmore.
John Power Collection.

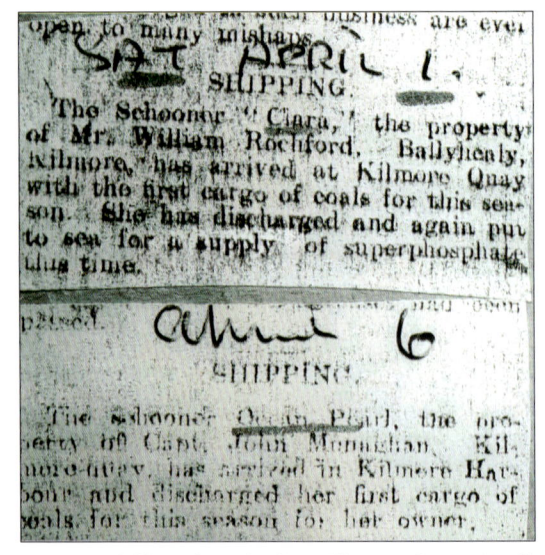

Notice of **Clara's** arrival at Kilmore Quay, April 1911. *John Power Collection.*

Clara, a two masted tops'l schooner of 69 tons, shown here in company with the three masted fore/aft auxiliary schooner **Crest.**
Courtesy of Austin O'Sullivan, Wexford.

Clara ashore at Kilmore Quay, Co. Wexford, November 1927.
W. Kelly Collection, Rosslare Strand.

half gale, with a heavy sea running. The **Clara** tied up at the quay.

However, in the heavy weather, she burst her forward moorings and drove towards the beach inside the harbour. Captain Furlong then set two topsails in an effort to save his ship, but then the aft moorings parted and she drove completely up on to the beach. She suffered extensive damage to her keel and some bottom planks were knocked out. The damage report stated that, *the tide now rises and falls in the vessel*. She was later salvaged and went back into service.

In 1923 her registration was cancelled when she had a motor fitted and she was re-registered as a motor vessel. On 28 October 1927, the **Clara** once again broke free from her moorings at Kilmore Quay and ran ashore close to the local coastguard station. This time, however, she was declared a total wreck and was dismantled where she lay.

CLARA & JESSIE
Number 29750. Code QGWH.

1844 Built at Abbeville, France. She was a two masted schooner with a female figurehead.

OWNERS
1868 Registered at Wexford; owner James Morris.
1879 Francis Morris.
1880 James Morris, Barrack St., Wexford.
1880 William Mangan, Station Master, who held 21 shares. J. R. Cooper and Henry J. Cooper both of Drinagh, Co. Wexford, held 21 and 22 shares respectively.

CREW 1881.
Captain: John Dowd.
Mate: James Doyle.
Sailor: Thomas Breen.
Boy: Andrew Bishop

> One of the prettiest little vessels owned in the port for many years was the little collier brigantine, "Clara & Jessie", 75 tons, owned by Messrs. J. & F. Morris, built in France in 1844, she remained in the coal trade until about 1890 and was commanded for a number of years by Captain J. Morris. Her dimensions are interesting as she had a much deeper draught than the average vessel of her size, having an overall length of 70 feet 6 inches, a beam of 21 feet 4 inches, and a draught of 14 feet 2 inches. She was one of the very few French built craft to be owned in Ireland. 0043

A descriptive report of the **Clara & Jessie**, c1890

Clara & Jessie, wreck sale notice December 1890. *Wexford People.*

Another wreck sale notice, for **Clara & Jessie**, dated December 1890. *Wexford Independent.*

The **Clara & Jessie** went ashore in the 'The Hole' near Rosslare on 17 January 1881. The Coastguard, who had been attending to the **Rambler** and her crew, saw the **Clara & Jessie's** predicament and knew that a similar fate as the **Rambler** was going to befall her. They were standing by, prepared. They fired a line by rocket but the crew of the stricken vessel were unable to use it and instead took to the ship's boat. All hands got ashore safely. **Clara & Jessie** was hard and fast in the sand and eventually broke up and became buried in the sand.

COLUMBINE
Number 8617. Code KCVL.

1834 Built at Schubenacadie, Nova Scotia. A 62-ton schooner.
1840 Registered at Wexford.

OWNERS
1865 Peter Sinnott of Summerhill and Robert Browne, both of Wexford.
1878 Sold to Paul Rogers of Carrickfergus, in part exchange for the **Excellent**. Rogers then sold **Columbine** to Paul English of Lisburn, in Northern Ireland.
1878 Registration transferred to Belfast.

CREWS
1863
Master: Patrick Hughes, 45, of Georges St., Wexford.
Mate: Darby Moran, 68.
Seamen: William Corish; - Hughes, 19.
Boy: James Quirke, 16. All of Wexford.

1864
Master: Patrick Hughes, as above, except age 67.
Mate: Darby Moran, 50.
ABs: William Stafford, 57; Patrick Sommers, 34.
Boy: John Carroll, 18.

On 5 December 1869, the **Columbine** sailed from Dublin for Wexford, with wheat for Davis of Enniscorthy. She was attempting to enter the Hantoon Channel of Wexford Harbour when she went aground at Frazer's Buoy. The weather was so bad that a pilot could not board the vessel, so the captain had attempted to get in himself. Captain Hughes of the **Columbine** was following another vessel in through the channel when she went aground. Fearing that his vessel would break up, the captain sent up distress flares for the lifeboat.

The lifeboat **Civil Service**, stationed at The Fort answered the call immediately. Due to the raging seas the lifeboat encountered great difficulty in getting the crew of the **Columbine** off and to safety. At the time they were rescued there was up to three feet of water in the hold. Captain Hughes had been in charge of the **Columbine** for thirty years and this was the first mishap that he ever had in her.

It was thought that she would become a total loss. However, **Columbine** was re-floated and carried on her career until January 1877, when her articles were endorsed: *this vessel laid up in Carrickfergus from 9 July 1877 to 6 October 1877. Sailed from Carrickfergus on 10 October. Arrived at Workington 12 October. Sailed from Workington 16 November. Arrived 3 October where she remains laid up.*

COMMERCE
No 21433 Code NGHT.

1834 Built at Milford. Registered: 79 tons.

OWNERS
c. 1834 Breen and Co., Wexford (Master: Captain Hammond).
1853 Captain T. Rossiter.
1865 J.T. Devereux of Wexford.
1885 John Codd, South Main St., Wexford.
1891 Wrecked on the Raven Point.

On 2 February 1842, the **Commerce** was anchored off Wexford Harbour in a fierce storm, when she slipped her cables, leaving her with no option but to run with the gale. As luck would have it, she drove across the channel and moored safely at Milford, Wales. In October 1891, the **Commerce** went up on the Swanton Bank at the Raven Point, reportedly due to an error by Pilot Carley, who mistook buoy markings in the channel. The cargo was salvaged but the vessel was wrecked.

COURTOWN LASS
No. 12538.

1850 Built at Gosport, Hants. 50 tons. Dimensions, 83.3x19.3x 10.6 ft. Original name, **Chichester**.

OWNERS (Wexford): Richard & William Massey and Richard Tomkins of Courtown, Co. Wexford.

1918 June: Garston to New Ross with coal, wrecked at Slade, Co. Wexford

Courtown Harbour, the Wexford home port of the **Courtown Lass**, was typical of the smaller ports around the coast of the county. The Harbour's shallow water or sand bars prevented vessels from coming alongside the quayside, so cargo was unloaded into smaller boats referred to as lighters. These were of shallow draft and therefore able to transverse the banks and shallow waters of the harbour.
 A description of the Arklow schooner, **Denbighshire Lass**, unloading her cargo at Courtown Harbour, illustrates how this was accomplished. The cargo usually coal, was discharged into lighters. These lighters were small vessels, manned by four or five men who would row out to the schooner and tie up alongside. The coal was unloaded in sacks and each lighter could take up to twenty, a total weight of one ton. The sacks were

manhandled from the schooner and as soon as the lighter had her full complement, her crew would row her to the quay. There was a tripod-mounted winch on the quay and the man operating it would load each sack onto a waiting horse and cart to deliver them to local coal yards for later distribution. Then the process began all over again until the schooner was fully discharged.

CREST
No 129725.

1903 Built at Marstal, Denmark as **Vigilant**, a three masted wooden auxiliary schooner of 118 tons. Dimensions 91.8x23.2.x9.2ft.

OWNERS
1920 Joseph A. Nolan, Waterford.
1923-1926 James Counsell, Arklow.
1934 John Rochford of Kilmore Quay, Co. Wexford.

In March 1936, the **Crest**, under her master, Captain Willie Bent, was at anchor off Rosslare Harbour in a gale, when she dragged her anchors and ran ashore on the beach. Rosslare lifeboat, the **KECF** was quickly on the scene but the **Crest's** crew decided to remain on board. It was a sensible decision as at low tide it was possible to walk out to the stranded vessel.
Rochford's ownership of the **Crest** was short lived. On 9 September 1941, the **Crest** was homeward bound from Cardiff to Kilmore Quay with coal, when she grounded on the Scarweather Sands in the Bristol Channel and broke her back. She stayed afloat but later sank. The crew took to the boat and were picked up by a passing ship, the mv **Oud**

Crest- An auxiliary schooner alongside the quay at Kilmore for the dedication of the new Kilmore Quay lifeboat, July 1927.

Beijerland, which landed them at Barry, South Wales. The crew consisted of Captain Willie Bent of Wexford, the Mate was John Rossiter of Kilmore and the Seamen were: G. Radford and W. Busher, both also of Kilmore.

CYRUS
Number 8639. Code KCWT.

1839 Built at Gloucester, a schooner 61 tons.
1883 Weight registered as 53 tons.

OWNERS
1865 Thomas Watkins of Hereford.
1879 M. Warren of Gloucester.
1887 Master Thomas Carr, 22 Carrigeen St., Wexford.

The **Cyrus** was lost off Clevedon, Somerset, on 2 September 1887. She went down with all hands. On 9 September, an inquest was held at Newport, on the body of Seaman John Hopkins of the **Cyrus**. Frank Wadding, who was a sailor on the schooner **Mite** of Wexford, identified the body and said that the last time he had seen him was in Wexford on 1 September. The **Cyrus** had left that evening, for Gloucester, with oats.

In October 1887, a local boatman saw a body floating near Clevedon Pier. He took it in tow and brought it ashore. Upon

Cyrus - a two masted tops'l schooner of 53 tons at anchor in Wexford harbour c late 1800s.

examination, the body was thought to be of a man of about 40 years, who was 5 ft 10 ins in height, and had the letters 'T C' tattooed on the back of his right hand. This is what identified him as Captain Thomas Carr. There was a knife found in a pocket plus a scapulars and a picture of the Sacred Heart. From these last two discoveries the police assumed, correctly, that the drowning victim was a Roman Catholic.

An inquest was held at a local farm house. After hearing the evidence of Edward Bacon, the boatman, and Police Constable Tilly, who had initially searched the body and removed it to the mortuary, the jury returned a verdict of 'found drowned'. Captain Carr's body was interred in Clevedon Cemetery, after a funeral mass, celebrated by Father Celestin, Vicar of the Franciscan Friary at Clevedon.

The crew of the **Cyrus** were all local Wexford men. They were: Captain Thomas Carr from Carrigeen St.; Edward Kinsella from John St.; John Hopkins from School St.; and J. Connors from Bride St.

D

DENIS CARTY
Number 3172. Code HSFL.

1833 Built at Newport, Monmouthshire, South Wales. A schooner; Dimensions 62x29x9ft, 87 tons, with a male figurehead.
1834 Registered at Wexford; J. Connors, master.

OWNERS
1834 Robert Carty, Birchgrove, Bree, Co. Wexford.
1835/6 Timothy Gafney
1847 Thomas Gafney
1854 Robert Smith and Thomas Devereux
1885 Thomas Hutchinson.
1886 Thomas Hutchinson sold 16 shares to John Tyghe and 5 to James Marlow.
1886 July: Thomas Hutchinson sold 6 shares to Simon Lambert.
1888 July: John Tyghe sold his 16 shares to John Hutchinson.
1893 Thomas Hutchinson sold his shares to John Hutchinson.
1894 October: James Marlow died and left his 5 shares to his mother, Catherine Kearns.
1903 November: Thomas Hutchinson, shipbroker, died and his estate went to William Hutchinson.
1907 Sold to Newport, Monmouthshire, South Wales
1921 Out of register

Note: Ships are held in 64 shares. Each share is 1/64th of the ship.

Denis Carty, a two masted tops'l schooner of 87 tons at anchor on a calm evening.

CREW 1891
Master: John Hutchinson, 43.
Mate: John Marlow, 45.
AB: Thomas Ryan, 21.
Cook: Thomas Kehoe, 20.
Also that year:
Mate: James Carroll, 31.
Ordinary Seamen: John Daly, 23; Charles Carberry, 22.
Boy: Patrick Murphy, 18; Boy, Thomas Kehoe, 18.

The **Denis Carty**'s original Wexford owner was Robert Carty of Birchgrove, Bree, Co. Wexford, a prominent leader on the rebel side in the great rebellion of 1798. After serving a prison sentence for his activities, he went back into business and one of his many interests was ship owning. The initial voyage of the **Denis Carty** to Wexford was the cause of much interest in the port, not least because her figurehead was said to be a depiction of Esmond Kyan, a rebel leader in the 1798 rebellion. Robert Carty died in 1836. It is said that the **Denis Carty** was named after his son, Denis.

In December 1842 the bodies of two sailors, Francis Doyle and Patrick Roach, were found dead on board the schooner **Denis Carty**, lying at Wexford Quay. An inquest was held in the County Courthouse by T.R. Hawkshaw, County Coroner to determine the cause of these deaths. The inquiry was told that Patrick Rowe and Peter Philips were walking down the Quay and stopped at the doorway of Mr Gafney's shop. Philips then went on board the **Denis Carty,** which was tied up nearby. He shoved the slide of the companionway and called out. Getting no response, he went below and found both men in their berths in the steerage. He laid his hands on Doyle's feet and found that they were cold. Then he went up on deck and called Pat Rowe on board, telling him that there was something wrong with Doyle.

Rowe went on board and found both men stiff and cold. He straight away went to inform Mr Gafney. Medical help was sent for and soon arrived in the form of Mr Cahill a local apothecary. Mr Cahill attempted to bleed both men but failed to get any blood from either man. He then declared them dead. Philips stated that earlier that day he had seen Doyle, who was the ship's boy, putting a cap on the funnel to prevent rain getting in. He (Philips) left the ship about 4 o'clock and could not say whether the captain came on board after that or not.

Thomas Connors, master of the **Denis Carty**, said that he had often found a very

Denis Carty, A share sale notice dated June 1836. *Wexford People.*

unpleasant sensation from the effects of the fire in the steerage. Mr Cahill confirmed that he had tried, unsuccessfully, to bleed both men one in the temple and the other in both arms, unsuccessfully. He supposed their deaths had been caused by suffocation. After hearing evidence from Surgeon James Furlong, who had performed a post mortem on the bodies, the inquiry concluded: *We find the deaths of Patrick Roach and Francis Doyle were caused by suffocation in consequence of a fire incautiously allowed to remain in the hold of the vessel upon which the hatches were closed.*

On Monday 2 May 1877 the **Denis Carty**, from Newport, was entering Wexford harbour, when she stuck on the Bar. Despite having the assistance of the tugboat, she remained fast. After being lightened, she was eventually got off. The *Wexford Constitution* reported that, *we regret to state that the Bar shows no sign of improvement; but as the winter season has passed and finer weather may be expected, fewer shipping accidents, we hope, will result.* They went on to say that they had learnt from *undoubted authority* that without the *unwearied exertions* of Captain Cogley, the Pilot Master and his pilots, there would have been many more accidents. Among his many accomplishments Captain Cogley had devised a system of signals to make approaching vessels aware of the position of the shifting sands, which were the cause of many tragic occurrences at the Bar.

Denis Carty- Report on her grounding at the Hill o' Sea, near Rosslare March 1906. *Wexford People*.

On 31 January 1887, the Welsh newspaper, *Western Mail*, reported that the **Denis Carty** had gone ashore at Breaksea but was re-floated. In June 1905, the she was on passage from Newport, with coal for Wexford. Coming down the Bristol Channel, she came upon a boat belonging to the **ss Kilkeel** in Milford Sound. Considerable wreckage was floating about. The previous Tuesday they had passed the steamer between the Nash Light and the Scarweather lightship and it seemed that shortly afterwards, that the **ss Kilkeel** had hit a rock. Later reports said that the crew had all been landed safely at Milford Haven.

The grounding of the Wexford schooner, **Denis Carty**, was reported on 31 March 1906. The schooner went ashore at the Hill O' Sea, midway between Rosslare Strand and Rosslare Harbour at 6 am on Sunday 11 March. She had left Newport on Friday 9 March, under her captain Thomas 'Lanigan' Walsh, with a cargo of coal for Wexford. She had to go into Milford for shelter and was forced to stay there, weather bound, for two weeks. When she finally arrived in the South Bay on the Saturday, it was impossible to cross the Bar, so she went to anchor off the Hill O' Sea, in comparative safety, abreast of the lighthouse. During the night the wind not only got up more severely but, more importantly, it changed direction to the North East, putting the **Denis Carty** in serious danger. The anchor chain held fast until about 6 am. By then, the gale was at its most furious and the seas were described by an onlooker as *running mountains high*. The cables parted and the schooner headed straight for the shore.

The crew, who had been standing by all night, were still at their stations and with a valiant effort managed to get some sail on. This was of little or no avail, as it was difficult, if not impossible, to manoeuvre in the face of the furious gale. Realising the hopelessness of their position, the men raised signals of distress The signals were seen by both the coastguards at Ballygeary and the lifeboat at Rosslare. Both responded but, before the lifeboat crew were assembled, the coastguards were seen to be on their way to aid the crew of the schooner, which was ashore by then. She struck bow first, about eighty yards from the shore on a high tide. Mountainous seas were breaking over her and but for the prompt action of the experienced coastguards and their lifesaving apparatus, there was a great danger that the crew were doomed. All hands were removed safely.

At the time of the report, she was still high and dry and showing signs of a lot of damage to her port side gunwales. Efforts were to be made to save her. She struck in nearly the same spot as the Danish schooner **Bonafide**, which had broken up there shortly before the **Denis Carty**. It was thought that the vessel could be salvaged. However, the **Denis Carty** did not break up as expected and eventually was pulled off the sand by the tug **Wexford** and brought into the quay. Her cargo was discharged and the ship was repaired. On board the **Denis Carty** that night: Captain Thomas 'Lanigan' Walsh; Edward Doyle; Michael Murphy; and James White, all of Wexford.

In 1885, the **Denis Carty** had come into the ownership of Thomas Hutchinson. She was to remain in the ownership of that family until 1907 when the long serving Wexford schooner was sold by William Hutchinson to Newport, to be used as a lighter. By 1921 she was out of register.

DIOLINDA
Number 119636. Code HPCG. In 1934 Code EIBX. In 1940 VSDM.

1909 Built as **Annie Reece**, at Appledore, Devon, by R. Cock & Sons.
A three masted auxiliary schooner of 150 tons, with a clipper bow, a figurehead and a square stern. Dimensions 99.1x22.7x9.4ft. Registered at Gloucester and managed by Albert Reece of Sharpness.
1922 Registered in Wexford to Captain Cardiff

Like many of the steel hulled schooners, she was commissioned by the admiralty during WW1 and fitted out as a 'Q' ship. After the war she was returned to her owners who sold her to the Dory Ship Company of Guernsey, Channel Islands, in 1918. There she was refitted, had a new auxillary engine installed and was re-named **Diolinda**. In 1922, Captain Cardiff of St John's Road, Wexford, bought her and registered her in the port. **Diolinda** traded under Captain Cardiff's ownership for 15 years, until he retired in 1935. During his ownership, **Diolinda** was well maintained and had the reputation of being one of the finest ships sailing these waters. Around this time down in the Indian Ocean, the Seychelles registered barquentine **Elizabetha** was wrecked and a replacement was required.

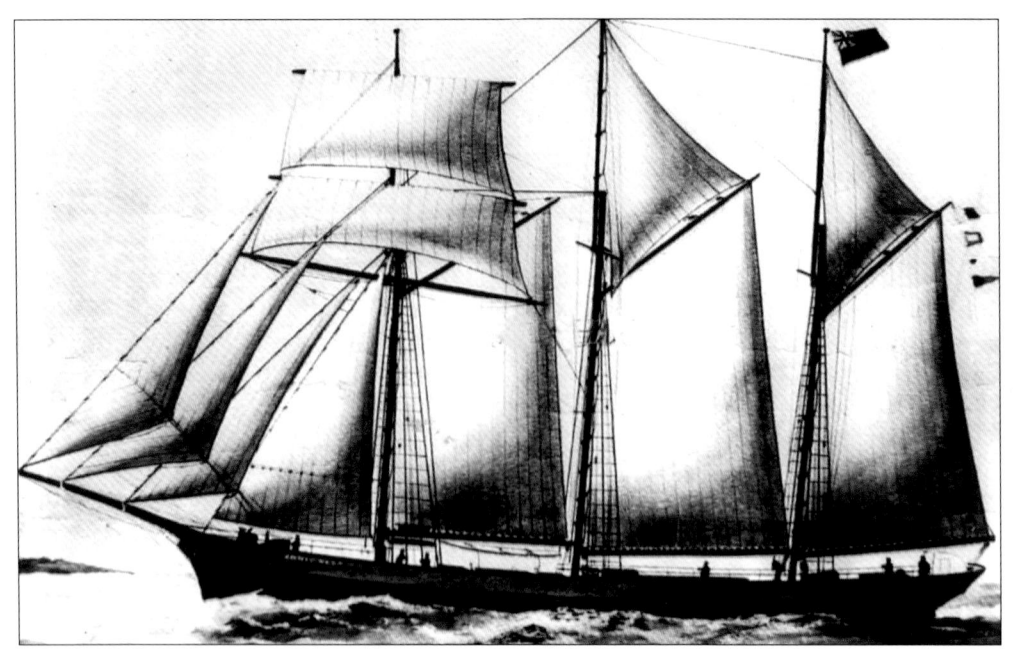

Diolinda- Depicted here as the **Annie Reece**, as built in 1909.

Her owners insisted that the replacement was to be small, fast, stylish and well built. They were told that such a vessel could be found in Wexford, Ireland. **Diolinda** was brought to Liverpool, inspected and classed A1 by Lloyds. This meant that she was considered capable of taking the hazardous trip down to the Indian Ocean. Under the command of her new owner, Captain T. Voss, and a crew of five men, she sailed for the Seychelles.

After 126 days of battling gale after gale on what was described as one of the hardest voyages undertaken, they arrived at Table Bay, Cape Town. The **Diolinda** underwent another re-fit in Cape Town and sailed for her new home. She sailed around the Cape of Good Hope and reached Mauritius in 36 days. She then began trading between the Indian Ocean Islands and her register was transferred to Port Victoria, Mahe, Seychelles.

That was the last Wexford heard of **Diolinda** until February of 1959, when Captain Mark Higgins of Thomas St., Wexford, master of Reardon Smith's mv **New Westminster City**, saw her in Port Victoria, Mahe, Seychelles. By this time, she had run aground, been re-fitted and put back to sea under new owners, a company called East African Navigators. **Diolinda** was reported lost by fire on passage from East Africa to the Seychelles in the 1960s. However, in 1971 two Wexford sailors, Donald Carroll of Mannix Place and Michael Scallan of Kennedy Park, who were on the mv **Irish Sycamore**, saw her still plying her trade in the Indian Ocean.

No more was heard of **Diolinda** until April 1986 when Wexford craftsman and renowned ship model maker, John Walker decided to make a model of her. Diligent as ever and knowing her last reported owners were in the Seychelles, he contacted the shipping authorities on that island and received details of her career from the President's Office of the Department of Transport and Marine Services.

The **Diolinda** had been re-registered in 1939 at Port Victoria, The Seychelles and given the new official number of 119636 and the call sign VSDM. Captain Voss was still

Diolinda- A three masted auxiliary schooner of 150 tons.

owner and remained so until his death in April 1955 when ownership of the vessel passed to his widow. In July 1956 the **Diolinda** was sold to Mr Habib Kasim Manji of Tanga and the **Diolinda** was re-registered in Mombasa. The Registrar of Ships in Mombasa still had her on their books in 2000, but only as a hulk lying in an inner harbour at Mombasa Port. Interestingly the name Wexford was still legible across her stern.

A waterline model of the **Diolinda**, made by Mr J. Walker of Wexford.
Courtesy of Brian Boyce, Rosslare Hbr. Maritime Heritage Centre.

DISPATCH
Number 427. Code HCSL.

1846 Built at St. Anthony's on Tyne, a brigantine of 145 tons; dimensions 81.9x20x12.2ft. Carvel built, with a figurehead.

OWNERS
1846 Richard Devereux and Matthew McCann, master.
1853 Devereux; J. Allen, master.
1880 J.J. Devereux.
1881 J. Kearon of Arklow.
1885-1896 J. Kingsberry of Belfast.
1896-1900 J. Elliott of Belfast.
1900 Donald McLean, of Avoch, Ross and Cromarty, Scotland.
1902 Harold Brown of Shoreham on Sea, Sussex.
1907-1914 P.T. Terry of Brighton.
1914 Out of register and broken up May that year.

Research initially gave the impression that there were two vessels named **Dispatch**, one a schooner and the other a barquentine, on the Wexford register, just one year apart. This did not seem feasible and further search indicated that there was just one **Dispatch**. Records state that in 1865 Devereux's **Dispatch** was a 145-ton schooner. She was registered as a coaster with Furlong as master. However, in 1866 the **Dispatch** had two differences: she was now a barquentine and was 195 tons, registered for Wexford to the Mediterranean area. The only conclusion is that the **Dispatch** was taken into the Dockyard, lengthened and re-rigged as a barquentine, trading between England and France and also on the Galatz run. Further research confirmed this.

    The **Dispatch** was unusual among Wexford sailing ships in that during much of her career she appears not to have been on a regular run but traded to wherever the business took her. Most, if not all, of the Wexford vessels ran a regular route: the colliers from Wexford to the Bristol Channel and back; the foreign going ships to Galatz in Romania and ports in between and back to Wexford or to North America. This appears not to have been the case with the **Dispatch**. A log of the **Dispatch**, which is in a private collection, indicates that she traded from England to various continental ports. Extracts from the log are reproduced in **Appendix 1**. The master of the **Dispatch** on these voyages was Captain James Carr of Carrigeen St. Wexford. Later he was master of the ill-fated **Cyrus**.

    In 1862, the **Dispatch** came to public attention, when a crew member took a case against the master of the ship, charging him with cruelty. In the 17th 18th and 19th centuries, discipline on deep sea sailing ships was harsh, to say the least. There were numerous tales of men being so severely treated by ships' captains and mates that they died from their injuries or jumped over the side of the ship mid ocean to avoid any further punishment.

    Many American vessels employed men known as 'Bucko' Mates whose main job was to beat obedience into the stubborn sailor. Discipline was similarly harsh on British ships. This truthfully cannot be said of Wexford vessels, even the Deep Sea ones. One possible reason for this is that all the men, Captains, Mates and Seamen came from the

Dispatch- A three masted barquentine of 145 tons, homeward bound from Galatz. Seen here off the Dardenelles c1870.

same town, the same streets in many cases, and had a lifetime acquaintance, if not friendship, with each other. However, vessels from the big international ports, such as Liverpool, had crews that were multinational and multi-racial and did not have this connection. Only once has a Wexford master been accused and charged with cruelty and that was in May 1862 when Pierce Wade, a crewman of the **Dispatch** of Wexford, charged Captain Michael Furlong of that ship with a series of aggravated assaults.

The case was heard at Wexford Petty Sessions. Mr Carr was acting for the complainant and Messrs Harvey and Waddy for the defendant. Mr P.J. Connell and Alderman J Walsh were on the bench and Mr Connell, presiding. Wade claimed that Captain Furlong assaulted him, wounded him, beat him with a hand-spike and tried to throw him over the side and drown him. These alleged assaults happened on two occasions and caused Wade to desert his ship at Sulina. Deserting a ship is an offence and the deserter is liable to be jailed, but Mr Carr pointed out to the Judges that the Merchant Shipping Act stated that if a man wishes to leave a ship due to the master's ill treatment, he can go before the British Consul, accompanied by the master, to plead his case. If the master refuses to go to the Consul with him he can leave the ship without being liable to the desertion charge. This Mr Carr argued, is exactly what happened.

We understand this photograph is of the **Dispatch** later in her career at Shoreham, England early 1900s.

In his evidence, Pierce Wade said that he had shipped on board the **Dispatch** on 1 September, 1861, as Cook/Steward for a voyage to Galatz. About seven weeks into the trip, the captain, in a fit of anger, grabbed him around the waist and tried to throw him over the fore-rigging. He wasn't able to do this, so he ran him aft, knocked him down and swore that he would throw him over the side and drown him. He only succeeded however, in getting his legs over the stern as he(Wade) held on to the stern chains for dear life until the mate came along and told the Captain to 'mind what he was doing' as Wade had severely punished a captain before who had ill- treated him.

About three weeks later, according to Wade, the captain became angry again as Wade did not have as much molasses as he expected him to have. This time the captain struck him with a hand-spike, knocked him to the deck and kicked him. He then followed Wade into the fo'c'sle and struck him with his fist. Wade also alleged that, at Sulina, as he was about to go to bed, he got a message from the Captain. When he went to see the captain he accused him of having left another Wexford vessel, the **Hope**, because he had committed robbery. Then, after using some abusive language, Captain Furlong broke a plate over his head, stuck a fork in his side and said that he would kill him. Wade then said that he asked the Captain to go to the British Consul with him, as was his right, but the Captain refused. So Wade left the ship and two days later found the Consul's residence. The Consul took note of his complaint against the Captain but refused to swear him in, saying that he could do that when he arrived in Wexford. The Consul then sent him home as passenger. On what ship he didn't say. Wade further stated that he had a discharge from the **Hope** saying his conduct was good. Wade also complained that the captain had fired a gun at John Nolan. This was part of his complaint to the Consul in Constantinople but this was said not to be considered here as it was nothing to do with Wade. John Nolan swore that the captain did not fire a gun at him but that it was usual to fire one in the evening.

Mr Harvey then began to cross examine Wade and said that it appeared to him the he did not go to the Consul until the **Dispatch** had sailed. He also questioned why it had taken Wade two days to find the Consul's house as it was not far from the ship and had a flag flying from the house. When Harvey asked Wade if the British Consul had not told him that Captain Furlong had been looking for him, Wade replied, *Not to my knowledge*. He also said that the captain had been drunk in a storm, but this was denied by three other witnesses. Wade did, however, admit to stealing some of the molasses.

Arthur Fortune, the mate of the **Dispatch** then took the stand and told the judges that he never cautioned Captain Furlong against striking Wade. In fact, he thought that Captain Furlong was more than kind to him. He did see the captain take hold of him at the stern of the ship but his legs were not over the stern. Fortune said that he assumed the captain was joking with Wade. He never heard the captain say that he would throw Wade over the side and he knew nothing about the hand-spike incident. He thought the captain may have been trying to frighten Wade. Wade had told him that he was going to the British Consul but he advised against. The mate further advised him to stay on the ship. He had heard about Wade being stabbed by the captain but that was in Galatz and a week after Wade had left the ship. The captain followed Wade ashore when he left the ship but was unable to find him. He also stated that the captain was perfectly sobre throughout the voyage and that there was only two dozen of porter on board when they left England. According to Mr Fortune, Wade was a bad cook, so much so that the crew refused to go to Constantinople unless he was discharged.

Charles Bishop, a crewman, corroborated the mate's evidence and said that he did not see the captain striking Wade with the hand spike but he did see one in the captain's hand. Neither did he see the captain strike or kick Wade or see him stab him with a fork. In reply to a question from Mr Carr, Bishop said that the captain could have struck Wade but he did not witness it. The next witness was a crewman named John Rossware. He corroborated the previous witness's evidence, adding further that he had heard Wade say *I will never be easy until I get that bugger's* [meaning the captain's] *neck broke in Wexford*.

The bench then retired for a few minutes and when they returned said that they were prepared to have more serious charges proved against the defendant. There had been an appearance of an assault but then it should be remembered that the boy [throughout the case Wade was referred to as a boy, but research indicates that he was about 30 years old. Perhaps it was his position on the ship that they were referring to] had given great provocation by his negligence. However, despite having said that they were prepared to have more serious charges proved against the Captain, the bench's decision was that the current charges had not been sustained and dismissed the case. Further research indicates that Wade never went to sea again and secured a job on the local docks.

Old hulk, possibly a Gabard, and a three masted barque at New Ross, c1880s.
National Library of Ireland.

Grosse Ile, late 1850s.

Quebec c1860.

Loading timber at Quebec, mid 1800s.

Quebec.

DORA

1835 Built at New Brunswick, 75 tons, a schooner.
1842 Registered at Wexford, owner, Richard Allen. (Joseph Fennell, Master).
1846 Out of register.

OWNER (1842): Richard Allen (Joseph Fennell, Master)

CREW
1845
All these served in the **Dora** at various times during this year.
Masters: John Rossiter, 30; Laurence McGee, 25; James Neville, 45.
Mates: John Campbell, 39; John Clancy, 28; Thomas Walsh, 50.
Seamen: Patrick Lynch, 27; Michael Bryan, 25; James Carroll, 21; Michael Dillon, 42; Thomas Murphy, 19. James Furlong, 23; Nicholas Dunne, 19; Martin Scallan, 41; James Mare, 22; Clement Busher, 31; Joseph Reilly, 27; A. Duggan, 27; L. Cousins, 20; John Howlin, 19; Nicholas Breene, 34; Maurice Gladwin, 20; Edward Rowe, 30; Mark Bent, 23.
Apprentices: Joseph Murphy, 20, Thomas Hackett, 18; M. Connor, 22; Owen Cash, 16.
Boys: Thomas Beck; Christopher Leonard, 19; Joseph Flood, 16; Patrick Coulan, 18; James Rowe, 14; S. Foote, 14.

DUNBRODY
Number 32842. Code RBTK.

1845 Built at Quebec, a barque of 458 tons. Dimensions, 109.8x26.7x18.7ft

OWNERS
1865 Anthony E. Graves of New Ross, Co. Wexford.
1872-1875 Francis P. Carrell of Cardiff.

Dunbrody was an emigrant ship out of New Ross and, like other New Ross ships on the transatlantic run, was renowned for the low mortality rate on her voyages. For example, on 22 January 1847, **Dunbrody** sailed for Quebec with 297 passengers. On arrival in Canada, only four deaths were reported. In the 11 years from 1847 to 1858, **Dunbrody** declared a total of seven mortalities on board; four in 1847 on the Quebec run, and three in 1853 on a voyage to Savannah, Georgia. It should be noted however, that these

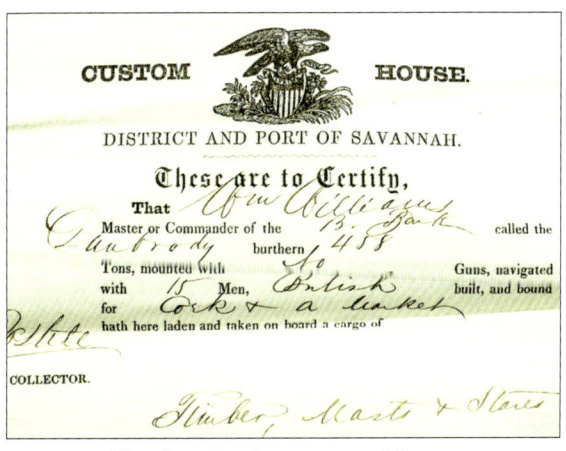

Dunbrody, clearance certificate.
Co. Wexford Archives.

Dunbrody at Quebec, 1859.
Courtesy of Myles Courtney, New Ross Street Focus.

Dunbrody. A three masted barque of 458 tons. Owned by Graves of New Ross is shown here anchored off Grosse Ile, Canada c1860.

figures are of those who died on board and take no account of those who died in Quebec, at Grosse Ile, or anyone who died shortly after disembarkation at Savannah.

An advertisement for a proposed voyage on or about 15 October 1853, under the command of Captain William Williams, extols the virtue of Savannah as a port of arrival. It states the **Dunbrody** to be a Packet Ship of 1000 tons, whereas her registration details give her tonnage as 458 tons. Possibly an exaggeration, possibly to instill confidence in the prospective passenger. Surely a 1000-ton ship was more likely to withstand the rigours of a transatlantic crossing than a vessel half her size. **Dunbrody** was built solely as a cargo vessel

> EMIGRATION TO
> SAVANNAH, UNITED STATES.
>
> The First-Class Superior Packet-Ship,
> *DUNBRODY,*
> WILLIAM WILLIAMS, Commander;
> 1000 TONS,
> Is intended to Sail from
> NEW ROSS TO SAVANNAH,
> WITH PASSENGERS,
> ON OR ABOUT THE 15th OF OCTOBER, NEXT.
>
> Savannah is a most excellent winter landing port for Emigrants, the climate is then mild and healthy, and labour of every kind is in better demand at much higher wages than are usually obtainable at New York—The passage to the latter Port is long and dangerous in winter, while to Savannah, it is safe and comparatively easy.
>
> In the neighbourhood of Savannah, land is cheap and fertile, and from it run lines of Steamers and Railways, which convey passengers to the North or West at low fares.
>
> For terms of Passage and all other particulars, apply to the owners,
>
> W. GRAVES & SON, NEW-ROSS;
> Messrs. T. & N. SINNOTT, Enniscorthy; or, to Mr. JOHN STAFFORD, 57, South Main-street, Wexford.
>
> ☞ Accommodation for first and second Cabin Passengers.
>
> New-Ross, 24th September, 1853.

Dunbrody- Notice of sailing from New Ross to Savannah, dated September 1853.
Co. Wexford Archives.

but, as a result of the famine of 1847 and the exodus of a considerable number of the population to North America, there was a great shortage of passenger vessels to carry them to their destinations. As a result, many transatlantic vessels, the **Dunbrody** included, were modified to carry passengers.

Also in 1847, another New Ross vessel **Lady Bagot**, sailed for St John, New Brunswick with 320 passengers and declared four deaths. Compared to other vessels from ports across channel on that run, that regularly reported 20 to 25 deaths, the

> A STRANGE VISITER.—On the night of the 3rd inst., as the bark Dumbrody, of New Ross, was on her homeward passage from Quebec, 950 miles from land, long. 30 W., one of the seamen observed a strange-looking bird attempting to roost among the shrouds. After many unsatisfactory efforts, it at length found a brief resting place on the main top-sail yard, to which one of the sailors quickly ran up and effected a capture. The bird proved, on examination, to be a very large owl, and created much surmise as to what unlucky wind could have blown it so far out of its latitude.

Report of a strange visitor to the **Dunbrody**.
Wexford People.

> **PORT OF CARDIFF.**
>
> MR. R. SHORT has been instructed to SELL by AUCTION, at the Exchange Rooms, Bute Docks, on MONDAY, JAN. 23rd, 1871, the Barque DUNBRODY, of Cardiff, 458 tons register, with all her stores, tackle, and apparel, as she now lies in the East Bute Dock, where she may be inspected. Sale to commence at three for four o'clock. The vessel and her stores to be taken with all faults as they now lie, without any allowance for weight, length, quantity, quality, or any defect or error in description whatever.
>
> Further particulars and inventories may be obtained of Mr. Francis P. Carrel, Ship Broker, Cardiff; or of Mr. R. Short, Auctioneer, Marine Surveyor, &c., 2, Stuart Street, Cardiff. 286

Notice a sale of the **Dunbrody** at the Port of Cardiff.
New Ross Street Focus.

numbers on the New Ross ships appear remarkably low.

Dunbrody had many masters over the years, including Captain John Baldwin, her first master, Captain John Williams, who succeeded Captain Baldwin, and Captain William Williams, who was born, 1815 in St David's, Pembrokeshire, Wales. The latter appears to have been her longest serving commander. There has been some confusion over the two Captain Williams, which is added to by the fact that they both married sisters in New Ross. Captain John Williams died at sea in the 1850s. Captain William Williams who retired from the sea and became a ship's chandler on the New Ross Quay, died at the age of 88 at his residence, Quay St., New Ross on 5 October 1899. **Dunbrody** was lost off the coast of Labrador in 1875. She is remembered today in the form of an exact replica moored at New Ross. It has justifiably become one of the main tourist attractions in the South East of Ireland and is a fitting memorial to the passengers and crew who crossed the Atlantic in the dark days of 'Black 47'.

> **LOSS OF TIMBER SHIPS.**
>
> We (*Manchester Examiner*) learn by cable of the loss of two well-known Liverpool and Quebec timber traders, both bound from Quebec to Liverpool, with full cargoes of timber. The first, the Calcutta, was wrecked on Magdalen Island, in the Gulf of St. Lawrence; crew saved. She was a fine ship of 1427 tons, built in Quebec last year, and owned by Messrs. W. H. Ross and Co., of Liverpool. ✭The second, the Dunbrody, was wrecked on the coast of Labrador; crew saved. She was a ship of 458 tons, built in Quebec in 1845, and owned by F. P. Carrell, of Cardiff. ✭
>
> SOURCE: The Monmouthshire Merlin November 1875.

The report on the wreck of the **Dunbrody** in the Gulf of St. Lawrence, November 1875.
New Ross Street Focus.

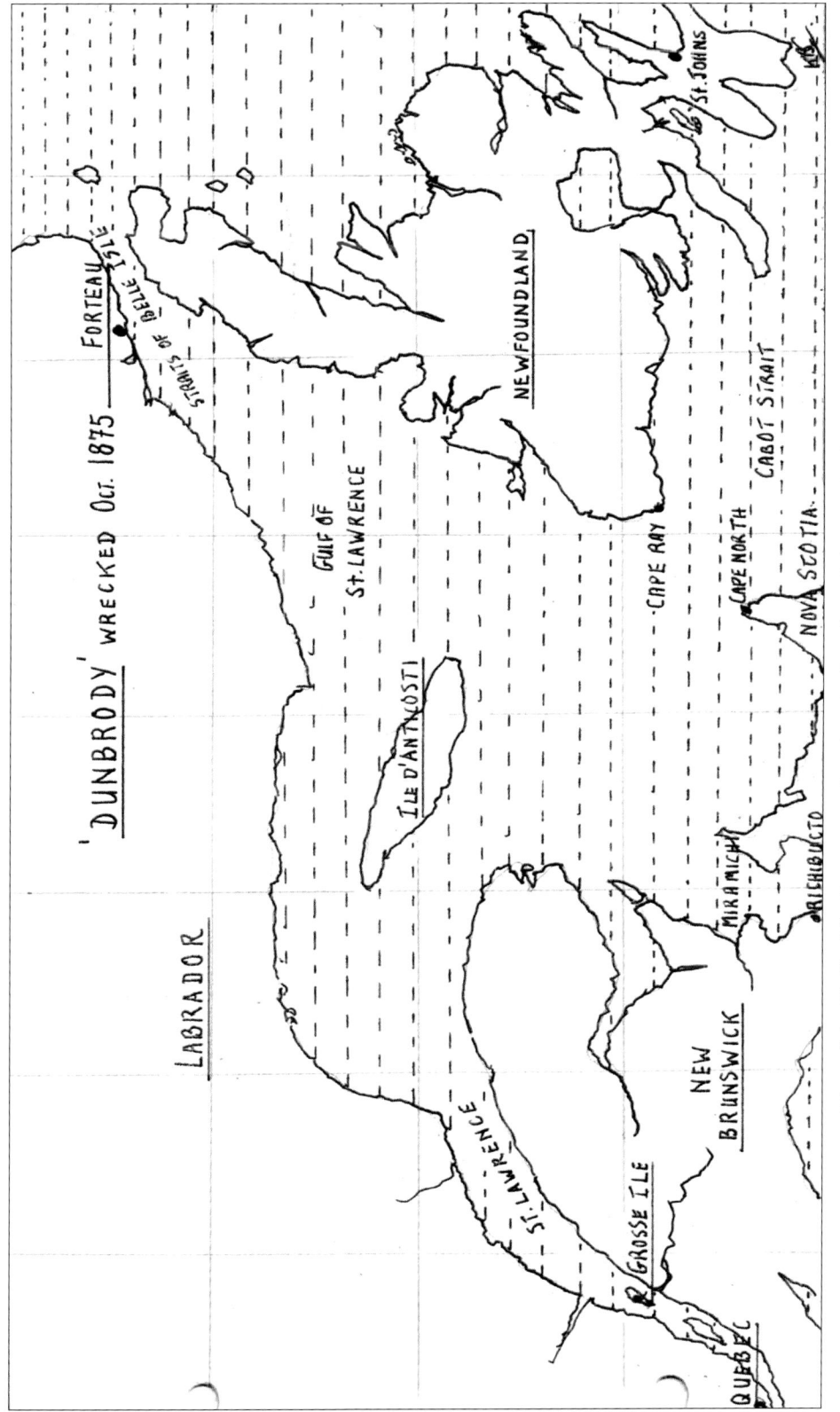

Map of the Gulf of St. Lawrence, showing the location of the wreck of the **Dunbrody**.

Dunbrody (II) The day of the launch of the famine replica ship **Dunbrody** at New Ross, February 2001.
Courtesy of the JFK Trust, New Ross.

E

EATON
Number 22844. Code NPDV.
1832 Built at Chester, a wooden schooner of 47 tons, with two masts.
Dimensions: 61.3x17.2x7.0 ft.

OWNERS
1865 Richard Owen, Bangor, North Wales.
1876 William Williams of Bangor, North Wales.
1879-1880 M. Devlin, Wexford
1880 Andrew Colfer of Carrig-on-Bannow, Co. Wexford.
1909 Simon Roche, Ballygow, Bannow, Co. Wexford.
1919 Cowman of Bannow.

On 29 January 1919, the vessel was owned by Cowman of Bannow and under the command of Captain Michael Morris of Wexford Town. She was lost after a collision with the British steamer **Glenorchy**, off the Breaksea Lightship off Barry, Glamorganshire, Wales, in the Bristol Channel. She was en route from Wexford to Cardiff with pit props. All hands were saved and brought into Barry. Mate Thomas Gratten was also from Wexford Town.

The report of the arrival of the **Eton (Eaton)** at the Bar o' Lough, Cullenstown, September 1911.
Wexford People.

Vessels Sunk Off West Wales.

The crew of the Wexford schooner Eaton were landed at Barry on Wednesday morning, the vessel having sunk in the Bristol Channel after collision.

The steamship Boah landed ten officers, men and crew of a French schooner found in a sinking condition off the Smalls.

Report of the Wexford schooner **Eaton** sinking near Barry, South Wales, 1919.

ECHO
Number 44130.

1863 Built at Weymouth, Nova Scotia by Savery, a schooner of 80 tons. Dimensions: 76.6.x18.3x9.7ft.

OWNERS
1870 John Barrington of Wexford.
1885 Thomas Harpur of Wexford.
1888 Harpur & Wickham, South Main St., Wexford.
1899 John Charles McCullagh, Paul Quay, Wexford.
1902 Sold to Liverpool and converted to a hulk; re-named **Taxi** in 1912
1915 Percy F. Clinton of Liverpool.
1917 Resolute Co. Ltd., Trafford Park, Manchester.
1921 Out of register.

CREWS
1864
Master: Michael Williams, 30.
Mate: James Power, 32.
ABs: Mathew Furlong, 34; Francis Lambon, 31.
Boy: Michael Neil, 15.

Previous crew signed off: ABs: Patrick Lawlor, 21; Bartholomew Fortune 17; Patrick Whitty, 27; John Browne, 23.

1870
Master: Michael Williams.
Mate: Patrick Kelly, 30.
ABs: Thomas Newport; Pat. Neville, 28.
OS: Michael Sinnott, 17.
Boy: Stephen Codd, 15.

In April 1887, the **Echo** went aground on Wexford Bar. She was being towed over the Bar by the tug **Erin** which was standing in for the **Ruby** which was in for survey. **Erin** did not have the power of the **Ruby** and was unable to pull her off but luckily she did float off the next day. In November 1894, Harpur and Wickham's **Echo** homeward bound from Newport, with coal, was struck by a gale while anchored off the Tuskar. She lost her anchor and chain, plus her main boom and yard, but was towed into the harbour the next day. Vessel hulked 1900.

ECONOMIST
Number 16677. Code MCLS.

1857 Built at Berwick on Tweed, Northumberland by Gowan. A two masted schooner of 98 tons. Dimensions, 78.4x21.0x9.2ft.

OWNERS
1865 James Fisher, Barrow-in-Furness.
1876 Joseph Fisher, Barrow-in-Furness.
1879 Alex Crawford, Glenarm, Co. Antrim.
1888 John Crawford, Belfast.
1889 P Neilson, Kirkcudbright, Dumfries, Scotland.
1891 John Codd, and James Murphy, both of Parnell St., Wexford.
1903 30 May. Sunk in collision in the Bristol Channel.

The **Economist** was so named because her design was said to make ballast unnecessary when sailing light. On 3 June 1903, the **Economist** was sailing along with two other vessels, the **Jane McColl** of Wexford and the **Eagle** of Waterford. They kept sight of each other until a thick blanket of fog came down. Shortly afterwards off Nash Sands in the Bristol Channel, the **Eagle** ran into the **Economist** and sank her. Captain James Murphy the part owner of the **Economist** was in charge at the time. When he returned home, Captain Murphy related to the local press what had occurred. He said that the weather was fine and there was a moderated breeze and they were making good headway during both the forenoon and the afternoon. The night was also fine and all went well until about half past eleven, when the crew saw a light ahead, bearing down on them. At the time Captain Murphy was in bed and he was summoned on deck immediately. The crew, realising the danger they were in, hailed the oncoming vessel, but there was no response. A few minutes later the collision occurred. The **Economist** was struck abaft the main rigging with such force that she foundered in around three minutes. She went down so fast that the crew were lucky to be able to climb onto the headgear of the **Eagle**. Nothing on board was saved and the crew had to leave their belongings behind them. The **Eagle** turned back to Cardiff Roads where the **Economist** crew were picked up by a tug and brought ashore at Barry Dock. They went from there to Cardiff where they were looked after by Captain Patrick Doyle of the **Mary Agnes**, who happened to be in port at the time. From there they travelled to Waterford on Monday and arrived home in Wexford on Tuesday. The **Eagle** had resumed her original course for Waterford, with little apparent damage, other than her fore yard jibboom had carried away.

EDITH ELEANOR
Number 85261. Signal Letters WFBD.

Built 1881 at Aberystwyth for H. Bridger, London, a schooner of 96 tons. Dimensions: 80.4x21.3x10.4ft.

OWNERS
1891 David Roberts of Aberystwyth.
1896 Humphrey Price of Aberystwyth.
1904 Richard Jones, Caernarfon.
1916 Patrick Donovan, Lamb House, South Main St. Wexford (Draper).
1916 8 May. Sold 16 shares to Edward Wickham (salvage contractor), Fort, Rosslare, Co. Wexford.
1916 20 May. 16 shares sold to James Wickham, Fort, Rosslare.

Edith Eleanor- A schooner built, 1881 at Aberystwyth.
Unknown artist.

1916 October. Sold to Capt. H. H. Bridge, 157, Half Moon Lane, Herne Hill, London. On 29 July 1921, en route from London to Galway with cement, the **Edith Eleanor** foundered 100 miles NW of the Wolf Rock, Cornwall. The crew landed at Sennen Cove, Land's End, Cornwall after 27 hours in their boat. She had been abandoned 80 miles NW of the Longships.

EDITH MAY
Number 73476.

1877 Built at Tarleton, Lancashire, by Peter Lund. A wooden schooner of 72 tons. Dimensions: 80.9x21.1x9.4ft.

OWNERS
1888 J. Platt, Liverpool.
1891 James Marlowe and John Tyghe both of Wexford, 32 shares each.
1896 June. Marlowe sold his 32 shares to Mrs Catherine Kearns of Paul Quay, Wexford and the following month Tyghe sold his shares to her, making her the sole owner.

> **SUPERIOR SCHOONER BY AUCTION.**
>
> TO BE SOLD BY AUCTION IN
> THE CHAMBER OF COMMERCE, CRESCENT QUAY. WEXFORD,
> By directions of the Administratrix of the late Captain CAHILL,
> On WEDNESDAY, the 29th NOVEMBER, 1893.
> 62/64 Shares in the Schooner "EDITH MAY," 72 Tons per Register, carries 150 Tons on 10 feet draft, shifts without Ballast, and requires only 15 Tons at Sea.
> This Vessel was built at Tarleton, Co. of Lancaster in 1877, and classed for 9 years. She is well and fully found, is in good repair, and ready to go to Sea.
> She can be inspected any day before the Sale where she lies near the Old Bridge, and a list of her Stores can be seen at the Office of the Auctioneers.
> Terms at Sale at Two o'clock.
> WALSH & SON, Auctioneers.
> Wexford, 6th November, 1893.

Edith May- Notice of auction of shares. November 1893.
Co. Wexford Archives.

1908 June. Catherine Kearns sold half of her interest in **Edith May** to Anna Eliza Horan of Commercial Quay, Wexford.
1909 January. Catherine Kearns sold her remaining shares to Mrs Charlotte Whelan, George St., Wexford. On the same date, Anna Eliza Horan sold her half of **Edith May** to a Catherine Hickey of Marlborough Terrace, Chippenham, England. This made Hickey and Whelan sole owners with 32 shares each.
1922 June. Catherine Hickey sold 26 of her 32 shares to the following people; Michael Horan, a publican, of Commercial Quay, 7 shares; Francis Horan, an engineer of Commercial Quay, 7 shares; Mary Josephine Horan, a spinster, of Commercial Quay, 6 shares; Katie Pettit, a married woman also of Commercial Quay, 6 shares.
1925 In March, they all sold their shares in **Edith May** to Captain George Murphy, Wexford and he sold her to J.J. Stafford, Wexford on the same day.
1933 J.J. Stafford sold **Edith May** to J. Rochford, Kilmore Quay, Co. Wexford.
1933 Captain E. Jones of Connah's Quay, Wales.
1947 Broken up. Registration closed.

On Tuesday 24 May 1904, **Edith May** ran into the Crescent Bridge on Wexford Quays. She had been under tow by the tug **Wexford**. When she was let go, she headed straight for the Crescent. It was said that had it not been for the rail tracks and the girders underneath, she would have gone straight through into the Crescent Quay. The only damage was to her martingale.

On 9 January 1915, the local newspaper the *Echo* carried a report that Captain McGrath's schooner **Edith May** *left the Crescent, looking very neat and trim after her repairs*. It was remarked that some months previously she had lost her masts and portions of her bulwarks in a heavy storm. The article said that she had been splendidly re-fitted in the Crescent by Wexford hands.

In August 1916, an inquiry was held into a complaint by Marlowe and Co. against Pilot Breen, regarding the grounding of their vessel **Edith May**. Marlowe's stated that there was plenty of water at the Bar at the time and vessels that drew more water than theirs got in without any problem. They also felt it unfair that the Commissioners charged them towage when, in their opinion, the grounding was the pilot's fault. Alderman Sinnott said that it was remarkable that the pilots can't bring in vessels, in fifteen foot of water.

Captain McGrath, master of the **Edith May** came before the Board and told them there was ten feet of water showing at the flag-staff on the Bar. His ship only drew eight feet, three inches at the time of the grounding. His ship was the first coming in and others who drew up to eleven foot came in directly after him without incident. He told the pilot that he was going too far north, but the pilot replied that he was trying to get his marks.

Captain Busher, of the tugboat, bore out Captain McGrath's version of the incident. He said that when he went to the assistance of the **Edith May** there was ten and a half feet indicated at the flag-staff. The secretary, Mr Jasper Walshe inquired of Captain Busher if there would be any difficulty getting the ship in if she was in the right position. Captain Busher replied that he didn't think there would. Captain Busher said that when she was pulled clear she sailed in over the Gull Bar herself. The Board decided that they could not proceed until they had interviewed the pilot in question but if he was found to be liable, he would be fined the cost of the towage lost, because they would have to

Edith May, two masted tops'l schooner of 72 tons, under sail off the Tuskar Rock Lighthouse.

return the towage charge to the Marlowes. The matter was deferred to the next meeting.

In December 1932, the **Edith May** was en route from Newport to Wexford, with coal, when she had to put in to Ballyhack after her foremast, main topmast and bulwarks had been damaged in a severe gale. The same year, **Edith May** was slowly entering Llanelly Harbour when one of the crew heard a cry from the water. When he looked over the side, he saw a man in the sea. He straight away shouted to let the captain know and he immediately altered course to get in close enough to throw a lifebuoy to the man in the water. The crew were getting a boat ready to launch when they heard another cry from the port side. Captain Bent seeing that the first man had got into the lifebuoy turned his attention to the man on the port side.

The operation was repeated and the second man got into the lifebuoy. The ship's small boat was lowered and two crewmen, J. Blake and F. Spanner, went to the aid of the two men and hauled them on board. Afterwards, they were transferred to the local pilot boat. It turned out that both of the men were Llanelly Harbour pilots and their boat had capsized. There had originally been three men in the boat but one had been picked up by the pilot cutter. It was fortunate for the other two that the **Edith May** had come along, as there were very fast currents in that particular place that would have carried both of them out to sea.

In 1933 **Edith May** was sold to Captain E. Jones of Connah's Quay, Wales. At the time, Captain Willie Bent was master and the local press noted that **Edith May** was the last of the Wexford sailing fleet. It was further noted that during her time on the Wexford register she was estimated to have crossed the channel almost 1,200 times. During World War Two, she traded between Douglas Isle of Man and Whitehaven. **Edith May** was broken up and her registration closed in 1947.

St John's, Newfoundland c1892

Shipbuilding at Prince Edward Island c mid 1800s.

Pictou, Nova Scotia c late 1800s.

Shipbuilding at St. John, New Brunswick c late 1800s.

EDWARD
Number 21421. Code NGHB.

1836 Built at Milford Haven, Wales by Hogan's, a schooner of 52 tons.

OWNERS
1836 Brennan, Wexford.
1865 John Lambert, The Faythe, Wexford.
1875 Patrick Joseph Doyle, The Faythe, Wexford.

Crew 1845 (at various times).
Master: John Lambert, 30.
Mate: Denis Howlin, 28; Michael Clancy, 20; William Godkin, 44
Seamen: James Lowney, 22; Nicholas Rowe, 19; James Moore, 16; Joseph Philips, 21; Jimmy Carroll, 31.
Boys: John McGrath, 14; Thomas Beek, 14; Christopher Codd.
Mariner: Patrick Roche, 29.

In November 1875, the **Edward** left Wexford for Ayr, with a cargo of beans. She was caught in gale force winds near Carlingford Lough and foundered. The crew had to abandon ship and were picked up by a steamer.

EDWARD PHELAN
Number 21405. Code NGDW.

1845 Built at Nova Scotia. A brigantine, carvel built of 72 tons. Dimensions 60x17x10ft. Registered at Wexford, November 1846.

OWNERS
1846 Edward Phelan of Enniscorthy. He died, 20 August 1861. His shares were sold to Edward Phelan of Carlow and William Prandy of Coolnaboy, Co. Wexford. **1861** 21 August. Phelan and Prandy sold the **Edward Phelan** to John Lambert and James Murphy, both of Wexford.
1863 11 August. Lambert and Murphy sold her to James Howlett of New Ross. **1864** 2 March. Howlett sold to her to Matthew Kent of Ballinamona, Co. Wexford.

CREW 1864
Master: Matthew Kent, 58; Michael Doyle, 35.
Mate: P. Hendrick, 24; Michael Heron, 30.
ABs: John Sutherland, 21; Thomas Crone, 26.
OS: Peter Mackie, 20; John Morris, 18.
Boy: James Walsh, 14.

On the 12 February 1859, the *Wexford People* reported that the **Edward Phelan**, of Wexford, with William Moore, master, was on her voyage to her home port, she discovered a brigantine in distress off the Bishops. Immediately the **Edward Phelan** bore down on the wreck, and found her to be the **Mary** of Waterford, with a crew of six men, bound from Cardiff to Waterford, with a cargo of coals. The vessel was in a fast sinking state, but after considerable exertion, the almost doomed crew were rescued from their fearful position, and brought safe into port. The **Edward Phelan** was lost at Wexford, 7 April 1868.

ELIZABETH COWMAN
Number 9372. Code KHBS.

1855 Built at Bristol, a barquentine of 129 tons. Dimensions, 84.3x20.4x11.7ft.
1875 Registered rigged as a snow.
1876 Registered rigged as a brig.
1882 Registered, rigged as a brigantine.

OWNERS
1865 Owners John Hodgsen, Whitehaven.
1867 Thomas Cowman, Whitehaven.
1879 John Blenkinsop of Whitehaven.
1882 Andrew Cullen of Bannow, Co. Wexford.
1897 Owner John Shea of Bannow, Co. Wexford.
1911 28 April. Registration closed. Vessel sold to Wexford Harbour Commissioners for use as a hulk.

Name board of **Elizabeth Cowman** on display near Bannow, Co. Wexford.
Jack O'Leary collection.

ELIZA BOND
Number 18225. Code, MKVW. Dimensions, 72x18x7.7ft.

1856 Built at Chester, a schooner of 71 tons.

OWNERS
1876 J.H. Barrow of Ulverston.
1897 G. Jones of Conway, North Wales.
1900 Mrs A. Jones of Conway.
1907 Simon Roche of Bannow, Co. Wexford.

Her captain was Clement Cox and she carried a crew of three, including the captain. On Thursday 16 October 1907, she sailed from Bannow at 5 o'clock in the evening, bound for Port Talbot, in a light breeze from the North and the weather fine and clear. She had neither cargo nor ballast on board. By 3 o'clock on Friday morning, they were nearing the Smalls light when the wind changed to a strong SE gale. Not having any ballast, they were forced to go with it and ran for Wexford's South Bay for shelter. They made the Bay at 8 am and went to anchor. Thirty minutes later, with the ship riding on a starboard anchor, she started to drag. After about a quarter of a mile she held again and stayed in position for another

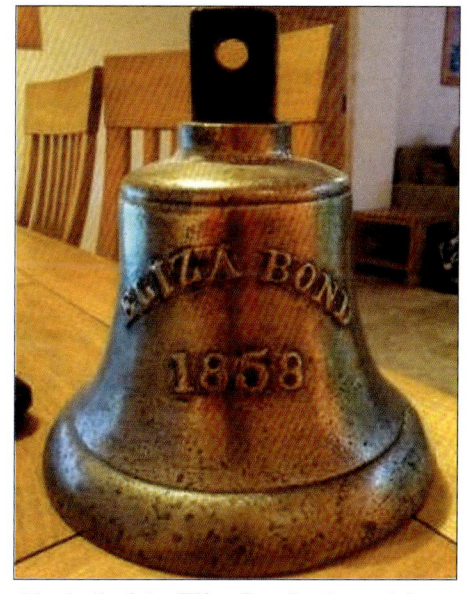

The bell of the **Eliza Bond** salvaged from the wreck.
Courtesy of Andy and Vicky Walsh- Maltby and Willie Wickham.

87

The two masted tops'l schooner **Eliza Bond**, 71 tons. Owned 1906 by Simon Roche of Bannow. Depicted here on a calm evening off Tuskar Rock Lighthouse.

ten minutes but then the cable parted and she drove ashore about 2 miles WNW of Rosslare Harbour Pier. The crew had managed to get ashore in the ship's boat, but as their ship did not seem to be in any immediate danger, they boarded her again.

At around one o'clock the **Eliza Bond** floated off and they went to anchor again. Somewhere in the proceedings she had shipped water so the crew got the pumps going but, after three hours of constant pumping, the water continued to gain on them. Later the wind changed to SSW and the captain thought it unsafe to stay on board for the night, so the crew went ashore again. At daybreak the vessel appeared to be settling down and at around 12 noon she foundered WNW of Rosslare Harbour Pier. The loss of the vessel was estimated to have cost her owner £300, a hefty sum in those days.

ELIZABETH WORTHINGTON
Number 56937.

1866 Built at Ulverston, Cumberlandshire, England by William White. A wooden schooner of 76 tons. Dimensions: 78.2x20.1x8.9ft. She retained her Lancaster registration until 1922.

OWNERS
1868 William Postlethwaite, Cumberlandshire.
1899-1918 Simon Roche, Ballygow, Bannow, Co. Wexford.
1929 Mr M. Cowman, Ballygow, Bannow, Co. Wexford.

In August 1898, the **Elizabeth Worthington** loaded coal in the Bristol Channel, she was due to sail the next day but a fire was discovered in her hold. After supper some of the crew went down below to find the timbers on fire. Fortunately, it had not taken too much of a hold and it was even more fortunate that it was found before they sailed. Had it not been discovered until they were at sea, it would more than likely, have been too late. She was unable to sail and had to undergo repairs. The master, Captain Neill had his wife and young child on board. The cause of the fire was put down to the men in the shore gang who had been working trimming the cargo. They had been using candles to illuminate the dark hold and simply forgot to extinguish them when they left. The **Elizabeth Worthington** was bound to Bannow with coal when she foundered in the Waterford River in 1900. She was, apparently, re-floated.

On 30 July 1929 **Elizabeth Worthington** was en route from Wexford to Newport, in ballast, when she sprung a leak. It was a serious leak and the pumps were unable to cope with it. The vessel was run ashore at Morfa Sands near Port Talbot in South Wales. In an interview in the local Wexford press, her master, Captain Patrick Doyle of Maudlintown, Wexford, told the reporter that, once the pumps were unable to cope with the incoming water, they ran for the beach and narrowly missed the Sker Rock. Once on the Morfa sandbanks, they had a three-hour struggle trying to keep their vessel from being carried back to sea on the ebb tide. The ship's lamps had been smashed so, in an attempt to attract attention, they soaked all of their clothes and anything else burnable in paraffin and set them alight. No one responded, so they set out to walk the six miles to Port Talbot, with only a vague knowledge of their actual position. They duly arrived

Elizabeth Worthington, owned by Simon Roche of Bannow shown under full sail outward bound off Hook Head Lighthouse c late 1890s.

at Port Talbot and went to the police station, where they were looked after.
The **Elizabeth Worthington** was a total loss. On board her were: Captain Patrick Doyle; James Kehoe, the mate; Patrick Reck, and James Cousins. Cousins was from Bannow; all the others were from Wexford Town.

ELLEN (1825)
1825 Built at Prince Edward Island; a brig of 95 tons.

1834 Registered Wexford

OWNERS 1834: Gafney & Co. (Master J. Shiel).

CREW 1845 (at various times in the year)
Masters: James Shiel, 39; Thomas Wickham, 31.
Mates: Thomas Lochan, 31; John Saunders, 30; S. Rossiter, 25; James Andrews, 30
Mariners: Matthew Finn, 26; Owen Blake, 23; William Blake, 22; Martin Doyle, 21
Apprentices: Matthew Rooney, 18; Anthony Meeney, 17; Patrick Morris, 17.
Others: Martin Bryan, 23; John Mc Donnell, 15; S. Cagney, 21; William Richards, 31.

ELLEN (1882)
Number 81530. Code EIJZ.

1882 Built at Bridgewater, Somerset by Prosser. A wooden schooner of 76 tons, with two masts. Dimensions 79.3x20.9x9.3ft.

OWNERS
1890 Wickham of Wexford, wine and spirit merchants, and Thomas Harpur of Wexford.
1898 October. Sold to J.F. Walsh (liquidator).
1910 Richard Kearon of Arklow. Manager James Byrne, The Brook, Arklow, Co. Wicklow.
1925 18 July. **Ellen** was at anchor at Lahinch, County Clare, in a SW gale, when two cables parted and she was driven ashore. She was later re-floated and in October 1925 she returned to Arklow.
1943 Broken up.
1944 13 September. Register closed.

ELLEN KERR
Number 27890. Code PTFH.

1860 Built at Perth, a schooner of 75 tons.

OWNERS
1865 Albert McLaren of Perth; Archie Smith of Argyllshire.
1880 Daniel McCormick of Port Glasgow.

Ellen Kerr- Two masted tops'l schooner of 75 tons. Built at Perth, Scotland in 1860.

1881 Registered at Wexford.
1882 Mrs Clement Morris, of Wexford and William Armstrong, of Wexford.
1881, **1883/1886/89/90** William Armstrong (Master: Murphy).
1894 Registration closed.

In June1882, the **Ellen Kerr**, sailing from Wexford to Newport, had to be towed into Minehead after her cargo shifted. Six months later on 1 January 1883, the **Ellen Kerr** dragged her anchor in Rosslare Bay. She went aground and the coastguard arrived and set up the Rocket Apparatus. They got Captain Rowe and his crew ashore safely. **Ellen Kerr** was re-floated sometime later. Three years later, in January 1886, a tragedy occurred off Tuskar. The ship's boy, Joseph Byrne, was trimming a lamp when a big sea hit and washed him over the side and he drowned.

Eleven years after the last reported grounding, the **Ellen Kerr** was not so lucky. On 8 January 1894, she went aground again. She left Milford Haven on 7 January, bound for Wexford, and anchored in Wexford's South Bay the next day. When they were shooting the anchor, someone heard the sound of water below decks. Martin O' Rourke, the mate, went below to investigate and found a large amount of water in the fore peak. They immediately started pumping but found that they were unable to gain on the incoming water. They then decided to beach her as close to Rosslare Pier as possible. However, due to the loss of her sails this plan failed and the **Ellen Kerr** went ashore further up the beach than planned.

As all of this was transpiring, the coastguards were observing it and had their Rocket Apparatus ready. Despite being prepared it took 5 attempts, before they got the breeches buoy in place on the ship. The first ashore was the ship's boy, a lad named Murphy. He was followed by O'Rourke, the mate, then a seaman named Duggan and finally Captain Murphy. The **Ellen Kerr** remained on the beach for some months until she was eventually blown up.

EMERALD
1838 Built at Barnstaple. A schooner of 81 tons. Registered at Wexford

1853 Registered at Wexford.
1857 Out of register.

OWNER 1853 P. Breen (Master: J. Reigh)

CREW 1852
Captain: Laurence English.
Mate: James Coughlin, 27.
Carpenter: Richard Mullet, 29 (Waterford).
Second Mate: Edward Parle, 26; Michael Aunon, 23 (Denmark); John Nielsen, 24 (Sweden).
Seamen: John Lister, 30 (Amsterdam); Abraham O'Reilly, 24; James Wilson* 20 (London); Patrick Nyland* 25 (Antwerp); John Lacey, 32; James Curran, 45; James Haddock, 24 (Biscayne); James Barry, 22; John Williams, 27 (Cork); Thomas Haigh (Drogheda); James Burne, 19 (Limerick).

Apprentices: James Roche* (Indentures signed, 14 March 1850); R. Kavanagh* (Indentures signed 2 August 1850); William Bermingham; William Murphy.

*Seamen James Wilson (20) and Patrick Nyland (25), together with Apprentices James Roche and R. Kavanagh, deserted in New York, May 1852.

EMERALD ISLE
Number15129. Code LRBN.

1841 Built at Wexford. A schooner of 86 tons. Dimensions: 63.7x20.4x9.3ft.

OWNERS
1840s RichardWalsh (Master: Peter Hall).
1853 Walsh & Co (Master: P. Rowe).
1870 William Gafney.
1890 Mr William Murphy, Carrig on Bannow.
1895 John Rochford, Kilmore, Co. Wexford, for breaking up.

CREW 1870
Master: J. Murphy, 64.
Mate: J. Kelly, 50.
ABs: William Kelly, 47; J. Maguire, 28.
OS: J. Hendrick, 17.
Boy: J. Breen, 15.

In January 1890, the **Emerald Isle** put into Wicklow Harbour in a disabled condition. She was bound from the Bristol Channel to Wexford with a cargo of coal. She got caught out in a fierce gale that had devastated the coast and arrived with all of her canvas carried away. Her master, Captain Moran said that it was only with great difficulty that they managed to make the shelter of Wicklow Harbour. **Emerald Isle** had left Penarth, along with the **Morning Light** and the **Ellen**, both of which made it to Wexford but in a very dishevelled state. The **Morning Light** had carried away her topsail and stay foresail, and the **Ellen** had lost two jibs, t'gallantsail and a lifebuoy.
In January 1892, the **Emerald Isle** was bound from Gloucester to Waterford with salt, when she went ashore at Tenby. After being lightened she was expected to float on the next tide. In1895 her owner, William Murphy of Carrig on Bannow died and the *Emerald Isle* was auctioned by his estate. At that time, she lay at Bannow Island. She was bought by John Rochford of Kilmore, for £10, broken up and her parts auctioned.

TENBY.

VESSEL ASHORE.—The schooner Emerald Isle, Wexford, laden with rock salt, is ashore to e north of Giltar. The vessel parted her bles when lying in Caldy Roads, and was ached at high water on Saturday night. The ew's depositions were being taken at the Coast uard Station when our parcel left.

Report on the grounding on the **Emerald Isle** c1892.

EMILY WYNN
Number 80233.

1881 Built at Caernarfon, by Richard Jones. A ketch of 65 tons, with two masts.

OWNERS
1882 John Roberts, Caernarfon.
1888 Harpur and Wickham of Wexford.
1900 12 May. Sold to Simon Roche of Ballygow, Bannow, Co. Wexford.
1908 28 May. Vessel unseaworthy and beyond repair.

On 14 January 1893 the local *People* newspaper reported that the **Emily Wynn** had sailed from Wexford manned totally by captains from owner Harpur and Wickham's fleet. At that time local sailors were in dispute over owners imposing lower wage rates on the sailors.

EMPIRE
Number 33079. Code RCTG.

1845 Built at Quebec. A barque of 729 tons.
Dimensions: 135x27.2x20ft.

OWNERS
Before 1857 Howlett, New Ross, Co. Wexford.
1857 Ware & Co., Cardiff.
1860 Rowland & Co., Cardiff.
1867 Thomas Plain, Cardiff.
1868 John Rowlands, Newport, Monmouthshire, South Wales.
1870 Out of register.

> In the month of June, 1852, The Empire proceeded to Quebec under the command of Edward Phelan, as master, with a letter of instructions from Howlett & Co., as follows:—
>
> "Capt. Edward Phelan, Ship 'Empire.'
>
> "New Ross, 31st May, 1852.
>
> "Dear Sir,—We wish you to proceed to Quebec with all possible speed, to which port the ship is insured, and also back to a safe port in the United Kingdom. On arrival at Quebec you will call on Messrs. Pemberton, Brothers, to whom you are consigned; they will use their best endeavours to charter you at the very highest freight of the day, giving a decided preference to the ports of Newport, Cardiff, or Sharpness Point in the British Channel. If a good thing cannot be had for those ports, you are next to turn your attention to Liverpool; but you are to make yourself well acquainted on arrival with the highest current freight of the day, and Messrs. Pemberton are not to charter without first consulting with you; and mind, it is no harm for you to stir them up, and see that they will obtain the very highest figure going; and it may so happen there will be flour freights offering that may pay better than timber, see also about this particularly. You will of course save your deck load, and try by all means to stow the ship to advantage. "Yours truly,
> "HOWLETT & Co."

SOURCE: The Exchequer Reports: Reports of Cases Argued and Determined in the Courts.

ERIN
Number 44126.

1862 Built at Arbroath, Scotland. A 2-masted schooner of 70 tons.
Dimensions 80.5x20x9.7ft.

OWNERS
1865 R. Devereux of Wexford.
1875 J.T. Devereux of Wexford.
1883 Mrs Clement Morris of Wexford.
1890 Clement Morris of Wexford.
1896 Register closed.

The schooner **Erin** of Wexford, laden with bricks, was wrecked at Dunany Point, Co. Louth in December 1895. All crew were saved.

Emily Wynn- A ketch built 1881 at Caernarfon, shown under sail off Hook Head Lighthouse.

Wexford Quay in 1926, two schooners **Agnes Craig** and **Emerald Isle** alongside.

CREWS
1863 January
Masters: Francis Larkin, 56; Patrick Connolly, 62.
Mate: Michael Hayes, 24;
ABs: Thomas Cullin, 27; Stephen Sinnott, 20; William Hayes, 23;
Boy: Michael Stafford, 17.

1863 July
Master: Patrick Connolly, 58.
Mate: Patrick Murphy, 33.
Seamen: Patrick Rossiter, 26; William McGrath, 23; Stephen Sinnott, 20.
Boy: Nicholas Stafford, 18.
Seamen: Francis Larkin, 30; James Corish, 25; Francis Stone, 19.
Larkin, Corish, and Stone signed on at New Ross, replacing Rossiter, McGrath and Sinnott, who paid off.

1888 Clement Cox of Lacken, Duncormick; Master Richard Barry of Lacken; Sailor Peter Keane.

ENERGY
Number 8467. Signal letters KCHM.

1850 Built at Nova Scotia. A schooner of 125 tons.
1850-1865 Registered at Wexford.
1867 Out of register.

OWNER Allen & Co. (Captain J. Fenlen).

ENTERPRISE
Number 44129. Code TRSV.

1863 Built at Elgin. A barque of 314 tons. Dimensions: 131.2x26.6x14.5ft.
1874 Out of register

1863-1870 OWNER: J.T. Devereux of Wexford.

CREW 1863 October.
Master: Captain James Codd, age 52.
Mate: Richard Scallan, 27.
Bosun: William Redmond, 21.
ABs: James Devereux, 21; Michael Murphy, 21; Thomas Neill, 21; John Murphy, 29; Edward Howlin, 23; and Michael Corish 30, who was also Cook/Steward.
Apprentices: Joseph Codd and Francis Lambert.

In late 1868, Pilot Stephen Larkin was charged with putting the barque **Enterprise** on the Hantoon Bank on 4 August, causing damage to the ship and expense to her owners.

Captain Smith of the **Enterprise** made the charges. After hearing evidence from Captain Smith, the ship's mate Mr Murphy; Anthony Ennis, master of the tug **Erin**; the Pilot Master and Larkin himself, the Board came to the unanimous decision:

We find that Stephen Larkin, Pilot was wrong in not giving up charge of the **Enterprise** *to the mate, who was acting as master, when he found the ship had been taken in tow and run for the Hantoon Bank, after he had told the mate and the Tug Master that she drew too much water to get in. We also find Stephen Larkin wrong in surrendering his judgement to the Tug Master and in piloting the ship after having stated she drew too much water. We therefore order Stephen Larkin, pilot, to be severely reprimanded for keeping command of the ship and the Pilot Master to be instructed to caution all pilots against a like error, for if such be repeated, the pilot offending will be severely punished if not dismissed.*

Murphy, the mate, of the **Enterprise**, who was acting master on the occasion, was judged to be at fault also for allowing his ship to be run for the Hantoon Bank, when the pilot told him she drew too much water to get in. Also for not making enquiry as to whose order she was got underway. Anthony Ennis, master of the tug **Erin**, who had her under tow at the time, was also judged to be at fault, as he knew that she was drawing 11ft of water when she should have been lightened to 10ft., and that she was waiting for another lighter.

Larkin had testified that he told Ennis that she was drawing too much but Ennis said he had not heard Larkin say that. But the Board stated that even if he had not heard Larkin he should still have acted with more caution, knowing that she was waiting for another lighter. In effect, all concerned were deemed to be at fault, but the acts of the Tug Master and the acting master of the ship had taken a considerable portion of the blame from the pilot.

ESPERANZA
Number 51264. Code PRCV.

1865 Built at Gorey, Jersey, Channel Islands by Le Sueur, as **Cupid**, of 77/80 tons. Dimensions: 87.2x19.7.x10ft.

1885 Registered as **Cupid** in Falmouth.
1886 Registered at Milford.
1909 Registered at Wexford

OWNERS
1899 W. Murphy, Main St., Wexford.
1909 Mary Murphy (Widow), 78 Main St., Wexford.
1911 July. Thomas Murphy, Hayestown, Co. Wexford, 22 shares; James Murphy, Thornville, 21 shares; Patrick F. Murphy, Main St., Wexford, 21 shares.

The Harbour Commissioners met to investigate a complaint against one of their employees, Pilot Duggan. The complaint was lodged in respect of the damage to the schooner **Esperanza,** when she struck the side of the quay, while under the control of the pilot. It appears that the vessel hit the quay when the pilot was bringing her alongside.

It was stated that this was not the first time that a vessel belonging to the owner of the **Esperanza**, William Murphy of Crescent Quay, had been in a mishap, when under the control of the same pilot. The master of the vessel, Captain Patrick Carty said in his statement that his ship was being towed part of the way by the tug **Wexford**. When the pilot slipped the hawser, she was going at speed. He failed to give the order to let the anchor go. Realising this, Captain Carty, let the anchor go without waiting for the pilot's order. He let out thirty-five or forty-five fathoms of chain but the vessel dragged the anchor and she struck her stem against the quay with force.

> **WEXFORD SCHOONER LOST.**
>
> The heavy fog which prevailed at sea last week has been the cause of many serious shipping disasters. On Saturday night the schooner Esperanza (Capt. James Carroll) bound from Newport to Wexford with a cargo of coal ran aground on the Nash Sands in the Bristol Channel and is likely to become a total loss. The Esperanza was one of the best schooners sailing out of Wexford and was owned by Messrs. Murphy Bros., Commercial quay, to whom the cargo was consigned. She was well known in the malt trade between Wexford and Dublin.

Report on the loss of the schooner **Esperanza**, May 1913. *Wexford People*

Pilot Duggan, in his evidence, said that the vessel sailed up a portion of the way and that she was not under tow. She only got a 'pluck' and was let go opposite White's Wall. The men were taking in sails and he was unable to see exactly where to drop the anchor, so he called out to the captain to have the anchor and chain ready and to have plenty of chain. The anchor was dropped but as there was not enough chain out, she dragged it. He said that there should have been thirty or forty fathoms out, but there were only about fifteen and therefore the anchor dragged. Had there been enough chain, the anchor would have held or otherwise it would have snapped or tore the vessel asunder. He blamed the **Esperanza's** mate for not having sufficient chain out. He told the board that if they would check the moored vessel, they would see that there was only about seven fathoms of chain out.

It was pointed out to Pilot Duggan that it was his responsibility to ensure sufficient length of chain was made ready and that he should take no one's word for it. A rule to this effect had been made by the Commissioners warning pilots, under penalty, that no vessel should be moored with less than forty-five fathoms of chain. The Harbour Master, Captain Brady, was instructed to inspect the vessel the next morning and determine how much chain was actually used. Next day he reported that she had only ten fathoms out.

In September 1905, James Gaul, a sailor from The Faythe was up in the crosstrees working on the rigging of the **Esperanza** at Wexford Dockyard, when the crosstree snapped. He fell 60 foot to the deck but the ropes of the rigging helped to break his fall and he was not seriously injured. The **Esperanza** was in for a re-fit at the time.

On 24 May 1913, **Esperanza** was en route from Newport to Wexford with coal. Her captain was James Carroll. The vessel was wrecked on Nash Point Sands, in the Bristol Channel and declared a total loss. All 5 crew were saved.

EXCELLENT
Number 55312. Code WSCG.

1868 Built at Gorey, Jersey, in the Channel Islands and re-built by Paul Rogers of Carrickfergus in 1877. A ketch of 59 tons, with two masts. Dimensions 79.6x18.6x8.6ft.

1877/1901 Registered at Wexford.

OWNERS
Before 1881 Peter Sinnott, Summerhill, Wexford, who held 32 shares, and Thos. Sinnott, Abbey St., Wexford, 32 shares.
After 1881 W. J. O'Keefe, maltsters, of Wexford.
James Doyle of Kilkeel, Co. Down.

CREWS
1877
Master: Thomas Green, 47.
Mate: Edward Stafford, 50.
ABs: Patrick Burn, 37; Michael Devereux, 27; George Macpherson, 30.
Boy: Thomas Bernie, 17.

This appears to be **Excellent's** first Wexford crew. Captain Green and Edward Stafford had come straight from the **Columbine** as had the Boy. Both Burn and Devereux's last ships had been Wexford ships, the **Rapid** and the **Tempest** respectively. It's likely that they were the delivery crew who brought **Columbine** to Carrigfergus and took command of the **Excellent**. Macpherson was a Belfast man, who joined in Carrigfergus and paid off in Wexford. Her first trip was from Carrigfergus to Ayr and from Ayr to Wexford.

1901
Master: Andrew Carty, 60.
Mate: James Williams, 29.
AB: James Dowd, 55.
OS: Peter Brien, 17.

1906
Master: Captain Owen Carty
Crew: James Carty; J. Walsh; J. Dowd.

1914
Mate: Mathew Murphy; Patrick Brennan.
AB: W. Whitmore.
Boy: Charles Carty.

1915
Masters: Joseph Cousins; Mathew Murphy; Robert Smith.
ABs: James Doyle; Nicholas Leigh; Thomas Somers; Patrick Whelan.
Mate: Nicholas Furlong; Patrick Pender.
Boy: Patrick Curran; Patrick McCormack.

1916
Boys: Stephen Smith; Edward Brennan (He went sick due to a septic finger and while he was off, his brother Moses Brennan shipped in his place).
AB: James Myrtle.

Excellent, a ketch rigged vessel of 59 tons, shown here signalling her code WSCG to the Coningbeg lightship off the Wexford Coast.
Courtesy Mr Des Murphy, Rosslare Hbr.

By the end of the year Myrtle was Mate and the boy Smith was AB.

1917
Mate: John Byrne.
Boy: Phillip Duggan;
Seamen: John Crosbie; Joseph Walsh; Nicholas Kelly, Abbey Street. Kelly was the only one whose address is given, possibly because there was more than one of the same name sailing out of Wexford at the time.

1918
Boy: John Flaherty.
Seamen: James Crofton; George Dixon; Philip Gaul; John Marlow. These last four are names long associated with Wexford seafaring.

1919
Boys: Nicholas Murphy; J. Hall.

1920
Boy: Philip Murphy.
Mate: John Smith.

1921
Boy: John Rossiter.

In July 1889, John Greene, age 18, of King St., Wexford was killed when he fell from aloft. He was working as the ship was in the River Usk entering Newport. Although the main sail broke his fall, he still sustained a fractured skull. He was dead before anyone could get to him. He was the nephew of the ship's master, Captain John Greene.

On 11 January 1906, O'Keefe's **Excellent** got into trouble in bad weather at Caldy Roads, near Tenby. The crew had to be taken off by the Tenby Lifeboat However the ship rode out the storm and the crew were able to board her again the next day. She was carrying pit props for Cardiff. Captain Owen Carty was in charge with a crew consisting of James Carty, J. Walsh and J. Dowd.

A ledger exists showing the accounts of wages paid out from 1914 to 1922. It all makes for fairly dry reading, but it does give an insight into rates of pay and other conditions. In 1914, a Captain's rate was £4-10 per month. By 1922 it had risen to £13-00 a month. Church dues for Easter and Christmas seem to have been deducted at source. It was taken from their wages at three shillings for the captain and one and sixpence from the ABs.

On 25 January 1926, the **Excellent** was sailing from Garston to Kilkeel with coal, when she foundered off the Great Ormes Head near Llandudno, North Wales. All crew saved.

EXPRESS
Number 82972.

1880 Built at Milford by John Reid. A schooner, carvel built, with one deck, two masts and a square stern, 89 tons. Dimensions: 81.3x20x10ft.
1897 Wrecked on the Arklow Bank.

OWNER Captain Laurence Murphy, 11 William St., Wexford.

CREWS
1882
Master: Michael Connors, 49.
Mate: James Maddock, 37.
Seaman: John Moore, 21.
Boy: Henry Cooper, 17.

1888
Master: Laurence Murphy, 11 William St.
Bosun: William Blake, 29 (Became mate later that year).
AB: Patrick Marlow, 21.
OS: James Volain, 19.
Boy: John Summers, 16.
Later that year:
Boy: John Wade, 15.
Mate: Richard Cullen, 52.
OS: John Bolger, 18.

1888 June
AB: John O'Connell, 29.
OS: James Howlin, 19.
Boy: John Summers, 16.

There were at least two schooners named **Express** on the Wexford register. One was owned by Devereux in 1839 and this one, built in 1880 in Milford Haven by John Reid and later owned by Captain Laurence Murphy, of William Street, Wexford. Captain Murphy was an experienced sailor and had spent some of his earlier career as mate on the Galatz run. He had served as mate on the **Alert**, among other vessels and at one time was master of the brig **Fame**.

According to the *Shipping Gazette* of November 1891, the **Express** of Wexford collided with the pier head at Cardiff in order to avoid the steamer **Grimsby** of St. Malo. No damage report was mentioned. In February 1892, Captain Murphy took a case in the Court of the Admiralty against the British and Irish Steam Ship Company, for damages arising out of a collision with one of their vessels. It appears that B&I's **Lady Olive** was outward bound from Dublin Port, when she ran into the **Express**. The Wexford schooner was lying alongside a steamer from which she was taking grain. The **Lady Olive** 'brushed' past her, squeezing her and dismantling her rigging. Murphy also alleged that the port side was damaged and claimed compensation of £413-18-10. B&I

Master's ticket issued to Captain Larry Murphy, owner/master of the **Express.**

admitted liability and lodged £150, but denied that any damage had occurred to the port side. Judgement was reserved.

The **Express** was still owned by Captain Murphy at the time of her loss in 1897. However, it appears that he had retired and that the ship was under the command of his brother, John. According to local legend the **Express** was in Dublin, weather bound, with a cargo of manure for her home port. Captain Larry was of the opinion that she should sail, despite the bad weather, and travelled to Dublin to take her home himself. This may or may not be true but he was definitely in command of the vessel. Also, the fact that there were five men on board indicates that the story may be correct. At that time, Wexford coastal schooners carried a crew of four, including the master There seems little reason for them to carry an extra hand on this occasion. Thus, the crew of the **Express** on that ill-fated voyage were: Captain Larry Murphy, his son James, his brother John, Myles Connors and another boy named James Kehoe.

The **Express** left Dublin on the morning of Saturday 27 March 1897. All went well until about 3.30 am when, in fog, the schooner struck the Arklow Bank. She was promptly brought about but this had the effect of driving her into shallower water and huge seas began to break over her. The captain immediately ordered the boat to be

Express, two masted tops'l schooner of 89 tons. Built 1880 at Milford, South Wales.
Courtesy, Mr Greg Murphy, New Zealand.

lowered and the gangway unshipped. As this was being done a massive wave struck them and the lifeboat was smashed to smithereens and Captain Murphy was washed away. The remaining crew took to the rigging and clung on there for dear life. There they were to remain for several long hours, saturated by the seas and frozen stiff. They had no means of alerting those shore side. They had neither flares nor rockets, so they hoisted a set of oilskins to the top of the mast, in the hope that someone would see it and recognize their predicament.

At around 5.30 am a steamer came up, heading northwards but even though the men in the rigging made as much noise as they possibly could, the crew of the steam ship did not see them. Around 9.30 am another steamer came up but also failed to see the **Express** crew. An hour later the Arklow lifeboat, **Frances &Charlotte** was seen approaching them. It was around 11.30 before they got close in to the wreck They soon began trying to get a rope to the men in the rigging. The first three attempts failed but the fourth was successful, and the mate, John Murphy, secured it to his nephew and he jumped into the sea.

The lifeboat men began to haul him towards them but the rope had fouled in the rigging and halfway across, it jammed. This left young Murphy in a precarious position and in danger of drowning. Someone on the **Express** saw this and after a quick conversation, a decision was made to cut the rope, allowing the lifeboat men to haul him on board, unconscious. The men on the lifeboat began to work on him and managed to bring him back to consciousness. The men who cut the line and released young Murphy must have known that by doing so they greatly decreased their own chance of survival but did it nonetheless.

In the meantime, the tide changed and in spite of their best efforts, the lifeboat could not get another line onto the wreck. Then, in a few minutes, the foremast, which the men were clinging to, collapsed. It hung over the deck at an angle of 45 degrees for about ten minutes and then went into the sea, bringing the men with it. The lifeboat rowed around for 20 minutes in the hope of finding some survivors but none were found. Then the ship broke up and the lifeboat returned to Arklow where young Murphy was tended to, in the home of James Tyrell. He was brought home by train, the following day, to his grieving mother and siblings.

Captain Laurence Murphy was a very highly thought of mariner. He was described as *upright and straightforward*. After serving his apprenticeship with the Devereux Line, he became master of their brig **Fame**. He remained with Devereux's until the company was broken up. Then he went to McCormack's of Dublin, to take command of one of their vessels. After that he took

CASUALTIES.
The schooner Mary Agnes, of and from Wexford, for Cardiff, collided in Wexford Harbour with the smack Express, of Wexford, with a cargo of malt for Dublin. Both vessels sustained slight damage to bows, and have returned for repairs.
A telegram from New York, on Tuesday night, states that the Magenta, from Cardiff for Bermuda, stranded at Bermuda, but was afterwards got off with assistance.
The ship Hudson, bound from London to New York, is reported by telegraph from Madeira to have collided with an unknown vessel and sunk. The crew were saved.
The Liverpool and Brazil mail steamer Horrox, from River Plate, has been towed into Cape Verde with main shaft broken by the steamer Jalande, of St. Meline. She will repair temporarily.

Collision report of the **Express** and **Mary Agnes**.

command of the East Indiaman **John Milton**, a 2,000 tonner, engaged in the tea trade to China. Leaving the **John Milton,** he commanded the **Connaught Ranger**, another vessel in that trade. After several years in the tea trade, he bought himself a schooner, **Alice & Kate** but lost her in Cardiff Roads in the late 1880s. He then bought the **Express** and later the **Topaz**. His brother, John, commanded the **Topaz** for some years before she was sold to O'Keefe's. Captain Larry Murphy was the only married man in the crew and was about 50 when he died.

A painting of the **Express** exists and is owned by Mr Greg Murphy of New Zealand, a descendant of the sole survivor of the **Express** tragedy. How this painting came to be is an interesting tale in itself. It appears that a former member of the crew of the **Express** was a prisoner of war of the Boers, in the second Boer War. One of his guards was a Murphy of Wexford and a relative of Captain Larry. The prisoner had a talent for painting and at the request of the guard, he painted this from memory.

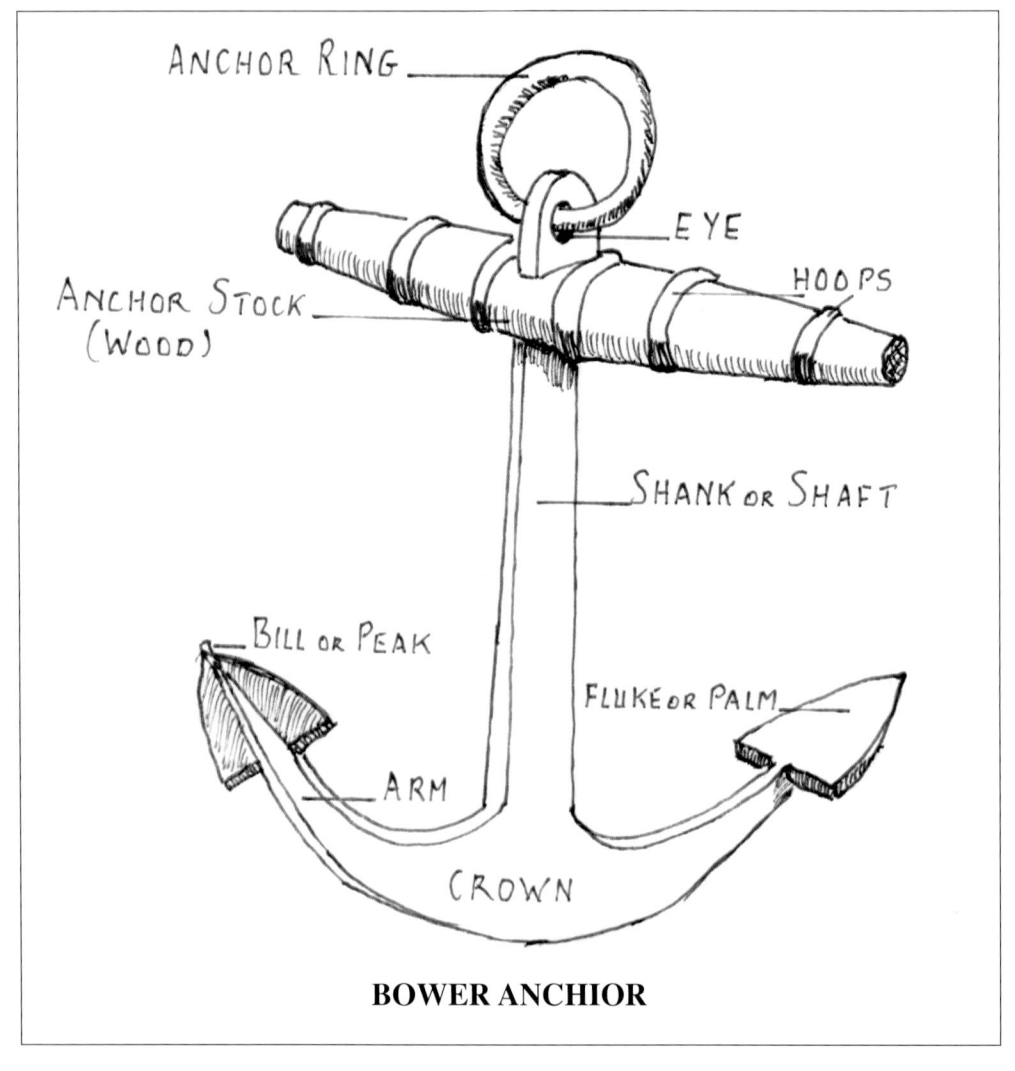

BOWER ANCHIOR

F

FALCON
Number 8471. Code KCHR.

1846 Built at New Brunswick, a brig of 219 tons, carvel built, with a male figurehead.

OWNERS
1848 Richard Devereux
1856 October. Sold to Michael Ennis of Wexford, merchant (Master: Michael Condon).
1856 30 October. Michael Ennis sold 16 shares to James Ralph Crosbie, shipowner, of Wexford.
1859 Register closed.

CREWS
1848
Master: William Hall, age 24.
Mates: Ed. Wickham, 35; Pat Dillon, 31.
Seamen: John Dillon, 24; Martin Rowe, 18.

1857
Master: Captain Edwin Hore
Mate: Patrick French
Seamen: James Howlin, John Clancy, and James Leary
Other: Frank Rowe
Boys: 2 unnamed, one acting as cook.

The **Falcon** appears to have been used by owner Richard Devereux as both a trading and a passenger ship in the late 1840s and early 1850s. On 18 April 1849, the *Morning Post* reported that the brig **Falcon**, under Captain Thomas Lambert, had left Wexford with 80 passengers, bound for Norfolk, Virginia and Baltimore, Maryland. The passengers were, the *Post* declared, *principally of the respectable class of farmers*. In May 1851, the **Falcon** was being advertised in local papers as being *a superior copper and copper fastened brig … having a spacious poop for cabin passengers and most comfortable accommodation for steerage passengers*. By June the same year local papers were reporting that the brig **Falcon**, was sailing under Captain Lambert *with ninety passengers for Norfolk and Baltimore. The passengers, chiefly young persons of a highly respectable class, and the majority of them belong to the town and vicinity Wexford*. However, in September 1851, the **Falcon**, along with several other ships, was seized by government officials in Baltimore and fined for violating a passenger law which required *a separate berth for each passenger and not more than two passengers for every 5 tons measurement of vessel*.

On 27 May 1854, the *Wexford Independent* reported that *Captain Thomas Lambert of the brig **Falcon** had died on 24 May at his house in the Faythe, after illness and in*

Devereux's brig Falcon.
Courtesy of Celestine Murphy, Castlebridge, Co. Wexford.

the prime of life. In 1857 Captain Edwin James Hore was the master of the **Falcon** which, by now, was in the ownership of Michael Ennis and James Ralph Crosbie and engaged solely in trade. In April 1857 the **Falcon** sailed for Quebec where three of the crew jumped ship. Suprisingly, they were prosecuted on their return to Wexford and their trial was reported verbatim in the *Wexford People* of 1 August 1857. The court proceedings are reproduced here in full as they throw considerable light on many aspects of life aboard a ship in the mid nineteenth century.

James Howlin, John Clancy, and James Leary (seamen) were charged with deserting the brig **Falcon** in Quebec. Mr Ryan prosecuted on the part of the owners of the ship, and Mr. Waddy defended. Captain Edwin Hore sworn, and examined by Mr Ryan. Captain Hore: *I am master of the brig* **Falcon**; *I recollect getting over the Bar of Wexford on the 22nd April last, bound for Quebec; the three defendants shipped in Wexford to go in the ship.* [Shipping paper was here produced, to which the signatures of defendants were attached.] *The* **Falcon** *proceeded on her voyage, and in four or five days after her arrival in Quebec, the whole crew deserted the ship; in consequence of this desertion, I was obliged to ship other men in their place, at a cost of £72 to the owners; I paid to some of the labourers 12s. 6d. a day, and to others 10s; I paid £10 sterling a month to the crew I shipped in their place to work the ship home.*

Mr Ryan handed witness the Log Book, and asked him was that kept in his handwriting. The Captain said that all the entries in it were made by him, and signed by his mate Patrick French. Mr Ryan then read from the Log Book the details of the desertion, and in conclusion stated that in the Act he found that the production of that Log Book was sufficient evidence to prove their case. Mr Coghlan (Collector of Customs) was sworn and proved to signing the articles, and to having seen it signed by the captain and the entire crew. Cross examined by Mr Waddy, Mr Coghlan said: *At the signing of the articles I did not hear anything about a proper cook being shipped; the whole crew are generally present when signing agreement; I cannot say if in this particular case such was the fact.*

The captain on being asked by Mr Waddy as to whether he saw all the crew sign the agreement stated that he only saw Frank Rowe sign it. Mr Waddy: *Now captain let me show you the log book, and now tell me is not that the touch of your name on it* (laughter). The captain identified his handwriting, which bore date 6 June, 1857, 9 o'clock am, and which stated the crew having deserted the ship in Canada on same morning. It was two hours after hearing the unfortunate circumstance that he made this entry.

Mr Waddy: *Why did you not make this entry on being told of the desertion?* Captain Hore: *I wanted to cool my temper.* Mr Waddy: *So then it takes two hours to cool you out of a passion* (laughter). Captain Hore: *I went up the town to go to a Magistrate, and also went to see one of the men in hospital, who had broken his leg the previous evening.* Mr Waddy: *But at any rate, as Canada is very warm, it took two hours to cool you down* (laughter). *You say all the crew deserted the vessel, now did you ever hear anything more unfortunate?* Captain: *I did not.* Mr Waddy: *I'm sure you didn't. I see by that Log Book that Pat French writes a bad hand for a mate.* Captain: *Well, he is not a school master* (laughter). *I never asked him to read anything for me but the Log Book, as I can read my own history (laughter). After I wrote the circumstance of the desertion he read it, and I read it. The reason why he read it after me was that he had a doubt of my honesty?*

Mr Waddy: *And will you tell the magistrates on your oath that you who it takes two hours to cool, would not knock down the man who should dare to doubt your honesty?* Captain: *I did not strike the mate for doubting my honesty. The mate keeps a Log Book of his own. I think the mate's log is wrote [sic] in the evening.* Mr Waddy: *So then you begin at the beginning.* Captain: *I can begin at any time. The cook I shipped did not know one rope from another, as he was never to sea before that voyage.* Mr Ryan: *They don't use ropes in making soup* (laughter). Captain: *Before we left the Island Side in Wexford harbour the crew did complain of the manner in which their food was dressed, but as I was satisfied with his cooking I considered the crew might also be satisfied, and I think the boy would do very well for dressing food for those who were not gentlemen, and the boy was a gentleman's cook before I got him.* Mr Waddy: *I suppose it was hay he was chopping then* (laughter).

Captain: *I admit I had to cook fish on the passage for my own use. There was another boy aboard who I often chastised with my tongue for not at once letting go a rope when I told him, but he was a superior boy at his business. The three defendants here during the voyage gave me the utmost satisfaction and the remainder of the crew were only middling. I cannot say whether the scale of provisions allowed the crew ought to have been hung up or handed to the crew. Never knew such to be done. I never heard of such scale being put in the forecastle, where all the men could see it. I am going to sea for the past 18 years and never heard this. I had no complaint of the crew on arriving in Quebec. I can't say why they deserted the ship.*

I had a conversation with the crew the evening previous to their deserting. They went up the town with the man who broke his leg and on returning they took their clothes and then deserted the ship. On that evening I did not hear them say they would leave the ship, and I did not say that they might go, and that I would get men cheaper. I was in bed when they returned to the ship and took their clothes. A man who worked as a labourer in the vessel told me so the next morning. Mr Ryan: *The crew of a vessel are not at liberty to take her boat without the captain's liberty, and for so doing they are liable to a penalty.*

Patrick French [the Mate] sworn and examined by Mr Waddy. Patrick French: *I am mate of the Falcon; the cook was very green; the three defendants were very good men; the crew complained continually of the cook not being fit to dress their food; I saw the captain cook some fish and some beefsteak; no man could be satisfied with the cook, as one day the meat would be raw, another day dirty, and another day undone. It was salt meat we used; I complained to the captain of the manner in which the food was cooked, and that the men were complaining of it, and he told me to tell them to let one of themselves cook; I did not see the men go away; I have frequently seen the scale of provisions hanging up in other ships.* Mr Waddy: *Why you know more than the Captain, you ought to be above instead of being under him* (laughter). Mr Crosbie: *There is no occasion for such scale being hung up in the Wexford vessels, as they are but too well kept.* Patrick French: *The Captain had an argument with me; he said that any man who would like to go away, he would not stop them; the three defendants were within hearing.*

A question as to the forfeiture of all or any part of the wages of the defendants bring raised, it was found that the tot was against the owners, as their [the defendants'] wives had been receiving weekly money some time after they had deserted from the ship. The Magistrates retired and in a short time returned into Court, on which the sentence of the Court was pronounced, that the defendants be imprisoned for six weeks without hard labor.

The brig **Fame**, built 1857 at South Shields, owned at Wexford by Devereux. Depicted here off the coast of Turkey, near Izmir, bound for Galatz.

In July 1859, Captain Hore was back in court having summoned a Nell Hayes for abusing him on several occasions in the public streets. It seems that Nell Hayes was the mother of 'Cocker' Hayes, a young man who had perished in the wreck of the **Pomona**. Young Hayes had been shipped on board the brig **Falcon**, but his mother had induced him to leave the ship, and had gone with him to Liverpool and there saw him shipped on board the ill-fated **Pomona**. It is not clear why she considered Captain Hore to be at fault in this, but the court proceedings clearly show a mother unhinged by grief although the press report is largely unsympathetic.

In the same month the *Wexford Constitution* reported that the captain of the brig **Falcon** (unnamed but presumably Captain Hore) had made a complaint to the Harbour Commissioners alleging that *the parties in charge of the dredge-boat had let a barge drop in the way of his brig whereby she struck on the bank and grounded*. This appears to have been the end of the **Falcon** as she was shortly afterwards out of register.

FAME
No 20248. Signal Letters MWHS.

1858 Built at St John, New Brunswick, a brig of 218 tons.
1876 Registered at Drogheda.
1880 Registered as 193 tons.
1890 Registered as barquentine.
1895 Out of Register.

OWNERS
After 1858 Devereux.
1876 John Chadwick, Drogheda.
A log of the **Fame** exists which covers a voyage from Wexford to Cardiff, then to Galatz and back to Wexford. It commences on Saturday 25 June 1870, and was kept by the Mate of the ship, John Murphy. It was an uneventful trip but provides a good example of the day to day running of a sailing ship. The extract from the **Fame**'s log is in **Appendix 1**.

FAVOURITE
1834-1835 Registered 59 Tons. Master: P. Hughes.

OWNERS
1876 John Cardiff and Captain Michael Cardiff, both of Wexford Town.

In December 1874, word reached Wexford Town that the local schooner **Favourite** was in trouble out in the South Bay. Immediately William Coghlan, Collector of Customs and William T. Taylor, another Customs official, left the quays to render assistance. It is not clear why Mr Coghlan and his companion rushed to the aid of the schooner, but Mr Coghlan was also Receiver of Wrecks around that time. By the time they had reached Rosslare, Mr Jago of the Coastguard and his crew had got out the rocket apparatus and were attempting to get a line aboard the **Favourite**, without success. Coghlan immediately sent a mounted messenger to the Lifeboat Station where the Coxwain, Mr Carty, another Customs officer, got the then new lifeboat **Ethel Eveleen** ready. But, unfortunately he was unable to raise enough men to make up a crew. This was due to the pilots on the Fort refusing to go onboard. Some, including Pilot Master Paddy Cogley, Mr Goodall and his son James and a Mr Boyle volunteered first off, but the launch had to be delayed until Mr Carty managed to procure the services of 11 local fishermen.

They launched the lifeboat and reached the stricken captain and crew of the **Favourite** and brought them ashore. It was said that had the fishermen of Rosslare not gone out to the schooner, all hands would likely have perished. Captain Ennis of the tug **Ruby** also arrived on the scene and helped tow the **Ethel Eveleen** out of the pounding surf after she had landed the schooner crew. Mr Coghlan was severely injured when operating the rocket apparatus, but was expected to make a full recovery.

> THE BARQUE "ELLEN."—We understand that this ship has arrived at Monte Video, from Liverpool, after a voyage of 59 days. The ship is manned by a crew who are all are Wexford men.
>
> THE WRECK OFF BALLYGEARY.—We are glad in having to announce that the schooner "Favourite," which we reported in our last issue as having been driven on shore near Ballygeary, has been floated off with little or no damage. The weather was very fine and boats were able to get alongside the vessel and take some of her cargo.
>
> COLLISION OF WEXFORD VESSELS.—On the 17th instant the schooners J P Taylor and Emeralds Isle came into collision at Passage East, Waterford, the damage done to both vessels being fortunately inconsiderable. The schooners it appears, were taking shelter at that roadstead, the weather not permitting them to enter this harbour where they were bound, and, while preparing for anchoring, one —the J P Taylor—having shortened sail for the purpose, they came into contact.
>
> TRADE WITH LIVERPOOL AND BRISTOL.—The Montague sailed on Friday for Liverpool, and as it is not intended she should return next week, the cargo was a large one, the greater portion consisting of articles intended for the Christmas markets; in addition to 500 sheep the freight was made up of very large consignments of fowl, &c, &c. The Briton, which sailed on Monday for Bristol, also took a large cargo of varied descriptions. She arrived here on Monday, yet which such celerity was the cargo shipped that the vessel was despatched on the following evening.

Report on the re floating of the schooner **Favourite** near Ballygeary, December 1874.

A few days later Captain Codd of the **Favourite** made a deposition before Mr W.T. Taylor. He said that the **Favourite** left Newport, Monmouthshire, on 1 December, with a cargo of coal for Mr Michael Quinn of Castlebridge, Co. Wexford. The next day, due to bad weather, they were forced to put into Milford. There they remained until 14 December when, about 7 pm, the wind changed NW, the ship beat about the South Bay of Wexford and came to an anchor about 11 pm. About 8 am on 16 December, they got under way to proceed to Wexford. They had no pilot on board and the wind was from the North. They hoisted colours for a steam tug and at about 11.45 saw a pilot boat beating up for the Bar. It seemed to signal them to leave the bay. This they attempted to do but, carrying all plain sail, they only got to an area known as the perch of the flats.

There was a heavy sea running and, at around 11am, the outer jib went. Then the sheets gave way, the pendant block was disabled, and the standing jib and the head of the mainsail gave way. They found themselves in a narrow passage and thinking that she would not be able to weather Splaugh Rock, they bore up for the bay and came to anchor about 2 pm, in an increasing wind. They let go both anchors. At 3 pm, the port anchor parted and at 4 pm, realising that the starboard anchor was unable to hold her, they slipped the anchor and ran for the shore and beached at Rosslare Strand, under Kilscoran, where she still lay. She was not making any more water than usual and it was expected to re-float her, which she did after being lightened.

In March 1876, the **Favourite** was wrecked off Mugglin Rock, north of Dalkey Island, while in the charge of a pilot. She was bound to Dublin with a cargo of wheat for Guinness and Co., under the command of Captain Michael Cardiff, who was the part owner. At the time of the casualty, she was in charge of a pilot named Tallant, who had taken over. He was from Kingstown (Dun Laoghaire). The night was dark and gloomy and the seas were running very high, when she struck the rock. Seeing that they were in a perilous situation the boat was lowered and Captain Cardiff, along with all five of his crew and the pilot, rowed to Bullock Harbour. From there they walked to Kingstown where they reported the accident to the Coast Guard.

The captain tried to procure a tug boat to go out and attempt to tow the **Favourite** off the rock but failed to get one. So they went out and removed any valuables they could from their vessel and left her to her fate. While most of this was happening the Coast Guards at Dalkey had seen the ship out at the rock and put out to the wreck. Finding her unmanned and seeing nothing could be done, they returned to their station. The loss of the vessel and the cost of her cargo was put at two and a half thousand pounds.

FLEETWING
Number 69886. Code WPNC.

1874 Built at Banff, Scotland by John Watson. A schooner of 78 tons, with two masts and an elliptical stern. Dimensions: 85x21x10.3ft.

1902 Registered at Wexford.

OWNER: J. J. Stafford.

CREW Jan. 1919
Master: Captain George Murphy of The Faythe.
Mate: James Carroll. Lost when the **Fleetwing** was wrecked in Caernarvon Bay.
Seamen: Patrick Whelan, Distillery Road; Matt Neill of Maudlintown and Thomas Murphy of High St.

Other crewmen who served on the **Fleetwing**:
Mate: James Imilt, 24.
Bosun: Moses Murphy, 26.
ABs: Patrick Dillon, 20; John Doyle, 26; Matt. Doyle, 26; John Culleton, 35; –? Harchild, 26; Patrick Lawler, 21; John Breen, 24.
Cook: John Keating, 28.
Cook/Steward: Peter Mernon, 35.
Apprentice: Patrick Harpur, 16.

In September 1908, the **Fleetwing** went aground at Rosslare Strand, just opposite Kelly's Hotel. Thomas and William Duggan of Whitehouse, Rosslare, spotted the schooner's predicament and along with Mr E. Moran, set out in Moran's boat to help. It was said that without the aid of the three local men the **Fleetwing** would undoubtedly have been lost. Luckily for all concerned it was nearly low water and it was thought that she could be got off when the tide rose. An anchor was secured some distance out to sea and the

Fleetwing a schooner of 78 tons. Built at Banff, Scotland in 1874. Grounded in Caernarfon Bay and became a total wreck in January 1919.

crew commenced to haul off the vessel. After some time, they succeeded in their endeavours and she refloated, apparently none the worse for her grounding.

By 1912 it seems a crewmen's union had been organised in Wexford. The *New Ross Standard* of 12 January 1912 reported that *the dispute between J.J. Stafford and the Union is being fought with great determination by both parties and during the week there were several incidents of sufficient importance to show the spirit animating the disputants. Three sailors arrived in Wexford on Wednesday with a view to the manning of the schooner **Fleetwing**, owned by Mr Stafford and taking her out of the harbour. The vessel, which was moored at the quay, was taken in tow by the tug **Wexford** and the men placed on board. But having been informed of the differences existing between Mr Stafford and the union, they decided not to sail in the **Fleetwing**, whereupon they left her and have since returned to Cardiff.*

On 10 January 1919, on passage from Newport to Wexford with coal, she went aground at Belan Point, Caernarvon Bay and became a total wreck. Captain George Murphy, and 3 crewmen were rescued. In a statement, Captain Murphy said that they had been at sea since the 27 December and had met with bad weather throughout. They had made several attempts to run for shelter but each time were thwarted by the raging gales. Eventually all their sails carried away and then they were driven ashore. Their predicament was spotted by Police Sergeant Jones of nearby Penygroess, who immediately went to where they were stranded. He found that owing to the horrendous winds and seas, it was impossible to even stand on the shore, much less try to to render assistance.

The nearest life saving equipment was 18 miles away in Pwllheli and although messages had been sent, no apparatus had yet arrived. However, it did arrive 6 hours after being sent for, having been hauled overland by four motor cars. By now the **Fleetwing** had been driven in, just twenty yards from the beach. Sergeant Jones and four other local men waded out to the stricken **Fleetwing**. They saw one man with his head hanging over the side of the ship. They grabbed hold of him and got him ashore with great difficulty. No one else was to be seen either on deck or in the water around the vessel. Hugh Evan Roberts, a local sailor got onboard the **Fleetwing** by means of a rope and inside he found four more men in bad condition, with three of them unconscious. He secured them, one by one to a rope and lowered them down. They were taken by car to the Caernarvon Bay Hotel but sadly James Carroll, the mate, died on the way. The others were looked after and later Captain Murphy was sent to a hospital in Liverpool, as a precaution. The remaining crew were sent home by The Shipwrecked Mariners Society.

FORTH
Number 8517.

1852 Built at New Brunswick. A barque of 200 tons. Dimensions: 93x20x13ft.
1852-1864 Registered at Wexford
1872 Re-registered as a brig, 167 tons (Owner Thomas Cumsky, Dublin)

OWNERS
1853: R.&R. Allen (Captain Gregory Cahill).
1870 John Meaze, Dublin. 174 tons
1871 Thomas Cumsky, Balbriggan, Co. Dublin.

CREWS
1863 August
Master: Daniel Cullen, 36.
Mate: Laurence Dempsey, 45.
Cook: Richard Delaney, 23.
ABs: Nicholas Cleary, 27; Con. Hilliard, 23; Stephen Sinnott, 20; Joseph Codd, 17; James Finn, 23; Simon Hatchell, 20; Richard Codd. 25; Patk. Loughlin, 34 (Dublin); William Galbraith, 23; John Sullivan, 32; John Marr, 21 (New Brunswick);
Apprentice: Martin Boyne, 17.

1864 August (Trip to the Black Sea, Sea of Azof and back to Continental Europe).
Master: Daniel Cullen, 36.
Mate: Laurence –??, 35.
Bosun: Nicholas Cleary, 27.
AB: Joseph Codd, 19; C. Hilliard, 22; Simon Hatchell, 20; Richard Codd, 25.
Cook/Seaman: Patrick Coughlan, 34.
Cook/Steward: W. Galbraith, 23; Ed. Sullivan, 30; John Marr, 21.
Apprentice: Martin Boyne, 20.

On 3 September 1852, the **Forth** signed on at Wexford for a voyage to the USA. In January 1862, **Forth** was one of five Wexford vessels frozen in at Ibrail on the River Danube. The others were: the **Ripple** (Captain Kelly), in ballast; the **Dispatch** (Captain Furlong), with wheat; the **Asia** (Captain Codd), in ballast and the **Selskar** (Captain Chandler). The **Forth** was carrying a cargo of maize. On 23 December 1862, the *Shipping Gazette* reported that the **Forth** of Wexford had been damaged by floating ice at Ibrail. She had been lightened of cargo and was being surveyed.

In March 1864, the **Forth** signed on a crew at Waterford. They signed 12 month articles and it appears the trip was for Galatz. It was a fairly uneventful trip, nothing untoward happened. Two men, A. Halch and W. Galbraith, reported sick in Cardiff. John Sullivan, from Kilrush, Co. Clare, went sick in Constantinople and was replaced by John Itward, a New Brunswicker. Halch and Galbraith would have been replaced, too but there is no indication of who replaced them. Reporting sick was not just a matter of declaring your illness to the ship's captain. Apart from convincing the captain, the sick man had to be seen by the British Consul, in whatever port the sickness occurred. Once the Consul had sanctioned that, the man was indeed sick. He was given whatever wages were due to him, and another man – having had his rates of pay and conditions explained – was signed on in his place.

In September 1866 the **Forth**, under Captain Rowe, arrived at Wexford from Llanelli, Wales, unknowingly carrying the dreaded cholera. The ship had been bound from the Welsh port to Belfast but, due to bad weather, was forced to run to her home port. They tied up below the Dockyard. During the trip from

Report on the wreck of the **Forth**, dated January 1887. *John Power Collection.*

Forth- a three masted barque of 200 tons .Built in 1852 at New Brunswick .Shown here on a calm evening at Wexford.

Llanelli, Robert Murphy, the mate, showed symptoms of the dreaded disease and was unable to carry out any duties. It appears that a day or two previously all hands had eaten (*with great gusto*, a report said), a mess of stewed cockles. Afterwards all hands, with the exception of Michael Bryan, began suffering with diarrhoea, some with severe pain. Despite this the captain was fully prepared to continue on the voyage, but the healthier members of the crew persuaded him to put in to Wexford.

The Mate's condition was worsening and the crew carried him to his home in Gibson's Lane. After that Captain Rowe went to inform Captain P. J. Doyle, Devereux's Marine Superintendent, of the situation. He at once directed that Dr Crean be called to attend the ship's Mate. Captain Rowe then proceeded home to his house in Maudlintown, where his condition worsened. The family called for Dr Crean, who after examining Captain Rowe expressed little hope of his recovery. Later that day Dr Crean again attended Captain Rowe but, despite the best attention, Captain Rowe passed away at 2 o'clock that afternoon, 10 September. Robert Murphy lingered on for some days but then, despite showing signs of strengthening, he, too, passed away. Then Michael Bryan, one of the men who had assisted in carrying Robert Murphy to his home, took sick and died on 13 September.

A later report said that Mrs Rossiter, Captain Rowe's sister-in-law, who had attended him in his final illness, was also suffering with cholera, but no further mention was made of her condition. The disease swiftly spread throughout the town and many households, particularly in The Faythe area, were devastated by it. In those days there were no adequate precautions available to combat the plague and many died within a matter of weeks. The disease was still alarming the authorities in mid November and a meeting was called of all the people of the town. A fund was opened to aid the suffering of the townsfolk. This was the second outbreak in Wexford that year. The earlier infection had been brought in from Liverpool.

The **Forth** was sold to Ayr in 1870.

FORTH
Number 27928.

1860 Built in Sunderland, 70 tons. Dimensions: 64.1x20x9.1ft.
1870 Registered at Wexford.

OWNERS
1870 James P. Devereux, Wexford.
1885 Michael Wickham, South Main St., Wexford.
1887 Harpur & Wickham, Wexford.

CREW (date uncertain)
Master: John Rowe, 36.
Mate: Patrick Terrill, 27.
Seaman: Patrick Marlowe, 24.
Boy: Francis Larkin 17.

The **Forth** was homeward bound with a cargo of coal from Ayr, when she was wrecked on the Blackwater Bank in January 1887. The crew were able to get ashore and reached Wexford that evening. She was commanded by Captain Patrick Saunders when she was lost.

Runcorn Docks.

Newport Docks, Monmouthshire, South Wales.

G

GEM
Number 20711. Code NCHR.

1848 Built at Leith, a schooner of 68 tons.

1860 Registered at Stornaway.
1863 Registered at Londonderry.

OWNERS
1863 Catherine Marlow, Wexford (Master: James Sinnott).
1865 Patrick Marley, Wexford.
1873 Mr Kearns, Wexford.
1873 Kehoe of Wexford.

CREWS
Date uncertain:
Mate: David Noonan, age 52.
AB: Christopher Williams, 22; John Redmond, 18.
Boy: Patrick Murphy, 16.
1873
Master: Captain Doyle;
Mate: John Corish.
Seamen: John Furlong; James Hayes.

The **Gem** was sailing from Ayr to Wexford when she struck the Dogger Bank, outside Wexford Harbour, on 4 September 1873, and became a total loss. A Board of Trade Inquiry was held at Wexford Courthouse. The inquiry was initiated to determine if the loss was the fault of her commander Captain Doyle. Mr Huggard, who appeared on behalf of the Board of Trade, opened the proceedings by handing the Court the order of the Board, empowering the inquiry into the matter. He read the preliminary statement of the master and told the Court that if, after hearing the evidence, they considered that the accident was the fault of the master, either by wilfulness or gross carelessness, then they should make the master liable for the costs of the inquiry. The captain was then asked for his certificate and he replied that he never had one.

John Corish was then sworn in and examined. He told the Court that he was mate of the **Gem** and had a certificate for Coasting and Foreign service. After hearing Corish's evidence, Anthony Ennis, Deputy Harbour Master was called. Then John Furlong, a member of the crew of the **Gem**. After hearing the evidence of both men, the Court was adjourned until the next day. The hearing was resumed the next day and Furlong was recalled to allow Captain Doyle to cross examine him. Anthony Ennis was also recalled and James Hayes, a sailor from the **Gem** was called for the first time.

Mr Huggard addressed the Court on behalf of the Board of Trade and said that the

Court, having carefully considered the circumstances of the case and hearing the evidence of all the various witnesses and the depositions of the master, found the master culpable. As the master did not have a certificate, they were unable to suspend him by withdrawing it, so they fined him five pounds, a portion of the cost of the inquiry.

GLENMORE
Number 21769. Code NHRF.

1858 Built at Garmouth, Scotland, a barque of 253 tons.
Dimensions: 106x24.6x14.2ft.
1863 Registered at Wexford.

OWNERS
1874 Richard Dexereux of Wexford.
1882 William John Lawson, Whitstable. Registered as a barquentine of 233 tons, in the port of Faversham.

CREW 1864
Master: Luke Sheil, 37, of New St., Wexford.
Mate: John Murphy, 52.
Bosun: Thomas Kane.
Cook: John Leary.
ABs: Patrick Kelly; Owen Lacy; Matthew Kavanagh; John Byrne.
AB: William Jones.
OS: Patrick Williams; James Edwards.
Apprentice: James Brown.

In May 1864, ABs Owen Lacy and Patrick Kelly, and Apprentice James Brown, were detained by police at Malta, for causing a disturbance ashore. Patrick Kelly had already been arrested 9 days previously by the Maltese police and sentenced to two weeks' imprisonment. They were therefore left behind, incarcerated or pending trial, when the ship sailed. Any due wages were paid to Lacy but none to Kelly as he was already in debt to the ship. The effects of all three were delivered to the office of the British Consulate. Edwards, Jones and Williams were taken on in their place

In July 1864, James Edwards fell overboard from the yard while unfurling the main top gallant sail and was drowned. As was customary at the time, his goods were auctioned among the crew. His effects were: 2 flannel shirts; 1 singlet; 2 caps; 2 pair of trousers; 2 pocket handkerchiefs; 1 pair of stockings; 1 pipe; 1 blanket; 1 bed box, and a tin box with 5 pictures.

GLYNN
Number 52533. Code JDHM.

1865 Built at Merioneth. A two masted wooden schooner, with a female bust and a square stern. Dimensions: 73x19.x9ft.

OWNERS
1882 Richards and Company, Porthmadog. Registered in Wexford.
1883 William Joseph Gafney, Wexford.
1885 Margaret A. Gafney, Wexford.
1889 Angela C. Gafney, Wexford.
1897 Edmund V. Barry, Middle Abbey St., Dublin.
1900 Staffords of Wexford.
1917 James French, Castlebridge, Co. Wexford.
1917 John Griffiths and Arthur E. Williams of Dinas Powys. Register transferred to Cardiff.

CREWS
1891
Master: Moses Boggan, 34.
Mate: T. Murphy, 40.
ABs: W. Murphy, 24; Martin Roche, 30; J. Blake, 22; R. Doyle, 21.
Boy: M. Rossiter, 21.
Later that year:
Mate: John Kehoe, 39;
ABs: Martin Rourke, 28; Richard Devereux, 26.
OS: James Carr, 15.

1911
Master: Patrick Doyle of Maudlintown, Wexford (born 1860).
Mate: Nicholas Dempsey (b. 1870).
AB: Nicholas Doyle (b. 1888); William Hall (b. 1879).
OS: Bartholemew Carty (b. 1887); Norman James Sharp (b. 1886) (Liverpool, first trip).

1915
Master: Patrick Doyle.
Mates: Nicholas Doyle; John McCabe.
ABs: George Curran; John Whilaw; Matthew Stafford.
OS: S. Doyle; Stephen Smith; John Scallon.

On 24 January 1889, the Nationalist MP William O'Brien, escaped from custody in Carrick on Suir, Co. Tipperary. He made his way to Wexford and the home of Dr Cardiff at Carrigbyrne. Also at Dr Cardiff's residence were two men O'Brien described as *two of the best Nationalists in all of Wexford*, Nicholas Codd of Barntown and John Bolger of Oylegate. Both of them drove to Wexford to arrange some means of getting O'Brien

Glynn, a two masted tops'l schooner Built 1865 at Merioneth, North Wales.
Artist unknown, courtesy of Captain Michael Doyle, Wexford.

'over the water'. Codd and Bolger returned about ten o'clock that night to tell them that all was arranged but they had to leave straight away. This they did and reached Wexford about two in the morning, stopping at the home of Captain Hugh McGuire. Also there was Captain Moses Boggan, *a wiry son of the sea*.

The collier **Glynn** was out in the harbour, standing by, under the command of Captain Boggan. Before boarding, according to O'Brien, they had *an hour's jollification* and at about three, they went *cautiously* across the quay to a little boat, which was tied up alongside. O'Brien slipped on the plank that was serving as a gangway to the little boat but managed to hang on and saved himself from falling into the water. This was the only mishap and soon Mr O'Brien found himself safely locked in Captain Boggan's cabin, where, he said *I was free to spend the remainder of the night in as much sleep as the rats would let me enjoy*.

At about eight in the morning, the crew came aboard and the **Glynn** prepared for sea. The tug **Wexford** came up and took them in tow to bring them over the bar. About two hours later, Captain Boggan unlocked the cabin door and told O'Brien that they were clear of the bar and it was safe to come up on deck. A very favourable wind was blowing and five hours later, an almost record time, the Welsh coast came into view. The next morning, they docked at *a drowsy little village named Porthcawl and went to a hotel owned by a Mr Lewis, a friend of Captain Boggan*. He agreed to drive them to Bridgend, from where O'Brien hoped to make his way to Manchester, where he was due to speak. Considering that O'Brien was a fugitive from the law, it could be assumed that his escape via Wexford would have been a secret but not so. Before her arrival back in Wexford, according to a report in the *Wexford Independent, The World and Garret Reilly know all about it now*. On her arrival back in the harbour, the **Glynn**, with her green burgee flying, was greeted with loud cheers and burning tar barrels.

The **Glynn** was shelled and sunk by gunfire from the German U Boat, UC-42, 32 miles NW of Les Hanois Light Vessel off Guernsey, Channel Islands, on 5 September, 1917. Reports say all hands were saved. She was on a voyage from Granville to Swansea with iron ore.

George & Susan, a two masted tops'l schooner of 100 tons. Built at Arklow 1875 and owned by Ed. Kearon of Arklow. In this interesting photograph of New Ross quay, c late 1800s the name **George & Susan** is just discernable on the schooner moored "bow on" to the quay.
The Laurence Collection, National Library of Ireland.

H

HANDY
Number 21445 Code NGJQ.

1841 Built at Wexford, a barque of 66 tons, carvel built. Dimensions: 62x15x7ft.

1865 OWNER: Richard Devereux, Wexford (Master: Peter Devereux).

CREWS
1852
Master: Patrick Fortune, 40.
Mate: Nicholas Devereux, 32.
Seamen: William Cahill, 24; John Connors, 32.

1870
Master: Thomas Rowe, 40.
Mariner: William W–?, 22; James Cullen, 22; Walter Leary, 23; James Leary, 24; Thomas Carberry, 24.

In 1869, the **Handy**, was sailing from Dublin to Wexford with wheat. She was anchored in the South Bay, Wexford, when her anchor chains parted and she was soon ashore. The crew were taken off by lifeboat and the ship was later re-floated with little damage. She was wrecked off Cahore in January 1871 but the wreck wasn't removed until October 1891, when it was considered an obstacle to Cahore Lifeboat.

HANNAH
Number 52884.

1865 Built at Conway, a schooner of 81 tons. Dimensions: 76x20x8.8ft.

OWNERS
It should be noted that although **Hannah** was owned in the following ports, she retained her original registry in the port of Preston.

1887 Edward Pyke of Liverpool; J. & F. Chadwick of Drogheda, Co. Louth, 68 tons.
1893 James Kavanagh of George's St., Wexford.
1894 Michael Kavanagh, George's St., Wexford.

CREW (All from Wexford town)
Master: Captain Williams.
Mate: James Williams (captain's son).
Seamen: Thomas White and James Doyle.

In January 1901, news reached Wexford that the local schooner **Hannah** was lost. The bad news was tempered by the news that Captain Williams, owner and master, and his

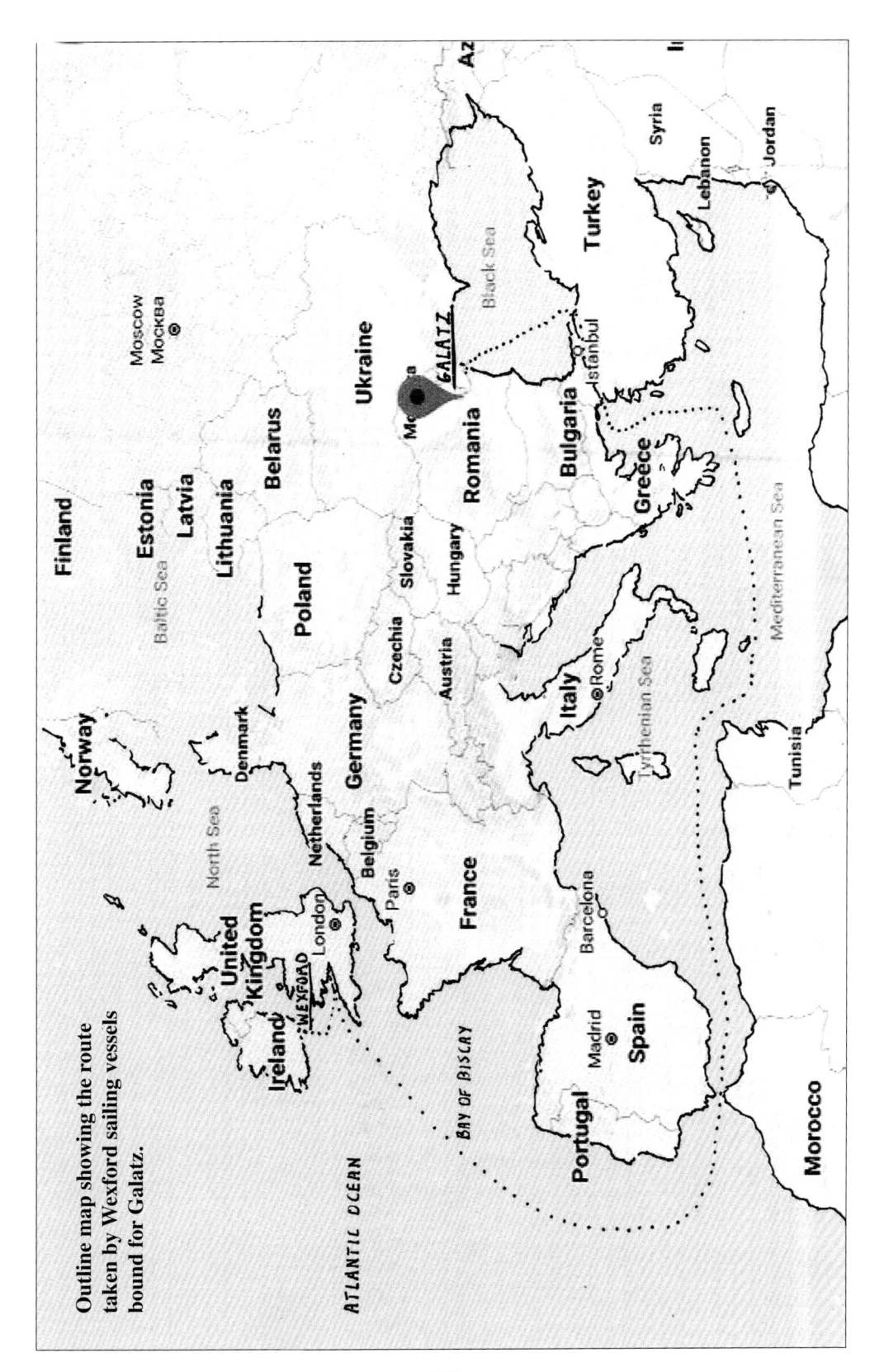

Outline map showing the route taken by Wexford sailing vessels bound for Galatz.

crew were safe. Due to bad weather, most of the Wexford fleet had been alongside for almost six weeks, some with cargo, and others in ballast. A break finally came and they decided to sail. The **Tempest**, **Charles Walker**, **Alice T**, **Star of Hope** and the **Glynn** all went over the Bar, with the **Hannah**. They had barely got over, when a fierce gale struck. They all proceeded on their way (to Newport, South Wales).

Eventually news came to Wexford that they all, with the exception of the **Hannah**, had arrived safely. Great uneasiness was felt at this news. However, shortly afterwards word arrived by wire from Queenstown, telling of the loss of the vessel but that the captain and crew were safe and had been brought into that port. They had been picked up by the Cork Steamship Co's ss **Moorhen** ex Liverpool for Antwerp and this is where they were landed. Although Captain Williams was reported to be badly injured, he was soon able to re-join his crew at Queenstown Sailors' Home, from where he recounted his experience.

He said they had left Wexford on a Sunday morning with the hope of making a fast passage as the wind was fair. They were about 8 miles outside the Tuskar, when they were hit by a massive squall that carried away the fore topmast and the foremast head, causing the spar to come crashing down on the deck and smashing a large part of the bulwark. They tried to jibe the ship, with the intention of getting her under the land and after some hardship had succeeded in getting within about 2 miles of the Lucifer Light Vessel, when another squall of hurricane force struck the **Hannah**, carrying away the mainmast. This in turn carried away the bulwarks, smashed the boat and threw the schooner over on her beam ends. She went over so far that they thought she would surely capsize. She didn't but now she was totally unmanageable.

Captain Williams had seen two steamers in the area and sent up distress flares, which were answered by the **Moorhen**. Captain Worsnop of the **Moorhen** offered to tow them to Waterford and, with this in mind, he sent over one of his boats with a hawser. The tow duly began. At 5 pm they were off the Tuskar, still in horrific weather and expecting the tow to part at any time. Captain Williams signalled the steamer to take them off. This was not an easy task in the dark with the type of weather they were experiencing, but Captain Worsnop, got a lifeboat in the water and it was manned by his 2nd mate and 4 sailors. After a struggle they got to the **Hannah** and brought the crew off and aboard the **Moorhen**.

The steamer still had the **Hannah** in tow but owing to the terrible strain it was under, the hawser soon parted and the schooner disappeared into the darkness. That night, with the winds and seas still in turmoil, the **Moorhen** was labouring heavily and her cargo shifted. So bad was the weather that Captain Worsnop kept his ship hove to for many hours, between the Lucifer and the Tuskar. The next day he had to hove to again and it was at this time that Captain Williams fell and broke his ankle and suffered multiple cuts and bruises.

The following day a dismasted schooner was observed passing eastward from Cardiff and driving through Cardigan Bay, before a fierce wind, with huge seas washing over her. A lifeboat was launched and they discovered it was the **Hannah**. She went ashore at Traeth-y-mount, on the Cardiganshire coast, near Aberporth in a good position and it was said that her condition was good and that it was hoped to re-float her. Two days later she went to pieces.

HANTOON
Number 49502, Code WDHC.

1861 Built at Rothesay, New Brunswick, a barque of 359 tons.
Dimensions: 123.2x26.1x14.9ft.

OWNERS
R.&R. Allen.
J. Devereux & J. Doyle.

CREW
Captain: John Neill* of the Shamrock Hotel, Anne St;
First Mate: Luke Sheil, The Fort;
Second Mate: Nick Bent, Byrnes Lane,
ABs: Jack Garrett* The Faythe; John Carley* Maudlintown; James Croften, Byrne's Lane; John Cullen* The Faythe; James Smith, Byrne's Lane; Thomas Luccan, Byrne's Lane
Cook: Mat Neill, Byrne's Lane.
Boy: John Kelly, Trinity St.

*Captain John Neill and ABs John (Jack) Garrett, John Carley, and John Cullen were lost when the **Hantoon** sank in 1881.

The **Hantoon** was lost on 26 December 1881, off Cape St Vincent, when she was run down by the steamer **Rothesay**. On 15 November 1881, the **Hantoon** left Galatz (Galati), Romania, bound for Queenstown (Cobh), with a cargo of 530 tons of maize and a crew of 11. Just before midnight on 26 December, she was about 50 miles north of Cape St Vincent, in fine weather and under full sail, making about 6 knots. Shortly before midnight, a green light was seen approaching her a little to the starboard and about 3 miles off. The **Hantoon** continued on her course until both vessels were within a short distance of each other. Suddenly all the steamers three lights appeared, then just as fast, the green light vanished. Almost immediately the steamer ran into the **Hantoon**, striking her on the starboard bow, just forward of the forerigging and cutting her below the waterline. When the crew of the **Hantoon** found that their ship was sinking, they clambered aboard the steamer, which turned out to be the **Rothesay** of Liverpool. She was bound for Port Said. One of the men failed in his attempt and was drowned. The **Hantoon** sank within three minutes of the collision and Captain O'Neill and two other men were still on board and went down with her.

The captain of the **Rothesay** had a boat lowered with four men aboard to search for any possible survivors from the **Hantoon**. After about two hours searching, all hope was abandoned and he ordered the boat back onboard. The 2nd mate of the **Rothesay**, who had been on the bridge at the time of the collision, appeared to be very agitated throughout these operations. After 3 hours he was nowhere to be found and what became of him was never known. An entry in his personal log indicated that his disappearance was not accidental.

On 1 February 1882, a Board of Trade Inquiry was held under the Merchant Shipping Act, to ascertain the cause of the accident. The Court decided that there was no doubt

Hantoon, a three masted barque of 359 tons. Built in 1861 at New Brunswick for J. Devereux of Wexford. Shown here in a "bit of a blow", with shortened sail c1880.

as to who was to blame. The Merchant Shipping Act stated that: *If two ships, one of which is a sailing ship and the other a steamship, are proceeding in such a direction as to involve risk of a collision, the steamship shall keep out of the way of the sailing ship and that the sailing ship shall keep on her course.* The 2nd mate of the steamer was found solely responsible. Had he given the order 'hard a port' rather than 'hard a starboard', the accident would likely have been avoided.

On 9 February 1929, the local Wexford newspaper, the *Free Press*, published the transcript of a letter written by **Hantoon's** First Mate, Luke Sheil to J. T. Devereux, owner, describing what happened. It was written in Lisbon on 31 December 1881 and it gives an insight into what occurred on that fateful night. It also provides an insight into the pandemonium which must have occurred on many sailing ships caught in similar circumstances.

It reads as follows: *I might as well let you know how the collision occurred. At 11.55 pm on the 25th inst, the man on the lookout reported a bright and green light on the starboard bow, about a point and a half, we bearing north with all sail set. Topmast and lower studding sail, wind ESE going about 5½knots, Cape St. Vincent at the time south 50 miles, boatswain's watch on deck.*

At eight bells watch was called. When Bent went on deck I heard him shouting 'Steamboat Ahoy'. I ran on deck partly dressed and saw a steamboat running right into us forward of the fore-rigging. Two or three seconds afterwards she struck us, cutting us more than half way through. Seven of us managed to get onboard the steamer, which we ascertained to be the **Rothesay** *of Liverpool. I was the last that escaped from the* **Hantoon**. *When the two ships swung alongside of each other I caught the railing around the poop forward of our mizzen rigging, the captain at the time abaft the rigging. I sang out 'Now is your time, this is the last chance'. When I got on the poop of the steamer I heard him sing out for a rope. I looked around for one, but not one to be found. The vessels then separated, and I neither heard nor saw any more.*

I should think that from the time we were struck until our lower yards were in the water could not be more than three minutes. Garrett fell between the two vessels and was killed. Carley was crushed and drowned in the forecastle; the boy delirious about the decks and afraid to leap for his life. There was not a single rope thrown over the side, everybody running to the starboard side afraid of the spars falling on their heads. The only things we found belonging to our ship were on the forecastle, a boom iron a piece of the foreyard arm, and one dog belonging to the topsail sheet sleeve hole.

The second mate of the **Rothesay** *had the watch at the time, and ported his helm on getting close to us, whereas if he had kept his course he would have gone well clear us on our starboard side. The rascal committed suicide when he saw what he had done. I wish he had done it the day before. Not one of us saved a coat. The watch on deck that had coats threw them off to make a jump, the cook with nothing but his shirt. We expect to remain here until an inquiry has taken place.*

By a remarkable coincidence all four men who were lost were named John, and by further coincidence, the steamer, **Rothesay** that ran them down carried the same name as the town where the **Hantoon** was built: Rothesay, New Brunswick.

HARVEST HOME
Number 81238.

1882 Built at Tarleton, Lancaster by Peter Lund, for T. Ashcroft. A wooden schooner with two masts of 79 tons. Dimensions: 88.4x21.4x9.6ft.

1882 Registered Preston.

OWNERS
1890-1894 Joseph Taylor, Lathom, Lancs. Registered as 80 tons.
1904 J. Rooney, Kilkeel, Co. Down.
1909 Gregory Devereux, Paul Quay, Wexford, 79 tons.
1919 16 March. The Douglas Shipping Co., Isle of Man.

In 1909, **Harvest Home** was under the ownership of Gregory Devereux of Paul Quay, Wexford. On 25 October at 10 am, she left Wexford in ballast, bound for Newport, Monmouthshire, under the command of Captain William Dunne. The wind was blowing a moderate breeze from the NNW. After crossing Wexford Bar, the wind increased and veered SW. They proceeded to the South Bay and went to anchor. Around mid night the wind was coming from the East and the second anchor was let go. The next morning, Wednesday 27 October, at 2 am, the weather was showery with a strong easterly gale and heavy seas and the port anchor began to drag. They hove the lead at 8 am and found they were in 8ft of water on the starboard bow, with a rocky bottom. The captain thought it wise to slip the anchor chains and head for the beach. This they did and the **Harvest Home** was driven ashore 2 miles NW of Ballygeary Coastguard Station (Rosslare Harbour). She was later refloated when the weather moderated. Ashore in the same area,

Harvest Home, a two masted tops'l schooner of 79 tons. Built 1882, Tarleton, Lancashire

This remarkable photograph shows no fewer than three Wexford vessels ashore in the South Bay near Rosslare in October 1909. Front to back they are, the **Harvest Home, Helen & Ernest** and **Zion Hill.**

at the same time, were, the Wexford ketch, **Helen & Ernest** and the Wexford schooner, **Zion Hill**. All were later refloated and resumed trading.

On Tuesday 14 November 1916, **Harvest Home** was under the command of Captain James Saunders, bound from Cardiff with coal for Donahoe of Enniscorthy. They left Cardiff at high water and, by 10.30 the next day, they sighted Tuskar Rock, two miles distant. They continued on course and made Wexford Bar, but they had missed the tide. The **Harvest Home** then made for Rosslare Harbour and arrived there at 1 pm, going to anchor. However, their position put them right in the course the mail boats used on entering and leaving the harbour, so they were forced to weigh anchor and move about 50 yards NW of the Pier Head. At this stage the weather was increasing and they were riding on the starboard anchor only. However, it was blowing so hard that at 3 am the port anchor was let go.

By Friday it was blowing a hurricane and they couldn't hold her. She dragged both her anchors, so it was deemed prudent to slip both of the cables and run for the strand. She ran up near the old lighthouse at The Hill o' Sea. The ship, cargo and crew were all safe. She was later towed into deeper water by the Wexford Harbour Commissioner's tug, brought into Wexford and repaired at the Wexford Dockyard.

On 28 March 1917, **Harvest Home** was sunk by gunfire from submarine **UC65** four miles north east of the South Arklow Light Vessel. She was enroute from Wexford to Garston, with timber. **Harvest Home** was one of the 10 vessels sunk by **UC65** that day. The Lightship **Guillemot**, on the South Arklow station, had observed at least some of these attacks and took it upon themselves to warn any other approaching vessels of the danger. This they did by flying signals to warn shipping that a submarine was operating in the area and warned them to stay clear. Obviously, the German U-Boat commander was not pleased that his actions had been seen and that his prey were being warned off, so he came up on the **Guillemot** and ordered the crew into their boat. Once the boat was away he put a team on board the lightship and placed charges in the hull. The charges went off but failed to sink the ship. He then sank it by gunfire.

The **Guillemot** was one of just two light vessels to be sunk during WW1. The **Guillemo**t crew were all from County Wexford. They were: Captain James Rossiter; crewmen: Paddy Cogley, Martin Murphy, Pat Gaddern, John Leader, and John and Pat Sinnott. Apart from the Sinnott brothers, who hailed from Courtown Harbour, the crew were all from Wexford town.

HAWK
Number 44122. Code TRSJ.

1861 Built at St Martin's, New Brunswick, a barquentine of 130 tons.

1861: Registered at Wexford.

OWNERS
1872-1876 R.&R. Allen of Wexford.
1878 Robert Tedcastle of Dublin, registered as 118 tons.

Hawk, a barquentine of 130 tons. Built in 1861 at New Brunswick. Shown here underway in the Mediterranean, bound for Galatz.

CREWS
1861
Master: Nicholas Roche, 39.
Mate: Robert Whitty, 24.
Cook/Steward: John Rowe, 21.
ABs: Nick Hayes, 28; Thomas Allen, 21; Matt McDonald, 28; James Kerr, 24; Wm. Miner, 26.
OS: Pat. Rossiter, 18.

1862
Master: John N. Kelly, 42.
Mate: Desmond Heron, 24.
Bosun: Wm. Kelly, 40.
ABs: John Costello, 23; John Stanford, 30 (deserted); James Larkin, 19; Daniel Price, 28 (Cardiff).
Cook/Steward: John Parle, 20.

On 26 October 1863, the British Consul at Constantinople certified that crewman Thomas Nugent of the **Hawk**, had been left behind on the grounds of sickness. After confirming that Nugent actually was sick, the Consul saw that any money due to him – in this instance 7 pounds 10 shillings – was paid to him. A man named Samuel Spring was taken on in his stead. It appears that 2 pounds 16 shillings and 6 pence, which was due to Spring from his previous ship, was, paid to the master of the **Hawk** in cash under the instructions of the British Consul.

HELEN & ERNEST
Number 74444. Code KCVF.

1876 Built at Cowes by White, a ketch of 51 tons. Dimensions: 66.4x18.8x7.1ft.

OWNERS
1905/1909 S. B. Weldon, Linziestown, Tomhaggard, Co. Wexford.
1911 John Ellis, Port Dinorwic, Carnarvonshire.
1918 Register closed.

In April 1904, **Helen and Ernest**, under Captain Walsh, unloaded coal at Carne. When she had completed her unloading and was in the act of putting out to sea, she went aground at the back of the pier. Fortunately, her position was not serious and she refloated without effort.

On Monday 25 October 1909, the **Helen & Ernest,** under the command of Captain Michael Smith of Maudlintown, Wexford, left Wexford Port at 10.30 in the morning. She had a cargo of 50 tons of oats, in bulk, for Hickman & Son, of Bristol. The weather was clear and there was a fresh breeze from the NW. After crossing Wexford Bar, the wind came from the South. They stood off until 8 pm, when the wind began to freshen and increase in force. Captain Smith thought it prudent to return to the South Bay for shelter. They dropped the starboard anchor there at about 10.30 pm. The next morning

Helen & Ernest, a ketch of 51 tons. Owned by Samuel B. Weldon of Tomhaggard, Co. Wexford. Shown here near the Lucifer Lightship, off the Wexford coast.

at 2.30, the gale was still increasing, so the port anchor was dropped. They rode it out there until 4.30 am on Wednesday when **Helen & Ernest** began to drag both anchors. By 7 am the wind was blowing a severe gale with heavy seas, from the E by S, when she struck ground.

Captain Smith decided that the only option open to him was to run for the beach, to save life and property. This he proceeded to do and she drove up onto the strand about half a mile north of Kilrane Railway Station. The crew landed safely in the ship's lifeboat. She was apparently refloated and carried on with her career until 1918. On 15 October 1918, whilst en-route from Runcorn to Howth, Co. Dublin with a cargo of salt, she was wrecked on the Point of Ayr, Flintshire.

HENRY
Number 8613.

1831 Built at Milford Haven, a smack of 61 tons.
1853 Registered as a schooner of 47 tons.

OWNERS
1831-1853 Walsh and Sons of Wexford (Master: J. Williams).
1865 Philip Walsh of Wexford.
1868 Richard Devereux of Wexford.
1874 J.T. Devereux of Wexford (47 tons).

CREW 1864
Master: James Hart, 55.
Mate: John Boylan, 47.
Seaman: James Kelly, 39.

The **Henry** was lost on the Barrels on 28 October 1874. She was in the charge of Captain Ambrose Butler. The crew took to the ship's boat but it overturned in the surf. They all managed to cling to the keel and were washed ashore safely.

LOSS OF A WEXFORD SCHOONER.—On Wednesday, the 28th inst., the schooner *Henry*, of Wexford, 46 tons register, Ambrose Butler, Master, and owned by J. T. Devereux, Esq., left here bound for Gloucester with a cargo of oats and barley. The morning did not look favourable, there was a nasty north east wind, springing up with a heavy sea rolling from the eastward. Still the master a very good seaman tried to make his passage, but after passing Tuskar found it impossible to do so, as the sea was too much for his small craft to contend with. He therefore prudently bore up for Carne roads, but while entering the passage between Carnsore point and Blackrock the usual course to the roads, the ship struck something but did not stop her way. The captain at first supposed it to be a rock, but on examining his chart considered it must be a sunken or floating wreck. As he often went through the same passage before he did not think it necessary to heave the lead, seeing the land on one side and Blackrock on the other. But the moment the ship struck he hove the lead, and found 3¾ fathoms; the ship drew but 9½ feet water; the ship sunk in ten or twelve minutes after striking, the crew having just time to get into their little boat; they pulled for the shore about a mile distant, and there had a most miraculous escape, the boat capsized in the surf and threw the crew out of her, but they managed to scramble ashore exhausted. The Captain is much bruised about the face; the poor fellows lost all their clothes and little effects.

Report on the loss of the schooner **Henry**, October 1874
John Power Collection.

HIBERNIA
Built at Wexford, 46 tons.

CREW 1845
Master: John Hore, age 57.
Mate: John Hore, 24.
Seamen: John Devereux, 70; Bill Gaul, 27; Joseph Dillon, 24.

HIBERNIA
1837 Built Prince Edward Island, a brig of 223 tons, carvel built.

OWNERS: Richard Allen, Wexford and Mary Allen, Latimerstown, Wexford. (Masters: William Neville, Patrick Ryan).

Hibernia was an emigrant ship, trading to Quebec and Miramichi. During 1845 she sailed on the coastal trade.

CREW 1845 (All Wexford unless otherwise stated).
Master: William Neville.
Mate: Patrick Ryan.
Seaman: William Cummins; James Stephens; Anthony McGuire; David Murphy; Patrick Kirwan (Waterford); Martin Byrne (Dundee); John Rogan (London); John Smith (Dundee); John Early (London); John Heran (London); Thomas Roche.
Apprentice: Joseph Percival; Owen Cash; Patrick Murphy.
Boy: Thomas Lloyd (Newport.); Henry Duggan.
Cook: Alexander Harrison.

HUNTRESS
Number 39063. Code SWRD.

1856 Built at Prince Edward Island, a schooner of 95 tons.
Dimensions: 84.4x20.9x9ft.

1863 Registered at Wexford.

Huntress. A two masted tops'l schooner of 95 tons. Built in 1856 at Prince Edward Island. Shown here at Douglas, Isle of Man.

OWNERS
Philip Walsh of Wexford (merchant) and Matthew Walsh of Dublin.
1862 October. Philip Walsh died.
1863 In January appointed to Richard Walsh of Wexford. Then sold to William Gillespie of Paisley, Scotland. Registration was transferred to Glasgow.
1911 Sold to France.

CREWS
1865
Master: C. Campbell, 35.
Mate: John Cahill, 45.
Seamen: Simon More, 42; Patrick Roche, 20.
Apprentice: John Ennis, 20.
Cook: Thomas McGrath, 70.
Later that year:
Master: Charles Campbell, 35.
Mate: G. Cahill, 25.
Seamen: C. Cahill; John Ennis, 21.
Boy: Thomas McGrath, 19.
Later the same year:
Master: John Rossiter, 36.
Mate: James Rossiter, 31.
Seamen: John Walsh, 25; John Byrne, 25.
Boy: James Devereux, 18.

HOPE

Number 20108. Signal Letters MVRK.

1835 Built at St. Martin's, New Brunswick, 71 tons.
1835 Registered at Wexford.
1874 Waterford. Owners J.W. Walsh and Patrick Lambert.
1865 Built at St. Martin's, New Brunswick, 71 tons.

Hope, a two masted tops'l schooner of 71 tons. Built in 1835 at Newfoundland. Owned in Wexford by Jasper W. Walsh and P. Lambert.

I

I'LL TRY
Number 1432. Code HJWL.

1865 Built at Bideford, a schooner of 65 tons. Dimensions 66.6x17x9ft.

OWNER: Gafney of Wexford.

1887 October. Lost on the Low Water Pier, Cardiff, during a gale. She was sailing from Newport to Wexford with coal. Three other schooners; **Water Lily** of Falmouth; **Sendre** of St. Ives and **Trevannance** were lost in the same place, in the same gale. The **St. Agnes** of Hull also foundered at anchor and three men were lost.

> **SULLY.**
> VESSEL ASHORE.—A vessel named the I'll Try, from Newport to Wexford with coals (Dowell, master), ran ashore in Sully Bay at two o'clock on Wednesday morning during a snowstorm. She is apparently undamaged, will float off the next tide, and proceed when the wind changes.

Report of **I'll Try** ashore at Sully Bay, South Wales.

INDEPENDENCE
Number 35175. Code RNLW.

1857 Built at New Brunswick, a barquentine of 134 tons.
1857/1863 Registered at Wexford.
1879/80 hulked.

OWNERS: R.&R. Allen, Wexford.

CREWS
1863
Master: Clement Morris, 25.
Mate: Arthur Fortune, 52.
Nicholas Rowe, ,21; John Murphy 23; Nicholas Rossiter, 26; John Butler, 20. 16 June 1863, John Harding signed on. It is likely that he signed on to replace a hand who had been declared sick or jumped the ship.

1864
Master: Clement Morris, 27.
Philip Savage, 19; Patrick Rossiter, 19; William Brennan, 21; Nicholas Codd, 21; James Doyle, 21; John Harrington, 23 (Queenstown); James Campbell, 19 (Dumfries); Thos. Clark, 47 (Crookhaven); Timothy Carty (Crookhaven).

James Doyle and Nicholas Codd, both 21 years old, went sick in Galatz. Harrington and Campbell were taken on in their stead. The British Consul General inquired into

Doyle's and Codd's claim of sickness and found them to be true. He granted them his 'sanction' to pay off. He ascertained that the two taken on in their stead understood the articles before giving them permission to sign on. Campbell deserted in Constantinople and then Carty was taken on to replace him.

In August 1871, **Independence**, sailing from Port Talbot to Cahore with coal, was driven ashore near Morriscastle. She had left Port Talbot on the 15 August with a cargo of coal to MrJohn Sinnott of Cahore and made Morriscastle on 17 August. The seas were rough and there was thick, heavy rain falling. The captain tried all that was possible to keep his vessel safe and secure but found it impossible to hold. He sent up distress flares. Within half an hour, the Coastguards of Morriscastle Station arrived and took the captain and his six crew ashore, by rocket apparatus. The next day the storm had abated and the captain and crew went back on board and got the pumps going and had most of the cargo discharged. That evening the ship was pulled into deeper water and safely anchored, having suffered no great damage.

INDUSTRY
Number 17573. Code MHFN.

1857 Built at St. John, New Brunswick. A brig of 188 tons. Dimensions: 108.2x 24.4x13ft.

1870 Registered at Wexford.
1890 Registered as a barquentine.
1912 Out of register.

OWNERS
1870 Richard Devereux of Wexford.
1890 Kearon of Arklow.

CREWS
1845
Masters: Patrick Lane, 30; Patrick Ray, 32.
Seamen: John Fortune, 41; George Roberts, 34.
Mariners: William Duggan, 20; John North, 21.
Boys: Patrick Kelly, 16; Patrick Murphy, 16.

1870
Master: Edward Tyrell, 40.
Mates: Thomas Cullen, 45; Charles W. Carey, 22.
ABs: John O'Leary, 25; John Doyle, 26; Thomas Meyler, 17; Michael Ericit, 23; John Hearon, 23; John Fitzpatrick, 23; Michael Kinch, 15.

1888
The crew was unchanged except for new hands: ABs Thomas Leary and Michael Regan.

When Russia declared war on the Ottoman Empire on 2 April 1853, the **Industry** was

Industry, built as a brig, shown entering quarantine harbour at Valetta, Malta. *Courtesy, Captain Michael Murphy, The Faythe, Wexford. Artist unknown.*

Industry, as a brig, 188 tons. Built at New Brunswick c1870. Owned by Richard Devereux of Wexford.

Industry re-rigged as a barquentine, shown here c1890 when owned by E. Kearon of Arklow.

at Ibrail. In early May, a Lloyd's telegram arrived at Wexford stating that all neutral ships, including lighters and tugs, had left both Galatz and Ibrail. However, the **Industry** of Wexford, under Captain Murphy, remained. No reason was given for this in the telegram but it seems that the **Industry** was delayed and was boarded by the Russian Navy and brought back to port where she remained for 12 months. The crew were sent home leaving one man, a Mr Kehoe, the mate, to look after the ship. Around the same period a telegraph arrived at the Underwriters Office stating, probably as a security measure, *that all ships arriving at this port (Odessa) will be boarded at Middle Fountain. The master and crew to tell all go below and the ship to be navigated to and from Odessa by Russian crews.*

In February 1861, the **Industry** was lying at the Albert Basin, Newry. Two seamen from the vessel were returning on board at a late hour, after carousing in the town, when one of them, Thomas Powell missed his footing, fell into the water, and was drowned.

On 22 October 1864, under Captain Howlin, the **Industry** was in the Bay of Biscay. She had begun to make water and then the pumps blocked, so Captain Howlin decided to abandon ship. This all hands did and they were picked up by the Italian brig **Teresina** and landed at Queenstown. Four days later the barque **Chandernagore** came up on the **Industry** and, seeing no activity, the captain sent his Second Officer and four hands over to see what was happening. Finding no one onboard and only 2 ft of water in the bilges, the Second Officer and his men took charge of the **Industry** and brought her into Falmouth. On inspection the cargo was found to be only slightly damaged. Mr Devereux had to pay a substantial amount in salvage to the men to get his vessel and cargo back. There is no mention of what he thought of Captain Howlin's decision to abandon a ship which was still found afloat four days later, neither is there any mention of what became of Captain Howlin.

At the end of February 1875, fierce gales hit the Wexford coast and caused severe damage to shipping. Among the vessels moored at the quays was the **Industry**. She broke away from her moorings and her captain James Murphy had a close call when trying to save her. A plank he was standing on gave way and he fell into the raging sea. Weighed down with a heavy coat and sea boots, he had great difficulty keeping afloat. The only other man present, Matthew Carr grabbed on to Captain Murphy by his coat, but the seas swept him out of his grasp. Carr then grabbed a hook that was nearby for such happenings, hooked the by now nearly drowning man and hauled him ashore. Captain Murphy was immediately brought to Mrs Carr's in Oyster Lane and Dr Creane was sent for. After a few days he was fully recovered from his awful experience. The only sign of his difficulties was a mark on his forehead, where he had been struck by the hook.

On 24 December 1888, the *South Wales Daily News* carried a report that the **Industry** of Wexford, bound for Galway, was found to have several casks of powder and shot aboard and was ordered to be detained. It is recorded that on the 6 December 1888, she was sold to E. Kearon of Arklow. At the time of her detention she was in Arklow ownership but apparently had not changed registration. There is no report on the eventual outcome to this incident. In 1902 the **Industry** was burnt at a wharf fire at Glasgow. Afterwards, in 1907, she was sold to Swansea owners.

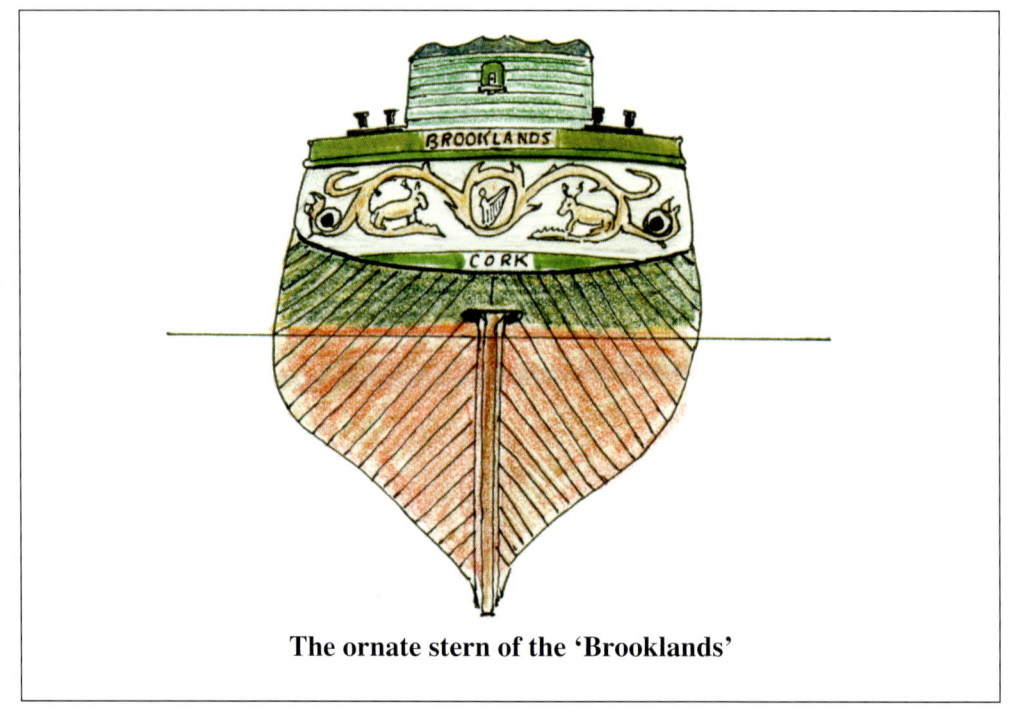

The ornate stern of the 'Brooklands'

J

JANE McCOLL
Number 60383. Code PDQV.

1868 Built at Rothesay, Isle of Bute, Scotland, by Robert McLea. A wooden schooner of 94 tons, with two masts. Dimensions: 81.2x20.4x9.4ft.

OWNERS
Before 1887 John McColl and Hugh Galloway of Glasgow, where she was registered.
1887 John and William Gilmore of County Down. John died in that year, making William the sole owner.
1891 William sold her to Samuel Armstrong of Wexford.
1907 Emilie Armstrong, Samuel's wife, became owner, with Samuel as Manager.
Later that year **Jane McColl** was acquired by James Billington.
1922 She was purchased by Robert F. Conway and Frances McGuire of Wicklow and the register was transferred to Dublin.

On 8 August 1908, the *Wexford People* reported yet another young sailor's death. His name was Patrick Lambert of William St. and he was an AB on the **Jane McColl**. The **Jane McColl** traded between Wexford and Newport and had not long tied up at Newport, when young Lambert got the job of bringing the captain, Joseph Doyle ashore in the ship's boat. They got ashore and the captain went about his business, leaving Lambert in the boat. That was the last anyone saw of him. It was surmised that when he was rowing around his ship he had got fouled up in one of the mooring ropes and knocked into the water. Another was that he had slipped going aboard and fell into the water, but whatever the cause, poor Lambert was never seen again.

In 1924, the **Jane McColl** was owned by Robert Conway of Wicklow and on 27 April that year, when bound from Garston to Wicklow with coal, she went on the rocks off Amlwch, Anglesey and sank. The crew were taken of by the local lifeboat.

JANE & FRANCES
1838 Built at Wexford, a schooner of 48 tons, carvel built.

OWNERS
Before 1842 J. Barrington, merchant, 16 shares; Richard Allen, merchant, 16 shares; Robert Sparrow, shipbuilder, 16 shares; Michael Jones, cabinetmaker, 16 shares.
1842 Hughes and Co., Wexford.
1844 Ed. Watson, Lacken, Duncormick, Co. Wexford.
1853 McCormick, New Ross.
1856 Out of Register.

CREWS
1844
Master: Richard Cox.

Jane McColl, a two masted tops'l schooner of 94 tons. Built, Rothesay, Scotland in 1868. Wexford owners included James Billington and the Armstrong family.

Mate: Walter Bryan, 61.
Seaman: James –?, 25.
Boy: Thomas Cox, 18.

1845
Master: Michael Cox, Duncormick, County Wexford, 34.
Mate: Walter Bryan, 61.
Seaman: Thomas Cox, 18.

JASPER
Number 70949. Code *NWGQ*.

1875 Built at Hylton, Co. Durham by William Richardson, as **Ruth Topping**, a barquentine of 296 tons, with a female figurehead and a round stern.
Dimensions: 135x27x12ft.
1891 Renamed **Ruth Waldron**.
1899 Renamed **Jasper**

OWNERS
1880 The Lancashire Shipping Co. of Bury.
1883 William G. Jarvis, Canning Place, Liverpool.
1891 O. Spearing & W.G. Waldron of London.
1895 O. Spearing of London.
1898 John Thomas Walsh of Wellington Cottage, Wexford.
1899 Jasper F. Walsh & F. J. Walsh of Wexford.
1904 Sold to The Italian Co. She was the last of the Wexford deep sea sailing ships and left Wexford on 2 June for Genoa.

CREW
Master: E. Clancy, Main St., 56.
Mate: R. Kellier, London, 21.
Bosun: D. Murphy, Faythe, 31.
Cook: Wm. Hess, King St., 55.
ABs: R. Kinshella, Michael St., 24; John Scallon, Upr. John St., 24; R. Clancy, Michael St., 20; OS: John Walsh, Castle Hill St., 18.
Boy: Ed. Scallon, Michael St., 14.
All from Wexford Town.

In July 1900, the **Jasper** was damaged in a collision off Cape Clear. She had left Wexford quays about two weeks before, bound for the St Lawrence River, to take on a cargo of timber. She was about 18 miles to the west of the island, in hazy weather, when they spotted a steamer astern, proceeding in the same direction. The steamer, Leylands Lines, **Winifredian**, was approaching swiftly. The steamer rang 3 bells, the signal to let bridge know that there was a vessel ahead and immediately the look out on the steamer was heard to shout *schooner right ahead, hard to port*.

Captain Clancy of the **Jasper** knew that at the rate the steamer was coming on, there

Jasper, a barquentine of 296 tons. Built, 1875 at Hylton, Co. Durham as **Ruth Waldron.** 1898 owned in Wexford by Jasper Walsh and re named **Jasper** after her owner. Seen here in November 1903 at anchor in Wexford Bay, offloading timber into the schooner **Zouave.** Paddle tug **Wexford** standing by.

was no possibility of avoiding a collision. The steamer hit the Wexford ship on the starboard side, carrying away anything that was in her course. The yards and topmasts were torn off and the side severely damaged. It soon became apparent that the **Jasper** was in no condition to continue on her voyage. Captain Clancy decided to return to the home port. With her rigging and main and mizzen masts practically gone, it was fortunate that they had fair winds on the way home. She arrived back in Wexford the following Tuesday morning. The **Winifredian** had proceeded on her trip to Boston. The local Lloyd's Surveyor, Robert Sparrow carried out a survey on the damaged ship and a representative of Leyland Lines also arrived in town, to carry out his own survey.

On 19 August 1903, the tug boat **Wexford,** under the command of her renowned master Captain Laurence Busher, made fast the tow rope and hauled the **Jasper** away from her berth and out into the river, for what was to be her last trip for her Wexford owners. With a long blast on her siren, the **Wexford** headed for the Bar, the first section of the **Jasper**'s trip across the Atlantic to Halifax, Nova Scotia. By the time she reached the Bar and was towed into the South Bay, all her sails were unfurled and she was in full sailing rig, ready for the long voyage ahead. She met fair weather along the coast but met with gales and storms out in the Western Ocean. Eventually, she reached her destination and began loading her cargo of 500 tons of deal for Walshe's sawmills. Then freshly watered and provisioned the **Jasper** set out for home.

The weather was good and the winds favourable and she made the South Bay of Wexford in eighteen days. As she was loaded to the gunwales she had to be lightened to enable her to cross the Bar. This was accomplished by the Dockyards Company's schooner **Zouave**, taking a good proportion of her cargo. She was then made fast to the paddle tug **Wexford** and was towed over the Bar and up to the quays on 2 December 1903. The crew were paid off the next day. After her discharge, the **Jasper,** was towed and laid up opposite the North Station, where she remained for some months before being sold to Italian buyers.

She was then renamed **Italia.** Her departure from Wexford the following June was a source of regret to many of the old sailors and to the port she had served so well. A month later, on 6 July, a Swedish ship arrived at the Port of Bristol carrying a lifeboat she had picked up, which was recognised as belonging to the **Jasper**. It was feared that she had been lost in the Bay of Biscay but later reports had her arriving at her destination. The **Jasper** ended her days as a coal hulk in Genoa Harbour in the 1930s.

The barquentine **Jasper** had served her owners well. On her final voyage her master was 29-year-old Captain J.J. Maddock of Fishers' Row (Byrne's Lane) Wexford, at the time a young, well-regarded master. Captain Maddock had taken command of the **Jasper** in July 1902, after her master Captain Clancy of Michael St. died and was buried at sea, while outward bound to Halifax. Maddock went on to an adventurous career at sea. He was awarded a medal by the Norwegian Government for saving the lives of crewmen from the Norwegian brig **Lillesand**. The **Lillesand** foundered in the Atlantic in 1916. Maddock was on the ss **Cluden**, when she was torpedoed off Cape Tenez, Algeria in October 1916. Captain Maddock, by then a resident of Rosslare Harbour, ended his career as master on the Rosslare/Fishguard mail boats.

Hulks in Wexford Harbour.
The National Library of Ireland.

JENNY LIND
Number 14251. Code LMJB.

1850 Built at Nova Scotia, a schooner of 55 tons.

OWNERS
1870 Hezekiah Hinkley of Liverpool.
1874 Peter Kearns of Wexford.
1891 Mrs. C. Kearns of Paul Quay, Wexford.
1892 James Marlow
1884/1891/1892 Registered in Wexford.
1899 Register closed.

CREW 1891
Master: James Marlow, 45.
Mate: James Smith, 42.
Seamen: Thomas Donnelly, 31; James Horan, 31; Nicholas Marlow, 28.
Boy: Patrick Murphy, 20.
Later that year:
Master: James Carroll, 32.
Mate: James Murphy, 40.
Crew: John Sell, 24.
Master: Richard Cleary.
Mate: James Cullen, 60.
Seaman: Andrew Cleary, 24.

It was January 1884 and it was blowing a strong SSE gale, with thick heavy rain, when distress signals were seen from the Fort, at the mouth of Wexford Harbour. At that time the RNLI Lifeboat was at Wexford Quay, so the Fort immediately sent up distress rockets which were seen from the quays. Immediately the RNLI's **Ethel Eveleen** was manned and put to sea. She was a 12-oared boat that also carried sails and had a very rough time getting over the east Bar in the high running seas. They were out searching for some time when the signals disappeared, leaving the lifeboat with little idea where the casualty was. After tacking about for a period, they went to anchor. Meanwhile the gale increased in ferocity.

When daylight appeared, they saw a schooner stranded on the Hantoon Bank. The **Ethel Eveleen** got under way again and bore down on the schooner, which was getting a severe battering from the seas. An anchor was let go from the lifeboat and she veered down on the wreck but, due to the high seas, she was getting knocked about by the waves and the first attempt failed. The second attempt was successful and the **Ethel Eveleen** got the captain and crew off. It transpired that the stranded schooner was the **Jenny Lind**, homeward bound from Newport to Wexford with coal. She was later successfully refloated. In April 1892, the **Jenny Lind**, then owned by James Marlow, loaded a novel cargo at Wexford quay. It was a cargo of turnips from the farm of Mr Peare of Kilmallock and destined for Messrs. McMahon of Newport. This was said to have been the first time such a cargo was shipped from Wexford.

On the 5 April 1905, the **Jenny Lind** was offered for sale by The Wexford Dockyard Company *as she now lies at White's Wall*.

JESSIE STEWART
Number 42549. Code KWSR.

1862 Built at Ardrossan, a schooner of 97 tons, with two masts.
Dimensions: 83.10x19.9x9.8ft.

1888 Registered at Wexford.

OWNERS
1865 Thomas Blackburn of Fleetwood, Lancs.
1879 Edmund Porter of Fleetwood.
1882 Porter's Shipping Co. of Fleetwood.
1888-1889 Martin Devereux, of Paul Quay; Patrick Lambert & Jasper W. Walsh.

CREW
Captain: Martin Devereux of Paul Quay, Wexford.
Mate: John Smith of the New Lane.
ABs: Wm. Edwards; Thos. Donnelly.
Cook: Michael Smith (son of the mate).
In early February 1892, the **Jessie Stewart** collided with the tugboat **Active** in Newport.

Jessie Stewart, a two masted tops'l schooner of 97 tons. Built 1862 at Ardrossan ,Scotland. Seen here in Wexford Harbour about to take a tow from the tug **Wexford.**
Courtesy of Mr Dave Dempsey.

Jessie Stewart, approaching the Lucifer Lightship off the Wexford coast.

The tug sank. It was reported that there would be an inquiry, held by the Board of Trade, to determine fault. However, on 18 February, she left Newport. homeward bound, when she met a fierce blizzard. It was thought that the **Jessie Stewart** would have been near Milford when the blizzard was at its fiercest and that visibility would have been so bad that Captain Devereux thought his only chance was to stay out in the open sea. Nothing was ever heard of her again.

JEWESS

Number 35558. Code RQDL.
1857 Built at Richibucto, New Brunswick, by David White, a schooner, 61 tons, with a figurehead and a square stern. She was named **Plantation**.
Dimensions: 57x18x9.3ft.

1863 Registered at Wexford as **Jewess**.
1908 Lost.

OWNERS
1863 Nicholas Fanning of Paul Quay, Wexford.
1888 William Murphy, Main St., Wexford.
1900s Breen; Greg. Rochford.
1907 Mrs William Murphy & Robert Hanton of John St., Wexford.
1908 Messrs Nunn.

CREWS
1863
Master: Martin Leary, 33.
Seamen: Thomas Carr, 30; Francis Murphy, 19.
Mate: John Moran, 30.
Boy: James Codd, 17.

1864
Master: Martin Leary.
Mate: John Connor, 28.
ABs: John Stanford, 37. John –?, 22.
Boy: Walter Breen, 15.

1870
Master: Martin Leary, 48.
Mate: Thomas Kavanagh, 58.
OS: Nicholas Cleary, 37; Henry Dollis, 19; John Furlong, 16.
Boy: Thomas Howlin, 14.
AB: Patrick Barry, 21.

In May 1881, the Cahore lifeboat **John Brooke** took the 5-man

> **GALLANT LIFEBOAT RESCUE**
> The lifeboat John Brooke, belonging to the Royal National Lifeboat Institution, and stationed at Cahore, co. Wexford, gallantly saved the crew of five men from the schooner Jewess, of and from Wexford, for Dublin, which had stranded south of Cahore Point on Monday in a strong wind and a heavy sea.

Report on the rescue of the crew of the **Jewess**.

crew of the **Jewess** ashore when she became stranded off Cahore Point. She was refloated and carried on her career until October 1908, when word reached Wexford of the loss of the **Jewess**. She had arrived in Dublin about three weeks before with a cargo of malt. After discharging her malt, she loaded a cargo of timber for Garston and was bound for there, when she ran into a gale. She put into Holyhead for shelter and, after the weather appeared to have improved, sailed again a few days later.

However, during that evening, heavy weather and fog came in again and drove her ashore at Moelfre, Anglesey. The crew burned torches to attract attention from the shore but no help was forthcoming. They got away in the boat and were lucky to get ashore as the boat was smashed to pieces as soon as they hit the beach. The ship was not insured. At the time of her loss she was owned by Messrs Nunn.

JONAH
No 15902 Code LVGC.

1838 Built at Preston, a schooner of 76 tons.

1870 Registered as 65 tons. Later registered at 50 tons.
1882 Out of register.

OWNERS
1865 George Lawson Jnr. of Lancaster.
1870 J.P. Devereux, of Rocklands, Wexford.

CREW
Master: John Murray, Faythe.
Mate: Joe Carberry.
AB: Murtha Whelan.
Boy: John Walsh.

On 9 March 1880, the **Jonah** went aground on the North Dogger Bank, Wexford. She was on a voyage from Dublin to Wexford and had left Dublin on the Friday 8 March. By 7 o'clock that evening, they sighted Blackwater Head NNW. About two and a half miles distant. The weather was hazy and, at about 8 o'clock, another light was sighted off the port bow but the crew were not sure if it was the **Lucifer** lightship or only a ship's light. A short time afterwards the schooner struck something lightly. Then the helm was put to starboard, to bring the ship's head to south and eastward, but this didn't work. All sails were then taken off with the exception of the mainsail, and a kedge (a small anchor) was then run out. The schooner still would not move.

At 9 o'clock, she began to make water and despite the pumps being used, the flow of the incoming water increased. The wind began to increase as well. The ship's boat was got ready in case she started to break up and distress flares were sent up. The flares were promptly answered by responding blue flares from the Fort. This put the **Jonah's** crew at ease as they knew help was on the way, should it be required. A quarter of an hour later a red light was seen approaching. It turned out to be the Fort lifeboat, **Ethel Eveleen**. The crew were taken off and landed at the Fort. It was hoped to save the cargo but there was no hope for the **Jonah**.

J P TAYLOR
Number 35193. Code RNPD.

1857 Built at New Brunswick, a schooner of 79 tons.

1858 Registered at Wexford.
1888 Out of register.

OWNERS
1864 Patrick Rowe and later Thomas Hutchinson, both of Wexford.
1887 Broken up at Crescent Quay.

CREWS
1864
Master: Patrick Rowe, 53.
Mate: John Sheal, 50.
Seamen: John Hamilton, 25; Sinnott, 21.
Boy: Francis Murphy, 19.

1881
Master: John Hutchinson, 22.
Mate: John Walsh, 33.
AB: David Murphy, 23.
OS: Francis Neville, 23.
In 1881 Captain Hutchinson made a claim against the Wexford Harbour Commissioners for damage suffered by the **J P Taylor** when she hit a rock in the river. The board referred the matter to their solicitors, Little and Elgee, for consideration. The solicitors replied that in their opinion there was no liability on the part of the Harbour Board. The vessel was in the charge of a harbour pilot and if there was any fault it was entirely his.

JOHN C WADE
Number 19106. Code MQNR.

1852 Built at Digby, Nova Scotia, 74 tons. She was a two masted schooner, with a scroll figurehead, and an eliptic stern. Dimensions 74 x19x9ft.

1882 Registered as a brigantine.
1895 She was brought into the Crescent Quay, Wexford for breaking up.
1896 Vessel declared unseaworthy and the register was closed.

OWNERS
1865 James Lewis Carvill, Newry.
1894 John 'Boss' Codd, of Parnell St., Wexford, master shipwright, and Patrick Lambert.
1895 Jan. Codd died and left his share of the ship to Captain Joe Murphy, who was master of the **John C Wade**. He was also the owner of a public house in Castle Hill St, now Kevin Barry St., in Wexford.

CREWS
1895
Captain: Joe Murphy.
Mate: Jemmy Hall.
Seamen: Jack Hall; Richard Murphy of the Faythe; Jem Doyle of Ram Street.

JOHN & MARY
Number 18357. Code MLKS.

1839 Built at Wexford. 19 tons.

OWNER 1845 Patrick Kirwan, Bannow.

CREW
Master: Patrick Kirwan, 24, Bannow.
Mate: Peter Brien, 45, Fethard.
Deckhand: Michael Farrell, 41, Bannow.

Despite being as small as some trawlers the **John & Mary** was engaged in the cross channel trade. In 1845, all her trips were from Bannow to either Pembroke or Neath and back.

John C. Wade, notice of auction, dated August 1884.
Wexford People.

JOSEPH FISHER
Official Number 54543.

1866 Built at Rothesay, by Robert Lea, a wooden schooner of 62 tons, with two masts. Dimensions, 78x20.05x9ft. First registered at Barrow.

OWNERS
1866 Joseph Fisher of Barrow.
1879 Alice Fisher of Barrow.
1888 John Fisher of Barrow.
1893 John McKenzie of Campbelltown.
1902 J.J. Stafford of Wexford.
1913 William H. Dann of Wicklow.

In early January 1906 a massive gale hit the whole of Britain and Ireland. The Wexford schooner **Joseph Fisher** was bound from Newport to her home port with a cargo of coal for her owners, J.J. Stafford. They made it to Milford Haven but at ten o'clock that night but, because of the strong winds blowing from the south east, Captain Neill thought that it would be best to beat up the harbour. He found, however, that due to the wind becoming so strong, his crew were unable to get the yards around. He therefore had to let go otherwise they would have been on the rocks.

Joseph Fisher, a two masted tops'l schooner of 62 tons. Built 1886 at Rothesay, Scotland, shown leaving Cardiff Docks, early 1900s, when owned by Stafford of Wexford.

During the time that they were taking the sails down, the vessel dragged further down the harbour until the anchors caught and brought her to a standstill. By this time, they were getting the full force of the sea coming in between Thorney Island and the Harbour's leading lights. They spent that night in comparative safety but, on the following day, the wind direction changed and the seas came in on them, causing their vessel to labour heavily. As night was coming on again, the wind veered a couple of points to the south and they were in grave danger of the cables parting and their vessel going on the rocks. The crew hoisted signals of distress, to let the local lifeboat know of their situation but the lifeboat was unable to get away from Angle Point. Luckily for the Wexford crew, a steam trawler was in the area and it came down and took the captain and crew to Milford.

On Monday Captain Neill went out to his ship and slipped her cables to have her towed to dock. It was thought that there was every likelihood that the anchors and cables could be retrieved. Along with Captain Neill, the crew were: Billy O'Rourke, mate; George Hess, AB; and John Doyle, OS. During WW1, on 15 September 1918, the **Joseph Fisher** was bound from Holyhead to Wicklow with coal when she was stopped 16 miles ENE of the Codling Light Vessel by Uboat UB64 and sunk by gunfire. The crew were allowed into the lifeboat and survived.

JUNE
Number 21406.

1824 Built at Polperro.
1845 Registered at Wexford.
1884 November. Broken up, certificate lost.

OWNERS
1848 Patrick Quirke.
1861 Robert Sparrow.
1861 September. Robert Acheson & John F. Hughes, Cork, shipping agents.
1872 October. John Penrose and Alfred Edward Allen of Cork, corn merchants.
1884 November. Broken up, certificate lost.

CREW 1845
Master: Patrick Quirke, 60.
Mate: Patrick Devereux, 48.
Seaman: Michael Boyle, 25.
Boy: Michael Murphy,17; George McCann, 18.

K

KATE
Number 8521. Code KCNB.

1853 Built at Wexford, a brig of 184 tons. Dimensions: 100x20x12.2ft.

OWNERS
1853 Patrick Doyle of Wexford.
1865 James Walsh of William St. (Master: Richard Devereux).
1871 Mrs Mary Greene, North Strand, Drogheda.

CREW 1870
Master: E.J. Bell (Certificate number 21304).
Mate: William Redmond, 28.
Bosun: Laurence Duggan, 26.
Cook: Patrick Murphy, 26.
ABs, James Murphy, 25; John Lean, 25; Patrick Corish, 19 (He was paid off injured at Holyhead, on 7 October); Michael O'Brien, 21.
Also that year:
Mate: Luke Shiel age 57.
Bosun: Edward Howlin, 28 (deserted at Cardiff).
Cook: Stephen Dalton, 32.
ABs: James Murphy, 20; Richard Gaul, 25.
Mate: William Redmond, 26.
Bosun: Patrick Breen, 28.
ABs, William Pierse, 20; Michael Duggan, 35; Richard Jones, 23.
Cook: Christopher Williams, 29 (Paid off sick at Soubine?).

In December 1874, the **Kate** was on a voyage from Memel to Belfast. She was off the Swedish coast, when she struck Stapleurs Rock and had to be abandoned. A Board of Trade Inquiry was held in Liverpool that concluded that the master, Richard Owens, was responsible due to carelessness in navigating his vessel. He mistook the light at Cape Stevens. He maintained that it was reported to him that the light was a revolving light, while both witnesses from the crew stated they told him it was a stationary light. The inquiry also said that the captain should have ascertained for himself that the light was stationary. In point of fact he was not within the radius of Cape Stevens and the light he had seen must have been the Fastenbro Light. The Court also remarked that he had never used his lead, nor was it ever on the deck. Captain Owens lost his licence for 3 months.

KATE
Number 28013. Code PTQK.

1863 Built at Weymouth, a wooden schooner of 78 tons. Dimensions: 88x19x11.2ft.

OWNERS
1870-1880 Bussell of Weymouth.
1883 William B. Gibbs of Cardiff.
1885-1910 Simon Roche, Ballygow, Bannow, Co. Wexford.
1915 Broken up, register closed as per advice from the deceased owner's executors.

In August 1903, a drowning tragedy was reported at New Ross (drownings at New Ross seemed to be almost a weekly occurrence). A thirty-three-year-old man by the name of John Fardy lost his life. It happened on the previous Saturday evening, when Fardy, described as a 'hobbler' and two others, Matthew Phelan, a pilot, and Moses Handrick, another 'hobbler', went down the river in a small boat, to board the schooner **Kate** of Bannow with a view to piloting her up the river. She was expected off Cheekpoint around that time.

When they arrived at their intended point the weather was very choppy. Although they sighted the schooner in the harbour, it did not see them. The **Kate** went through the Barrow Bridge, and the pilot and the hobblers took off after her. The little boat was no sooner clear of the bridge than a sudden squall caught them and capsized their boat. Their plight was spotted by two mechanics, working on the bridge, who immediately launched a small boat and put out to save the men in the water. They picked up Handrick and Phelan and went after the third man, Fardy. They threw an oar to Fardy, who was a non-swimmer. He held on to the oar for some minutes but, before the small boat could get to him, he let go and sank beneath the waves. He was a married man and the sole supporter of his parents. Strangely, the **Kate,** the vessel they had set out to meet, arrived at Ross, never knowing anything of the tragedy that had occurred in her wake.

KETCH
Number 99732.

1894 Built at Fairlie, Ayr. A wooden-built ketch of 56 tons. Dimensions: 69x19.7x8.5ft.
1921 Auxillary engine fitted

OWNERS
1894 William Fife & Sons, Fairlie, Ayr.
1907 J.J. Stafford of Wexford.
1911 A.F. Sutherland, of Thurso, Caithness.
1920 A. Savage of Portaferry, Co. Down.
1930 W.H. Jewell of Appledore, Devon.
1938 S.J. Beara of Appledore, Devon.
1940 Arthur Hamlyn of Bristol.
1946 broken up Appledore.

Little is remembered of the **Ketch** apart from the fact that she was the only vessel on the Wexford register to be called after the type of rigging she carried. She did, however, make the news in January 1906, when still under the ownership of Fife of Fairlie. She was en route from Plymouth to Wexford with a cargo of Patent Manure for J.J. Nolan of Enniscorthy, Co. Wexford, when she went aground near the Dogger Bank.

Ketch, a ketch rigged vessel of 56 tons. Built, 1894 at Fairlie, Ayr.

The **Ketch** arrived in the South Bay, Wexford at 10.30 in the morning on 24 January 1906 and dropped anchor. Three days later, on Saturday 27 January, they weighed anchor at 5 o' clock in the morning and got underway for Wexford Harbour. The morning was clear and there was a fresh breeze from the SW. At 6.30 am, she was about 2 cable lengths away from the second Bar Buoy off the Dogger Bank, when she 'took the ground'. By now there was a strong north-going tide that forced the **Ketch** further on the bank. The captain contacted his brokers ashore. They advised him to jettison some cargo, to save the ship.

Ketch, by 1907, owned by Stafford of Wexford.

    The crew threw about 20 tons of cargo over the side but it made little difference, they were still stuck hard. About 11 that night the weather had turned very bad and the captain decided to take to the lifeboat. This was still Saturday night and they remained by until Sunday morning. They appear to have boarded a Milford trawler the **Christina**, which was also firm on the ground. At 9.30 that morning, the tug **Wexford** was heading for the **Ketch,** seemingly with the intention of putting some of their own men onboard. The **Wexford** passed the men in the **Christina**, towing the **Barbara Moir** and put 3 men onboard the **Ketch**, before her own master could reach her. It seems likely that the **Wexford** put the men on the **Ketch** so that they could claim salvage. In the meantime, the crew of the **Ketch** had been picked up by the Fort Lifeboat, **James Stevens No. 15**, and landed them. They had to walk to Wexford. The captain of the **Ketch** declared that he had not abandoned his ship but left for safety and was returning to it when the tug put men onboard. Shortly afterwards, the **Ketch** came into Stafford's ownership.

    During WW2, **Ketch** was used as a barrage balloon anchor barge at Falmouth. In 1946/ 47 she returned to her Appledore owners, Samuel J. Beara; the vessel was uneconomical to repair and was broken up.

L

LADY BAGOT
1842 Built at Quebec, a barque of 442 tons with a square stern.

OWNER Graves of New Ross.

The **Lady Bagot** was mainly engaged from New Ross to Savannah, Georgia, carrying emigrants out and usually cotton back to Liverpool for the Lancashire cotton mills. On 18 December 1845, the *Cork Constitution* published the following letter taken from the Quebec Mercury. Punctuation is as published.

To the Harbour Master:
Quebec-Brig Atlas, Thomas Hobson, from Quebec, ten hands, sailed on the 20th day of August with a cargo of timber for Sunderland. When off the Bird Rocks on the 28th day of the same month, I fell in with a heavy gale of wind from the south which continued 24 hours. During the gale the vessel was making a great deal of water. On the 30th day when off St. Paul's, the vessel was keeping both pumps constantly going. On the 17th Sept. in lat. 48.58 n long. 18.10 w, at 3 pm running under double reefed topsails and foresail, a heavy sea struck the vessel on the larboard quarter, which took away the bulwark and started the vessel's whole frame. At 6 pm split both topsails, the crew not being able to leave the pumps as the water was gaining on them, the topsails were left hanging to the yard. On the 18th at 1 am sounded the pumps and found 8 feet of water in the hold. At 4 am the vessel was beginning to lose the use of her helm. At 10 am gave the pumps up and made preparation for the tops.

When in the act of getting the water and stores up into the tops, one of the men saw a vessel to the windward standing to the WSW. I hoisted the ensign Union down. Shortly after, the captain of the vessel discovered the signal and instantly bore down to our

> THE BOMBARDMENT OF SEBASTOPOL.—Some idea of the terrific reverberation from the opposing batteries at Sebastopol on the day of the opening of the bombardment may be formed from the statement of the respectable master of the Glendalough, in writing home from Eupatoria to the proprietors of that fine vessel, Messrs. Graves and Son, of New Ross. He observes—"Although at the time 30 miles distant from the scene of the engagement, the ship was kept in a continual tremor by the unceasing cannonade at Sebastopol." The Glendalough was engaged in carrying provision stores from Eupatoria to Sebastopol, for the use of the allied armies.— *Kilkenny Moderator.*]
>
> SOURCE: The Welshman 8th December 1854

Report of the **Glendalough** at the bombardment of Sebastopol, 1854.

Lady Bagot, a three masted barque of 442 tons. Built. 1842 at Quebec. Owned by Graves of New Ross. Shown here anchored at Quebec. Mid 1840s.

assistance. When the vessel was within a mile of us the **Atlas** *brought to athwart the sea and took a long list, where she remained for two minutes, then she took a sally and fell gently over on her beam end, the crew all clambered upon her side, where the sea broke with great violence over us. The master of the vessel seeing our critical situation immediately got his boat out t and sent second mate and two hands to our assistance, but in consequence of the sea being so high the boat was in great danger of coming too close to the wreck, but the second mate of the vessel having a line in the boat, he threw it towards the wreck, which we missed the first time, the sea running so high and the water washing over us we could not see it, but the second time I succeeded in getting it and made it fast to the wreck, and took the bight of it and went one by one off the wreck, but the boat being small and the sea high, they could take one at a time, leaving six on the wreck.*

After the four men were safely berthed on board of the barque **Lady Bagot** *of New Ross, one of her crew refused to go for the remainder of the men on the wreck. The Captain instantly asked for volunteers but none would volunteer to go. The Captain first giving charge to the Mate determined to save the remainder and reckless of his own life went into the boat himself, and succeeded in bringing the remaining six of the crew from the wreck. After we were safe on the barque* **Lady Bagot**, *Mr Williams, commander, treated us more like brothers than shipwrecked seamen, to whom we shall for ever be grateful for his kindness on board. For the space of seven days he acted the real Samaritan to those who were ill and had wounds. Wishing Capt. Williams every success on his future voyages, for whose welfare I shall ever pray.*
Thomas Hobson, Master
Signed on behalf of the crew of the brig **Atlas.**

Captain Hobson, quite rightly spoke very highly of Captain Williams. His well wishes for future voyages were well placed. In later years, Captain Williams retired from the sea and opened a ship's chandlers on the quay of New Ross.

Almost two years after that exciting episode, **Lady Bagot** left New Ross for Savannah,

Lady Bagot, Port of Savannah light duty certificate, dated October 1847.
Courtesy of Peggy McHale and Kieron Cronin, Waterford Institute of Technology.

on Thursday 21 October 1847. She arrived at her destination on 21 December. During her time berthed at Savannah, a sailor, William Simpson fell down the hold and had to be hospitalised. He returned for duty on 6 January 1848. Another sailor, Michael Moran, was arrested and jailed for fighting and for drunkenness. Two other men, Joseph Irving and David Cooper, were also charged with drunkenness. This was not an unusual occurrence on a ship in port, as you will note throughout this book.

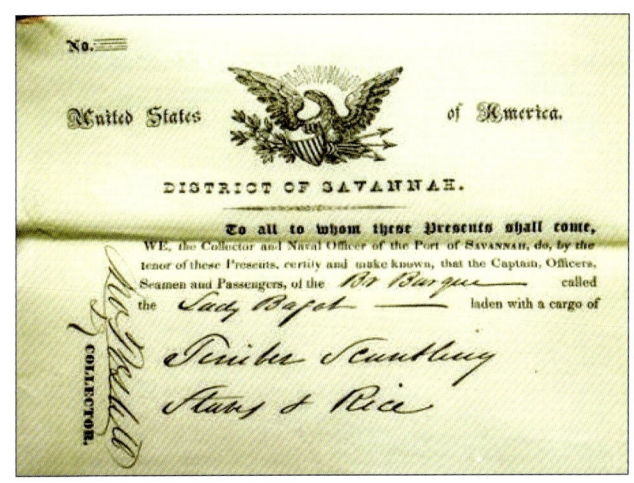

Lady Bagot, Port of Savannah goods certificate, dated January 1848.
Courtesy of Peggy McHale and Kieron Cronin, Waterford Institute of Technology.

Lady Bagot left Savannah on 24 February 1848, with a cargo of timber, molasses, and rice. The log reports that the men were kept busy caulking the decks, and repairing sails. The weather must have been fair, but one ominous entry noted that they were manning the pumps.

On 1 March the log noted: *at 2pm awful squalls split the foresail - 3 pm a complete hurricane. Sea making a fair sweep over the ship, washing water cocks, spars and ropes overboard. Cabin door washed in and filled the House so that the tables and chairs were all afloat. Sea water in the Starboard gangway and took the master fore and aft and was going over the rail when one of the men catched [sic] him by the hair of the head. Likewise washed a dog overboard.*

4 pm: Slued up the main topsail and hove the ship under storm. All hands to the pumps. Strong gales with a high sea washing over the ship, fore and aft. All men lashed to the pumps.

6 pm: the man at the wheel was washed off and greatly hurt. All hands still kept to the pumps and complaining of being greatly fagged out. Midnight sounded four feet of water in the hold.

Thursday, 2 March. *This day set in more moderate with a very high sea running. Ship still set before the wind. Leak still gaining.*

8 am: Sounded the pumps at four feet and a half. Made one more effort to clear the well but found the leak still increasing.

9 am: showed a sail ahead. Made all possible sail which proved to be the American ship **Oregon***, bound for Havre. Captain Healy very kindly kept his ship hove to, until*

was came up and asked the master if he wanted any assistance and if he wanted to be taken off the wreck. Captain Anderson asked him if he would lay by him until morning. When he asked the American captain this favour the crew all came towards Captain Anderson and said that they had done their best endevours to save the ship but they found the leak gaining and their strength failing fast. They told him they could not hold out any longer as they had been on since noon on Tuesday to the pumps without any rest and no chance of saving the ship.

They asked him to leave the since there was a chance of saving their lives, which Captain Anderson was loathe to do, but at last consented when the carpenter reported eight and a half feet of water in the well. He then asked the American captain to take us off. Then the Chief Officer of the **Oregon** and four men launched their boat to come to our assistance, to the great risk to their own lives for to save ours from a watery grave. We all got safe on board the ship by 4 pm. The ship had at that time settled down in the water very much. They took a few sails and ropes and set fire to the ship. Sounded the well when they left the ship and found nine feet in the hold and the last sight we saw of the **Lady Bagot** she was sunk to her chains in water.

Earlier that year on 20 July 1847, the Enhanced Parliamentary Papers on Ireland quoted H.M. Emigration Agent, St John, New Brunswick who wrote the following:

Government Emigration Office St. John.
20 July 1847.
Sir,
I have the honour to enclose Ship Return No. 47 for the barque **Lady Bagot** *which vessel arrived here yesterday from New Ross, with 337 passengers. The passengers by this vessel were unusually clean, and all in excellent health. I found on inspection, that the vessel was exceedingly well ventilated, and that the master had paid real attention to the cleanliness of the passengers.*

They came aft in a body while I was on board and thanked the master for his kindness to them during the voyage, in granting them extra allowances of rice and other comforts when necessary, in furnishing and administering medicines, and for unremitting and constant watchfulness of himself and his ship's company over all who were in the least indisposed.

The high health and spirits of the passengers by the **Lady Bagot** *may be attributed, under providence, to the benevolence and generosity of Captain Anderson, who deserves great praise.*
I have, & c
(signed) M.H. Parsley
H.M. Emigration Agent.

The Honourable John S. Saunders,
Provincial Secretary.

While the above letter does seem a bit flowery and over the top, it is a fact that ships of

Port of Savannah, Georgia, mid 1860s.

the Graves Company had a much lower mortality rate than any of the other vessels from the larger ports of the UK., such as Liverpool. This can be attributed not only to far better food, and more hygienic conditions on board the New Ross vessels but also to the fact that Graves vessels carried surgeons on board.

LANDSHIPPING
Number 21428. Code NGHM.

Built at Landshipping, Lawrenny, Pembrokeshire, a schooner, carvel built, of 63 tons. Registered at Wexford.

OWNERS
1843-1852 Thomas Connor, MM., 32 shares and John Hore, Mariner, 32 shares.
1860 John Knight of Gloucester and William Washbourne of Frampton-on–Severn, 32 shares.
1867 Out of register.

CREW 1852
Master: John Hore.
Mate: John Devereux, age 33.
Seamen: Nicholas Laffan, 22; – Lambert, 40.

LERWICK
Official Number 21431. Code NGHR.

1835 Built at St. Martins, New Brunswick, a schooner of 55 tons.
1837 Registered at Wexford
1874 10 August. Broken up.

OWNERS
Before 1853 Laurence Kavanagh and Thomas Connors.
1853 May. Kavanagh died and his widow Catherine and the Reverend John Pendergast (Catholic Priest) were appointed executers. Probate of Laurence Kavanagh's shares in the **Lerwick** was granted to them on 2 May 1853.
1856 Connors died on 17 May 1856. His shares went to his widow Anastatia Connors. On 19 May 1856, Anastatia Connors sold her shares to Catherine Kavanagh and on 10 December 1856, she sold 32 shares to Edward English of Wexford.
1867 Patrick Morris of Wexford.
1871 Michael Fortune of Slade, Co. Wexford.

On 12 June 1841, Captain Patrick Dillon of the **Lerwick** was charged, before the Reverend Thomas Pope on information supplied by the Harbour Master, with dumping ten tons of ballast overboard into the channel leading to the river Usk. He was convicted and fined 5 pounds and costs.

In September 1842, Captain John Keogh of the **Lerwick** lost his life in Bristol Docks. He was crossing over several vessels to get to the **Lerwick**, when he slipped and fell into the dock. He was dead before any aid could be given. Another Captain Keogh, who seems to have been the brother in law of Captain John, died on the brig **Native** around the same period (See **Native**).

> At the Office of T. J. Phillips, Esq.
> Patrick Dillon, master of the schooner Lerwick, of Wexford, was charged before the Rev. Thomas Pope, on the information of the Harbour Master, with throwing ten tons of ballast overboard into the channel leading to the river Usk.—Convicted in the penalty of £5., and costs.

Report of the fine to the **Lerwick**.

LUCINDA JANE
Number 21407. Code NGFC.

1838 Built at Wexford, by Hingstons. A schooner of 77 tons, carvel built with a female figurehead. Dimensions 65.5x19x9.8ft.
1888 Lost near the Hill O' Sea, Rosslare; Register closed.

Lucinda Jane, a two masted tops'l schooner of 77tons. Built 1838 at Wexford. Outward bound, on the River Mersey, with a cargo of coal from Garston to Wexford.

OWNERS
1838 Mr Moore of Rowe Street
1838 Nicholas Whitty, merchant, Wexford. He died in 1854 and his shares went to George Whitty (RC Priest).
1882 Nicholas Fanning, Wexford.
1888 William Murphy, South Main St., Wexford (Master: Captain Patrick Carty).

CREWS
1845
Master: Edward Rowe, 32.
Mate: James Flaherty, 43.
Seamen: Thomas Devereux; William Codd, 18; Thomas Rossiter.
Boy: Edward Connolly.

1864
Master: Patrick Carty, 35.
Mate: Robert Breen, 25.
Seamen: Patrick Sinnott, 22; Patrick Whelan, 21.
Boy: Nicholas Dayley, 15.

Lucinda Jane was built in Wexford in 1838 by Hingston's, at their ship yard at the corner of Church Lane, on the landward side of Wexford Quay. She was built for a Mr Moore of Rowe Stret. By all accounts it was an eventful launch. To get her into the water, the road had to be broken up and timbers laid across to the quays. However, half way across the road, the **Lucinda Jane** ground to a halt. It took hours to get her across to the water's edge, but eventually she made it.

In February 1888, the **Lucinda Jane** left Wexford with a load of corn for Arthur Guinness and Company, from Breen and Son of Castlebridge. She got as far as the Arklow Bank but, due to strong winds, she had to turn back and run for Wexford's South Bay to seek shelter. Reaching there she went to anchor and remained anchored until both of her chains gave way. There was a strong east wind blowing and the master decided to run for the beach, deeming it to be the safest option for his ship and his crew. She went ashore near the Hill O' the Sea, near Rosslare.

The coastguards had seen the ship's predicament and estimated correctly where she would come ashore and were waiting with their rocket apparatus ready. They got all the crew ashore safely, some without even getting their feet wet! However, their vessel was declared a total loss. Great praise was given to Mr Connibeare of the Coastguard, who was in charge of the operation.

M

MARGARET ANN
Number 62702.

1868 Built at Barrow by Ashburners, an auxiliary schooner of 77 tons. Dimensions: 78.2x19.5x8.1ft.

OWNERS
1870 William Ashburner of Barrow.
1879 Thomas Ashcroft of Hesketh Bank, Lancashire.
1890 John Coppack of Connah's Quay, Flintshire.
1902 Mrs B. Gibbons of Bootle, Lancashire.
1904 J. Angus & J. Gibson of Bootle, Lancashire.
1907 Alex Wilson of Kirkbrightshire, Scotland.
1918 Patrick Donovan of Lamb House, South Main St., Wexford.
1918 16 December. Wrecked in Freshwater Bay, Milford Haven.

The **Margaret Ann** left Briton Ferry on the 14 December 1918, with a cargo of coke, in bulk, for William Doyle of Wexford. Captain Tommy Morris was in command and the weather was fine and clear. They used her auxiliary motor until they came to Helvick Head, off Co. Waterford. Then they stopped the motor and came along under sail. At midnight a strong SW breeze sprung up and they had to shorten sail. They took in the topgallant sail, the main gaff topsail and the outer jib. At 3 am they were off St Govan's buoy in a freshening wind. Rather than try to make Milford, they instead hauled to wind and tacked the ship.

The next day, Sunday 15 December, it was still blowing a moderate gale with rough seas. Still tacking and after filling the topsail, they were about to reef the mainsail when the foremast went. They then put her helm down to get her head to the wind, when the mainmast went. The broken masts and spars were cleared away as best they could. They tried to start up the auxiliary engine, only to find that part of the mainsail had jammed in the propeller. Despite many attempts to clear it, the mainmast wouldn't budge. This left them in a very precarious position, running free in a very rough sea. They burned lights from 3 am until 8 am in an attempt to attract attention.

At about 8 am the ss **Mungo** of Newry came up and bore down on them. They got a hawser on board, made it fast, and the **Mungo** began to tow them towards Milford Haven. The seas were still very rough and just as they spied Milford, the windlass broke. It was now 11 am and the **Margaret Ann** was drifting towards the shore, without any hope of saving her. All the crew got on board the **Mango**, with difficulty. The **Margaret Ann** went down about ¾ of a mile from the shore, a total loss. The **Mungo** took her crew to Sharpness.

MARGARET & MARY
Number 55422

1867 Built at Perth, Scotland by the New Shipbuilding Co. A two masted schooner of 97 tons, with a female figurehead and a square stern. Dimensions: 79x21x9ft.
1915 19 November. Wrecked on Raven Spit, North Dogger Bank, Wexford,
1915 Certificate lost with vessel.

OWNERS
1870 K. Matheson, Lockalsh, Ross-shire.
1885 Duncan Matheson, Lockalsh.
1888 James Smith of William St., Wexford.
1894 Margaret Smith of 5 William St., Wexford.
1897 James Smith of Commercial Quay, Wexford.
1913 J.J. Stafford of Wexford; James Sinnott of Wexford.

CREWS
1891
Masters: James Smith; John Cahill.
Mate: Nicholas Saunders.
ABs: J. Smith; John Smith; Patrick Clancy.
Boys: N. Marlow; James Murphy.

On Monday 25 August 1907, the **Margaret & Mary** arrived in Wexford, under tow by a cross channel steam tug. The previous Thursday, she was homeward bound with a cargo of coal for an Enniscorthy merchant, when the already choppy weather worsened and her main mast snapped in two, bringing the rigging down with a mighty crash. Captain Smith, her owner, was at the wheel at the time. Fortunately, no one was hurt. About three months later the, **Margaret & Mary** went aground near the Fort as she was approaching Wexford Harbour. Captain Smith sent up signals to the Fort. They phoned Wexford and Captain Busher was out to them as fast as possible. The tug had great difficulty getting them off but succeeded in their task after some hours, aided by the pleasant weather and calm seas.

In January 1914, the local press reported on an inquest which was held in the Vivian Arms pub in Swansea, into the death of Patrick 'Butt' Walsh, cook of the **Margaret & Mary,** who drowned in The North Docks Basin, when he and another man were returning to their ship. The publican gave evidence that Walsh and his companion, an AB named Tope, were in the pub that night and that both had a good deal to drink. Tope told the jury that Walsh tripped over a mooring rope and fell into the water and that he (Tope) was too drunk to help him. The jury returned the verdict of 'death by drowning'. Captain William Dunne of Parnell St., Wexford, was in command of the **Margaret & Mary** at the time.

In February 1916, a meeting of the Wexford Harbour Commissioners was held, to inquire into the loss of the **Margaret & Mary** on 19 November 1915 on The Raven Spit. Mr J.J. Stafford a member of the Commissioners, who was also the owner of the **Margaret & Mary**, stated that he wanted to ask Pilot-Master Breen why his vessel was lost on the Bar. He said that his vessel was lost over a couple of months ago and it was

Margaret & Mary, a two masted tops'l schooner of 97 tons. At anchor in Wexford Harbour c1900, discharging coal into a Slaney Gabard. Paddle tug **Wexford** tied up alongside the quay.

WEXFORD SAILOR DROWNED

SAD ACCIDENT AT SWANSEA.

On last Thursday night a sailor on board the Wexford schooner, Margaret and Mary, a native of the Faythe, named Patrick Walsh, was accidentally drowned at Swansea. At the time of the accident the vessel, which belongs to Mr. James J. Stafford, Wexford, was being discharged of a cargo of grain. It is stated that Walsh when boarding the schooner, slipped off the gangway and fell into the water. Capt. Dunne and the other members of the crew vainly endeavoured to save the man, but he is said to have disappeared at once. The body, which was found about an hour afterwards, was removed to the morgue, and an inquest was held on Saturday before the town coroner and a jury, when a verdict of "death by misadventure" was returned. The unfortunate man, who was about 40 years of age, was the chief support of his mother, for whom much sympathy is felt.

Newspaper report of the drowning of Patrick Walsh, January 1914.

time he had an explanation from Pilot-Master Breen.

Breen came in front of the committee and told the chairman that he had sent the pilot boat out between 9 and 10 o'clock on the date in question. She got about half way down to the Narrows and could not get much further, due to the tide coming south. Neither could she hove down to the vessel due to the big sea that was running. Pilot-Master Breen was of the opinion that they would wish to wait until the tide was slack. After questioning Breen and considering his evidence, the Board concluded that the pilots could not board the **Margaret & Mary** until she had gone aground. Mr Stafford was not in complete agreement with this decision but decided he would not take any further action.

The wreck remained there until July 1916 when the Harbour Commissioners discussed the possibility of removing it as it was an obstacle to navigation. Wickham Brothers of the Fort tendered to remove it providing they could obtain the necessary explosives and military permission to use them.

The schooner Margaret and Mary, with barley from Wexford, arrived in the West Basin, Cardiff, on Thursday. She experienced bad weather on the passage homewards, causing the cargo to shift, choking the pumps, and damaging the bulwarks and stanchions.

*News report of a bad trip of the **Margaret & Mary**.*

Margaret & Mary name board on display at Rosslare Harbour Maritime Heritage Centre.
Courtesy of County Wexford Archives.

MARIA
Number 1483. Code HKDT.

1832 Built at Barnstaple, a schooner of 69 tons.

1845 Registered in Wexford.
1862 22 January. Vessel foundered off Hook Head. All hands lost, including two unknown men who shipped in Waterford.

OWNERS
1845 J. Carr of Trinity St.
1856 Registered to J. Ralph Crosbie, 24 shares; James Carr, 24 shares and James Roche, 16 shares.
1858 Jan. Roche died and his shares were left to Mary Murphy. She sold her shares to the other two owners.

CREWS
1845
Master: John Cousins, 34.
Mate: Thomas Bolger 42.
Seamen: Nicholas Cousins, 22; John Murphy, 47.
Apprentice: James Hamilton, 18.
Boy: Patrick Curran, 18.

1852
Master: James Carr, 54.
Mate: William Rowe, 42.
Seamen: Nicholas Murphy, 34; Thomas Edwards, 20.

1862
Master: J. Carr, 62.
Mate: C. Moore, 48.
Boy: Michael Moore, 16.

MARIA REID
Number 45589. Code RCWN.

1865 Built at Perth, Scotland. A two masted schooner of 76 tons. Dimensions: 81x21x10ft.

OWNERS
1867 Peter Reid of Wick.
1885 David Sutherland of Wick.
1887 Registered at Wexford.
1888 Thomas Harper and M. Wickham of Wexford. Owners declared bankrupt. J.F. Walsh and Alex. Knox McIntire (assignees) sold the ship to F.J. Walsh of the Wexford Dockyard Company.

Maria Reid, a two masted tops'l schooner of 76 tons. Built 1865 at Perth, Scotland. Depicted passing the Blackwater Lightship, off the Wexford coast.

1899 May. Wexford Dockyard Co. sold her to Stephen Codd of the Faythe.
1913 21 Jan. Stephen Codd died and his shares were left to his widow, Mary Codd.
1930 Owner died. The **Maria Reid** was left to rot. Registration cancelled.

CREWS
1911
Masters: Stephen Codd, 104 The Faythe (born 1855); Thomas Kehoe of Michael St. (b. 1842).
Mates: James Doyle (b. 1856); Nicholas Morris (b. 1852); Paul Murphy (b. 1842).
ABs: Nicholas McGrath (b. 1889); John Booth (b. 1891); Wm. Harpur (b. 1881); Thomas Nolan (b. 1867); Peter Kehoe (b. 1872).
Boys: Patrick Mernagh (b. 1891); Philip Doyle (b. 1893); Patrick Furlong (b. 1894); John Kehoe (b. 1876).
OS: William Rossiter (b. 1870); Nicholas Murphy (b. 1871); James Murphy (b. 1875); James Nolan (b. 1868); John Kehoe (b. 1876); (John Kehoe's first trip).

On 10 March 1891, the schooner **Maria Reid** (Captain Thomas Kehoe), from Newport with coal, was driven ashore between Rosslare Coastguard Station and Rosslare Pier (Ballygeary) in a gale. She had been riding at anchor in what was described as a 'high running sea', when her anchor chains parted and she drove ashore. The coastguard had great difficulty effecting a rescue as the lifesaving apparatus had to be hauled overland, through rough terrain, but in the end all hands were saved. The **Maria Reid**, after

Maria Reid at the Crescent Quay, Wexford.

removing much of her cargo in bags, which were sold to Mr Murphy of Kilrane, was re-floated within days.

John Carroll, a seventeen-year-old sailor from the Faythe, was drowned off the **Maria Reid** on 4 October 1920. The ship was lying at Cardiff's West Dock when the fatality occurred. At the inquest held by Cardiff City Coroner Mr W.L. Yorath, Captain Denis Murphy master of the **Maria Reid** stated in evidence that he had last seen the boy alive on Monday 4 October when they were having breakfast. Half an hour later the cook-boy asked him if Carroll was with him as he could not be found. Captain Murphy promptly made inquiries and then sent the mate out in a small boat to check the water around the schooner to no avail.

John Gaul of the Faythe Wexford, an AB on the **Maria Reid** gave evidence that at 8.30 a.m. that morning he had seen young Carroll bailing water out of a punt that was moored to the schooner. A heavy shower came on and he (Gaul) ran for shelter. Someone suggested the Carroll should come on board out of the

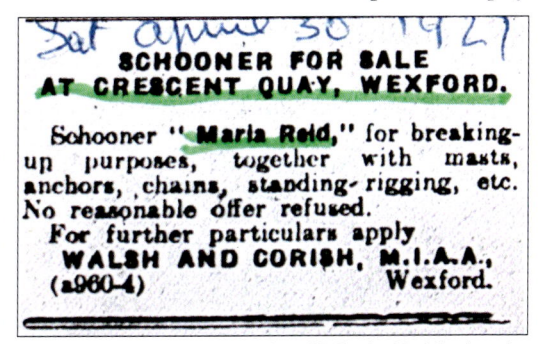

Sat April 30 1927
SCHOONER FOR SALE
AT CRESCENT QUAY, WEXFORD.

Schooner "Maria Reid," for breaking-up purposes, together with masts, anchors, chains, standing-rigging, etc. No reasonable offer refused.
For further particulars apply
WALSH AND CORISH, M.I.A.A.,
(a960-4)   Wexford.

Notice of upcoming sale of **Maria Reid**, dated April 1927. *John Power Collection.*

183

Maria Reid, laid up in the Crescent Quay. mid 1920s.
Courtesy of Mr James Maloney, Carne.

rain and when the cook-boy went to look for him he wasn't in the punt. The police were informed and they began dragging the water around the ship and three hours later Carroll's body was recovered from under the bow. Gaul said that it was possible that the boy had fallen out of the punt when he was trying to board the schooner. The death was attributed to drowning and the coroner recorded a verdict of accidental death. John Carroll was the son of Captain James Carroll, of the Faythe, Wexford. His father later laid a claim for compensation against the owners and was awarded two hundred pounds. In 1931 the owner died and the ship was abandoned. Registration was cancelled. The **Maria Reid** was moved into the Crescent Quay and remained there for many years until she was moved to her final resting place. The skeleton of **Maria Reid** lies today behind the Wexford RNLI building at Wexford Quay.

MARQUIS OF ELY

Number 8667. Code KDCS.

1804 Built at Aberystwyth, a schooner of 71 tons.
1852/1857/1863 Registered at Wexford.
1888 Out of register.

OWNERS John Connors (snr), 64 shares; Mrs O'Connor; P.J. Doyle, Wexford.

CREWS
1863
Masters: James Kean, 51; Richard Wafer, 27; Patrick Cullen, 35.
Mate: Nicholas Sinnott, 51.
Seaman: Martin Hayes, 20.
Boy: James Moran, 16.

No Year
Master: James Barry, 60.

Mate: John Murphy, 27.
Seaman: Michael Barry, 17.
Mariner: Philip Byrne 22.

MARY

Number 8743. Code HKDT.

1851 Registered 31 tons.

1851 Sold to Peter Hewson, and James Nolan, mariner.
1863 11 May. John E. Petitt, merchant
1867 11 September. Sold to Maurice Byrne of Wicklow.

CREWS
1865
Master: Peter Hewson, 60.
Mate: James Nolan, 55
Boy: John Murphy, 20.

MARY AGNES
Number 49504. Code JSMF.

1865 Built at Wexford for J. T. Devereux. A wooden schooner of 95 tons, with two masts. Dimensions: 84x21x10ft.

OWNERS
1867 J.T. Devereux
1870 James Murphy of Rosslare.
1883 J.E. Barry, of Dublin.
1888 John E. Barry of Crescent Quay, Wexford.
1889 John E. Barry(snr) of Middle Abbey St., Dublin; James Murphy, Anne St., Wexford.
1903 August. Sold to Thomas McDermott, 17 City Quay, Dublin.
1915 November. Bought by John. T. Young.
1918 Alfred Thomas Sidall, 13 James St., Cardiff.

On Friday 7 January 1870, a young Wexford man named William Murphy, lost his life when he fell from the bowsprit of the **Mary Agnes,** when she had been caught out in a storm.

On 29 December 1914, the **Mary Agnes** left Wexford at 2 pm, under the command of Captain Thomas 'Lanigan' Walsh, bound for Bristol with a cargo of 120 tons of oats in bulk. She had a crew of five. At 7 pm the same day, she went to anchor in the Bay. The wind was blowing WSW with a strong breeze. During the night the wind changed, blowing from the south and increasing to gale force. **Mary Agnes** remained at anchor in the same position.

The following morning the wind veered around SE and remained at gale force. At about 6.30, the **Mary Agnes** started to drag her anchors. As she came across the opening of the bay, her starboard anchor chain parted. With only one anchor now holding her, she began to travel faster. Captain Walsh was left with only one choice; he let go the Port cable and headed the vessel for the beach, where she grounded. As luck would have it she came ashore abreast of Rosslare Coastguard Station and all hands were swiftly taken off by the lifesaving apparatus. The **Mary Agnes** was refloated shortly afterwards.

On 14 January 1919, en route Morlaix to Cardiff, in ballast, **Mary Agnes** was trying to enter Falmouth Harbour, to shelter from an easterly gale, when she struck rocks near Pendennis Castle and broke up. The master and crew were saved.

MARY & BETTY
1818 Built at Lancaster, a schooner, 102 tons.

1822 Registered as a brig of 114 tons.
1820 OWNERS Allens of Wexford.

On 25 October 1820, **Mary & Betty** went aground on the way into Liverpool, when under the control of a pilot. She was carrying a cargo of beans and wheat and also had passengers. Captain Lambert, his mate and two of his men were lost along with four passengers. The passengers who perished were Philip Walshe of Knocktruth, Wexford; a man named Pierse of Rathaspeck, Wexford; Walshe, a cooper of Slippery Green, Wexford and Leary, a butcher also from Wexford.

Apparently the locals came and plundered the ship while the survivors were clinging to the rigging for their lives. The plunderers ignored the plight of the people in the rigging until they had taken all they could from the ship, then they went to the aid of those in the rigging. The mate was one of those rescued from the rigging but shortly after he was put to bed in a nearby house he died. The rest of the survivors were looked after by some Wexford residents of Liverpool, who also got together and paid for the burial of the dead and acted as pallbearers.

MARY BLAIR
Number 8485. Code KCJQ.

1854 Built at Nova Scotia, a barquentine of 146 tons. Dimensions: 89x20x10ft.

1854 Registered at Wexford.

OWNERS
1862 14 July. Richard Devereux and Richard Joseph Lawrence Devereux & Co. **1862** 17 July. Hugh Jamieson of Leith (North), Scotland; John Bessey Hylton (shipowner), Great Yarmouth.

MARY ELLEN
Number 28901. Code GCKR.

1860 Built at Conway, by Luke Roberts. A schooner of 64 tons. Dimensions: 74.4x19.9x9ft.

OWNERS
1865 John Jackson of Preston.
1888 Thomas Jackson of Preston.
1889 Simon Roche of Ballygow, Bannow, Co. Wexford.

On the 24 February 1904, reports that the **Mary Ellen**, a Dublin schooner had been run down and sunk in the Bristol Channel proved untrue. It was discovered, on enquiry, that there was no schooner of that name, registered in Dublin Port. There was, however, a schooner of that name on the Wexford register and it was to her that the report referred.

Mary Ellen was owned by Simon Roche of Bannow. She was run down by the steamer ss **Innesmoor** with the loss of one life, that of a 19-year-old sailor, Joseph Stafford, from Kilmore. The unfortunate young lad was below when the collision happened and made a determined attempt to get up on deck but got jammed in the 'scuttle' (the entrance to the forecastle head) and all attempts to get him out proved useless. The master and mate were landed at Barry on the following day.

Pursuant of the Merchant Shipping Act of 1894, on 20, 21, and 22 July 1904, a formal investigation was held at the Town Hall, Cardiff, to inquire into the cause of the accident. Mr Vachell appeared for the Board of Trade and Mr Miller for the master and chief officer of the **Innesmoor**. Captain John Roach of the **Mary Ellen** and the mate of the vessel, along with the pilot of the **Innesmoor**, attended but were not represented. The court was told of the **Mary Ellen's** registration details and informed that she had one lifeboat and three new lifebelts, along with some older belts. The boat was stowed on the fore hatch and two tackles, one from the fore and the other from the main rigging, were for getting her out. The **Innesmoor** was described as an iron screw steamship of 1,263.37 tons gross. She was rigged as a schooner and her official number was 79644.

At 6.30 pm on 17 February 1904, the **Mary Ellen** left Wexford, in ballast for Newport. Her crew consisted of three men, namely the captain, mate and an ordinary seaman. They arrived off Barry the following evening, and soon after the wind died and the tide began to fall. The captain worked the vessel inshore but he was unable to make any progress, so he let go his anchor. It was about 7.30 pm and they were about three quarters of a mile south east of Sully Island. It was a fine night with a slight breeze from off the land. The riding light was up and the mate remained deck on watch. The captain went below to his cabin and sat by the fire. The ordinary seaman went forward and turned in. At around 10 o'clock the mate saw the two side lights and the masthead light of a steamer about three quarters of a mile away. This later proved to be the **Innesmoor**. The mate soon decided that there was the fear of an accident, so he called out the captain and the ordinary seaman and then started to clear the lifeboat away.

Captain Roach came on deck, saw the steamer's lights and ran below to get his cap, returning immediately. As he came out of the companionway, he heard a shout from the steamer and in an instant the steamer struck the **Mary Ellen** between the fore scuttle (the entrance to the accommodation) and the windlass, cutting the schooner's bow right off. He was helping the mate to get the lifeboat out, when he heard the young ordinary seaman call out: *Is that you captain? I am jammed here*. He called the mate over and they found the ordinary seaman jammed in the fore scuttle, which had been forced into a V shape by the impact.

The ordinary seaman had been caught above his hips as he tried to escape from the forecastle. They were trying to pull him free when the ship foundered. He went down with the ship and both the master and the mate took to the rigging. The master to the forerigging and the mate to the aft. They were soon washed off their perch as the schooner sank beneath the waves. All of this happened in a space of 5 minutes, from impact to sinking. Both of them were in the water for 20 or 30 minutes when the **Innesmoor's** boat picked them up.

The **Innesmoor** was in the charge of a Cardiff pilot named Johnadab Bowen, who took her to the Ranie Spit Buoy. At this point the pilot's duties would normally cease.

Mary Ellen, a two masted tops'l schooner of 64 tons. Built in 1860 at Conwy, North Wales Outward bound from Barry, South Wales, off Penarth Head, c1900.

The pilot was to leave the steamer as soon as it was possible for a pilot boat to take him off. On rounding the buoy, the steamer was put full ahead, about eight or eight and a half knots and put on a WSW course. About 10.30, after they had passed the buoy, both the master and the pilot saw a bright light ahead, about three quarters of a mile away. This light, it turned out, was the **Mary Ellen's** riding light.

Both the master, Captain William Steele and the pilot were on the bridge at this time and both assumed that the light ahead was a pilot boat coming to pick up Bowen, so the course was altered directly towards the light. The captain was watching the light and soon became doubtful that it was a pilot cutter, so he took out his telescope and realised that it was in fact, a small sailing vessel at anchor. He told the pilot that it was a small ship and the pilot immediately shouted to the helmsman 'hard-a-port' and the master rang the telegraph to 'stop' and straight away to 'full speed astern'. The **Innesmoor** started to come round to her port but was unable to clear the schooner and struck her on the starboard bow. The master of the steamer got a boat in the water promptly and picked up the two survivors. They told the men in the boat that there was no point looking for their third hand as he went down with the ship.

After hearing all the evidence, the inquiry concluded that the primary cause of the collision was the captain and the pilot mistaking the riding light of the schooner as the light of a pilot cutter. They decided that, while the **Mary Ellen** was navigated with proper and seamanlike care, and was at anchor and displaying her light in accordance with regulations, it was not so with the **Innesmoor**. The cause of the accident was that both the captain of the **Innesmoor** and the pilot wrongly identified the light of the ship for that of the pilot cutter. Despite this conclusion both men were exonerated of any culpable negligence. However, the Court was of the opinion that *more promptitude* should have been shown in the use of glasses when the light of the **Mary Ellen** was first sighted.

A year before her loss, **Mary Ellen** had been sent out from Wexford Quays to lighten the steamer **Alliance**, to help her get in over the Bar. After removing some of the steamer's cargo of superphosphates, **Mary Ellen** anchored off the **Alliance** for the night. Along with her normal crew, **Mary Ellen** carried six stevedores to help transfer the cargo. Telephone communications had broken down between Wexford and the Fort and there was no sign of the **Mary Ellen**. The authorities in town assumed that the schooner had been blown out to sea, by the gale that had sprung up and they were correct. What happened was that the lighter, which had been towed out by the tug **Wexford**, was moored alongside the steamer at about four o'clock in the afternoon. The stevedores immediately began to transfer the cargo over to the **Mary Ellen** and by around 5.40 had got about twenty tons aboard.

Then a nasty swell got up and the vessels began to roll. It was decided that the two ships could no longer stay tied up alongside each other and the steamer went astern. The winds continued to rise and then the **Alliance** started to drag her anchor. Around the same time the **Mary Ellen**'s anchor chain, with about forty fathoms out, parted. Her small anchor was out as well but this proved useless in the gale. They shipped the anchor and let the schooner out before the wind. By now it was dark and soon the lights of the Tuskar Rock and all other lights were lost to view. Neither captain nor crew onboard knew their position, but thought that they were near the Long Bank.

After passing the Lucifer Lightship, a tremendous sea hit them, carrying away their lifeboat and clearing the decks of any gear. They were unable to see the compass, catching only the odd glimpse of it when a lull came along and this they managed by lighting matches and using candles!! By this time, her sails were gone too and she was running under 'bare poles'. At 12.40 they rigged up a double fore sail and a standing jib and headed for the channel. Or at least what they thought was the channel, as there were still problems with the compass and still there were no lights to be seen. Around about 1.20 they spotted the South Arklow Light Vessel and later, towards daybreak, they sighted land but had no idea where it was.

The **Mary Ellen** was running along with the wind when Lambey Island and Howth Head came into view. It was still blowing a gale, up to hurricane force, so they headed out back into the channel. The wind eventually dropped and she beat about and headed for the shore line. The next day, Saturday, they sighted the Kish lightship and when they reached it, they made for Kingstown (Dun Laoghaire) Pier. But the wind was still blowing hard North West so it was decided to go further south. They passed Bray and made for Wicklow, where they raised signals for a pilot. One came out and brought them safely into harbour. They had been more than thirty hours at sea, battling hurricane winds in a little schooner, which was neither rigged out nor prepared for this kind of ordeal. The captain, Nicholas Walsh, remained at the wheel throughout the entire thirty plus hours.

The Arklow schooner **William Martin** at New Ross.
The National Library of Ireland.

Workshop at Graves Timber Works, New Ross. c1880s.

MARY & GERTRUDE
Number 58203. Code PBDM (later EIFT).

1867 Built at Connahs Quay, Wales by Ferguson and Baird. A two masted schooner of 75 tons. Dimensions: 80x20x9ft.

1867 Registered at Chester.

OWNERS
1867 William Hancock, Hawarden, Flintshire.
1888 Fred L. Hancock, of Hawarden, Flintshire.
1891 James Stafford of Wexford.
1891 Joseph Cullimore, (32 shares).
1896 J. Stafford.
1904 Richard Kearns of Arklow.
1909 John Kearon, Fair Green, Arklow.
1911 Richard Kearon, King's Hill, Arklow.
1923 Thomas Greally, Market Square, Wicklow.
Her final owners were, James Doyle, Patrick and Ellen Byrne of Arklow and Thomas Gregory of Wicklow.
1934 16 January.The **Mary & Gertrude**'s registration was cancelled and after a long lay up, she was broken up.

CREW
Master: George Murphy of the Faythe (b.1860).

Mary & Gertrude. A two masted tops'l schooner of 75 tons. Built, 1876 at Connah's Quay North Wales. At Bridgewater, Somerset, at low tide.

Mary & Gertrude, under full sail in the Mersey.

Mate: Bart. Carty (b. 1864).
ABs: John O'Connell (b. 1858); N. Pender (b. 1865).
Mate: N. Delaney (b. 1870).
AB: Michael Brien (b. 1872).
Boy: Thomas Carroll (b. 1878).

On 3 March 1900, the Wexford schooner **Mary & Gertrude**, under Captain George Murphy, owned by Stafford's of Stonebridge, was in a collision in the Bristol Channel. She was homeward bound from Newport, with a cargo of coal. She was beating about off Penarth Roads when an outward bound steamer ran into her, hitting her abaft the forechains. At first Captain Murphy thought the damage was serious and got his crew into a lifeboat which had been lowered from the steamer. However, closer inspection showed that the damage to the vessel was not as serious as first thought, so they boarded her and were taken in tow by a tug, which happened to be in the area. The tug beached her and she was then brought into dock for repairs.

In December 1894, when a fierce gale disrupted many local schooners, the **Mary & Gertrude** suffered the greatest hardship. She was on her way home from Newport, Monmouthshire and had put into Milford. She left Milford on the Friday night and was well out in the channel when the gale struck. Her topsail was blown to shreds and a

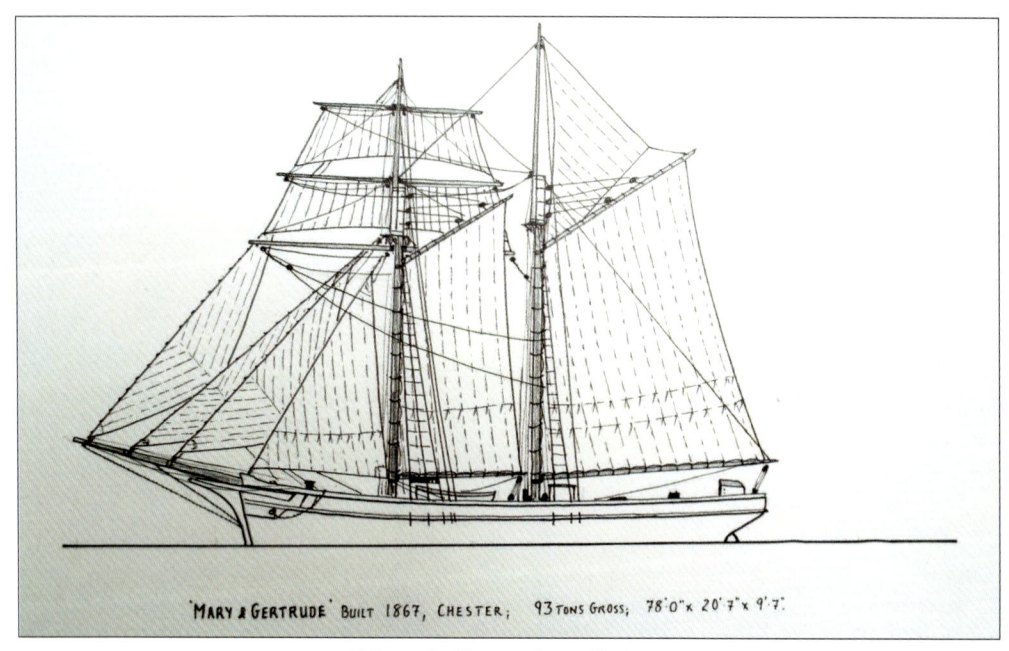

Mary & Gertrude, sail plan.

large piece of her bulwarks were stove in. Two large water barrels came adrift and began rolling around the deck. Attempts to secure them were at first unsuccessful but eventually at great risk to their own safety, the crew managed to get them under control. When the winds eventually subsided it was discovered that they had no water and had to wait until Sunday, when they reached Wexford, before they could replenish their supply.

The following month, January 1895, James Carroll, mate of the **Mary & Gertrude**, was missing, presumed drowned. The ship was tied up at the Wexford's Crescent Quay and it seems that Captain Murphy and a boy by the name of Bernard Lacy were in a cabin with Carroll (It's not clear if this cabin was ashore on the wall or on board the ship). At eleven o'clock it was Carroll's turn to go 'on board' (hence the confusion). Shortly afterwards the boy went above and when he saw Carroll was not there, he called the captain. Carroll's home was checked first in case he had gone there on an errand, but there was no sign of him.

There was a howling gale blowing at the time and it was assumed that either Carroll lost his footing on the slippery gangway or was blown over the side by the wind. His body was later recovered on the shore of the North Slob. Carroll was aged 35 years, married, with 3 small children, and from the Faythe.

MATILDA
Number 58737. Code LWTB.

1870 Built at Selby by James Banks for J. Rhodes of Goole, 73 tons. Dimensions: 82x20x9ft.

1919 Fitted with a parafin motor

OWNERS
1900 S. Renny of Arbroath.
1919 S. Gould of Plymouth.
1921 W. Skilton of Plymouth.
1925 Richard J. Tomkins (farmer), Eleanor Massey (a married woman), both of Courtown Harbour, Co. Wexford.

The Courtown Harbour owned vessel **Matilda,** got into serious trouble in bad weather at her home port, in July 1925. She had arrived off Courtown, with a cargo of 170 tons of coal and went to anchor at her usual place, about 500 yards from the shore. On board were Captain Richard Massey, Mate William Godkin, and ABs Patrick Kenny and Peter Sinnott, all natives of Courtown. The following morning, Sunday, people ashore noticed that the crew were working continuously on the pumps. Apparently, she had dragged her anchor and this had the effect of loosening her beams and she was taking in water. At 3 o'clock distress signals were flown, causing great excitement among the large crowd, which had gathered on the shore. The local Civic Guard Superindent O'Neill immediately sent a car to Arklow for the assistance of the lifeboat and at the same time telegraphed Rosslare. Unfortunately, they found that the Arklow boat was not available, but that the Rosslare men, under Cox Ned Wickham and 2nd Cox James Wickham, had put to sea. The Rosslare lifeboat **William Evans** was the first motor powered lifeboat on the Wexford coast and was based, at this time, in Wexford Harbour.

At 5 pm the **Matilda** sent up further distress signals. Seeing this and despite the very high winds blowing, a party of volunteers attempted to launch a large ship's boat from the slip but she was damaged before getting off the slip. Just then the sail of the Rosslare lifeboat was seen rounding Cahore Point and shortly after Coxswain Wickham brought her close in to the ship. Captain Massey told them that he was not going to abandon his vessel and only required assistance to relieve his crew, who had been manning the pumps for twenty-four hours and were exhausted. A number of men on the shore agreed to take the place of Massey's crew and were brought out along with some food, to relieve the sailors.

When the weather abated the **Matilda** was brought in and repaired. She continued her trade until 11 December 1928 when, enroute from Bridgewater in Somerset to Dublin with cargo of bricks, she was run down and sunk by the trawler **Joseph Button** when entering Milford Haven. Patrick Sinnott was the only one to survive. Lost were: Captain Richard Massey; his nephew, William Massey, who was the ship's cook; and the mate, Peter Sinnott.

MAUDE ANNIE
Number 42243. Code TJBF.

1860 Built at Richibucto, New Brunswick. A brigantine.

1861-1863 Registered at Wexford, 114 tons.
1894 Broken up.

OWNERS
1863 Hugh McGuire.
1867/1870 T. Hutchinson of The Faythe. Wexford.

CREWS
1863
Master: Christopher Cahill, 63.
Mate: Hugh McGuire, 30.
Seamen: Kenneth Savage, 19; John Furlong, 21; Michael Murphy, 31; John Cahill, 50.
Boy: William Devereux, 18.

1864 14 April. Signed on at Ardrossan for the Mediterranean and the Black Sea (articles were changed as the previous period of articles had run out).
Master: Christopher Cahill, 60.
Mate: Hugh Maguire, 32.
Abs: John Carty, 45; William Murphy, 41; John Mcgrath, 32; John Leacy, 18.
Cook: James Smith, 17.

1870.
Master: N.J. Neville, Castle St., Wexford, 35.
Mate: Nicholas Cullen, 58.
Abs: John Furlong, 31; John Power, 46; Moses McGrath, 36.
Boy: Peter J Murphy, 16.

Later the following signed on:
Abs: Owen Lacey, 25; James Cunningham, 21 (Belfast); William Bruce, 20 (Dundee); John Neilson, 35 (Stockholm).
Lacey, who had come to the **Maude Annie** from an American ship, was paid off in Oran, Algeria 'under mutual agreement'.

Later again the following signed on:
ABs: James Kearns, 30; John Murphy, 20;
Boy: Wm Doyle, 17.

The **Maude Annie** signed Deep Sea articles on 4 July 1870 for a voyage from Wexford to Cardiff and from there to Oran. The voyage seemed to have been uneventful until at Oran on 28 August, when Owen Lacey was stated to have *committed a brutal assault on John Furlong by challenging him to fight then knocking him down, belting him and kicking him in the most brutal manner*. The following day Lacey was brought before the British Consulate and was discharged. The day after that, 30 August, a Swedish sailor was taken on in Lacey's place, at the required monthly rate of two pounds fifteen shillings.

It is interesting to note the menu that applied on all deep water vessels of the time. Each man's entitlement consisted of:

Maude Annie, a brigantine of 114 tons. Built 1860 at Richibucto, New Brunswick.

Bread: 1lb per day;
Beef: 1¾ lbs on Sunday, Tuesday, Thursday and Saturday;
Pork: 1½ lbs on Monday, Wednesday and Friday;
Flour ½ lb per day;
Peas: ½ pint, Monday, Wednesday and Friday;
Tea: ¼ ounce daily;
Coffee: ½ ounce daily;
Sugar, 1lb per week;
Water: 3 quarts per day.

It should be said that the list above was the ideal but was not always what the sailors actually received. To cover that eventuality, articles were endorsed with the following notice: *Substitutes may be given at the Captain's option; sweetening on Duff Days or for rice or barley.* 'Duff' is a mixture of flour and yeast, put into a bag and boiled until it reaches a certain consistency. If the poor sailors were lucky a handful of raisins was thrown into the mixture and this became 'Plum Duff'.

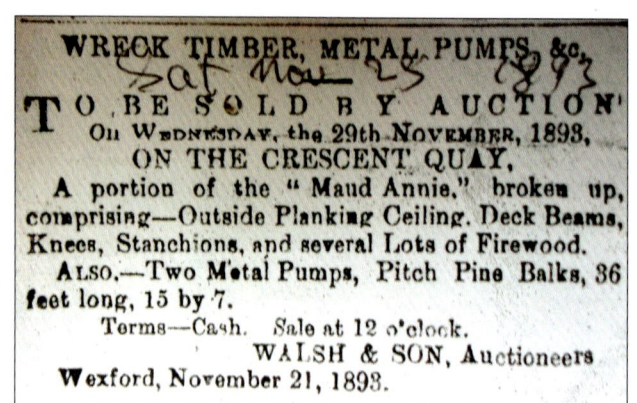

Notice of "Wreck Timber Sale" of the **Maude Annie**, dated, November 1893. *John Power Collection.*

Out of his 3 quarts of water per day, which the sailor carried strapped around his waist, he had to give some to the galley as his share of the water used for cooking. Personal hygiene would also have been an issue. Obviously the old sailing ships did not have the luxury of crew washrooms or lavatories. Perhaps this song composed by Nicholas Saunders, Bosun of the Wexford barque, **Saltee** describes the sailor's daily menu better:

Three days a week salt beef and duff, three days salt pork and peas. Three quarts of water daily, to drink and boil the peas, and make the tea and coffee, you know you'll get your whack of lime juice and vinegar. According to the Act, on Saturday you get salt beef, Molasses and boiled rice, a pound of biscuits daily, two ounces of sugar weighed nice, a quarter ounce of coffee, an eight of an ounce of tea. That was the sailormen's menu, on board the barque **Saltee***.*

In January 1877, a south-east gale flooded the quays and lower streets in Wexford town. The brigantine **Maude Annie** was driven ashore at the Hill o' the Sea, while the **Lucinda Jane** rode it out in the bay, along with a Norwegian vessel. After being lightened of some cargo she was re-floated (coincidently, 38 years later, the **Lucinda Jane** was lost in the very same spot where the **Maude Annie** went aground). The roadway on the pier at Kilmore Quay was broken up and the landing slip severely damaged as were many of the local fishing fleet.

MAY QUEEN

Number 49507. Code HFRQ.

1867 Built at Wexford, a barque of 345 tons. Dimensions: 130.2x23.9x16.4ft.

1890-1891 Re-rigged as a barquentine.

OWNERS
1867-1870 J.T. Devereux of Wexford.
1884 William W. Robinson, Westland Row, Dublin.
1890-1891 John H. Bull of Newhaven.
1902 The London and Tilbury Lighterage Contracting and Dredging Co. Ltd. and converted to a barge
1905 Register closed. Vessel a hulk.

In May 1873, James Keaton, a cook on the **May Queen** was charged at Cardiff Police Court with desertion. On the advice of the magistrate, he was returned to his ship. On 14 January 1879, **May Queen** signed on at New Ross for a voyage to the Black Sea and the Sea of Azof.

CREW 1879,
Master: James Smith, 38. Certificate number: 32556.
Mate: John Smith, 47. Certificate number: 87025.
Bosun: Robert Smith, 24.
Cook/Steward: Thomas Walsh, 30.
ABs: Thomas Saunders, 23; William Bolger, 21; Nicholas Cullen, 25; John Furlong, 25; Thomas Lambert, 18; John Marlow, 20; Harry Holland,19.
OS: Thomas Anglin, 19; James Williams, 15.

The vessel arrived at Ibrail on 15 April and her articles were deposited with William Watson the acting British Vice Consul on the following day. On 30 April the Vice Consul added the following endorsement to the articles:

I hereby certify that the within named William Anglin has been discharged and left behind on the alleged grounds of his death by drowning in the River Danube in this port on the 18th instant and that I have inquired into the matter and find that the allegation is true and that nine shillings & six pence balance of wages due to him to that date and his effects have been taken charge of by the master. Further that I have sanctioned the engagement of Harry Holland upon the terms within the written agreement and that I am satisfied that he fully understands same and that he signed same in my presence.

Poor Anglin's effects were listed as: 1 chest containing 8 white flannel singlets, 7 pair of drawers, 5 coulard [sic] shirts, 7 dungaree jackets, 6 pair of stockings, 3 pair trousers, 1 towel, 1 pillow, 2 covers, 2 shoe brushes, 2 story books, 1 prayer book, 1 needle case, 1 small bag containing, 1 looking glass, 1 belt, 1 suit of oil clothes, 1 blanket, 1 quilt, 1 bed tick, 3 pairs of boots. This appears to be a remarkable amount of clothes for an Ordinary Seaman on a nineteenth-century sailing ship but that is the list of effects on the official agreement.

The Grain Race

The **May Queen** was on the Galatz service and was one of three vessels that took part in 'The Grain Race' from Galatz to Wexford. The other two ships were the **Saltee** and the **Hantoon**. Wexford's Grain Race began on 3 February 1881, when all three of the barques left Wexford Quays together. In those days, departures of the Galatz men always attracted enthusiastic crowds of relatives and friends, to wish the men 'Bon Voyage'. On this occasion, with all three leaving together, the quays were packed. When the vessels were pulling away from the dock, the shanty men roared out the well known capstan shanty 'Rio Grande' (pronounced Ryo) and the men at the capstan answered with the chorus and so did the crowds on the quay wall. Imagine, if you would, a couple of voices calling out, 'Say was you never down Ryo Grande' and hundreds of voices responding 'Way Ryo'. A sight and a sound to behold, no doubt.

Once they were clear of the docks and the tugboats got lines aboard, the outward bound vessels dipped their flags to the crowd and they were on their way down the harbour and out over the Bar. All three were bound for Cardiff to load coal for the coaling stations and then the **Saltee** set out for Malta, the **May Queen** for Alexandria and the **Hantoon** for Odessa. Once they had unloaded their cargoes or more likely their ballast and loaded their new cargoes at their respective ports, they then all sailed for the same destination, Galatz. A typical day on these 'Galatzers': apart from the men on watch and the watch below, all other hands turned to at 5.30 in the morning. They started by washing down the decks, assuming that the weather wasn't already doing it for them. After that, the work continued with overhauling blocks, repairing and making sails, setting up rigging, scraping and painting.

On that particular 'Grain Race' trip the **Hantoon** met bad weather in the Bay of Biscay, outward bound. On the 16th day out, the **Hantoon** passed through the Straits of Gibraltar and into the Mediterranean and fine weather. A few weeks later she reached the Dardanelles. There was a curfew on ships going through the Dardenelles Strait and the **Hantoon** was a little late, so one of the forts guarding the passage sent three shots from a cannon across their bows, just to remind them. They went to anchor and the next morning the captain had to go ashore to have their bill of health signed, essential before being allowed to pass through, and to pay the cost of the three shells which worked out at three pounds. Then, once the formalities were dispensed with, they set out across the Sea of Marmora and into the Bosphorus.

This section of the voyage took 3 days, one of which was spent in Constantinople (Istanbul). Then they went up the Black Sea and arrived at Odessa. There the crew had to turn to and start unloading their cargo of 500 tons of coal. Unloading the cargo and then cleaning out the holds took 3 weeks, then, most likely in ballast, the **Hantoon** sailed back down the Black Sea and a week later arrived at the port of Sulina, at the mouth of the mighty Danube. The morning after arriving at Sulina, they commenced the long 98 mile haul up the Danube to Galatz. This was often far from a pleasant undertaking. There was just one tugboat plying the river but the cost was too prohibitive for small vessels to engage it. Normally mules were employed to do this job but it was not always possible to obtain them. In such cases the task had to be carried out by the crew themselves. It is not apparent how it was accomplished on this occasion but it was not uncommon on calm, windless days, for the crews to go onto the shore and physically haul their ship by means of ropes.

The ropes had to be made fast up high, near the mast head, so as to avoid becoming

J.T. Devereux's **May Queen**, built at Wexford 1867, a three masted barque of 345 tons.

tangled up in the undergrowth of bushes, briars and bamboos. The undergrowth was so high in places that the men hauling the ship could barely see the mastheads. Added to that, they had to tramp through muddy brooks and swamps, sometimes up to their waists in mud and slime, with their legs and even their faces cut and torn by branches of thorns. Even worse than the cuts and scratches from the briars, were the mosquitoes. Numbering in their millions, they attacked constantly. The men often found it difficult to see through the swelling around their eyes, caused by their bites. Their legs were in a worse condition. Then, to add to their discomfort, the occasional enormous snake slithered across their paths. This tow involved all hands with the exception of the captain, the pilot and the ship's cook. At meal times the ship would be moored bow first to the bank and a stake driven into the soft soggy ground to tie up to. The crews would rest up for the night and next morning at 6 am, after coffee and later breakfast, it began again. This awful task went on for up to 3 weeks! Such an onerous and an unhealthy task in the hot, clammy, mosquito ridden Danube Delta, must have had a detrimental effect on the crew's health.

When the **Hantoon** reached Galatz, they were delighted to find the **Saltee** and the **May Queen** already there. They were four weeks in Galatz, living high on the hog for certain: dining on fresh food for the first time in weeks and having the occasional 'run ashore' for refreshments. The crew would also purchase presents for the people at home. Apparently the gifts favoured mostly by the people at home were: fur caps, tobacco, scent, cigars, and muskrats' tails! It is easy to imagine why the first four would be so popular but less easy to picture what the fifth was to be used for. Another perk for the Galatzmen, the captain, in particular, was the purchase of casks of dried fruits, which were brought home and sold to local businessmen. The crew were also involved in this enterprise but in a much lesser capacity than the captain. They had to club together the buy a cask or two whereas the captain had the resources to buy in bulk.

Once loaded, all three vessels left Galatz on the same day, under sail, when possible, but often drifting with the current, which always ran down to the Black Sea. The first to reach the Bosphorus was the **May Queen**, followed shortly afterwards by the other two. All three spent a day in Constantinople before they crossed the Sea of Marmora then on through the Dardanelles and into the Mediterranean. They had been able to keep close together until this juncture but then lost sight of each other for three weeks.

The **Hantoon** arrived at Gibraltar, to find the **May Queen** and the **Saltee** already there. The former had been there for three days and the latter for two, both waiting for favourable winds. Favourable winds are essential to get through the Straits. After three more days cruising back and forth, occasionally speaking to each other, the winds changed easterly and all three passed through. The next day, they lost each other again. Three weeks later, on 21 July 1881, the **Hantoon** was off Ballycotton, Co. Cork. The next morning, at around 3 o'clock they were passing the Tuskar, when they spotted the **May Queen** four miles to the leeward. At 10 'clock, they stopped just inside the Long Bank to take on a pilot, as did the **May Queen**, which was barely 3 ship lengths behind them. Thus ended Wexford's 'Grain Race' The **Hantoon** was the victor, the **May Queen** second and at 2.30 that afternoon the **Saltee** arrived in the bay.

At the time the three barques reached the South Bay, they were drawing between 15 and 16 feet of water and therefore had to be lightened to allow them to traverse the Bar. This was accomplished in this instance by 6 schooners, which were towed out by Devereux's steam tugs and no time was spared transferring some of the grain to lighten the homecoming barques. This was a labour intensive job. Each lighter carried a crew of 5 and 10 corn porters which, along with the crews of the barques, involved up to 150 men. When the job was completed the tugs lined up all of the ships and towed them in over the Bar and up to the quays. They were received with great acclamation and jubilation from the waiting crowds. The arrival in the Bay would have been signalled by the Pilot Station, flying the Devereux house flag from their flag pole. This could be seen from all over town, so it wouldn't have been long before everyone knew that the 'Galatzers' were in the Bay.

Once the ships were tied up and everything safely stowed, the men would jump ashore to greet their wives or sweethearts and friends. The next morning all hands went to Devereux's office to sign off and collect their hard earned pay. The crews and porters from the lighters would also be there to collect their pay. Then the merriment began. The more prudent shopkeepers in town arose early that morning and shuttered their windows lest they be accidently smashed by the revellers. This uproarious going on could last for days until they all had let off steam or run out of money. Naturally, not all the homecomers were like that. The quieter among them celebrated in their own way, usually with a few drinks, a dance and a good feed of oysters in one of the many taverns in Oyster Lane. It is certain that the even quieter ones just went home to be with their loved ones.

The 'Grain Race' to Wexford also heralded the beginning of the end for the Wexford to Galatz service. Five months later, on 26 December 1881, the **Hantoon** went down in the Bay of Biscay, with the loss of four men. She was run down by the steamer **Rothesay**. By 1888, when Galatz was declared a closed port, the **Saltee** was already on the North American trade and the **May Queen** had been sold out of Wexford hands.

MENAPIA

1841 Built at St John, New Brunswick. A barque of 280 tons, carvel built, with a female figurehead.

OWNERS: R. Allen; M. Allen; J. Quinn and Thos. White (Master J. Quinn)
1852 16 Feb. Sold to John Hatchell Brennan, of London, shipowner.

MENAPIA

Number 1003. Code HGDT.

1853 Built at New Brunswick, a barque of 358 tons. Dimensions: 115.5x23x15.6ft.

1854 OWNERS R.&R. Allen and Rev. Thos. White (Master: Laurence English).

In the mid 1800s, as the tide of emigration increased, ship owners, never the ones to miss an opportunity for a profitable enterprise, began vying with each other for business. In 1847/48, at the height of the famine, notices extolling the superior services of each company's vessels, appeared in the local press. One, for R &R Allen's **Menapia**, promised the prospective emigrant the following:

THE REPUBLICAN.
BY J. L. LOCKE & CO.
F. W. ALEXANDER, ASSOCIATE EDITOR.

SAVANNAH, GA.
SATURDAY MORNING, JAN'Y 19, 1850.

☞ Cotton was not the only commodity in demand on Thursday:—the British barque *Menapia*, Capt. Rossiter, arrived from Wexford, Ireland, with 83 emigrants of the better class of Irish peasantry; among whom were some valuable mechanics, blacksmiths, carpenters, &c. The women were decently dressed, full of health and spirits, and seemed to attract attention, for the vessel had scarcely made fast at eight o'clock in the morning, when bids for servants commenced from the wharf. Stout rosy cheeked girls went off briskly at four to five dollars a month, but towards ten o'clock as the stock became reduced, the article rose to seven and eight, at which the market closed firm.

Capt. Rossiter gives a very creditable account of the demeanour of his passengers during the voyage.

Announcing the safe arrival of the **Menapia** to Savannah, January 1850.
County Wexford Archives.

EMIGRATION TO SAVANNAH.

THE Favourite Barque *MENAPIA*, JOHN HAYES Commander, burthen 500 Tons, will sail from WEXFORD with Passengers for SAVANNAH, about the 21st NOVEMBER.

The *MENAPIA* landed ALL her Passengers at Quebec on the 26th of September, being the THIRD time that she conveyed Passengers to America in the present year, and each time landed all in good health, not a single death having occurred on board of her, which is sufficient proof of the care taken to insure the Health and Comfort of the Passengers.

The *Menapia* sailed from Quebec, on her return to Wexford, the 9th October, and may be expected here early in November—on her arrival, the EXACT DAY of Sailing will be announced.

Captain HAYES's care and attention last voyage gave universal satisfaction.

For freight or passage, apply to
R. M. & R. ALLEN, or
Mr. J. DEVEREUX, Enniscorthy.
Wexford, Oct. 24, 1850.

EMIGRATION DIRECT FROM NEW ROSS, TO NEW ORLEANS AND SAVANNAH.

FOR NEW ORLEANS,

THE Splendid first class Packet Ship "EMPIRE," Burthen 1400 Tons, MICHAEL KEANE, Commander, will sail from NEW ROSS for NEW ORLEANS, on the 20th day of NOVEMBER next, and will be followed by the favourite and fortunate Passenger Ship "JOHN BELL," Burthen 900 Tons, MICHAEL CLARKE, Commander, to be dispatched for

SAVANNAH,

on the 5th day of DECEMBER next. The "*Empire*" has just returned from America, after performing her voyage out and home, in the short space of Three Months and Twelve Days, and both Ships landed their Passengers in a highly satisfactory manner, and without a case of sickness on Board.

The necessary supplies of Provisions and Water will be put on Board, and served out regularly during the Passage, and the Ships fitted up for the reception of Cabin, Second Cabin, and Steerage Passengers in the most approved manner, and careful attention paid to Ventilation.

An early application is necessary to Secure Places by those Ships, and it may be well to observe that Emigrants cannot too highly appreciate the advantages of sailing direct from home, and particularly from the Ports to which the Ships belong. It however, frequently happens unfortunately for themselves, they are induced to go to Liverpool with a view of saving some trifling sum in the passage; but on landing there, and long before arriving at their Ports of Destination, they discover such was not the wisest course for them to have taken.

For Passage and all information, apply to
HOWLETT & Co., New Ross.
Mrs. COONEY'S, John-street, Wexford.
JAMES DEVEREUX, Grocer, Enniscorthy.

Notice of the upcoming sailing of the **Menapia,** from Wexford to Savannah, Georgia, October 1850.
Wexford People

Emigration to the United States. The well known barque Menapia, Commander Stephen Rossiter now discharging a cargo of timber at Wexford from Quebec, will sail from the above port on Saturday November 10th with passengers for Savannah and Charleston. Each full passenger by this vessel will receive per week, 1lb of pork; 2½ pounds of biscuits; 1 lb of wheaten flour; 7 lbs oaten meal; 2 ozs tea; ½ lb of sugar; ½ lb of molasses; and 21 quarts of water.

Savannah and Charleston are the best ports for emigrants to reach at this season; they are as near the states of Ohio, Tennessee and Kentucky, Indiana , Illinois and all central parts of the States, as the most Northern ports of New York, Boston, etc.; and as the rivers that run by Savannah and Charleston do not freeze during the winter, emigrants can travel much cheaper, and will suffer much less privation from cold than if they emigrated by the more northern routes; and as winter is the time when works are mostly executed in these localities, persons wishing for employment would be more certain of obtaining it on their arrival than at New York or Boston etc. For freight or

The three masted barque **Menapia**, built, 1841 at St John, New Brunswick for Allen's of Wexford. Seen here in the Straits of Gibraltar, mid 1880s

Courtesy of Mrs Eithne Agar Sinnott, Wexford.

passage apply to R. M. Allen, Wexford.

On 23 April 1854, during the Crimean War, the **Menapia,** under the command of Captain Whitty, was caught at the bombardment of Odessa. Two other Wexford vessels, the **Selskar**, under Captain Chandler and the **Wexford**, under Captain Codd, were also caught. All three vessels were given a naval escort to Constantinople. Captain Codd reported to his owners (R.&R. Allen) that he had been at anchor between the shore batteries and the Franco-British Fleet, when the firing commenced. The only loss he suffered was an anchor and thirty fathoms of cable and a shell had torn away the fore top mast shrouds.

At this period, Wexford vessels traded to Galatz in Romania for corn and Odessa was one of their ports of call. This trade commenced in 1837 when the previously closed Galatz was declared a free port and closed in 1888 when the free designation was revoked. Many of Wexford's barques, barquentines and brigs were then modified and sent trading to the southern states of the USA, carrying passengers out and cotton back to the English mills, or to the Canadian Provinces for timber.

At another period in her career, **Menapia** traded on the coast of 'Dead Ned', as the coast of West Africa was known. She loaded a cargo of cheap trinkets, colourful cloth and cheap jewellery at Liverpool and traded with tribal chiefs, up the rivers and creeks of the West Coast of Africa. In return they received small quantities of palm oil. This was the toughest trade that any of Allen's vessels engaged in, with many of the crew falling victim to malaria and blackwater fever in the mosquito infested swamps and rivers.

The **Menapia** was lost off the coast of Georgia.

MERMAID
Number 49510.

1869 Built at Wexford, a schooner of 87 tons, with two masts. Dimensions: 74.6x19.8x10ft.

OWNERS
1870 J. P. Devereux of Wexford.
1885 Thomas Harper of Wexford.
1888 Harper & Wickham, South Main St., Wexford.
1898 William Harland, Tranmere, Cheshire. Converted to a barge.
1964 15 Feb. Register closed.

In October 1897, Thomas Neill of Bride Street, Wexford was seriously injured when he fell from the mast of the Wexford schooner, **Mermaid**. She was discharging ballast at Newport, Wales when the accident occurred. Neill broke both his arms in the fall but was not thought to have suffered any internal injuries. Believed lost during an air raid on Liverpool Docks in World War 2.

Mermaid, a two masted tops'l schooner of 87 tons, built, 1869 in Wexford for Harpur & Wickham.

MISS WILLIAMS
Number 80232. Code MCJS.

1880 Built at Port Dinorwic, North Wales by Rees, Jones and Sons. A two masted schooner of 79 tons, with a figurehead of a woman's bust and an elliptical stern. Dimensions: 77.7x21.1x9.7ft.

OWNERS
1882 R. Jones, Port Dinorwic.
1888 H. Williams, Anglesey.
1902 Thomas Brown, Connah's Quay.
1904-10 Margaret Hutchinson, Wexford (Master: Captain T. Hutchinson).

On 18 May 1904, Captain Thomas Hutchinson, owner and master of the **Miss Williams**, wrote to the Wexford Harbour Commissioners, claiming a refund of 30 shillings. Apparently, on 28 April, he was leaving port under the command of Pilot Peter Furlong. When it came time to drop the pilot, Captain Hutchinson was not able to see the pilot boat and was therefore obliged to take Pilot Furlong with him. It then cost him thirty shillings to send Furlong back and this was the refund he was applying for. The Act of Parliament governing such occurrences, required that the owner of the vessel would send the pilot back. Over carrying a pilot was not a totally unusual occurrence. Pilots went aboard to bring vessels out into the South Bay only to find that, once they were out there, the weather changed for the worse making it impossible to disembark from the outgoing schooner.

Captain Maddock told the Commissioners that the pilot boat was otherwise engaged at the time, out in the South Bay. It was putting pilots on to vessels ready for the next morning. Had Captain Hutchinson waited twenty minutes, they would have come alongside him. But he also admitted that the weather was so bad, by then, it was doubtful if they could have taken the pilot off. After a debate it was decided to pay Captain Hutchinson the thirty shillings but not before the Mayor asked if it was true the **Miss Williams** was sailing one man short that day, which it seems it was. The inference seems obvious but nonetheless no further remarks were made.

On the 21 February 1921, en route from Newport to Wexford with coal, she went ashore. She got off the next day, but was still taking in water and she sank 3 miles south of Curracloe Coastguard station. Her registration was closed.

N

NAIAD
Number 37681. Code SGBC.

1862 Built at Hopewell, New Brunswick, by N. M. Bennett. A wooden schooner of 74 tons, with two masts, a billet head and a square stern. Dimensions: 79.7x22x8.6ft.

OWNERS
1865 J. Read of Nova Scotia.
1872 John Hy. Tuke of Arklow
1887 William Murphy of Carrig-on-Bannow, Co. Wexford.
1895 November. William Murphy had died earlier in the year. His shares were left to Philip Murphy of Waterford.
1895 September. Andrew Ffrench of New Ross.
1896 Andrew & Jane Ffrench (joint owners).
1898 February. J. Bagnal Boyd, of Kiltra Hse., Wellingtonbridge, Co. Wexford.
1902 February. Thomas Boyd of Kilkenny, 32 shares.
1917 September. Thomas Boyd died and his shares went to Caroline Harriet Crosby Burthill.
1917 October. She was sold to James Child Gould of Merthyr Hse., Cardiff.
1917 Wrecked off France.

CREW 1891.
Master: Matthew Carr of Oyster Lane, Wexford.
Mate: Patrick Sinnott.
AB: Michael Morris.
OS: John Sinnott.
Boy: John Devereux.

CREW
Master: Matthew Neil, 39.
Mate: Rich. Bent, 49.
AB: Patrick Roche, 22.
Boy: James Murphy, 18.

The **Naiad** arrived at Bannow on the 21 April, 1891 and was laid up at the Bar o' Lough for repairs. Captain Carr paid off at Bannow on 23 April 1891 and the crew on 30 April.

Messrs. Jones & Company of New Ross and Bannow, Co. Wexford, bought the schooner **Naiad** from Captain French of New Ross. They intended to use her in their coal business. Mr Bagnell Boyd, managing director of Jones and Co. had begun importing coal into Bannow and had found it difficult to get ships over the bar and into the port. However, the **Naiad** was of a shallow draught and more suited to Bannow than other vessels. The **Naiad** had previously been owned by William Murphy of Bannow.

On 26 July 1896, the **Naiad** met a severe SW gale off the Saltee Islands. All sails were set and later they were all shredded. A steamer out of Waterford came along and took her in tow to Waterford and later brought her to New Ross. In March 1903, New Ross lived up to its reputation as a dangerous port for sailors trying to get aboard their ship in dock, when two men from the **Naiad** (Captain Marlow), were almost drowned. The men, Messrs Sinnott and Roche, were boarding their ship when they both missed their footing and fell into the river. They were rescued by some quay workers. Judging by local papers at the time, falling into the river seems to have been a regular occurrence at New Ross. Hardly a week went by without some poor unfortunate ending up in the drink and not all were as lucky as these two sailors.

On 25 November 1917, en route from South Wales via Falmouth, with coal for Cherbourg, the **Naiad** was wrecked at Villeroille, France. Of the 5-man crew, there were no survivors.

NANNY WIGNALL
Number 56705. Code JGMF.

1868 Built at Irvine, Ayr, Scotland for J. Wignall of Fleetwood. A two masted schooner of 84 tons, with a full female figurehead and an elliptical stern. Dimensions 84.2x20x10ft.

OWNERS
1879 Wyre Shipping Co. of Fleetwood.
1885 John Amer of Fleetwood.
1885 John Morris of Skerries Co. Dublin.
1902 William Dunlea of Dungarvan, Co. Waterford

Nanny Wignall, alongside, possibly at Bristol.

Nanny Wignall, a two masted tops'l schooner of 84 tons. Built 1886 at Ayr. In 1917 she was owned by Mary Kate Stafford of Wexford.

1903 Eileen Dunlea.
1916 Stafford of Wexford.
1917 Mary Kate Stafford, Cromwell's Fort, Wexford.
1918 9 March. Sunk by submarine gunfire in St. George's Channel, 14 miles SE of Tuskar Rock.

During her time in Dungarvan, she was said to be one of the finest schooners in that port and the cross channel ports.

On 9 March 1918, **Nanny Wignall** was homeward bound from Cardiff with coal, when she ran foul of a German submarine. The submarine surfaced, bore down on the schooner and opened fire on them. The first salvo brought some of the rigging down and wounded James O'Neill, the ship's boy. The Captain, Matt O'Neill, gave what assistance he could to the boy and concluded that the best he could do was to abandon ship.

He went aft to assist the other two men to get the boat into the water. At this stage Laurence Smith, the deckhand, was hit. They got the boat into the water and away from their sinking vessel. Once the crew were clear, the Germans carried on shelling the **Nanny Wignall** until she finally sank beneath the waves. The crew were in the boat for 6 hours before they fetched up on the Wexford coast.

NATIVE
1840 Built at Wexford, a brig of 300 tons.
1850 Registered as 227 tons
Native was an emigrant ship.

OWNERS
1845-1847 J. Allen (Master: Captain Patrick Joseph Doyle).
1850 Breen & Co., Wexford (Master: Doyle)

An account of the scene at the departure for Norfolk, Virginia and Baltimore of Allen's brig **Native**, Captain P.J. Doyle, states that:

*On Tuesday evening the brig **Native** sailed from Wexford port with emigrants for Norfolk, Virginia and Baltimore, USA and bore away from their beloved Ireland many highly respectable inhabitants of Wexford with their families, as well as many comfortable persons from the rural districts. In fact, they all had the appearance of ladies and gentlemen. All day the quays were crowded with a well dressed decent concourse of people, grieving, taking leave and sorrowfully observing the affecting scene. There is one consolation, as is always the case with Mr Devereux's, that the brig **Native** is accommodatingly fitted up; the provisions necessary for the voyage abundant, with an experienced and obliging commander, Captain Patrick J. Doyle .*

Judging by the notice from Allen's (see above) and the description of the departure of the Devereux ship, the scene of the departure and the list of provisions provided by Allens, are far removed from the usual depiction of famine time emigration we have become used to . There were no starving people in rags being herded on to coffin ships, and this was "Black '47", at the height of the famine.

It has been said that the atrocity of 'Black 47' had little effect on Wexford and that the population of the Barony of Forth actually increased during that period. Certainly, this description of the emigration of well dressed, comfortable people seems to bear that theory out. Another astonishing fact from that time was that foods, such as oats, barley and wheat, were still being exported, weekly, from Wexford to England! Surely had the famine had any debilitating effect on the local population they would have risen up and rioted to prevent the export of essential food.

In September 1842, Captain Denis Keogh of the Wexford brig **Native** was reported to have died in Havana, from 'the disease prevalent there'. Another Wexford town man, Thomas Barry, also a member of the crew of the **Native**, died around the same time. Other crew men were said to be suffering also. The nature of the disease was never stated but it was likely cholera.

On 2 March 1850 en route from Seaham to Hamburg with coal the **Native** stranded near Spikerwood.

NEW ZEALAND
Number 42654. Code TKQM.

1861 Built at New Brunswick. A barquentine of 134 tons.
Dimensions: 98.1.x24.2x9.7ft.

OWNER Hugh McGuire (Master: Captain John Cahill).

On 17 July 1875, as the result of a report that there was a shipwreck near Ballygeary (Rosslare Harbour), the local Collector of Customs and the Lloyd's Agent proceeded to the reported site. There they found a large barquentine had gone ashore. It turned out to be the **New Zealand** of Wexford, bound for New York. The coastguards at Rosslare had attempted to get a line aboard by the rocket apparatus but due to it being a very dark night, they were unable to fire it accurately. However, in the daylight all hands were landed safely. Later she was re-floated.

On 25 January 1879, the **New Zealand** was abandoned, after a collision with the barque **Star Beam** near the Welsh coast. The crew were picked up by the barque. She was taken under tow. The tow rope parted and she went ashore at Trewent, Pembrokeshire and was a total wreck. The crew were landed at Cardiff.

NORA
Number 76109.

1868 Built at Boston, USA. A schooner of 85 tons.

1880 William Goddard of London.
1883 Patrick Lambert & Jasper Walsh, Wexford.
1885 September. Lost on the Bar.

In September 1885, the schooner **Nora** of Wexford, was lost on the Bar, whilst in the charge of Pilot Michael Blake. The inquiry that followed found that the **Nora** drew 11 ft of water and although the signal flags showed that there was only 10 ft at the Bar, the pilot attempted to bring her in but put her aground. Lambert & Walsh put in a claim for one thousand pounds in compensation.

NORTHERN LIGHT
Number 18689. Code MNTV.

1857 Built at Tarleton, Lancashire, England by John Bannister. A schooner of 61 tons, with two masts: a woman's bust figurehead and a round stern.
Dimensions: 76x18x8ft.
1871 Registered at Preston.
1895 Dundalk.

1917 OWNER Patrick Donovan of Lamb House, Wexford.

On 6 December 1917, **Northern Light** left Cardiff with 108 tons of coal for George Stafford of Wexford. The weather was clear and it was blowing a moderate breeze from the WNW. She hove to in Cardiff Roads, waiting for a favourable wind, and left at 1.30 pm on 11 December. The following day, she brought up in Dale Roads, Milford Haven at 6 am. She set out for Wexford at 10 am on 18 December in a moderate SE. breeze. All was well until 2 am the following day when the wind changed direction to ESE and increased in force.

On Friday 21 December, it was blowing a full gale from the SE. The **Northern Light** had passed the green buoy at the entrance to Wexford Harbour and was attempting to go about when the traveller of the mainsail carried away and the mainsail split. The other sails had already blown away. It was impossible to manoeuvre the vessel and the only option was to let an anchor go. The starboard anchor was dropped and the port anchor was let go shortly afterwards. This held the vessel for about 1 hour but with the rising tide and the wild seas around her, she began to drag both anchors, for a short distance. Just then a steam trawler came up and got a line on board the **Northern Light** and began to tow her. But as soon as the strain came on, the hawser snapped. The Fort Lifeboat, **James Stevens No. 15**, came up and passed another line from the trawler to the schooner but that also snapped.

The **Northern Light** was now totally adrift in rough seas and beached abreast of the Watch House, on the Curracloe side of the harbour entrance. The crew were taken off by the lifeboat and landed in Wexford. The prospects of saving the vessel were unknown. In the end she was declared a total loss. At the time of her accident **Northern Light** was still registered in Wexford but owned by Captain D. Bride of Exchange Buildings, Cardiff. Her master was Victor Belmont.

NORTHUMBRIA
1847 Built at Pictou, Nova Scotia. A barque of 560 tons.
Dimensions: 98.1x24.2x9.7ft.

OWNERS
Howlett and Co., New Ross, Co. Wexford.
1853 Holmes of London.

O

OCEAN MAID
Number 28996. Code QCTB.

1861 Built at Fraserborourgh, Aberdeenshire in Scotland by Websters. A schooner of 97 tons, with two masts and a square stern. Dimensions: 79x21x10ft.
Registered at Peterhead.
1882 Registered at Dublin.
1906 Registered at Wexford.

OWNERS
1876 James McRae, Lockalsh, Argyll.
1883 William Darragh, Summerhill, Wicklow.
1906 William Noble, Fraserborough, Aberdeenshire
1907 Patrick Byrne of the Bull Ring, Wexford.
1908 6 March. **Ocean Maid** wrecked near Rosslare Harbour in a severe gale.

Mr P. Byrne of The Bull Ring, bought the **Ocean Maid** from her owner, Captain Darragh of Arklow, for one hundred pounds. She was sent into Wexford Dockyard for a re-fit, which cost a further six hundred pounds. In July 1906 she returned from Newport with coal, on her maiden voyage for her new owner.

Yet another great storm hit the coast in March 1908. Two schooners were driven ashore at the west side of the pier at Rosslare Harbour: the **Ocean Maid** and the **Denbighshire Lass** (Arklow). The Wexford vessel had left Newport on 25 February and had to put into Milford three days later. Leaving at 5 o'clock in the morning of 5 March, she arrived at 3 pm that afternoon in the South Bay, Wexford, with a fresh breeze from the SW. During the night, the wind speed increased to gale force and at 5 am it turned north, increasing further. With the force of the wind and the raging seas, the port anchor chain parted, followed 30 minutes later by the starboard anchor.

They then hoisted the standing jib and the boom jib and Captain Kehoe took the wheel and headed his ship for the beach. He successfully beached her near Rosslare Harbour. The coastguards, under Chief Officer Mulligan, proceeded at once with the rocket apparatus, to render aid to the crews of both vessels. They lost no time establishing contact with the 4-man crew of the **Ocean Maid**. They immediately got a line on board and the crew lashed it to the main mast. Captain Kehoe ordered his three crewmen to go ashore in the breeches buoy. They were all safely transferred ashore with no damage, apart from a thorough soaking.

Captain Kehoe then began to secure himself into the breeches buoy. But, for whatever reason, he failed to secure himself properly. He gave the signal to the coastguards to haul him ashore and everything seemed to go well until he was about 20 yards from the ship, when it appeared that he threw his hands up in the air and to the horror of all who were watching, slipped out of the buoy into the water. With his weight gone from the buoy, the cable of the apparatus went into the water and the poor man was seen to grasp at it but he was unable to keep hold. Two of the coastguards, at great personal risk, waded out to the body and brought it ashore. All possible attempts were made to

March 1908, **Ocean Maid** and the **Denbighshire Lass** were both driven ashore near Rosslare Harbour. The **Ocean Maid** became a total loss, the **Denbighshire Lass** was re floated.

resuscitate the unfortunate man but all to no avail.

A reason put forward for Captain Kehoe's demise was that as a man of 67 years, and after the grueling ordeal he had gone through, he was completely exhausted. Although this was his first trip on the **Ocean Maid,** Captain Kehoe was an experienced seaman and had commanded many Wexford schooners. He was from Michael Street in Wexford Town. The **Ocean Maid** was a total loss.

While all this was going on the coastguard had managed to get a rope onto the **Denbighshire Lass** but in the meantime the Arklow men lowered a small boat and got themselves ashore. Shortly afterwards the **Denbighshire Lass** came ashore about 20 yards from the Wexford schooner. She was later re-floated.

OCEAN PEARL
Number 19447. Code MSRK.

1858 Built at Tarleton, Lancashire, England by Roger Bannister.
A schooner of 47 tons. Dimensions 73x18.6x7.3ft. 1902 converted to a ketch.

OWNERS
1865 James Ashcroft of Barrow-in-Furness.
1879 James Taylor, Hesketh Bank, Lancashire.
1880 Robert Wright of Hesketh Bank.
1888-1897 Patrick Rochford of Kilmore Quay, Co. Wexford.
1889 John Monaghan, Kilmore Quay, Co. Wexford.
On 17 February 1904, the ketch **Ocean Pearl** of Wexford, was reported to have burst both her anchor chains and broke adrift at Kingstown (Dun Laoghaire) Harbour. She was spotted by the keeper of the Bailey Light, flying distress signals. He phoned Howth Lifeboat which put to sea and reached her near Lambey Island. The lifeboat took the crew off and towed the **Ocean Pearl** safely into Howth Harbour. **Ocean Pearl** was under the command of Captain William Cox of Wexford.

Accounts for the Ocean Pearl
Crew wages for master, mate, man and boy for 30 days came to £9-15-00. It was broken down in the following manner: Master, £4; Mate, £3; Man, £2 5s- and the Boy got the last 10 shillings. Other expenditure came to £5 16s, a total of £15-11s. Ninety-five tons of coal were loaded @ 5 shillings per ton, which came to £23 15s. So the master didn't make a lot of money on that particular trip! Unless of course, he squeezed another shorter trip in between. The stores are accounted for, as are the wages. So too, is the destination but there's no mention of the duration of the trip. A trip to Newport and back hardly took a month, unless the weather was bad.

Log of the Ocean Pearl
The weather certainly played an important role in a trip, from Arthurstown, Co. Wexford, to Porthcawl, South Wales, by the **Ocean Pearl** in October/November 1916. The details come from a small notebook headed 'The Log of the Ketch **Ocean Pearl** of Wexford'. It is written in beautiful clear handwriting by, most likely, Captain Monaghan himself, and gives a good example of some of the trials and tribulations of the small sailing ship

Ocean Pearl, a two masted tops'l schooner of 47 tons, later converted to a ketch. Built 1858 in Tarleton Lancashire. Shown here signalling her code, MSRK, to the keeper on Tuskar Rock.

captain. The log commences at Arthurstown on 27 October 1916, and is transcribed here as originally written.

October 27: *We commenced loading oats in bulk alongside quay at Arthurstown Harbour. Weather sets in very bad, blew gale, south and veering south, east to north, east. Took very little cargo in. Heavy seas breaking over quay. Held vessel on to mooring all right. Pumps attended to, ship not making any water.*

October 28: *We took in some more oats, weather still bad and blowing very hard, southwest. Pumps seen to, ship making no water.*

October 29: *This day being Sunday, no work done. Pumps seen to and ship making no water.*

October 30: *Took in some more oats today. Wind strong westerly, squally weather. Pumps attended to. Ship making no water.*

October 31: *Took in more oats today. Weather still squally and very bad. Wind westerly. Pumps attended to, ship makes no water.*

Captain John Monaghan, owner/master of the **Ocean Pearl.**
John Power Collection.

November 1: *Today a holiday here and no work done. Strong west wind and raining. Pumps attended to, ship making no water.*

November 2: *Taking in more oats and completed our cargo. Wind westerly, moderate weather. Pump attended to and ship making no water. So far, all was fairly normal, then the weather changed.*

November 3: *Weather unsettled, wind veering west, southwest. Pumps attended to, ship making no water. Weather got worse a morning proceeds, blowing a heavy gale and rain. Wind southwest, veering west. Pumps attended to, ship making no water. Vessel rolling against the quay and grinding and chaffing her side. Cut up three ropes for extra fenders to help save ship and her cargo. Parted all moorings forward about 1 pm, pulling a large stone bollard up out of the quay and vessel dragged it about 30 fathoms through the mud. Vessel now being adrift and afloat was carried by the force of gale right out of Arthurstown Harbour and being dismantled forward had to run vessel up on to beach to save ship and cargo from being lost on rocks near Coastguard Station. In doing this we shipped our stern moorings, stream anchor and chain cable which was lost in 6 fathoms. Whilst on beach had great difficulty in keeping vessel from going broadside on. The heavy sea running during which time all our rails, stanchions, stern pipes, fixings, chucks got broken. Hawspipes started, Windlass strained, bits started, winch started, stern damaged, ship's boat smashed up and ships bottom damaged. When the tide ebbed we ran a hawser from off the stern to the quay with help and assistance of men from the shore. Weather still very bad, vessel was on beach all night. Pumps attended to at all times and vessel found to be making considerable water.*

November 4. *Weather moderated and we got vessel off beach with assistance of boat and men, into harbour of Arthurstown again and moored her alongside the quay. Pumps regularly attended to, ship making water. Weather bad during afternoon, strong southeast winds.*

November 5. *Strong weather, wind about northwest, a gale at times. Pumps attended to and ship makes water.*

November 6. *Very bad weather, wind veering southwest to southeast. Plenty of rain. Pumps carefully attended to and vessel makes water. Went to Waterford and noted protest during afternoon (?).*

November 7. *Wind southwest, very bad weather. Pumps attended to and ship still makes water.*

November 8. *Wind west and veered northwest, got vessel out of Arthurstown by warping and then set mizzen and sailed down to anchorage at Passage East to wait favourable weather to make our voyage to Bristol. Let go anchor about 5 pm. Pump attended to, vessel still makes water.*

From 8-20 November gales and rain battered the coast and the **Ocean Pearl** remained at anchor at Passage East, weather bound. Every day the pumps were kept working and gradually the logs shows that she was making less and less each day, until on 19 November, he reports that the vessel was 'making no water'. On 20 November, the winds moderated and we take up the log again from that date.

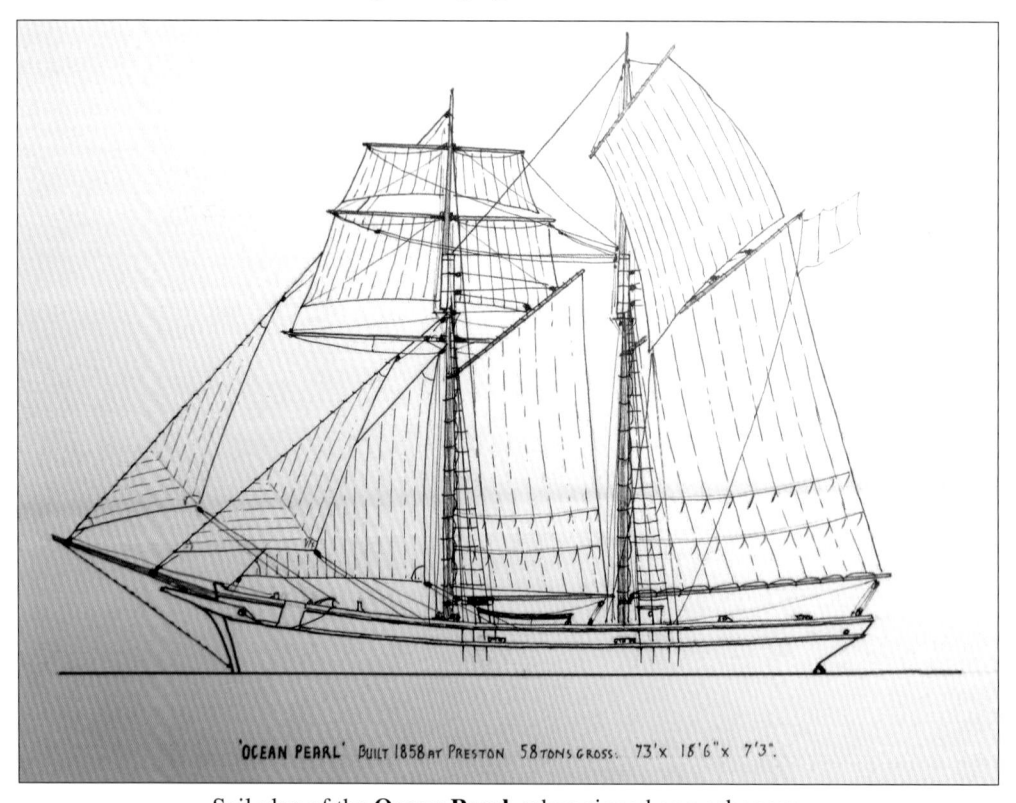

Sail plan of the **Ocean Pearl,** when rigged as a schooner.

November 20. *Weather moderated west from northwest. Hove up our anchor about midday. Set canvas and sailed right out to sea. Proceeded on our passage to Bristol. Weather mild and a steady breeze, northwest. Pumps attended to carefully and the vessel still makes water.*

November 21. *Strong northwest winds, which died away. Let go anchor about 5 pm, in Barry Roads. Pump attended to carefully and vessel making water.*

November 22. *Hove up anchor about 10 am. Light wind about west and freshening as we got near Spit Buoy. About 4 pm, the tugboat **Sylph** picked us up off Portishead and towed us to Bathurst Basin, Bristol. Got moored in Basin about 6 pm. Pumps carefully attended to. Heavy rain.*

November 23. *Got vessel down to berth and ready for discharging. Weather dirty and raining. Strong westerly wind and gale at night. Pumps carefully attended to and vessel still makes water.*

November 24. *Commenced discharge of oats to R.F. Webb, corn merchant. Cargo seems in good order, a little rain occasionally, and west wind. Pump carefully attended to and vessel makes water.*

November 25. *Completed discharge of oats about 1.30 pm. Strong west wind all day. Pumps carefully attended to and vessel still makes water.*

November 26. *Today is Sunday, no work done, wind northwest light and fine weather. Pumps attended to, vessel makes little water* (Log ends).

As you can see, under normal circumstances the trip from Ireland to Bristol should have taken about one day but thanks to the weather, this particular one took, from the time of loading to the time of discharge, almost a month! This meant, of course, that the master was paid for a job that should have taken a week or so, but actually took a month. More than likely he loaded coal in some of the Welsh ports for the return trip. In normal circumstances he would have had made three cross channel trips in the same time period, each time bringing back a load of coal, but this time he could only manage one. If something similar happened during the period covered by the accounts above, it's easy to see why that trip made no profit. So it's possible that through bad weather those accounts were for a one-month trip.

There is no certain indication who the crewmen were, but there are four men mentioned in an account of wages. Besides Captain Monaghan himself (£4 per month), there's John Blake (£3 per month), John McCabe (£2) and Richard Blake (10 shillings). At the end of the log there is a note that a John Cousins shipped aboard on 7 April 1919, at £3.10s a month and that John McCabe shipped on 11 July 1921 (he was still there on 27 May 1923).

Captain Monaghan owned at least two vessels in his time, the **Ocean Pearl** and the **Alice Latham**. When he died in the early 1920s, **Ocean Pearl** was tied up in Bannow Bay, where her skeleton lies to this day. In July 1930 her certificate was cancelled and the registration closed.

OCEAN SPRAY
Number 42253.

1860 Built at Miramichi, New Brunswick, a brig of 250 tons.

1864 Out of register

OWNER R. Devereux, Wexford (Master, Kehoe).

Little appears to have been documented about this vessel. Apart from the usual arrival and departure notices in local newspapers, the first report of her abroad is a letter of complaint from Gravesend dated 10 July 1862 to the editor of the *Wexford Independent*. The correspondent is a Captain R.R. Browne, captain of the vessel, **Trabolgan**. Part of the letter is as follows:

Dear Sir, will you please to report that on the 22 of June in Lat. 41', 28' N and Long 36' 8 W (or about half way) spoke the brig, **Ocean Spray** *of Wexford, from Wexford to Baltimore, out 24 days, Captain Kehoe, by the* **Trabolgan** *from Columbo.*

Dear Mr Greene, I was much surprised to find when I sent a boat to the above named vessel, that I could not procure a paper of any kind, and I am surprised that captains go to sea without a large file. I was, at the time I boarded this vessel, 110 days at sea, without having any news, and would have given freely a guinea for one of yours. I am sure one of us would have given 2 for the Times, but not such a thing of any sort on board. I am quite sure if the Masters would apply to you on the eve of their sailing, especially when bound south, you would let them have some spare ones.

Captain Browne then went on to report the loss by fire of the Spanish vessel **Reina del Scirano**, from Liverpool to Manila, about 500 miles off the coast of Africa. But the principal reason for his letter seems to bemoan the lack of the *Wexford Independent* or any other newspapers, on the **Ocean Spray**.

The **Ocean Spray** was reported arriving at New York from New Ross on the 28 November 1862 and departing there on 28 January 1863. After that nothing is heard of her.

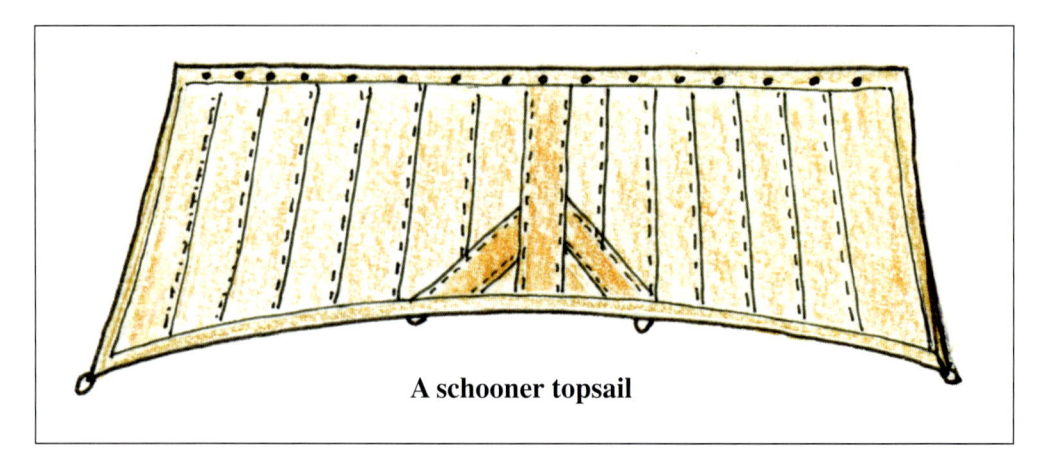

A schooner topsail

P

PEARL
Number 3066. Code HRSJ.

1835 Built at Barnstaple. She was a sloop, carvel built of 44 tons.

1847 Registered at Wexford. George Murphy, master.
1863 October. **Pearl** was lost off the Isle of Arran, on passage from Devon to Skerries.

OWNERS
Nicholas Whitty, merchant, of Wexford.
1859 July. Joseph May. M.M. and James McTiernan, merchant, both of Skerries, Co. Dublin.

This is the first Wexford registered vessel in which the authors found crew working as 'Sharemen' This means that they weren't paid a wage but took a share of any profits, after a voyage. This may have been the practice where her last owners and crew were from.

CREWS
1845
Master: Christopher Cahill, 58.
Mates: Patrick –?, 30; Richard Allen, 44.
Seaman: Martin Larkin, 22; Martin Lawler, 21.
Boy: –? Cahill, 18.

1863 (This crew all lost when **Pearl** sank in October)
Master: John Gilch, 60.
ABs Nicholas Gilch, 50; Thomas Shines, 18.

PERSEVERANCE
Number 81236. Code PJBW.
1882 Built at Freckleton, Lancashire by P. Rawstrone, a schooner of 78 tons. Dimensions 84x21x9ft.

OWNERS
1890 Mrs M. Ashcroft of Lancashire.
1892 Joseph Taylor of Lathom.
1896-1897 H. Bennett of Shotton, Connah's Quay.
1898 Murphy and Nunn, South Main St., Wexford.
1907-1910 Mrs M. Murphy, South Main St., Wexford.
1913 Thomas Murphy, Hayestown, Wexford.
1918-1923 Edward Maynard, Overton, Plymouth.
1924 William E. Rae, Castlemaine, Co. Kerry and Thomas Rooney, Rush, Co. Dublin

In January 1901, **Perseverance** had a narrow escape from destruction when she went aground on the Bar. The tug and the lifeboat went to her assistance but, because of her dangerous position, could not get alongside. Luckily she floated herself clear later and was brought up to the quay. She was in ballast from Dublin. Nothing else of note seems to have happened to her until July 1905, when a sailor named Barty Whitmore jumped over the side as the vessel was leaving the harbour. His fellow crewmen launched the boat and brought him back onboard.

In 1917 **Perseverance** was commanded by Captain Thomas Newport. On the 24 March of that year, the ship left Swansea, bound for Wexford, with a cargo of coal for Boxwells of Drinagh. At around noon that day the wind, which had been blowing from the NE, backed to NW and continued so until the following day when, just as they were making Milford Haven, it went to the NW. They remained in Milford until 8 April at 8 am. Leaving in a South Westerly breeze, it was a good trip and they made the Tuskar Rock that evening at 8 pm, and the South Bay the next day at 5 o'clock in the morning.

Making for the Wexford Bar under a single reef mainsail and in a fresh breeze, the **Perseverance** caught the ground at the east end of the Dogger Bank. The crew backed the yards and lowered the mainsail and the vessel's head paid off. The sails were re-set and the **Perseverance** made back for the South Bay, where they went about again and made back for the Bar. At this time the mate, Mathew Murphy, was at the wheel, steering as per master's instructions. About 7 am, she again caught the ground on the Dogger Bank, about half a mile further north from where she first hit. The mainsail was lowered and the topsail backed, but this time, although her head paid off, due to the tide, she did not move and remained stuck on the Bar.

Perseverance, Tied up at an unknown location, possibly one of the Bristol Channel Ports.

Perseverance- a two masted tops'l schooner of 78 tons. Built, 1882 at Freckleton, Lancashire. By 1898 she was owned by Murphy & Nunn, South Main Street, Wexford.

The Wexford Lifeboat, **James Stevens No. 15**, came out and ran out two anchors and assisted the crew of the schooner to jettison some of her cargo. After ditching about 50 tons, and with the tide in their favour, the lifeboat crew tried to pull the **Perseverance** off the bank, but she wouldn't budge. After about an hour trying to get her off, the hawser on one of the anchors parted and it was decided to lighten her some more. They jettisoned another 20 tons and the next day came back to have another attempt. High tide was at 8 am and they tried to refloat her then but she still remained fast. Finding that the situation was hopeless, the **Perseverance** was abandoned and the crew were landed at Wexford by the lifeboat. She was declared a complete wreck, but apparently re-floated.

In May 1932, **Perseverance** was en-route from Clanakilty Co. Cork to Newport, in ballast, when, due to light airs and fog she sought shelter off Milford Haven, but the wind and current drove her ashore on Skomer Island. The crew manned their ship's boat and rowed over 8 miles to Hakin Point. The vessel became a complete loss.

PERSEVERANCE (June 1832, not the same as the Perseverance above)
Luke Sheil a sailor on the brig **Perseverance** of Wexford, was posted missing. His hat had been found at the Crescent Quay, giving rise to serious alarm among his friends. His body was later found in the river opposite the Crescent.

Grass to be paid for before the Horse is led out.
Rath, April 27th, 1840.

FOR SALE,

THE following VESSELS, which are all in good order and well found; have been, and are constantly employed in the Grain Trade.

Schooner PILOT,

Built at Laurenny, Milford, in 1835, 56 Tons new, 66 Tons old measurement length 52, 5 tenths, breadth 16, 2 tenths, depth 9, 3 tenths.

Schooner SWIFT,

Built at P. E. Island, in 1832, 72 Tons new, 83 tons old measurement, length 59, 3 tenths, breadth 16, 9 tenths, depth 9, 9 tenths.

Sloop FAME,

Built at Arman,' in 1833, 45 Tons new, 50 Tons old Measurement, length 46, 6 tenths, breath 15, 1 tenth, depth 8 feet.

Sloop INDUSTRY.

Built at Shoreham, County Sussex, 43 6/9 Tons old measurement, length 50, 2 inches, breadth 14, 9, depth 8 feet.

Apply to Messrs. BREEN and DEVEREUX, Wexford, or Mr. WILLIAM CARSON, Dublin.
Wexford, April 24, 1840.

Sale notice for the Pilot, Swift, Fame and Industry,
Wexford People April 1840.

Wexford Harbour, late 1800s, showing many aspects of interest, including a schooner at the Ballast Bank, either loading or discharging Ballast; the round top buildings of the Wexford Dockyard and the steam train at the old South Station loaded with farm machinery, likely from Pierce's Foundry.

PETREL
No.54532

1865 Built at Kingston, Moray. A schooner, 74 tons. Registered at Lancaster.

OWNERS
1870-1880 Fisher's of Barrow;
1884 Michael Williams, M.M. Wexford;
1884 Dec. Michael Kavanagh, and Nicholas White of Kilmore, Co. Wexford.
1885 to Mary Carroll, Summerhill, Dublin, 11 shares, Mike Williams of Wexford, 8 shares, Nicholas Quinn of Wexford, 5 shares.
1889 6 April. White sold his shares to Michael Kavanagh and to Mary Carroll of the Cottage, Kilmore, Co. Wexford
1889, 2 Feb. Quinn died. Administration granted to Mary Williams, widow of M. Williams.
1889 Sold to the Isle of Mull
1891 Stranded and broken up, Isle of Bute,
1892 Out of register.

In April 1888, a young sailor, Michael Doyle of Maudlintown was killed on board the **Petrel** at Newport, Monmouthshire when the lashing of the anchor chain gave way. The inquest was held at the Talbot Hotel, Newport. The coronor was told that Doyle was assisting to haul in the anchor, which had fouled, when an iron bar that had been put in the anchor chain flew out and hit Doyle in the forehead. He was knocked instantly unconscious and removed to hospital where he died. A verdict of 'Accidental Death' was returned.

CREW 1845.
Master: Patrick Hannon, 44.
Mate: W. Morris, 25.
Seamen: S. Carley, 29; S. Sinnott, 27; John Wade, 29.

PILOT
Number 17298. Code MGCF.

1835 Built at Lawrenny, a schooner of 75 tons. Dimensions 64.9x16.5x9.2ft.

OWNERS
1854-1875 J.T. Devereux of Wexford.
1882 William J. Gafney of Wexford.
1884 Gafney died and left the **Pilot** to his daughters; Mary, Margaret and Angela.
1889 Out of register.

Crew 1845
Master, William Cousins, age 30; Mate, Thomas Hayes, 35; Seamen, Michael Cullen, 26; Thomas Moore, 23; Mariner, James Duff, 20.

Crew 1888
Master, Moses Boggan, age 30; Mate, Thomas Murphy, 36;OS, Thomas Furlong, 22; Boy, John Daly,18.

In November 1873, the clipper ship **Nagpore** from Calcutta, put into Queenstown on fire and out of control. She collided with various other vessels, one of them being the **Pilot** of Wexford. Newspaper reports stated that the captain of the **Pilot** was knocked over the side and drowned but that proved incorrect. Although that did happen to the captain of another vessel. The **Pilot** was however damaged. In the end, to protect others vessels in the harbour the Coastguard had to fire on the clipper and sink her.

In November 1875, bound for New Ross from Dublin, the **Pilot** broke free from her anchor in the South Bay of Wexford and went ashore at Ballygeary (Rosslare Harbour). The crew were all taken off by rocket apparatus. The **Pilot** was undamaged and later refloated.

In February 1888, the **Pilot** ran aground at the point of the Fort. Even though the position she grounded at was considered a dangerous shoal, it was thought that she would float on the next high tide. This is apparently what happened as on February 29th Walsh & Sons, Auctioneers, announced that the hull of the **Pilot** plus two masts; wire standing rigging; two chains and anchors, were to be sold at Commercial Quay on Wednesday March 7th 1888.

On March 10th 1888, a note to the Registrar General stated that the **Pilot** had been dismantled and sold and would not put to sea again.

PORTIA
Number 44191. Code TSDB.

1861 Built at Bridport, a barque of 298 tons. Dimensions 122.x24.5x14.7ft.
1862 Registered at Wexford.
1865-1870 Owner Richard Devereux of Wexford.
1875 Mrs Mary Wilson, Addiscombe, Surrey.
1885 Out of register.

Crew 1862
Master: Patrick Ryan, age 39.Mate: Michael Nevill, 26.Bosun: Francis Larkin, 28.Carpenter: Joseph Kelly, 43.Cook/Steward: John Leary, 40.ABs: John Byrne, 35; Martin Williams, 21; James Sinnott, 20; Moses Murphy, 21; David Samuel, 22; Henry Nelson, 27: Joseph O'Bryan, 26; John ?, 22.Bosun: John Ryan, 34.

Leary, Byrne, Williams and Sinnott, deserted in New York in July 1863. Moses Murphy was hospitalised. Samuel, Nelson, Ryan, O'Bryan and John ?, were taken on in their place.

Previously, in April 1863, James Fanning,a crew member was sentenced to two weeks imprisonment at Malta, for desertion. He was due no wages and in fact was two pounds two shillings and two pence in debt to the ship. Any effects were brought to the store at the Consul Generals Office, to be returned to him on release.

Gaetano Baldachino, a Maltese aged 40, was taken on in his stead.

According to the articles, the Mate, Michael Nevill also deserted on that trip. Another crewman, whose name appears to be William H. Johnstone, was paid off in Malta because of his inability to do his job because of sickness.

Also on that trip were the following men, George Lambert, 32 Wexford; Peter Carty, 21 also Wexford; James Leros, 22 of Malta; Francis Power, 24 Liverpool; William Warren, 24 Plymouth and another 30 year old whose name and country of origin is indecipherable.

There were also two apprentices on board, Robert Ryan, aged 19 (Captains son, perhaps?) and Joseph Codd, age 14.

On October 23rd 1863, Baldachino and Leros paid off in Malta "by mutual consent" and two men were taken on in their place.

Portia signed on at New Ross, on the 9th February 1864, for a voyage to the Black Sea. Her master was Patrick Ryan. She carried a crew of eight including one apprentice, Laurence Murphy.

Nine years later, on 11th of July 1872, **Portia** signed on at Wexford for another voyage to the Black Sea and Galatz. It was to be a fairly eventful trip.

Crew 1872
Master, Martin Dunne, Mate, John Murphy, 29,Bosun,Thomas Smith, 22, ABs,George Murphy,32;John White,22;James Clancy,23;William Roach,26;Richard Carley, 22;James Johnson,37.Boy, William Walsh, 16.

On September 11th William Roach was brought before the magistrates at Malta for refusing to do his work on board ship. A substitute was brought on in his place.There was no notification of the magistrates decision.White,Clancy and Carley deserted, or "jumped ship" at Malta and Joseph Irvin, Lewis Smith, James Johnson and William Walsh were discharged. Irvin and Smith by mutual consent and Johnson and Walsh by reason of sickness. It is not apparent when the former two joined the ship but the latter two were on board since the voyage commenced. Isabella Mizzi, Angelo Blasinich, Giuseppi? And Paolo Cassan all from from Malta signed on September13th and another man, James A.Southerland from Bombay signed on October 12th at Constantinople. Paolo Cassan's time on the **Portia** was short lived as, on the 5th of October he was drowned at sea.He was furling the main top gallant sail when he fell overboard from the yard. Then on October 12th Southerland was discharged at Sulina on the grounds of sickness. Miles Codd, a Wexford man whose last ship was the **Saltee** then joined at Sulina, as AB.

PRINCE ALBERT
1841 Built at Wexford, carvel built, 133 tons.

On March 3rd 1841, a Saturday morning at 8.30, the schooner **Prince Albert** was launched from the yard of Edward Hingston, Wexford. She was built with timber from the woods of Newtownbarry (Bunclody).
1841 Owners Richard Devereux of Wexford and Patrick Breen of Castlebridge, Co. Wexford. David Roche was master.

The vessel was said to be most pleasing to the eye, with an elegant bust figurehead and 'other appropriate decorations'. It was also said to be the second of a number of vessels which were to be built at Mr Hingston's yard for Devereux and Breen. Hingston's yard was situated on the site of the present day Church Lane Car Park.

PRINCESS
Number 15119. Code LQWT.

1841 Built at Wexford. A carvel built schooner of 67 tons, with a female figurehead.
1865 Owner R. Devereux of Wexford.
1875 John T. Devereux of Wexford.
1885 Patrick Ryan of Wexford. Master, Laurence Butler.
1887 Out of register.
Crew 1845
Master: Laurence Butler, age 51: James Williams, 34.Mariner: James Hayes, 23; John Duggan, 17; Nicholas Butler, 18.Apprentice: James Finn, 21.

Crew 1870
Master, Thomas Neill, age 47; Boy: Michael Connolly, 15.Master: John Neill, The Faythe, Mate: John Breen, 52.AB: Michael Hamilton, 19.OS: Nicholas Bent, 18.Boy: Nicholas Breen, 14.

The Wexford registered schooner **Princess,** left Milford Haven on the 30th April 1885, under the command of Captain Daniel Barlow, with coal for Dublin. Shortly after leaving, she was "spoken" by another Wexford schooner but was never seen again. About three months later, a decomposed body was washed up near Courtown Harbour, Co. Wexford. This was identified as that of Captain Barlow. The identification was made by a watch on the body with Captain Barlow's name inscribed on it. The remains were interred in Courtown, as they were considered too badly decomposed to be transported to Wexford.

PRINCESS LOUISE
Number 63862. Code KLQF.

1871 Built at Perth, a 58 ton wooden schooner. Dimensions 71.7x19.9x9.5ft.
1880 Owner Joseph Hunter of Barrow.
1889 Alexander Gordon of Annalong, Co. Down.
1904-1924 Alexander Purdy, Annalong, Co. Down.
1924 Captain George Murphy, The Faythe, Wexford.

April 19th 1924.
Six Hours Struggle Against Waves and Storm
Three Wexford town sailors diced with what looked like certain death, when their schooner **Princess Louise** ran into a terrific storm, after leaving Cardiff, bound for their home port.

They were Captain George Murphy of the Faythe and Maudlintown men: Patrick Murphy and Thomas Smith.

Describing their experience, Captain Murphy told how the vessel had left Cardiff on the Friday afternoon, when a ferocious gale blew up forcing them to turn back at The Nash to seek refuge in Cardiff Roads, where he dropped anchor. The gale strengthened throughout the night and the vessel began to drag both her anchors, driving her towards Cardiff Sands. Despite valiant efforts by the three men, she became fast on the bank, turning their already dangerous situation into a perilous one.

When the tide turned, they saw that the vessel's sides had been strained and in addition to the seas breaking over her, they now had to contend with the inrush of water below decks. It was shortly after one o'clock, when the crew took to the pumps and they continued pumping away until eight o'clock.

- Captain George Murphy, Owner/Master of the **Princess Louise**
Courtesy of Veronica Murphy Mazzola of Florida USA.

Soundings were being taken at intervals and showed that despite regular pumping, the volume of water in the holds was increasing, leaving Captain Murphy with only one alternative, and that was to take to the boat. By then the ship was beginning to break up and the exhausted crew had great difficulty in getting the small boat away safely. In fact it took them fifteen minutes to get clear, just as their ship broke up. A tug boat came to their aid and brought the thoroughly exhausted men into Cardiff, where they received aid and a change of clothing before leaving for home.

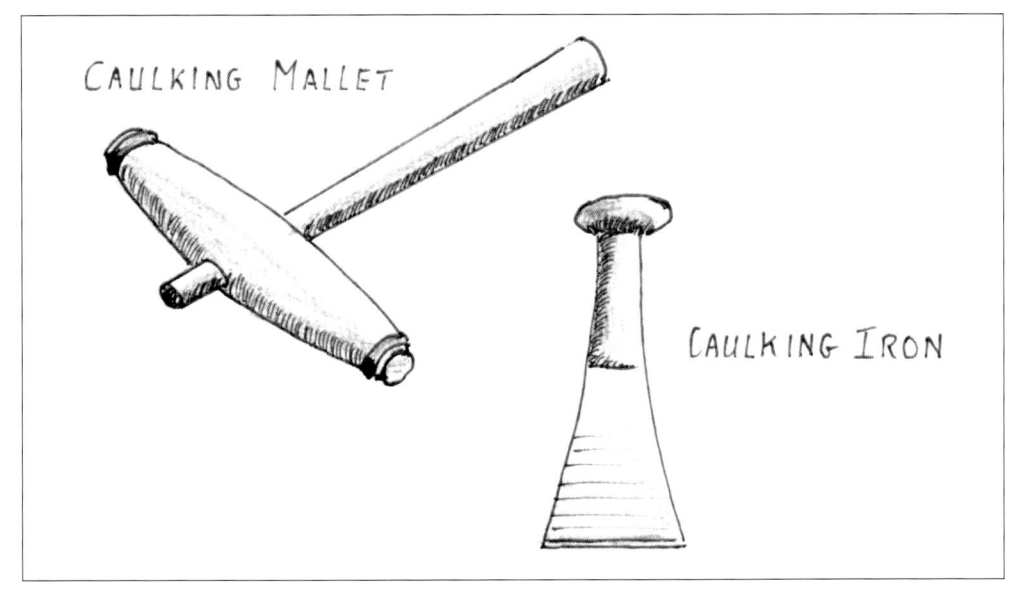

Courtown Harbour with two schooners and a dredger anchored off.
The National Library of Ireland.

Courtown Harbour.
The National Library of Ireland.

Wexford Dockyard c1890.

The **Feodora**, a sailing yacht, owned by Pettigrew of Wexford.
Jack O'Leary Collection.

Wexford Harbour Regatta, 1890s.
Jack O'Leary Collection.

Loading a sailing ship at New Ross, by tipping cargo from a rail wagon, c1900.
National Library of Ireland.

The Newport, Monmouthshire schooner **Gleaner** at anchor in the river at New Ross, with two fishing smacks tied up alongside. Late 1890s.
National Library of Ireland.

Captain Thomas "Lanigan" Walsh, master of the **Rambler** and many other Wexford schooners.
Courtesy the late Liam Walsh of Wexford.

Sale notice for the **Ranger** by auction, dated March 1868.
Wexford People.

Schooner **Ranger**, sale notice, April 1868.
Wexford People

236

R

RAMBLER

Number 15138. Code LRCF.

1822 Built at St. Martin's, New Brunswick, a schooner of 49 tons.
1835-1844 Registered at Wexford.
1865 Owner Rev. George Whitty, Castlebridge, Co. Wexford.
1876 Patrick Lambert of Wexford.
1876 Nicholas White, Kilmore Quay, Co. Wexford.
1882 Out of register.

Crew 1835
Master: Thomas Wickham, 25.Mate; James Keating, 30.Seaman; Gerald Harding, 35; Patrick Rowe, 30.Boy; Nicholas Bawn, 18; Michael Bent, 15.

Crew 1870
Master: Owen Carty, 35.Mate; David Morris, 40.AB; Pat Rossiter, 25.Boy; Thomas Murphy, 16.Seaman; John Walsh, 30.OS; Thomas Roche, 20.

Rambler left Llanelli on the 15th January 1881, with coal for O'Keefe of Wexford. She met bad weather near Tuskar Rock. Captain Thomas Walsh was in command.
On Monday the 17th they spoke **Clara & Jessie,** who was also bound for Wexford. They concluded that they could not make Waterford Harbour for shelter, so they both made for the South Bay off Wexford. They both came to anchor at 9 am in a SExE wind.
On Tuesday at mid-day, the weather was stormy and the **Rambler's** starboard anchor chain broke. With the weather changing to ExS, she began to drag and hove into two and a quarter fathoms of water. They slipped the cables and hoisted the standing jib and she wore round before the wind. At 2 pm the **Rambler** struck and the seas continuously broke over her. The crew were taken off by the Coastguard Rocket Apparatus. Evidently the **Rambler** was refloated.

In March 1875, the **Rambler** was abandoned in a gale off the Welsh coast. The crew were picked up the next day and brought into Llanelli.

RANGER

Number 21414. Code NGFP.

1843 Built at Prince Edward Island, a carvel built schooner of 71 tons. Billet head Dimensions 64x17x9ft.

1843 Registered at Wexford. Master: Patrick Marley. Owner Denis Kenselagh.
1861 On 20th November, Kenselagh died, his shares went to Catherine Cosgrove.

1868 15th May, to Patrick Devereux, Jasper Walsh, Nicholas Fanning, and R.D. Crean.
1874 Owner J.T. Devereux, Wexford.
1888 Out of register,

Crew 1864(January)
Master: John Murphy, age 48.Mate: James Murphy, 60.Seaman: Patrick Green, 35; Denis Devereux, 30; Rowland Crane, 21; John Marley, 28; Thomas Wadding, 28; Martin Murphy, 20.

Crew 1864(July)
Master: John Murphy, 48.Mate: John Martin, 38.Seamen: John Breen, 40; Lambert, 21.Boy: William Connolly, 18.

RANGATIRA

Number 59221.

1869 Built at St. Martin's, New Brunswick, a schooner of 107 tons. Dimensions 85.3x25.3x7.7 ft.
1869 Owner William Henry Rourke of St Martin's, New Brunswick.
1872 Hy. Weston Wilson of St John, New Brunswick.
1879 William J. Gafney of Wexford.
1885 Miss Margaret Gafney of Commercial Quay, Wexford.
1889 George Harry, M.M. and Ed. Nichols, both of Penzance, Cornwall
1889 On 11th July, Henry James Bennett of Penzance, Cornwall, became the sole owner.
1889 She was broken up on 18th. October.

At a meeting of Wexford Harbour Commissioners, held at the Ballast Office in April1878, a letter was read from the Board of Trade, stating that they had received a communication from the Receiver of Wrecks, Wexford concerning the stranding of the **Rangatira**, on the Dogger Bank. The stranding happened on the 9th of the previous month and had been attributed to the fault of the pilot in charge of the vessel at that time. The Board requested the Commissioners to take whatever steps they considered correct and to inform them of their decision.

Apparently on the morning in question, the **Rangatira**, under the charge of Pilot Breen, took the ESE Bar and immediately struck and drifted onto the Dogger Bank. She remained there until the 17th. The vessel only got off the

Rangatira, a two masted tops'l schooner of 107 tons, built, 1869 at New Brunswick. Note heavily patched sails.

238

Two Wexford schooners, **Rangatira** and **Caledonia** alongside at Wexford.

bank by having the greater part of her cargo thrown over the side. Even then she had to be assisted by the steam tugs, **Erin** and **Ruby**.

At the time of the grounding, **Rangatira** was drawing 9 ft 6 ins of water and there was 10 ft 4 ins on the Bar.

Pilot Breen gave evidence stating that the vessel had the proper marks when she struck. She took the ground in the "hollow" of a sea. When she struck her head "fell off ", she lost way and became unmanageable.

The Commissioners having fully investigated the case instructed the secretary to inform the Board of Trade that they had failed to find any lack of caution on the pilot's part and therefore no blame could be attached to him.

RAPID

Number 10156. Code KMHB.

1856 Built at St. John, New Brunswick, a brigantine of 142 tons.
Dimensions 90.7x22.9x11.6ft.
1865-1891 Owner Allens, Custom House Quay, Wexford.

Crew
 Master: Michael Murphy, born 1852.Mate: Edward Dwyer, 1856.ABs: Andrew Sinnott, 1853; Michael Cullen, 1864; Jas Sinnott; Thos. Leary.OS, Bernard Pender, 1874; Bernard Lacey, 1871; George Murphy.Mate: Jas. Atkinson, 1860.
On the Galatz run c1870, Captain Patrick Kelly.

Crew 1862
Master; Thomas Cooney, 34.Mate; Thomas Marlow.AB; John Moran, 25; Patk. Fitzgibbon, 24; Thomas Parr, 26;William Wallace, 22; William Wallace, 32.OS; Charles Lambon, 20; Edward O'Brien, 17.

In October 1862, the **Rapid** was at Alicante, where Thomas Parr deserted.
The British Consul inquired into this desertion and finding it true sanctioned the employment of another sailor in his place. The other sailor was a William Wallace, a Liverpool man.

The following January 1863, another crewman, P. Fitzgibbon was paid off by mutual consent. He was paid whatever money was due to him and another sailor was taken on in his place. By a remarkable coincidence, this new hand was also named William Wallace, a 22 year old Glaswegian. Having two men with identical names must have been confusing but any confusion would have been short lived because, on March 18th 1863, Charles Lambon and both William Wallaces were discharged with the Consul's sanction. Guinell, Love and Cummings were signed on in their stead.

The **Rapid** was at Cardiff on Tuesday, July 3rd 1866 when William Jefferes jumped ship. Three weeks later on the 25th, the ship's cook, John Lacy, from Cork was, *Knocked off unable to work with his limbs swelled and no use of his right arm* .He was given a good discharge.

The **Rapid** was at Passage East on March 2nd ,1866 when James Leary was sent home to Wexford,for being sick and unable to continue the voyage.

On June 14th 1876, the **Rapid** was discharging coal at Morriscastle, Co. Wexford, when she broke her moorings and ran ashore at Sinnott's Gap. The situation was seen by a coastguard, who immediately summoned the rocket apparatus. The rocket connected with the ship and they took off the crew. The captain and 1st mate refused to go. At daylight the next morning, they changed their minds and agreed to be taken off. The **Rapid** was re-floated at the first opportunity.

The brigantine **Rapid** was sold in February 1899 to the Congested Districts Board.

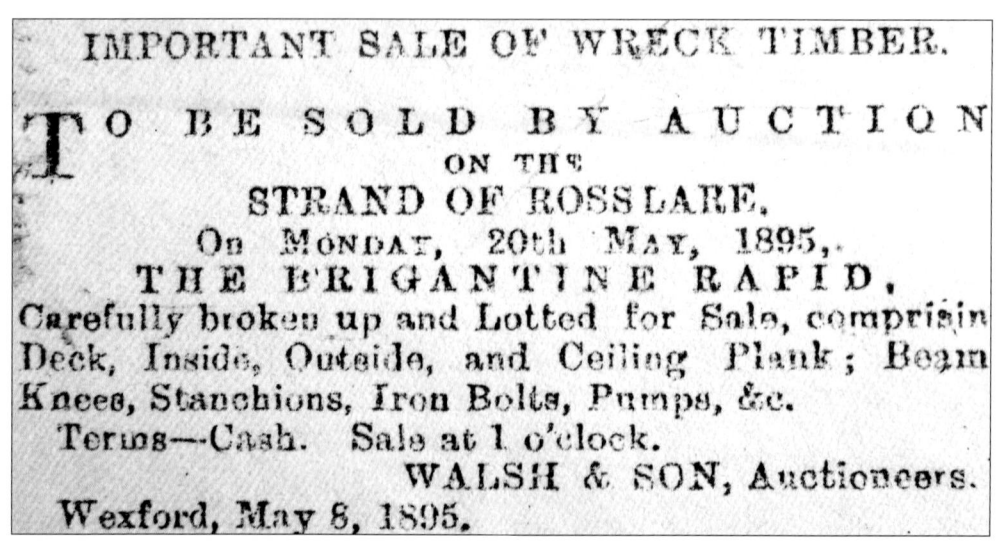

> **IMPORTANT SALE OF WRECK TIMBER.**
> **TO BE SOLD BY AUCTION**
> ON THE
> **STRAND OF ROSSLARE.**
> On MONDAY, 20th MAY, 1895,.
> THE BRIGANTINE RAPID,
> Carefully broken up and Lotted for Sale, comprisin Deck, Inside, Outside, and Ceiling Plank; Beam Knees, Stanchions, Iron Bolts, Pumps, &c.
> Terms—Cash. Sale at 1 o'clock.
> WALSH & SON, Auctioneers.
> Wexford, May 8, 1895.

Rapid, notice of wreck timber sale, May 1895. *Wexford Independent*.

The Wexford Dockyard.
Courtesy, Mr Dave Dempsey, Wexford.

RECRUIT

Number 61483.

1870 Built at Cornwallis, Nova Scotia, a schooner of 131 tons. Dimensions 90x24x8ft.
Owner **1872** Ebenezer Bigelow, Cornwallis, Nova Scotia.
1879 Jasper W. Walsh, Wexford.
1897 Francis J. Walsh, Crescent Quay, Wexford.
1900 Patrick Lambert of Trinity St., Wexford.

1899 In May, the schooner **Recruit** under Captain P. Doyle, made a remarkably fast trip cross channel. She left Wexford on the Tuesday, loaded coal at Llanelli and was back home, tied up at the quay on the following Saturday. She then sailed the following Friday from Wexford to Ayr, a distance of 290 miles, in ballast, and despite bad weather made good time. She unloaded her ballast and loaded a full cargo and was back in Wexford, on the next Friday.

On February 7th 1900, the local press reported that the Wexford schooners **Recruit** and **Jane McColl** collided off the Lucifer Bank Lightship. Both were homeward bound, the former from Newport and the latter from Llanelli, both with coal. The **Recruit** sank. It appears that they had sighted each other at about three o'clock, near the Blackwater Lightship. The collision happened about an hour later. The **Jane McColl** was going with the wind, while the **Recruit** was beating about. The stem of the **Jane McColl** struck the **Recruit,** driving hard into her fore rigging on the starboard side, with great force. They continued to strike against each other for some time until the foremast of the **Recruit** collapsed and fell into the water. It also hit the deck with great force as it fell. The master Captain Doyle realising the danger to himself and his crew, got himself and all hands on board the **Jane McColl** with all haste. Within twenty minutes the **Recruit** had gone down in thirty fathoms of water. The following day the tug **Wexford** visited the site but no traces of the vessel could be found.

The **Recruit** was owned by Patrick Lambert of Trinity Street, Wexford. At that time, the **Jane McColl** was owned by William Armstrong of Wexford.

At the end of August 1900, the Court of Admiralty, Dublin heard a case for compensation brought by Patrick Lambert, Coal Merchant of Trinity St., Wexford, against Mr Samuel Armstrong of Wexford, for the loss of his vessel **Recruit** due to a collision with Armstrong's vessel, **Jane McColl.** Captain Edward Doyle of the **Recruit** and his crew were examined and described how the collision had occurred.

According to their evidence, the **Recruit** was on a starboard tack, while the **Jane McColl** was on a port tack. They maintained that according to the rules of the road at sea, it was the duty of the **Jane McColl** to keep clear of their vessel. A man named Jeremiah Corbett, a barber by trade, who had joined the **Jane McColl** as a passenger at Newport was then examined, as a witness for the plaintiffs. He told the Court that at the time of the collision the captain of the **Jane McColl** was down below in his cabin.

In their defence Captain Walsh and his crew of the **Jane McColl** told the Court that the **Recruit** had altered her course so suddenly that it was impossible for them to avoid her. However, after weighing up all the evidence, it was held that the **Jane McColl** was entirely to blame for the collision. The damages were to be assessed by the court the following November.

Recruit, a two masted tops'l schooner, of 131 tons. Built, 1870 at Nova Scotia. Seen here approaching Tuskar Rock Lighthouse.

RELIANCE

Number 49503.

1865 Built at Perth, a schooner of 86 tons. Dimensions 80.3x20.6x10.6ft.
1867-1876 Owner John Codd, Oyster Lane, Wexford.
1885 Wm. Coghlan of Wexford.
1888 Patrick Ryan, South Main St., Wexford.
1891 Thos. Hutchinson of Wexford. First Wexford Mutual Marine Association Ltd.

Crew 1891
Master: Thomas Hutchinson, 31.Mate: Paul Murphy, 40.ABs: John Rossiter, 28; John Blake, 26; Thomas Brien, 24.OS: Thomas Murphy, 20.

On October 9th 1889 Welsh newspapers told of a dismasted schooner seen in trouble in Newport Bay some three miles off the land, near Carregdydriod, two days previously. It turned out to be the **Reliance** of Wexford, Captain Hutchinson in command, bound from Wexford to Newport, Monmouthshire, in ballast. The Newport lifeboat, **Clevedon** was called out immediately but due to the low tides her services were not available until some hours later. When she did arrive at the casualty, according to the newspaper report, the mate of the **Reliance** misjudged the closeness of the lifeboat and jumped into the sea to get on board it but drowned in the attempt. However, according to the local Wexford papers, the mate, James Breen was lost from the **Reliance** when he was working on the jiboom and was washed overboard when a big sea engulfed the ship.The vessel had both of her masts blown away and was in serious trouble. The **Clevedon** got alongside and brought the remainder of the crew of safely, but they were unable to return to Newport and the gale drove them into Cardigan Bay. The crew then headed for Cardigan and landed at St. Dogmael's Coast Guard Staion, where Mr Buchan the chief officer of the coastguard treated both crews hospitably and supplied them with dry clothes and food.

The **Reliance** was so badly damaged that she had to be towed back to Wexford, by a Welsh steam tug. They brought her to the Bar where the local tug **Wexford** took over and brought her into the harbour and up the river where she went to anchor.

In March 1902, **Reliance** was lost off Angle, near Milford Haven. She was bound from Cardiff to Wexford with coal. She was at anchor when she was run down by the Milford trawler **Othonia**. There was no time to launch the boats but, it wasn't necessary, as the crew were able to just step on to the deck of the trawler.

RIPPLE

Number 10159. Code KMHF.

1856 Built at New Brunswick, a brig of 143 tons. Dimensions 91.7.x22.1x11.5ft.
1865-1870 Owner R.&R. Allen of Wexford.

Crew 1856
Master: Patrick Kelly.
Mate: John Neil,
Cook/Steward: William Murphy.
ABs: Patrick Rossiter; Patrick Fortune. Two apprentices, Lynch and Jackson also signed on.

Crew 1870
Master, Sam Jeffares, 37, certificate number, 23922.
Mate, John Morris, 22.
Cook/Steward, John Lambert, 30.
Abs, John Fortune, 43; James Smith, 23; James Redmond, 30.
OS, Joseph Morris, 19.

24th May 1869 Thomas Cullen was entered in the official log book for refusing an order of the master to rig out the top mast studding sail boom. Being logged normally resulted in a monetary fine but there is no indication to what Cullen's punishment was.

On the 16th January 1870, the **Ripple,** under Captain Samuel Jeffares, hit a submerged rock near Tuskar, at about 3 am and was lost. She was homeward bound from Ibrail, on the Danube, with a cargo of Indian corn.

She left Ibrail on November 4th 1869 and reached the Wexford coast in good though hazy weather. At 3 am on January the 16th she struck the rock known as the Mahoon, the scene of many a shipwreck. The captain and crew abandoned the ship straight away, thinking that she would immediately break up. The exhausted crew arrived at Wexford at 3 pm after rowing the whole way. All they had was the clothes they were wearing. She had left Constantinople on the 19th November 1869. She met bad weather and as a result was taking some water but nevertheless made Ballycotton on the 14th January. On the 16th they sighted Carnsore Point and set a course for Wexford. Due to the weather, they were unable to fetch the Bay but were kept away to the north of the Tuskar. That evening they spoke the Lucifer Light Vessel. The ship then wore and stood away to the southward. The captain instructed the mate to have him called when Tuskar was bearing SSW and he went below. Owing to dense fog, at 1.30 the light was obscured and at 3.30 breakers were seen ahead. The helm was put hard up but due to the stillness of the breeze the vessel would not obey the helm. Shortly after the Tuskar light was seen, almost overhead and the **Ripple** was dashed against the rock. The crew took to the jolly boat and rowed around for a while to see if it was possible to get back on board, to rescue their effects but it was not possible, so they struck out for Wexford. Later the captain put the loss down to the fog bell on Tuskar not being used. The cost of the loss was put at 2,000 pounds. The cargo was insured but the vessel was not. All hands were officially signed off at Wexford on the 29th of January 1870.

ROSSLARE

Number 35477. Code KPTC.

1864 Built at New Brunswick, a barque of 386 tons. Dimensions 132.2x27.7x15.5ft.
1865 Owner J.J. Walsh of Wexford.
1867-1879 J. Coghlan, MD, Main St., Wexford.
1879 William Coghlan, Wexford.
1882 Out of register.

On December 8th 1874, the **Rosslare** was leaving Amsterdam under tow from the steam tug **Harlem** when a steamer, the **Bereniece** ran into her causing her considerable damage. The steamer ran into the port bow and carried away all the upper works, with the cathead and forecastle decks and five planks below the covering board, the stanchion top rail and all the iron work attached.

In March 31st 1876 Martin Byrne, a long serving Mate under Captain English, was recorded by H.M. superintendant at Hull to have died on the 27th of that month of congestion of the lungs. He was 34 years old.

In March 1877, the **Rosslare** arrived in the South Bay from Darien, Georgia, USA, with a cargo of pitch pine for the yards of J.W. Walsh. Her commander, Captain English, reported a fast passage of 37 days, during which they ran into a fierce gale, before clearing the American coast. On passage they fell in with the barque **C.P. D.** of Fleetwood, who were short of provisions and were able to assist them. Other than that, the trip was uneventful. Almost two years later, on February 6th 1879, the **Rosslare** arrived in the Bay, after what was described as "a very long and severe voyage" but nonetheless she sustained no damage.

On November 21st 1877 she signed on for a voyage described as *Wexford to Cardiff thence to Kingston, Jamaica in the West of India Islands or to any port in the continent of Europe between Le Havre and Hamburg or within the Baltic or Meditereann (Black Sea inclusive) and back to a final port of discharge in the United Kingdom.Probable duration of the entire voyage not excceding eighteen months.*

The crew on that occasion were,
Laurence English, Master, certificate number 74934.
Patrick Walsh, 35, Mate, certificate number, 23582.
ABs, Joseph Carberry, 54;John McClean,20;Samuel Gaul,30;Robert Furlong, 22;James Murphy,24;Aidan Cogley,19.
OS, James Moran,16 ;Peter Boyle,17;Richard Scallan,16.
Boy, John English, 11. (This seems to be a remarkably young age for a ship's boy, in the later 19th century .The likeliehood is that he was the captain's son.)
On May 20th 1878 all, except Captain English, paid off at Rotterdam, with the sanction of the British Consul.

With the exception of Joe Carberry, who signed back on, a foreign crew, consisting of 1 man from Jersey and 5 from Rotterdam then joined the **Rosslare**.

Seen here passing the Anatole Hissar Fort, at the entrance to the Bosphorus en-route to Galatz is the Wexford three masted barque **Rosslare**, c1860s.

ROVER

Number 21432. Code NGHS.

1840 Built at Barnstaple, a schooner of 65 tons. Dimensions 74.1x18.7x9.5ft.
1865 Owner R. Devereux, Wexford.
1875 J.T. Devereux, Wexford.
1883 John Codd, Wexford.

In December 1866, the **Rover**, under Captain James Murphy, broke away from her moorings in Tenby Roads, during a storm, and was lost at Baglan Point. She was from Saundersfoot to Wexford. Captain Murphy and his crew; M. Rowe; John Rowe and Joseph Brien, were all saved.

ROYAL VISITOR

Number 42249.

1860 Built at New Brunswick, a barque of 339 tons,
1861/1862 Registered at Wexford.
Managing owner, Richard Devereux, North Main St., Wexford.

Crew 1862
Master: Thomas Hull, 45.
Mate: Andrew Rossiter, 39.
Bosun: Edward Murphy, 36.
Cook: William Stafford*.
ABs: Richard Murphy, 20; William Gladwin, 38; Nicholas Murphy, 24; Thomas Doyle, 21; Edward Blake*, 20; William Sinnott *.
Boy: Peter Corish. 19.
Apprentice: James Murphy.
* These men were reported to have deserted in New York on the 16th December 1862, and there is no indication that they ever came back onboard before sailing. All the others were lost on passage home from New York in 1862.

On the 10th October 1862, the crew mentioned above, signed on at New Ross, for a voyage designated as *From New Ross in Ireland to New York, Baltimore or any other part or parts in the United States of America or Canada and back to a final port of in the United Kingdom or Continent, the period not to exceed twelve months,*

This was commonly known as Twelve Months Articles. The **Royal Visitor** arrived at New York on the 16th December 1862, and it seems that Richard Murphy, Stafford, Blake and Sinnott 'jumped ship' almost straight away.

Deserting or ' jumping ship' was not an uncommon event in those days, nor was it uncommon right up to the 1950s and '60s. The reasons for jumping ship were many and varied; a spirit of adventure; the other man's grass was always greener; drink; getting and staying so drunk in one of the many drinking houses or houses of ill repute. These places abounded in the "Sailortowns" near the docks, all over the world. Another hazard was having his drink 'spiked ' by an unscrupulous boarding master and waking up on another ship bound out for God knows where.

A whole book could be written about boarding masters and the 'services' they supplied to the sailorman. Generally he was not the sailor's friend. There were a few good ones, but they were in the minority. There were also the horribly bad conditions which a sailor had to endure. Including rotten food, miserable wet quarters and in many cases discipline bordering on sadism. Whatever the reason, these men jumped and fortunately for them, there is no record of any of them returning before sailing.

According to the law, three men were taken on in the place of the deserters but there is no reference to them on the articles.

On Wednesday January 7th 1863, the **Royal Visitor** arrived at Baltimore and sailed from there on the 9th. On January 23rd the Cork Examiner picked up a report from the Baltimore Sun, that the **Royal Visitor,** ex New York for Wexford, was in distress. She was reported as passing Sandy Hook, where she met a severe gale. There does not appear to have been any mention in the local press, until nearly two months later. On April 18th 1863, the Wexford Independent carried the following:-

*The anxious fears created by the non-arrival of the barque **Royal Visitor** of this port, the property of the Messrs. Devereux, and the painful suspense induced by her continued absence, are fast giving way to what, we fear, may be with too much justice called, well ground despair.*

*Though it is painful to have to write it, yet, we fear, that she may have met the same melancholy fate as the **Ocean Spray**. The **Royal Visitor**, under Captain Hull, with twelve hands on board, left Baltimore with wheat on the 12th of February, for Wexford, and has not since been heard of. Even should the vessel be still afloat, the relatives of these men are subjects for our compassion, but should she be lost, they deserve our profoundest sympathy. Compared with the loss of life and the misery it entails, the mere mercantile loss sinks into insignificance. We are happy to find that Messrs. Devereux intend replacing these two fine vessels and that already a fine barque, the **Enterprise**, of 650 tons, has been added to their already numerous fleet. This firm employs nearly 200 seamen, on the home and foreign trade, which necessarily circulate a large amount of money through the town. It is therefore most satisfactory to find that their enterprise has not been abated by these two sad disasters.*

And that was it. As far as can be ascertained, the **Royal Visitor** was never mentioned again.

S

SALTEE
Number 49501. Code WDHB.

1863 Built at Weymouth, Nova Scotia. She was a barque of 285 tons with 3 masts and a scroll figurehead. Dimensions: 114x26.4x14.9ft.

OWNERS
1864 R.&R. Allen, Wexford.
1870 R. Devereux, Wexford.
1870-1884 Jasper Walsh and Patrick Lambert; Manager, Robert Sparrow, 41 North Main St., Wexford; Captain John Smith.

CREWS
1863
This appears to be her delivery crew to Allens.
Master: John Kelly (St. Patrick's Square, Wexford).
Mate: S. Bell, 56 (From Dundee).
Cook/Steward: A. Lunn, 19 (St. John's).
Seamen: W. Moor, 25; E. Murray, 27; S. Booth, 20; S. Devine, 32; T. Coward, 50; C. Duff, 48; P. Redmond, 23.

Date unknown
Master: John Devereux, Fisher's Row, Wexford, 47.
Mate: Laurence Devereux, 54; Henry Dollis, 58.
OS: Pat Parle, 17; James Lambert, 48.
ABs: George McGrath, 38; Stephen Larkin, 20; Martin Lane, 23; John Furlong, 18; Stephen Crosbie, 21; John Walsh, 23.

1878
Master: Joe Codd.
Mate: Dick Bent.
2nd Mate: Paul Murphy.
Cook: Zakariah 'Akey' Quinton, Cook.
ABs: John Cullen, John Hutchinson, Moses Boggan, Patrick Kelly, Tommy Luccan.
Boy: Joe Hopkins.

1888 (Final voyage)
Master: Captain John Smith.
Chief Officer: Richard Bent.
Cook: William Hesse
Bosun: Nicholas Saunders.
ABs: Andy Sinnott; Jack Cassidy; Jack Hagen; Henry Ryan.
OS: Laurence Smith (Captain's son).

The **Saltee** was one of the fine sailing vessels on the Galatz grain trade. When that trade ceased **Saltee** and other vessels were modified, for the timber trade to Canada's Maritime Provinces.

At Christmas time 1868, the **Saltee** was at Sulina and according to the log book a boisterous time was had by some of the crew. Three ABs were logged for being ashore without leave and fighting when they did arrive back on board. Earlier, in Malta on 25 December, the Bosun, John McGrath had to be left behind in hospital with a badly injured leg. There is no indication how this happened. The log just said that he was ashore and got his leg *badly hurted*. He was paid off and Henry Radford, AB was taken on in his place.

On the 14 August 1878, the **Saltee** left Wexford Harbour, for a voyage to Cardiff and then on to Galatz. They arrived at Cardiff, where the **Saltee's** masts were condemned and a new set had to be purchased and installed. To facilitate this operation, the cargo had to be discharged. Eventually they got away on a voyage that was to take ten months. On the return trip, before they reached the Dardanelles, the cargo of grain had shifted and the pumps were choked up. They put into a small side harbour, where they had to remain for three weeks. During that time the cargo had to be removed yet again and loaded into lighters. When everything was sorted out, they were allowed to proceed on their way home. When they were out in the open sea, an Austrian barque drifted across their bows, taking the jib boom away with her. A new jib was rigged up from a spare spar and the next day they set sail for their destination, New Ross, Co. Wexford. There all hands, with the exception of the boy, Joe Hopkins, paid off and went home.

Nicholas Murphy who served on the Wexford barque **Saltee.**
Courtesy of Eithne Martin, Wexford.

The **Saltee's** crew on that trip were all seasoned sailors, with the exception of the Boy, Joe Hopkins. This was his first full trip to sea. He had previously run away to sea, and had joined the Norwegian ship **Telefon** at Liverpool but had been taken off her in Cardiff by relatives and sent home. He was an apprentice printer at the time on the *Wexford Independent* and was soon back at his job. However, his guardian realised that he was not happy and, after much discussion, it was decided to let him go to sea again. So, on 14 August 1878, he signed on at Wexford. Joe Hopkins went on to an adventurous career at sea and eventually ended up living in Australia, where he resumed his apprenticeship and finally became a qualified printer. At least two of that crew, Moses Boggan and Tommy Luccan went on to become masters. While still an AB, Luccan went on to join the **Hantoon** and was onboard when she was lost in the Bay of Biscay. The **Saltee's** trip concluded on 24 March 1879, at New Ross, Co. Wexford.

The **Saltee** left Wexford on the 31 January 1884 for Cardiff, to load coal for Cadiz, Spain. It took them three weeks to battle their way across a stormy Bay of Biscay but they arrived intact. At Cadiz, they loaded salt for St John's, Newfoundland and had a pleasant trip until they came to the Grand Banks. There they ran into a severe gale and lost one of their boats and had others damaged. Three days later they arrived at St John's and were greeted by many Wexford men, including the Goodall brothers, who were related to the family that lived in William Street House. After a few weeks of being treated royally by the Wexford exiles, they set sail for a small Canadian port in the Gulf of St Lawrence called Sault-au-Cochin where they loaded timber for Wexford. After another pleasant voyage lasting 25 days, the **Saltee** arrived at Wexford on 31 August 1884.

Eleven days later, she sailed once again, first to Cardiff to load coals for St Vincent in the Cape Verde Islands. St Vincent was one of the coaling stations, where steamers called for 'bunkers', ie, coal to fuel their engines. At the time there were no docks and the coal had to be loaded into lighters. Unloading 400 tons of coal into lighters, under a gruelling hot sun, was not an easy task. One of the problems the **Saltee** encountered there, was pilfering of cargo by native boys. Their tactic was for two of them to start a fight. While the sailors were watching, the rest of them would roll the larger pieces of coal over the side into the water, to be recovered once the ship had sailed. Once the first fight had ended, another one would commence and more coal would be rolled over the side. This, of course, fooled no one and the antics of the pilferers, provided the sailors with some amusement.

Once the cargo was discharged, the crew then took on about 150 tons of ballast from a lighter and set out from St Vincent to Appalachicola, Florida, in the Gulf of Mexico. Again, on the outward bound trip, they met fine weather and had a mostly uneventful trip. However, one night, off the West Indies, the watch below were woken by a voice roaring out *All hands on deck to shorten sail, quick!* The men jumped out of their bunks and ran up on deck to be greeted by the worst weather many of them had ever experienced. The thunder roared, the winds shrieked and lightening flashed all around the ship and she was lying almost on her beam ends. The pieces of the two upper top sails and the main sail were completely lost.

All hands sprung into action and after two and a half hours of gruelling, hard and dangerous work, under very trying conditions, everything was safely secured and the men fell exhausted into their bunks. The watch was called again after an hour and all hands were back on deck. They reached Appalachicola without further incident. They loaded a cargo of pitch-pine and sailed for home on the 25 February 1885. On 1 March, the **Saltee** struck a coral reef in the Gulf Stream and was almost lost but got off and then for the next 30 days battled through one heavy gale after another, which drove them sideways across the Atlantic. One Sunday about half way over, they lost 23 stanchions and the bulwarks were smashed in on the deck. The boat davits swung in and pierced the aft hatch and the cabin skylights. The rudder head was sprung which left her unmanageable and more 'like a raft than a vessel'.

The crew worked hard all that day and into the night, trying to keep the water out and the masts in place by nailing canvas over the holes and rigging spars for bulwarks and coiling spare sails around the hatches and bandaging the rudder head. About a week later, she looked so bad that a passing steamer spoke the **Saltee** and asked if they wanted to abandon her. They decided to stay and they eventually reached Wexford Bay, bruised and battered but not broken. The **Saltee** arrived on 4 April 1885, after a hard 38-day battle across the Atlantic Ocean.

The Wexford barque **Saltee**, built in 1864 at Nova Scotia, is depicted here in the process of being manually "warped" up the River Danube en-route to Galatz to load grain for Wexford.

Galatz, c late 1850s.

The **Saltee's** final voyage began of 12 September 1887. They signed on at Anne St. Customs House, Wexford and left for Cardiff in ballast. At Cardiff, they unloaded the ballast and loaded 466 tons of coal for St. Thomas in the West Indies. After departing Cardiff on 24 September, they met rough weather and head winds for the first half of the trip but once they were south of Madeira, they got into the North-East trade winds and the rest of the trip was pleasant enough. They berthed in St Thomas on 19 November, 58 days out of Cardiff. For some reason, probably to save expense, the crew had to discharge the cargo themselves. With the stifling hot weather, working under the hot tropical sun and still eating the same old ship's fare, one by one the crew came down with fever. Because so many of the men were sick, a job which would have taken local stevedores two or three days, took three weeks. In the end, locals had to be employed to complete the job anyway.

When the coal was out, they took on ballast and set out for Brunswick, Georgia, USA. She arrived there on 27 December. Once the ballast was cleared, pitch pine logs were loaded for Wexford. On 2 February 1888, the **Saltee** set sail for home. She met the Western trades and after a good trip of 42 days' duration, arrived in Wexford Bay on 13 March. Her master, Captain John Smith signalled for a pilot to take her into the harbour, and at noon the same day, Pilot Robert Breen boarded her. She then proceeded into the south bay, where she went to anchor. At this stage she was drawing 13 ft 5 ins aft and 12 ft 3 ins for'ard. It was deemed prudent to lighten her to get her over the Bar. The lighters came, lightened her and she then drew 12 ft 4 ins for'ard and 12 ft 10 ins aft. The next day they signalled for the tug to bring her up. The tug arrived about 6.30, the weather was fair but occasionally squally. The **Saltee** was taken in tow and reached the Bar about 3.30 or 3.40 that afternoon. At the time the signals at the Fort showed that there was 13ft of water at the bar, but in fact there was about 5ft more than was shown.

Arriving at the Bar, the **Saltee** had her fore and aft sails set. About 8.30 pm the squalls hit and it appeared that the tug was unable to keep the ship's head to the marks, and the **Saltee** took to the south side, struck the ground and banked heavily. The tug stayed alongside her for some time, but realising that there was nothing more they could do for her, they left. At 11 pm, 3 ft of water was found in her hold. Signals were made for the lifeboat, which arrived and brought the crew of 9 men ashore. During the night the weather worsened and the **Saltee** was lost.

As is usual under these circumstances, a Board of Trade Inquiry was held into the loss of the **Saltee**. It convened in Wexford Courthouse on 4 May 1888, before Colonel Miller, R.M. and Naval Assessors, Captain Bragg and Captain Washington. Mr Huggard appeared on behalf of The Board of Trade; Mr Elgee for the Harbour Commissioners; Mr Cooper for the captain of the **Saltee**; Mr O'Flaherty, for Lambert and Walsh, the owners, and Mr Taylor on behalf of The Pilots Association of the United Kingdom.

Mr Huggard stated that: *The pilot attributed the loss of the ship to the tug not being able to keep her head to the marks owing to the squall coming on, whereas the master of the **Saltee** attributed it to not being able to keep her in the fairway. But the tug master said there was no want of power on the part of the tug. There were 11 pilots and a boy at the fort and they were assisted by 4 harbour pilots who take vessels down the harbour. On account of the Bar constantly shifting after storms, Captain Cogley, Pilot Master takes soundings and he will explain how this is done.* (Captain Cogley was not in charge at the time of the incident with the Saltee)

In addition to the signals mentioned there is a danger signal but the pilots are left to exercise their own judgement when this is up. The high water is the same here as Llanelli, unless there is a SSW or E wind when it is a little longer. On this day the signals were in charge of Captain Cogley's son, a boy of 16, but Captain Cogley said he was perfectly competent to undertake the duties, and that he was often in charge of them before.

Another view of the Port of Galatz.

The cause of Captain Cogley's absence was that he was sent by the Harbour Commissioners to South Shields to bring over the new tug **Wexford**. Two pilots were away onboard vessels, 1 sick which left only 6 on station. He would offer the master of the **Montague** steamer as a witness in order to depose as to the state of the sea; and to give his observations as to the **Saltee** and her chance of getting over the Bar at the time; also Pilot Brady, who was in charge of the Pilot Station, and Mr Briggs, a Customs Officer that was on board. It was ordered that all witnesses, unless holding Board of Trade Certs should leave the court.

Mr James Stafford, examined by Mr Huggard said he was acting as manager of the **Saltee**; she was not insured, her cargo was insured for £425 and her freight for £163. In his evidence Captain John Smith told the court that he was the master of the **Saltee**, and that she had a registered tonnage of 265 tons. He said that she left Brunswick on 1 February 1888, at about 10.30 in the morning with 9 hands onboard, and with a cargo of pitch pine for Wexford. They arrived off Wexford at about 8.10 am on 14 March. Pilot Robert Breen boarded and brought the ship into the South Bay. He then gave details of the amount of water she drew. He further stated that the pilot gave him no directions but said that he wanted her lightened before she went in. They got her ready for lightening and next morning proceeded to lighten her. Lightening was completed by about 4 or 5 that evening.

He told the court that he was a native of Wexford but had not sailed out of the port for some time and that he had shipped out of Cardiff. He was of the opinion that the tug master was doing his best and that if he himself had been in charge of the vessel without a pilot he would not have attempted to have brought her in. But the pilot was in charge of the ship and that if he thought that there was anything wrong he would have taken charge from him.

Robert Breen, the pilot who had charge of the **Saltee** attributed the loss to the tug not being able to keep her head to the marks, owing to the squall coming on. He said that the vessel was steered by his directions and that it was no part of the master's duty to interfere with this unless he saw something wrong. *I blame the squall for the casualty. Vessels come in with from 6 to 10 ins less than their draft when water is smooth.* He said he calculated by the Manx Almanac that the vessel was too deep for'ard to come into the harbour without being lightened. He also maintained that it was not usual for a ship to draw more water for'ard than aft. It was usual for a large vessel to strike as she comes over the Bar. He did not mention this to Captain Smith as it was not the practice to tell Wexford masters, as they already knew this.

The inquiry found that the wreck was caused by trying to get over the Bar on a falling tide and with insufficient draft. They were unable to state, from the evidence given, that the tide gauge at the station correctly registered the water on the Bar. The sea was moderate at the Bar that morning, wind blowing NNE to NE, with a squall and a moderate sea, but rising. Having regard to the draft of the vessel the court concluded that the pilot was not justified in trying to bring her over the Bar and that the ship was not navigated in a proper and seamanlike condition. As to the question of whether the master was in default and if any blame attached to the pilot, the inquiry concluded that considering that the pilot told the master to lighten the ship to 12ft 10ins, he (the pilot) must have known the ship's draft and the master, knowing that the signals at the station were for 13 ft only, was not justified in allowing the pilot to attempt crossing the Bar. Mr Breen, the pilot was deemed mainly to blame for the casualty. They made no judgement regarding costs.

Consequences

On 21May 1888, as a result of the Board of Trade Inquiry, Wexford Harbour Commissioners suspended Robert Breen for three months, without pay (This must have been the start of Breen's misfortunes in the Pilot Establishment. On the 20 November 1888, Breen's pilot's licence was revoked. He had been appointed in June 1879). On the same date, Mr Brady, who was the Acting Pilot Master in the absence of Captain Cogley, was suspended for two weeks for leaving the station without a qualified pilot (Captain Cogley's son who manned the signals on the day of the loss was not employed by the Commissioners).

Captain Blake, Tug Master, had stated to the inquiry that he had doubts about the manouvere the pilot was undertaking but did not communicate these doubts to the pilot. For not informing the pilot of his reservations he was censured by the Committee (This did not have any detrimental effect his career as since the loss of the **Saltee** and before he was censured he was appointed both Pilot Master and Tug Master). There is no record of Captain Smith being censured.

SAMUEL DIXON
Number 17024. Code MDVT.

1782 Built at Witton, Cheshire, a schooner of 46 tons.
1881 Rebuilt by the Wexford Dockyard Co., to 38 tons. Dimensions: 67x16.6x6.7ft.

OWNERS
1865 J.W. Walsh, Crescent Quay, Wexford.
1872 Nicholas White, Kilmore, Co. Wexford and Thomas Hutchinson, Wexford.
1903 Out of register. Vessel broken up at Wexford.

CREW 1891
Master: Joseph Cousins, 35.
Mates: Patrick White, 41; Thomas Blake, 25.
OS: Thomas Ryan, 24; James Carty, 19.
Boys: Patrick White, 19; Martin Blake, 16; Thomas Keith, 16.

In January 1870, the **Samuel Dixon** was inbound to Wexford Port, when she struck the Long Bank and remained there for 30 minutes. She was being battered by the waves and taking in water. The pumps were kept going constantly but the sea kept gaining. The arrival of the steam tug **Ruby** saved the crew from what would have been a perilous position. The tug took them in tow and she was run up on the beach, near the Dockyard. She was carrying a cargo of slate from Porthmadog.

Little more was heard of her until 1894, when the **Samuel Dixon**, under the command of Captain James Marlow, went ashore at Carne, Co. Wexford. It seems that they had begun unloading her cargo of coal, when a strong easterly wind blew up. She broke her moorings and swung around into shallow waters and grounded. She still had most of her cargo on board and the impact stove in part of her bottom. She immediately

Samuel Dixon, a tops'l schooner of 38 tons. Built 1782 and rebuilt in 1881 when owned by Nicholas White of Kilmore Quay, Co.Wexford.

filled with water. This put her in a perilous position but fortunately the wind veered around again to North West making it possible to remove the remaining cargo.

Samuel Dixon lost her main boom in a storm, homeward bound from Newport. She was owned by Captain Hutchinson and was under the command of Captain Walsh.

SCOTIA QUEEN
Number 57186. Code KPCQ.
1867 Built at Windsor, Nova Scotia by William Pratt. A barque of 413 tons. Dimensions: 130.3x29.3x12.9ft.

OWNERS
1870 George Smith of Nova Scotia.
1880 Alex Gillies of Glasgow.
1885-1888 William Murphy of Wexford.
1888 Transferred to Hull owners.

On 5 March 1877, the **Scotia Queen**, en route from Glasgow to Trinidad, went aground at Dunaverty Rock, Southend, on the Kintyre Peninsula. Two days later, after jettisoning

Scotia Queen a three masted barque of 413 tons. Built 1867 at Nova Scotia. Pictured here under full sail.

some of her cargo, she was towed off and brought to the Clyde for inspection. Although the damage was not deemed to be too serious, her cargo was transferred to another vessel and it must be assumed that the **Scotia Queen** remained on the Clyde. No further incidents in her career are apparent until 11 March 1888, when under William Murphy's ownership. At 2 am the **Scotia Queen** was off the coast of Cuba, when she went aground on a coral reef, near Cape San Antonia. Shortly afterwards a group of 'salvers' came on board and with the help of the crew began to throw some of her cargo of mahogany over the side in an attempt to lighten and thereby float her off the reef. Their efforts were not successful and the **Scotia Queen** remained hard aground on the reefs.

Later in the evening, the wind got up and the salvers, being natives of the area and knowing how much these winds could increase, refused to stay on board. The reef was also 22 miles from the shore and any hope of help in a gale would be minimal. Taking all this into consideration the crew also decided to leave with the salvers, and after taking the sails off their ship, they lowered the boats and struck out for land. After a long hard row, they eventually got in under the land and sheltered. The crew had intended to return to their vessel the next day but the storm maintained its intensity, making the journey impossible.

The next day the storm abated. The men made for their ship only to find when they arrived at the site of her grounding, that there was nothing to be seen. The **Scotia Queen** was gone! Their consternation can only be imagined. Their ship was hard aground when they left her two days before and now there was no sign of her. After some time scanning the area, someone spied a dot out on the horizon. They deduced that it had to be her, so undaunted the bold crew set out to row towards it.

After another long hard row they came up on the ship, which was indeed, the **Scotia Queen**. After working herself off the reef, she had drifted over 15 miles. The crew boarded her and were ready to sail, but here it became complicated. The salvers were still with them and had boarded the **Scotia Queen** with the crew. The complication was that the salvers had control of the sails which had been removed from the ship and refused to hand them up until they had been paid an amount of money. The equivalent of 100 pounds. The captain didn't have that much money onboard and offered them a promissory note for the amount, which they declined. They would only accept hard cash.

After some consultation, it was decided that the mate of the **Scotia Queen** would go to Havana to appraise the British Consul of the situation and to verify that the claim being made by the salvers was a genuine claim. The mate, accompanied by some of the salvers, set out on the four-day journey to Havana. They duly arrived at the Consulate but when the mate verified that the salvers were entitled to the payment for the sails, the Consul replied that he had no funds for such a purpose. After hanging around for a few days, the salvers got tired of waiting and got ready to leave but refused to bring the mate back to the **Scotia Queen**.

At this stage, the Consul began to think that the captain and crew of the **Scotia Queen** might be in danger from the salvers, so he sent a sloop to look after them. However, before she arrived, word was sent from the Spanish Admiral at Havana that the **Scotia Queen** had sailed. No one knew how she had got her sails back from the salvers. They had remained to keep a guard on her while the others were in Havana, but they must have been overpowered by the crew, otherwise they would not have enough sail to effect an escape.

Concern was expressed about the condition of her bottom, after going up on the reef, but others thought that due to her being over 40 hours at sea after she re-floated and showing no ill effect, that she was fine. **Scotia Queen** was not expected at her first port of call, Goole, for at least two weeks. Evidently she made Goole safely, discharged part of her cargo there and arrived in Wexford in May 1888, safely, to discharge a cargo of timber for Michael Ennis, Timber Importer. She obviously fitted in another trip to the Americas for timber and arrived back in Wexford in August 1888 with another cargo of timber for Michael Ennis. She vanished from the registers in 1889. There is no record of what became of the mate. It seems he was left in Cuba, but more than likely he procured another ship to get him home.

SEAFLOWER
Number 1259.

1825 Built at New Brunswick, a schooner of 61 tons, with a carved figurehead.

OWNERS

1836-1842 Registered at Wexford: Owners Thomas Connick and David Cullen, both from Wexford.
1852 John Cullen (John Codd, Master). Connick sold his shares to John Codd.
The **Seaflower** sailed to and from Wexford for Glasgow with beans. She ran ashore at Arklow, on 16 November 1852. She was full of water and expected to become a wreck. The crew were saved.

SEAFLOWER
Number 41769. Code TGBN.

1858 Built at Prince Edward Island, a schooner of 52 tons, with a female figurehead: Dimensions 66x17x7ft.

OWNERS
1860 Matthew Stafford of Drinagh, Wexford.
1867-1904 Thomas Hutchinson of Wexford.
1904 William McCormack of Clarence House, Kingstown, Dublin.
1916 Registration closed. Vessel broken up.

CREWS
1864
Master: Thomas Hutchinson, 29.
Mate: Edward Kennedy, 35.
Seaman: Edward Kelly, 26.
Boy: Martin Murphy, 18.

1870
Master: Thomas Hutchinson, 41. He was also the owner.
Mates: Francis Wafer, 39; Richard Wafer, 38.
ABs: Thomas White, 35; Pat Roche.
Boys: Laurence Walsh, 16; Thomas Sutton, 19; Pat Wafer, 15 (1st trip).

Mr Thomas Hutchinson of Henrietta St, Wexford, complained to the Harbour Commissioners that on 9 February 1870, his vessel the **Seaflower**, was run into by the ketch, **Two Sisters**, when she was being towed over the Gulbar. It seems that both vessels and another boat were under the command of pilots, when the accident happened and they were being towed in by the tugboat. Hutchinson's vessel sustained damage to her main rail, top gallant, bulwark and to one main stanchion. He also stated that on 11 February, his vessel, this time moored at the quay, was run into again by the same ketch! This time she damaged the main rail and bulwarks on the other side. He estimated the damages at thirteen pounds and said that after due consideration he thought that both collisions could have been avoided.

Captain Busher, of the Tug **Wexford**, was called before the Board. He said that blame could not be attributed to either of the pilots. He said that at the time there was only ten and a half feet of water at the Gulbar and that the **Seaflower** touched bottom and would not steer. She was then run into by the ketch. The pilot was called to give evidence and after that the Commissioners issued the following order:

*After hearing the statements of the the tug master and pilots with regard to the collision of the **Seaflower** on the 9th inst., while in tow with the **Two Sisters** and the **Sarah Ann Ruskell**, we find that the collision occurred in consequences of the **Two Sisters** [the **Seaflower** ?] taking the ground and not steering. We also find the pilots and the tug master in no way to blame. With regard to the collision on the 11 February by the **Two Sisters** running into the **Seaflower**, moored on the quay, the pilot Roche stated that the*

Seaflower, a tops'l schooner of 52 tons Built, 1858 at Prince Edward Island. (Artist unknown)
Courtesy of Tom Harpur, Parnell St. Wexford.

*master of the **Two Sisters** did not obey his orders, which were to give twelve fathoms range of chain. Therefore, there was not sufficient chain to bring up the vessel in time to avoid collision.*

SELSKAR
Number 21437. Code NGJC.
1853 Built at St. John, New Brunswick, a brig of 285 tons.
Dimensions: 93.6x20.6x12.6ft.
OWNERS
1865 Allen Brothers of Wexford.
1870 John Meagher of Dublin.
1872 Patrick Delargey of Cushendall, Co. Antrim.
1879 John Webster of London.
1880 Port of register, London, 182 tons.
1882 Out of Register.

Captain Patrick Chandler oversaw the building of **Selskar** and went on to command her for 20 years. During that time, he brought in the first and the only cargo of cotton ever landed in Wexford. Captain Chandler also had the distinction of landing two cargoes of sugar from the West Indies, considered to be an unusual cargo for the Port of Wexford.

   Selskar was one of the three Wexford vessels caught up in the bombardment at Crimea in 1854. In July 1863, Frank Rowe, a seaman, was charged at Cardiff with desertion from the brig **Selskar**, that at the time was lying in the West Docks. Captain Chandler gave evidence that Rowe went backwards and forwards to the vessel but did not do his work. The bench found that the Articles entered into, did not bind the captain and dismissed the charge. No mention was made to Rowe's position but it is likely that he was discharged.

SHAMROCK
Number 15125. Code LRBH.

1838 Built at Barnstaple, a carvel built schooner of 82 tons, with a figurehead.

OWNERS
1842. R. Devereux (David. Roche, Master).
1856 Oct. R. J. Devereux,16 shares; Laurence Devereux, 16 shares; William Aloysius Caulfield, 16 shares (all merchants); and Thos. Connors (shipwright), 16 shares.

CREW 1845
Master: David Roche, 48.
Mate: John Byrne, 19.
Apprentices: Patrick Bolgcr, 20; John Scallan, 16; Denis Devereux, 17.
Seaman: Thomas Codd, 19.
In December 1869, the **Shamrock** was reported to have foundered in the river Barrow at New Ross while en route to Wexford with a cargo of barley. However, it apparently

was refloated as, at Christmas 1878, Devereux's **Shamrock** went ashore on Lambay Island, off Dublin and became a complete wreck. She was bound from Glasgow to Wexford with coal.

SIBYL
Number 9349. Code KGWF.

1830 Built at Wexford, a schooner, 99 tons.

OWNERS
1831/1845/1851 John Barrington, 32 shares, Simon Lambert, 32 shares.
1860 April. Lambert sold to John Leared and Robert Stafford.
1861 May. Leared died, his shares went to Stafford;
1865 John Barrington of Wexford.
1868 Feb. Stafford sold to PatrickLambert, merchant of Wexford.

CREWS
1845
Master: John McClane, 29.
Mate: Joseph Moran, 34.
Seamen: M. Carley, 22; James White, 22; Patrick Breen, 42.
Apprentice: Edward Carroll, 18.

1864
Master: Clement Busher, 38.
Mate: Bartle Carty, 34.
ABs James Mulligan, 28; Patrick Doyle, 25; James Busher; James Doyle, 19; Bernard Smith, 22; Richard Hughes, 20; William Gaul, 25.
Boys: Henry Kelly, 18; Peter Murphy.
Also that year:
Mate: Laurence Devereux, 44.
ABs Laurence Neill, 24; John Breen, 23; Simon Furlong, 19; William Garret, 25.
1877 Evans Byrne, Master.

On 1 January 1831 **Sibyl** *was boarded and robbed by pirates in the Bosphorus*. This information was endorsed on her articles and no other reference was made.

On 27 April 1877, the **Sibyl**, under Captain Evans Byrne, was lost near Tacumshane. She was on a voyage from Portsmouth to Wexford with a cargo of 155 tons of super phosphate for Devereux of Templeshannon, Enniscorthy, Co. Wexford. The ship was 4 miles E.N.E. of The Lizard when they started to take water. Both pumps were put to work. With four men pumping constantly she made the Tuskar, but by then she had 5 feet of water in the hold.

The captain tried to make for the South Bay but in the end had to run for the Chour near the seaward side of Lady's Island Lake. At this stage the crew refused to pump anymore so the captain told them he would run for the shore. This he did and they made land at Rosstoonstown near Tacumshane. All hands were got ashore by line but the **Sibyl** was a complete loss.

SKER
No 44121

1846 Built at Marshallstown, Nova Scotia, a schooner, carvel built, 61 tons.

1846 Registered at Wexford.

OWNERS Allen Bros.
Captains: Patrick Ryan (15 Aug 1847); Laurence English (21 April 1847); Joseph Fennell (14 Dec. 1847); Henry Dobbin (19 July 1848); John Campbell (5 February 1849); Christopher Cahill (6 September 1851); Joseph Fennell (27 April 1852); Laurence Cahill (6 April 1854); John Murphy (24 November 1854); Francis Morris (16 May 1856); John Reilly, High St., Wexford (24 June 1864).

CREW 1863
Master: John Reilly, 28, High St Wexford;
Mate: J. Murphy, 45.
ABs William Atkinson, 20; Robert Carty, 22.
OS Michael Crean, 18.

Sker went aground at Arklow Bay in a storm in February 1855, but was later re-floated. On 31 January 1869, she was driven ashore in the Waterford River but was re-floated again, and, in September of the same year, she lost both of her anchors at Cahore, Co. Wexford and was driven ashore, to be re floated yet again.

William Cousins a sailor on the **Sker** was charged at Cardiff on 14 April 1871 with cutting and wounding Martin Kerwin, a shipmate. Both men were walking up Bute Street when a row broke out. Cousins pulled out his knife and attacked Kerwin, almost severing his nose. He was arrested and committed for trial.

The **Sker** finally met her end on 16 December 1876 when she struck the Splaugh Rock off the Wexford coast. After a while she got off again only to run up on the Carrig Rocks. This time she sank. The captain stated that he mistook the light on shore, south of Greenore Point, for the light recently erected on the pier at Ballygeary (Rosslare Harbour.) Another Wexford schooner the **Samuel Dixon** was following the **Sker** and she, too, went up on the Carrigs but got off with just the loss of her rudder. She was towed into Wexford Harbour in a sinking state.

This was not the first time that a ship mistook the two lights. Shortly before, an English vessel, the **Star**, struck the Splaugh Rock and was abandoned by her crew, who were taken in tow the next morning by the Wexford Harbour Commissioners tug, **Ruby** under Captain Anthony Ennis. The **Star** was from Port Talbot with a cargo of coal for Gafney's of Wexford.

SLANEY
No 21412 Code NGFL.

1837 Built at Wexford, a schooner, 90 tons. Dimensions: 65x17x 10ft.

OWNERS
1865 R. Devereux, Wexford.
1872 J.T. Devereux.
1883 Wm. Armstrong, Wexford.

CREWS
1845.
Master: Francis Larkin, 36.
Mate: Wm. Larkin, 41.
Seamen: Wm. Murphy, 37; Peter Doyle, 28.
Apprentice: Dennis Campbell, 19.
Others: John Murphy, 17; –? Murphy, 24.

1864
Master: M. Rowe, 35.
Mate: James Murphy, 40.
ABs: Simon Hatchell, 36; John Murphy, 26; Thomas Carr, 20.
Boys: Thomas Pender 20; Richard Roach, 15; R. Cousins, 20.

1881
Master: Nicholas Dempsey.
Mate: Michael Rowe, 50.
AB: Edward Clarey, 23.
OS: Joseph Murphy, 18.
Boy: Larvis(?) McGrath, 15.

On 26 September 1883, the **Slaney** was at anchor in Milford Roads in a fierce gale. She parted her anchor chain and drove ashore at South Hook Point, Milford Haven. Captain James Carr and his crew were rescued by lifeboat. Vessel became total loss.

> **WRECK AT MILFORD HAVEN.**
>
> The schooner *Slaney*, of Wexford, was totally wrecked near Milford on Wednesday. Three of the crew were rescued by the Angle lifeboat, and the remainder got ashore on the rocks.

Slaney wreck notice, 1883.

Wreck of the Wexford schooner **Slaney** at Milford Haven, September 1883.

SPRAY
No. 44124.

1861 Built at Carleton, St. John, New Brunswick by John Thompson. A schooner, 82 tons. Dimensions: 77x 18x 8 ft.

1861 Registered at Wexford.

OWNERS
1861-1891 Robert Allen; Mrs M. Allen, Wexford.
1900 Captain Jemmy Storey, The Faythe, Wexford.
1902 Out of Register.

CREWS
1863
Master: Matthew Neill, 35, of William St., Wexford.
Mate: Nicholas Murphy, 45.
AB: Francis Wafer, 30.
Seaman: James Carberry, 25.
OS: Patrick Sinnot, 18.

Later that year:
Master: Matthew Neill, 35, of William St., Wexford.
Mate: Nicholas Murphy, 45.
ABs Edward O'Brien, 24; Michael Shannon, 20.
Boy: Patrick Redmond, 17.

1864
Master: Matthew Neill, 36.
Mate: Nicholas Murphy, 46.
AB: Patrick Codd, 22.
Others: Nicholas Baron(?), 18; William Cra–?, 35.

The second half of 1864 was atypical of the normal run of the Wexford coastal schooners. From 10 July the **Spray** went from Bristol to Newport; on 25 July she sailed from Newport to Wexford. Then on 15 August she left Wexford for Whitehaven. She sailed from there on 17 August for Briton Ferry, then from Briton Ferry she arrived to her home port on 5 October. Sailed from Wexford on 24 October for Whitehaven, and from there she sailed for Newport and then back to Wexford, arriving on 29 December.

In February 1899 the **Spray** rescued the crew from the sailing ship **South Australia** which had foundered off Lundy Island. The crew were in a lifeboat for twelve hours before the **Spray** came upon them. They were transferred to a steam trawler that brought them into Swansea. Only the cook of the sailing ship was lost.

Here moored at Wexford Quay is the schooner **Star.** Built 1833 at Lawrenny, Milford Haven.

The **Star** again at Wexford Quay berthed ahead of a steamship from the Waterford Steamship Company, possibly the ss Menapia.

STAR
No. 21410 Code NGFJ.
1833 Built at Lawrenny, Milford, a schooner, 78 tons. Dimensions: 63.5x16.9 x8.1ft.

OWNERS
1852-1856 John Connor Snr. of Wexford.
1856 John Connor died; shares to widow, Ellen Connor.
1856 Ellen Connor sold eight shares to Evan Byrne, M.M. of Wexford.
1865-1867 Ellen O'Connor of Wexford.
1875 J. P. Devereux of Wexford.
1885 Thomas Hutchinson, Henrietta St., Wexford.
1887 Broken up at Ferrybank.

CREWS
1852
Master: Thomas Rowe, 26.
Mate: John Hayes, 32.
Seaman: George Molloy, 20.

1864
Master: Kearns , 50, of Chapel Row, Wexford.
Mate: Edward Brown, 30.

In September 1879, the **Star** was en route from Cardiff to Wexford and had to return to Penarth Roads with all of her sails blown away in a heavy gale.

Damage report to the Wexford schooner **Star,** 1879

Auction notice of the sale of the masts/ spars etc. of the schooner **Star,** 1887.
Co. Wexford Archives.

STAR OF HOPE
No 55423 Code JBMW.

1867 Built at Perth, by Mc.Pherson and Geddes, A schooner, 90 tons. Dimensions: 80.3x21.3x10ft.
1871/72/73 Registered at Banff.
1904 Vessel sunk after collision with the **s.s. Fernside**.

OWNERS
1868 William Reid of Portgordon, Banffshire.
1883 Matthew Weston, Cheshire.
1884 Joseph Codd, MM, of New St. (Parnell. St.),Wexford.
1896 John Carr, 43, Parnell St.
1897 Jane Codd of 39 Parnell St.
1902 J. J. Stafford Wexford & J. Bolger of Ferns, Co. Wexford.

CREW 1891
Master: Joseph Codd, 62.
Mate: J. Doyle, 22.
OS: J. McCabe, 22.
AB: James Quirk, 22.
Boy: Michael Murphy, 20.

The **Star of Hope** was run down by the steamer **Fernside** on Wednesday 5 October 1904. She was in ballast bound for Newport. She had left Wexford on the previous Tuesday and was making good progress. Early on Wednesday morning she was off Bull Point, three miles from Ilfracombe, when the steamer collided with her. At the time, the master, Captain Thomas Kehoe, and one hand, Edward Clancy were on deck, and realising that a collision was imminent, began shouting and waving their hands at the approaching steamer. But it was to no avail as the steamer came on and ran into the port side of the **Star of Hope**'s bow. She began to settle immediately.

The other two hands on the schooner, Bernard Quirke and John Molloy were watch below and, hearing the commotion, they ran up on deck. Seeing their predicament, they both jumped onto the steamer. This all occurred at about 4 in the morning but it was not until around 7.30 that Captain Kehoe abandoned all hope of his ship surviving and left her in one of the **Fernside's** lifeboats. The steamer's captain accepted full responsibility for the accident.

Report of the collision of the schooner **Star of Hope.**

On 18th of October 1889, the Wexford lifeboat **Ethel Eveleen** rescued five crew from the Wexford schooner **Star of Hope** which had grounded on the Dogger Bank outside the entrance of Wexford Harbour. The **Star of Hope** was later re-floated, repaired and returned to service.

SWIFT

No. 21443 Code NGJM.

1846 Built at Prince Edward Island. A schooner, carvel built, 62 tons. Billet head.

1835/1841, 1845 Registered at Wexford

OWNERS
1847 John Carr, 22 shares; James Carr, 21 shares; John Cullen, shipowner, 21 shares.
1854 John Cullen (now Master).
1856 Nov.Cullen died and his shares went to his widow, Mary Cullen.
1865 Margaret Cullen of Wexford.

CREW 1845
Master: Nicholas Fallon, 35.
Mate: William Atkins, 38,
Seamen: Matthew Sinnott, 34, Patrick Cogley, 22.
Apprentice: James McGrath, 18 (Indentures signed, 6 Dec. 1844, Dublin)

In August 1859, Michael Madden a Cook/Steward on the **Swift** drowned when he was going ashore to buy stores for the ship. One side of the gangway was shorter than the other and the unfortunate Madden fell in. John Smith a crew member of the **Swift** gave evidence at the inquiry to that effect. Madden left a wife and 3 children in Wexford.

On 21 Dec 1872, the **Swift** was lost near Newcastle, Co. Down when en route Wexford to Glasgow with a cargo of beans. The crew of 5 were saved by the Newcastle lifeboat, **Reigate.**

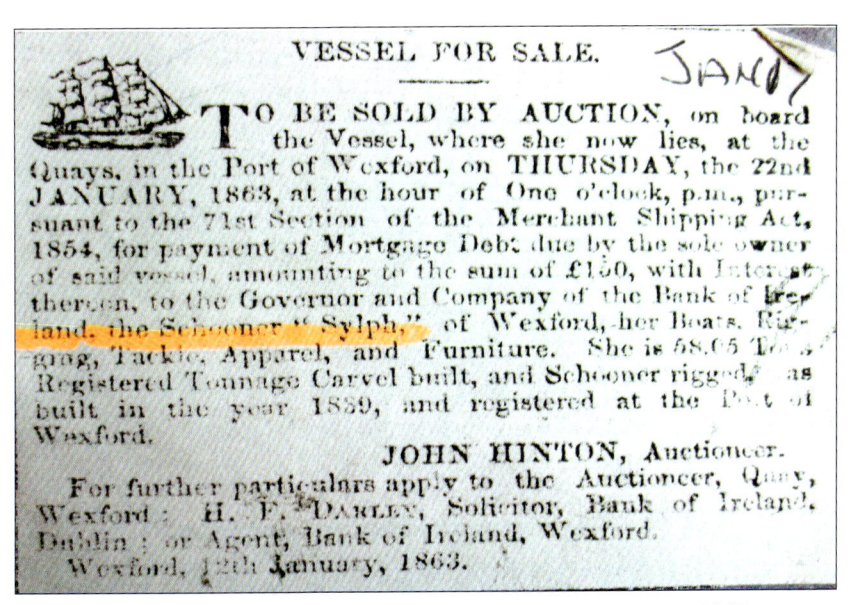

Auction notice of the sale of the schooner **Sylph**, January 1863.
John Power Collection.

T

TELEGRAPH
No. 41861, Code TGKQ.

1859 Built at St. John, New Brunswick. A schooner, 92 tons. Dimensions: 78.0x21.8x7.4ft.

OWNERS
1865 Wicklow Copper Mine Co. of Dublin.
1875 William D. McCormick of Kingstown, Co. Dublin.
1876 William Joseph Gafney of Wexford.
1885 Miss Margaret Gafney of Commercial Quay. Wexford.
1889 Miss Angela Gafney, of Commercial Quay Wexford; Thomas Hutchinson of Wexford.

CREW
Master: John Whealan, Parnell St, Wexford (born 1846).
Mate: William Murphy (b. 1860).
AB: Patrick Kavanagh (b. 1862); Martin Rourke (b. 1862).
OS: William Devereux (b. 1871)
Others: Thomas Breen (b. 1868); Francis Wafer (b. 1864); Peter Brien (b 1860); William Hess (b. 1844); James Blake (b. 1874).
Boys: Myles Dalton (b. 1871); William Higginbotham (b. 1874) (First trip).

Hutchinson's **Telegraph** went aground at the entrance to Wexford Harbour in February 1892. She was homeward bound from Newport with a cargo of coal, valued at £110. She had a rough passage from the Welsh port and was attempting to cross the Bar when she hit the ground. Captain John Whelan of Parnell St., Wexford, was in command and he and his crew did all they could to prevent the grounding but the heavy seas and strong winds made their efforts ineffectual. She went up on the Dogger and started taking water immediately. The crew remained with her until the last minute but, once they realised that there was little they could do to save her, they took to the boats.

The Fort lifeboat was launched but by that time the crew had reached safety. The **Telegraph** was previously owned by Gafney's and had not been long under Hutchinson's ownership when she met her end. At an inquiry held by the Harbour Board to determine how the loss occurred, as she was in charge of a pilot. Captain Cogley, Pilot Master and Laurence Murphy, the pilot concerned, gave their evidence. The Board concluded that Laurence Murphy was at fault for trying to bring the ship over the Bar at two hours flood, taking the weather conditions at the time into consideration. Captain Cogley was told that he ought to be stricter in seeing that the rules of the Commissioners are enforced

One month later it was reported that the wreck of the **Telegraph** was causing an obstruction to vessels coming in and leaving the harbour. The owners, Hutchinson's were ordered to remove it forthwith. Possibly as a result of this order, a fishing cot belonging to a military pensioner named Hayes was working on the hull of the

Telegraph. The cot, under the control of Paddy Carroll and 3 hands, had a small boat in tow. They made fast to the **Telegraph** but for some reason they later cast off from it and, as one of the men described it, the cot gave *a wrong sheer, all on account of the wind and grounded herself up on the bank she straight away started to break up.*

All 4 men clambered into the small boat. All that transpired was seen by Tom Wickham of the Fort and he, with his two sons Michael and James, along with Pilot Michael Brady, went to the rescue. They reached the small boat just as she was about to be swamped and took the 4 hands off. Carroll later publicly thanked the Wickhams and Brady and said that but for their prompt arrival they would have likely lost their lives.

TEMPEST
No. 20247. Code MWHR.

1857 Built at Milford, Pembrokeshire, a schooner, 59 tons. Dimensions: 77x20 x10.2 ft.

OWNERS
1865 Nicholas Whitty of Wexford.
1879 P. J. Roache of New Ross Co. Wexford.
1891 Harper & Wickham, Wexford.
1898 John O'Neill of William St. Wexford, M.M. (for £280).
1910 Peter O'Neill, M. M. and Maria O'Neill, both of William St. Wexford.
1914 to William Massey, of Courtown, Co. Wexford.
1916 James Billington, Sth. Main St., Wexford.
1922 Thomas McDonald of Dublin.

CREWS
Unknown date
Master: Murtha Foley.
Mate: Richard Phelan.
ABs: Patrick Cousins; James Kavanagh.
Boy: Anthony Duggan
1864
Master: J. Lambert, 45.
Mate: Rich. Ryan, 37.
Seamen: J Neil, 26; Robert Evans, 29.
OS: J. Murphy, 24.
Boy: P Lambert, 17.

1864 (January)
Master: J. Lambert, 45.
Mate: Michael Rowe, 38
Seamen: Patrick Lambert, 35; Edward Howlin, 38; Patrick Waden, 28.
Boy: Patrick Clancy, 17.
Other: J. Lambert, 41.

Captain Murtha Foley c1867- 1904.
Master of the Wexford schooner
Tempest.
Courtesy of Liam Ryan, Fethard on Sea, Co. Wexford.

1864 (1 July)
Master: John Lambert, 45.
Mate: Edward Ryan, 37.
Seamen: James Neil, 26; R. Brown, 29.
OS: John Murphy, 24.
Boy: Patrick Lambert, 17.

On the morning of Saturday 15 February 1864, the **Tempest** under Captain John Lambert ran ashore on the West Pier when she was leaving Kingstown (Dun Laoghaire) Harbour, bound for New Ross. She remained on the rocks there until the next rising tide floated her. She was damaged slightly.

In June 1891, the **Tempest** ran into the ketch **Bertie** of Bristol, Bridgewater to Waterford, off St. Govan's Head. The **Tempest**'s bow sprit and a large portion of her head gear carried away. However, she was able to stand by the **Bertie** and took her crew off and landed them in Milford Haven. The Bristol ketch sank.

The Welsh newspaper *Evening Express* reported that on 20 September 1910, the Spanish vessel **St Outon** was swinging in the River Usk when she struck the Cardiff steamer **Rosaleen** moored at the Liverpool Wharf, forcing astern and driving her into the Wexford schooner, **Tempest**. The **Tempest** had her bow stove in and her boom broken.

In January 1923, while en route from Newport, Monmouthshire with coal for Clonakilty, the **Tempest** was at anchor in Milford Haven when she was run into and sunk by the steam trawler, **Charles Boyes**. She was apparently raised after this incident and sold for scrap. Registration closed 5 April 1924.

TIGRIS
Official No. 11604 Code KTHN.

1837 Built at New Brunswick. A schooner, 85 tons. Dimensions: 62x17x 9 ft.

1839-1845; 1859 Registered at Wexford

OWNERS
John Hatchell Brennan, shipowner of London.
1865 J. T. Devereux of Wexford.
1865 J.H. Nicholls of Falmouth.

CREW 1845.
Master: John Ennis, 46
Mate: – Bert, 28.
Seamen: S. Cleary, 56; James Douglas, 17
Apprentice: Nicholas Ennis, 29.
Others: William O'Shea, 21; William Siberly (?), 31; James Kelly, 25
Boy: Richard Ennis, 14.

The **Tigris** left Ibrail, a small port in Romania, on 17 November 1847 and made

Constantinople two days later. She left there on 24 November and arrived home on 6 February 1848. Due to reports of cholera in Constantinople, she was immediately placed in quarantine, as the law demanded. Because of some unexplained oversight by the captain, the vessel was still in quarantine on 24 March. On that day, Dr. Coughlan was taken out to the **Tigris** by the Customs to ascertain whether or not she was clear of the cholera. When he went aboard he found that the Mate had died and all of the crew were *more or less ill*. However, on examination he concluded that it was not cholera or any other contagious disease that had incapacitated the crew and killed the Mate and the **Tigris** was allowed to come into the quay.

For some few days later, no further attention was paid to the crew as the assumption was that their incapacitated condition was just from fatigue or exhaustion. However, the Captain sent for Dr Coughlan who examined him and his two sons, who were also members of the crew of the **Tigris**, and diagnosed that all three of them were suffering from the effects of lead poisoning. An inquiry was launched and it was discovered that all the pork and salt beef that made up the principal food on the ship was held in a lead cistern. Three days after this discovery, the Captain died. An inquest was held a few days later when Doctors Coughlan, Cardiff and Crane gave evidence that they had examined the body of Captain John Ennis and it was their opinion that he had died from scurvy and that all the rest of the crew were suffering from the same disease and that their constitutions were *deteriorated* by having eaten provisions that were kept in a leaden cask.

Nicholas Cullen, a member of the crew, told the inquiry that they had left Wexford on the previous July and had loaded the meat there. He thought that some of it was American and that they had loaded further supplies of meat in Constantinople, Malta and Tulsk. They had no significant sickness on the way out and it never happened until they were in the Straits of Gibraltar, homeward bound. They were all feeling sick on the way home and the mate, Henry French died when they entered quarantine. As soon as the ship was allowed out of quarantine and permitted to dock all the crew, with the exception of Joseph Codd, the 2nd apprentice, went home. No reason was given why Codd stayed onboard. Richard Ennis, the captain's son and also a crew member gave similar evedence as those who preceded him.

The conclusion of the inquiry was that ' We find that the said John Ennis died in consequence of having eaten meat which was kept in a leaden cistern onboard the schooner **Tigris**. No further reports were made regarding the **Tigris** so it must be assumed that all the others survived. The **Tigris** was subsequently sold in 1865 to Falmouth shipowners and on a voyage from Falmouth to Liverpool was driven ashore and wrecked near Blackwater Head on the 23 March 1866.

TOPAZ
No, 36827.

1860 Built at Prince Edward Island by Longworth. A schooner, 90 tons.
Dimensions: 84x19.6x9.8ft.

OWNERS
1870 Richard Devereux of Wexford.

1883 Laurence Murphy of Wexford.
1885 William O'Keefe of Wexford.
1889 Thomas J. O'Keefe of Wexford.
1894-1910 William J. O'Keefe of Wexford.
1911-1912 Francis Mumford of the Scilly Isles.
1914 Richard Abel & Sons Ltd. of Liverpool.
1929 Out of register and vessel broken up.

CREWS
1863,
Master: James Murphy, 35.
Mate: James Lambert, 40.
ABs: Nicholas Dempsey, 25; Patrick Ryan, 40; John Murphy, 22.
OS: Thomas Bolger, 17.

Principal trips in 1863 were from Dublin to Barrow in ballast, Barrow to Cardiff with iron ore and Cardiff to Wexford with coal. Then Wexford to Barrow in ballast, returning to Wexford via Newport to deliver iron ore, and then on home to Wexford with coal. This pattern was repeated throughout 1863 with the occasional run to Liverpool and at least one to Lancaster.

CREW undated
Master: James Murphy.
Mate: James Mulligan, 37;
Seaman: James Byrne, 35;
ABs: Patrick Roach, 33, John Campbell, 20; John Golding, 23; John Connor, 22; Stephen Connor, 20.
Boy: James Furlong, 18; Nicholas Brennan, 16.

In September 1879, the **Topaz,** en route from Cardiff to Waterford, was caught in the same gale that had disabled the **Star,** had to return to Penarth Roads with her jiboom blown away. Both vessels had left together and had to return the following day.

On 1 September 1902, Thomas Breen, mate of O'Keefe's **Topaz**, died at Newport, South Wales. He had been admitted to the local hospital reportedly suffering from confluent smallpox. His condition had improved and he was expected to convalesce for about six weeks but experienced a sudden change in his condition that caused his demise.

On 7 March 1909, the Liverpool Maritime Board convened to hear charges against Mr R.E. Simmons, former first mate of the steamer **Karina** of London, for failing to stand by the Wexford schooner **Topaz**, that had been run down by the **Karina**, contrary to The Merchant Shipping Act. Section 422 of the act stated that it was the duty of the master or an officer of a vessel to render assistance to any ship that had been in a collision with and to report the incident to the authorities.

The **Topaz** had left Wexford on 3 August the previous year, with a crew of four, bound for Newport, South Wales, in ballast. She was off Tuskar at around 11.45 that night in thick weather and showing all lights. The captain, who was sounding the

The paddle tug **Wexford** with the tops'l schooner **Topaz** under tow out of Wexford Harbour.
Jack O'Leary Collection.

The tops'l schooner **Topaz.** Built 1860 at Prince Edward Island. Shown here "high and dry" on the river Parrat, Bridgewater, Somerset.

mechanical foghorn, suddenly saw the masthead and starboard lights of a steamer looming up on them a short distance away. The steamer struck them on the port bow, turning the little schooner (she was only 76 tons.) right around, and then continued on her way. The crew of the **Topaz** called out to the steamer but she just carried on her way, ignoring the cries for help.

In evidence Patrick Doyle, master of the Wexford vessel, told the Board that the first he saw of the steamer was a light approaching from the starboard quarter. He did not hear the steamer blow her whistle. She came on until she struck the schooner on her port bow. Doyle said that as soon as he saw her still coming on, he went to the wheel and sent his son down to wake the watch below. After she struck he thought that they were going down and all hands shouted for help. At this time the **Karina** was just across their bow.

The mate of the **Topaz** said in evidence that he turned in at about 8.40 pm and before he went below he made sure that all lights were properly showing. When he was called on deck at around midnight, he saw the steamer bearing down on them. Simmons of the **Karina** said that his ship was going at around 13 knots and that he did not notice any shore lights during his watch. He called the second officer at about midnight and then went along the saloon deck on the starboard side. As he was going along he looked over the side and spotted a sail about 20 yards off. He saw no lights, neither did he hear any order given to the wheel, or any sound except the flapping of the schooner's sails. As far as he was concerned, they did not come into contact with the **Topaz**. He did say that after the vessel crossed their beam he thought he heard a cry and that it sounded like the usual cry heard when a ship is too near the nets of a fishing boat. He also saw a red light after they had passed the vessel but was not aware of any collision.

Joseph Brown, an AB on the **Karina** who was on the chief officer's watch, told the Board that he had taken the wheel at 10 o'clock. It was a foggy night and got worse as the night progressed. He also said that the whistle was not sounded throughout his watch. Neither did he get any orders other than the course until the time the schooner was upon them. Then the chief officer gave the order to *hard a port*. Something then came into contact with them. He then saw the schooner as she was passing alongside them after the collision. No lights were visible on the schooner.

After the crash he saw the chief officer looking over the side. He then heard shouts of *help* but the next order he got from the mate was *Steady*. Apparently, after the collision had been reported, a reward had been offered for information in identifying the steamer involved and it was suggested by Mr Simmon's representative that, as Brown had been ashore since the incident, with only his Board of Trade money of £1 a week to live on that the reward offered was the reason for Brown's evidence, which was contrary to that of the mate. However, Thomas Doherty, a lamptrimmer on the **Karina** gave similar evidence to Brown's and stated to the Board that he had only been ashore for a week and knew nothing of the reward.

After hearing further evidence from both the crew of the **Karina** and the **Topaz**, the Board dismissed the charges against the chief officer. The **Topaz** was subsequently sold to the Isles of Scilly.

TOTTENHAM

OWNER 1843 Hartrick, New Ross.

In 1843, in a Parliamentary Report titled *Tobacco Smuggling in New Ross,* the ship **Tottenham** was mentioned as having been seized twice with smuggled tobacco on board. The owners of the ship were given as: George Hartrick, Standish Hartrick, James Howlett (another name prominent in New Ross ship owning), and the rather grandly named, Horatio Nelson Jones.

The crews were named as: James Browne, John Gunnet, Edward Hutchinson, James Brawders, Timothy Carey, John Russel, and James Ryan. It appears that both ships were released on payment of a fine. None of the owners were charged.

Barque

Fore & Aft Schooner

2 Masted Tops'l Schooner

Yawl

Ship

Snow

U

UNDINE
No. 21403. Code NGDT.

1849 Built at St John's, Nova Scotia. A brigantine, 105 tons. Dimensions: 71x18x10. 5ft.

OWNER Richard Allen.

CREW 1864,
Master: James Kelly, 39 of John Street, Wexford.
Mate: James Codd.
Seamen: James Rucards (?) 25; William Allen, 25; Edward Brien, 36.
Boy: Patrick Codd, 19.

Allen's brigantine **Undine** went ashore in a fierce gale on Saturday 5 January 1867. She had left Newport, Monmouthshire Sth Wales with a cargo of coal on 1 January in fine weather until Friday night then the weather changed to gale force winds. The **Undine** anchored in the South Bay on Saturday morning and, due to the beating she was receiving from the heavy seas, her beams opened and soon there was six feet of water in her hold and all hands had to man the pumps.

   The winds increased to hurricane force and began to drive the vessel before it despite both anchors being out and the ship in excellent anchorage. In the end she broke both anchors and careered up on the beach, 4 miles south of Rosslare Point. All hands were forced to take to the rigging and were clinging on there for about an hour when one of the masts gave way. One by one they dropped into the water, some never to surface again.

   One of the boys survived by hanging on to a few feet of a spar that brought him ashore while the other got ashore without any assistance. Patrick Carty, the mate, attempted to swim ashore and almost made it until a big wave swamped him and he was never seen again. The two who survived were James Moran and Miles Codd. Lost were: Captain James Kelly, Nicholas Lacey, Patrick Carty and James Ennis. The **Undine** was a total loss.

A schooner under reefed fore and afters

V

VENUS
No. 44127 Code TRSP.

1862 Built at Wexford, a brig, later re-rigged as a brigantine, 225tons. Dimensions, 113.0x24.1x13.0ft.

OWNERS
1863 The Whitstable Shipping Co.
1866 April. Collided with and sank the **Jane.**
1911 27 Dec. Vessel was lost en route from Newcastle to Ramsgate with a cargo of coal when she collided with the Swedish steamer **ss India**, off the Essex coast. All hands saved.

VERNON
No. 35232 Code RNSQ (1935 EIGK)

1857 Built at Dorchester, New Brunswick, a schooner, 97 tons. Dimensions: 83x20.5x9.2ft.

OWNERS
1865 Hartwell B. Crosby, St John, New Brunswick.
1868 John Reynolds of Arklow.
1870 James Kearns of Arklow.
1893 Ed. Kearns of Arklow.
1909 Thomas Kearns of John St. New Ross. Co. Wexford.
1911-1940 Thomas R. Brown, Knowle, Bristol. Converted to a barge.
1941 Vessel broken up. Register not closed until June 1953.

VICTORIA
No. 21444 Code NGJP.

1837 Built at Wexford; a cutter, carvel built; 19 tons.

1857 Wrecked

OWNERS John & Edmund Roach.

CREWS
1841
Master: Martin Rowe, 45.
Mate: John Rossiter, 40.
Mariners: Nicholas Sinnott, 21; Thomas Martin, 20; Daniel Dillon, 25.
Boy: Patrick French, 18.

Vernon of New Ross and Arklow.
Painting by Reuben Chappell.

1845.Sept.
Master: John Cahill, 54;
Seamen: Peter Cullen, 42; John Furlong; John Cahill; Daniel Byrne; Stephen Kehoe.

VICTORIA
1837 Built at Barnstaple, a schooner.

OWNER: John T. Devereux, Wexford (Master: Thomas Rowe, Mate: O' Dowd) Wrecked at Portrane, Dublin when she ran onto rocks in a gale in January 1854. All hands including the two mentioned above plus four seamen and a boy were lost. She was bound from Liverpool to Dublin.

VILLAGE BELLE
No. 77395.

1878 Built at Barnstaple, Devon, 95 tons. A schooner. Dimensions: 82.1x 21x 10.3ft.

OWNERS
1882 J. Landy, Skerries, Co. Dublin.
1918 Mr P.J. Donovan of Wexford.
1920 J. Tyrell of Arklow.
1922 T. Kavanagh of Arklow.
1933 Register closed.
1934 Broken up at Arklow.

Village Belle, a three masted fore and aft schooner of 95 tons. Built 1878 at Barnstaple

The **Village Belle** was returning to Wexford, from Newport in October 1919, with a cargo of 150 tons of coal, when she ran into the same gale that had decimated the **Fleetwing**. They anchored in the Bristol Channel to try to ride it out. A large drifter came along and took the crew aboard for their safety. When the storm blew itself out they returned to find the **Village Belle** intact, not seriously damaged as they had feared. The **Village Belle** arrived at Wexford Quay a few days later. 1922, she had an engine fitted.

Damaged cargo notice of the schooner **Village Belle,** *November 1919.*
Wexford People.

VISION
No.25788. Code, PHLD.

1846 Built at Nova Scotia, a schooner, carvel built, female figurehead, 143 tons.
1849 Registered at Wexford.

OWNERS
R. Devereux, Wexford (John O'Connor, master).
1862 22Dec. Sold to John Duncan &Co. of Elgin. Registration transferred to Banff.

VICTORY
No 11602 Code KTHL
1838 Built at Nova Scotia, a schooner 70 tons.
1853 Registered.
1866 Wrecked at Poulshone.

OWNERS
1853-1866 Matthew Cooney, 32 shares; Edward Browne, 32 shares. Browne died leaving his shares to his wife who sold to Thomas Rowe. Cooney died June 1863 leaving his shares to Richard Howlin and Patrick Hayes.They sold to Rowe.

VIVID
No.21401. Code, NGDR.

1850 Built at St John's, a schooner.

1850 Registered at Wexford, 83 tons.

OWNERS
1850-1874 R.&R. Allen of Wexford.
1877 Margaret Lambert & J.F. Walsh, F.J. Walsh of Wexford.
1898 Staffords of Wexford.
1900 Out of register.

CREWS
Jan./June 1864
Mate: William Larkin, 60.
ABs: George Curran, 33; William Goodwin, 22;
OS: John Murphy, 20.
Boy: William White, 19.

July/Dec. 1864
Master: John Butler, 29.
Mate: Peter Hayes, 37; William Larkin, 60; Michael Hayes, 24; Barnard Corish, 52.
ABs: Henry Marks, 24; Peter Neill, 25; Thomas Newport, 22; Michael Shannon, 22.
OS: William White, 18;
Boys: Michael Devereux, 16; William Bulger, 16 (First trip).
Later that year the crew were:
Hayes, Larkin, Neill, Devereux, Corish, Bulger.
Also signed on at that time were: William White, 18; F. Hayes, 24 and –? Shannon, 24.

VULCAN
No. 21448. Code, NGJP.
1834 Built at Wexford. A cutter, carvel built, 41 tons.

OWNERS
1843 Harvey Boxwell of Wexford, 64 shares; later Mary Wheeler of Roxborough Cottage, 48 shares; Edward Wickham, 16 shares (Master: John Radford)
Later shareholders included, Robert Hughes of Ely Place, 32 shares; Thomas Fortune of Ferrybank, 16 shares; Edward Wickham 16 shares (Wickham also the Master).
1858 John and Richard Doyle of Skerries, Co. Dublin. Registration transferred to Dublin.
1878 Out of Register.

In 1853, Patrick Ray, master of the **Vulcan**, lying in Cardiff Roads, was going aboard another Wexford vessel, the **Marquis of Ely** which was lying near Powell's Wharf on the Bute Road, Cardiff, when he was attacked by 2 men. They knocked him down and stole his watch and some money. Captain Ray had intended to sleep on the **Marquis of Ely** and board his own vessel in the morning. Both men were captured and sent to trial. A guilty verdict was delivered and both were transported for 10 years.

W

W.S. HAMILTON
Built 1834 at Sunderland. A barque, 298 tons.

OWNERS
1838 R. Potts of Dublin (Master: W. Carson) Dublin-Liverpool route.
1840-42 Armstrong of Liverpool (Master: D.Brown) London to China.
1846-1853 Howlett of New Ross (Masters: Black, Phelan, Murray) Cardiff to the United States; Clyde to the Black Sea;
1857 Out of register.

WAVE
No 44123.

1861 Built at St. John, New Brunswick. A wooden schooner, 67 tons. Dimensions: 76.4x17.9x9ft.

1861 Registered at Wexford

OWNERS
1861 John Barrington, Wexford (Master: Murphy).
1883 William Boxwell, Sarshill, Kilmore, Co. Wexford (Master: Busher).
1887 William Murphy, Main St., Wexford.
1907 Mrs Mary Murphy, Main St., Wexford & Robert Hanton of John St., Wexford.
1910 Mrs Mary Murphy of Crescent Quay, Wexford.
1913 Out of Register.

CREWS
1864 June
Master: Martin Codd, 44, of Carrigeen, Wexford.
Mate: Patrick Crosby, 44.
ABs: Patrick Saunders, 33; John Lambert, 23; Murtagh Whelan, 25; Laurence Carroll, 23.
Boy: William Codd, 16.

1864 Dec.
Master: Martin Codd, 29.
Mate: Laurence Carroll, 23.
Seamen: Martin Whelan, 23; Stephen Sinnott, 44; John Green, 20.
Boy: Patrick Codd, 15.

On 14 August 1892, the **Wave**, under tow by the tug **Wexford**, and under the command of Pilot Brady, was stranded on the Swanton Bank in Wexford Harbour. A special meeting was convened by Wexford Harbour Board to inquire into the circumstances of the stranding. Captain Hugh McGuire was in the chair and the members of the committee were: Mr John E. Barry J.P; Patrick Lambert; P. O' Dwyer (who was taking his seat for the first time); James Marlow; Thomas Hutchinson; and T.C. Stockdale. The witnesses examined were: Captain Busher of the **Wave**; Pilot Michael Brady; Captain Laurence Busher, Tug Master; and Captain Cogley, Pilot Master.

Having heard the evidence fully, the Committee concluded that it was an accident and blame could not be attributed to either pilot or tugmaster. Captain Cogley, however, was directed to instruct his staff to feel satisfied in future that the vessel was out of danger before they let go the tug hawser, and Captain Busher, of the tug, was requested not to blow the whistle to 'let go' until he, too, was sure that the vessel could cross the Bar safely.

In November 1907, reports reached town of two vessels that were caught out in the South Bay in a raging storm. One was a local schooner, the **Wave**. She then owned by Murphy and Nunn and was homeward bound from Newport with a cargo of coal. Captain Patrick Carty was in charge and she carried a crew of three. The **Wave** had left Newport on the Tuesday morning and, making good time, she arrived in Rosslare Bay that evening. By this stage the weather was beginning to blow up and they were forced to go to anchor, it being impossible to get in over the Wexford Bar in such conditions.

All day Wednesday and Thursday they had to stay at anchor and the weather began to deteriorate. At about quarter past five in the morning one of her anchor chains gave way, leaving her with just one to keep her secured. Soon after, that anchor started to drag and then it, too, parted. This left the ship at the mercy of the heavy seas and roaring winds and left Captain Carty with little choice other than to run for the shore. At six o'clock she grounded.

The watchman at the local coastguard station had been observing all this and as she struck he called his mate from his bed and they began to rouse the people from the neighbouring houses. In about fifteen minutes, some forty men, coast guards, naval reservists and local fishermen were assembled at the life saving apparatus ready to render assistance. Within minutes of that the apparatus was on its way to the nearest point on land to the stricken schooner. The rocket was fired to the **Wave** but it fell about fifteen yards short. The next big wave drove the schooner alongside the apparatus and one of the men onboard got hold of a boat hook and hauled the line onboard. However, once the line was onboard the coastguard saw that there was not enough line to enable the men on the ship to secure it and to enable the coastguard to haul the men ashore safely. So they had to splice another length of line to the existing one to give it sufficient length to rescue the men onboard. This was done with the utmost speed.

By now the four men on the **Wave** were in an exhausted condition, having battled tremendous seas for nearly three days. When the line reached them none of them were able to secure it in the proper position, which is immediately below the lower yard. Instead they had to lash it to the bottom of the mast. This was not satisfactory, possibly because it meant that the men were too close to the water when being hauled in, but nonetheless it worked. The men were brought ashore with just a small wetting. However, the captain, who was naturally the last man to leave his vessel was not so lucky. By the time his turn came the schooner had moved even closer to the shore and that, of course, made the hawser slacker, in fact it was touching the water.

The signal 'all right' was given and they proceeded to haul the captain in. He had not been hauled very far when the breeches buoy capsized, turning him head over heels.

He was in the water with his head under and his feet up in the air, and this was how they hauled him ashore. It is probable that he would have drowned were it not for the prompt action of two young Rosslare lads who realised his position and rushed down into the sea and dragged him ashore. He was almost unconscious and was brought to the farm of Mr Patrick Byrne at Hill O' the Sea where he was looked after by Dr Anglim and subsequently removed to Wexford Infirmary.

The other vessel in the bay at the time was the **Young Hudson** of Annalong, Co. Down. She was more fortunate than the **Wave** as her anchors held her fast throughout the gales. The crew, however, were not confident that the lines would hold and sent up distress signals. The Rosslare lifeboat, **Tom & Jenny** answered the call and brought the crew ashore. The local papers were full of praise for the seaworthiness of the **Young Hudson** describing her as 'one of the finest of her kind, even though the seas were running mountains high, it took not the slightest effect on her'. But there was a sad ending to this tale. The **Young Hudson** sank at anchor a few days later and was considered a total loss.

As for the **Wave**, she was still high and dry out near the Hill O' the Sea and the owners were trying to figure out a good and cheap way to get her cargo unloaded. In the end they decided to give the job to anyone who wanted to work at it! This news spread like wild fire and in a short time the beach at Rosslare was full of cots, about nineteen of them each with four hands, all anxious to help get the schooner lightened. By two in the afternoon, she was about eighty tons lighter, and at 2.15 the tug pulled her off into deeper water.

On 27 December 1907, James Walsh, of John Street, Wexford, mate of the **Wave**, was reported missing while the vessel was in Custom House Dock, Dublin. No sighting of him was reported or any word of his whereabouts heard and the **Wave** was forced to sail without him. The following month, January 1908, there was still no trace of Walsh and the **Wave** was back in Dublin. She was coming alongside at Custom House Dock when a body came to the surface, possibly disturbed by the movement of the ship coming alongside.

When the body was brought ashore, Captain Patrick Carthy of the **Wave** had no difficulty recognising it as James Walsh, his missing mate. At the inquest that was held, Captain Carthy gave evidence as detailed above and told the Coroner that when Walsh went ashore the previous month his vessel was tied close to the wall. Mr James Walsh, father, identified the body as that of his son who, he said, was a married man of 25 years of age. The medical evidence was to the effect that death was due to drowning and that was the verdict that was returned.

Almost 3 years later the **Wave** was yet again in trouble. She sailed from Wexford on 22 December 1911, bound for Dublin with a cargo of Malt, in bulk, for Guinness and Company. Captain Michael Smyth was in command. She left the quay on high water at 7.30 am. Weather clear and fine with a light breeze from the S.E. The weather was gradually getting worse with the wind now blowing more from the East. At 11am, the **Wave** passed between the Money Weights and the Rusk Buoys under double reefed sails. Still the wind increased in force and they took in more sails. About 3.30 pm they sighted land. The ship was still on course, steering ENE in an increasing gale and under 'small canvas'.

Seeing land off the port bow they tried to stay the vessel but she wouldn't stay. They tried a second time with the same results. By this time the fore and aft sails had blown away as the ship came into the wind. The captain then squared the yards and, in an effort to save lives, ran his ship for the beach. She beached north of Mizen Head, in Ardanairy Bay, Co. Wicklow and the crew all got ashore safely in the ship's lifeboat. However, the **Wave** was considered a total loss.

WEXFORD
1829: Built at Quebec, a barque, carvel built, female figurehead, 280 tons.

OWNERS 1841: Allens of Wexford (Master: John Slattery).

CREW 1842
Master: John Slattery, 41.
Mate: D. Brown, 47.
Seamen: Thomas White, 29; Denis Doyle, 28; Laurence English, 21; Alexander McLofty*, 24; George Malloy, 20; Robert Forest, 24.
Cook: –? Conran, 45.
Carpenter: Patrick Furlong, 23.
Apprentices: Thomas Creighton, 18; Thomas Murphy, 19; Thomas Lambert, 20.
*McLofty was an Antrim man who jumped ship in Quebec and was replaced by Robert Forest, from Waterford.
The **Wexford**'s principle trade seems to have been Wexford to Savannah with emigrants and back to Liverpool with cotton, although as can be seen above, she also traded to Quebec. This trade was probably emigrants out and timber back. That trade was prevalent until the more accessible, pleasant, temperate, climate of Savannah was realised. Unlike Quebec, Savannah did not ice up in winter and remained open all year round.

WEXFORD
No.16021.Code, LVRB.

1851 Built at New Brunswick, a barque, 307 tons. Dimensions: 105x26x16ft.

OWNERS
1851-1868: R.& R. Allen, Wexford (Master: Captain Larry English). Gloucester to Savannah route.

On 9 February 1861, the barque **Wexford**, bound for Savannah, was hit by a massive sea 70 miles south-west of Tuskar Rock and three men were washed over the side. The three men, Neville, Campbell and Duggan, were all natives of Wexford. The ship put back into Queenstown for repairs. **Wexford** was one of the three local ships caught in Constantinople at the outbreak of the Crimean War in 1854.

Captain Joseph Codd of the Faythe, Wexford, master of the ship **Wexford**, for Brazil and the Southern States of America, died in Savannah, Georgia in 1879, from a disease contracted in Brazil.

Three masted barque **Wexford**

A note from her registration papers says: *and seized upon the high seas and brought into the port of Sydney, Cape Breton as bearing ship*, but gives no date.

WILLIAM THOMPSON
No. 15205.

1843 Built at Glencaple, a schooner, 66 tons. Dimensions: 63.3x18.7x9.6ft.

OWNERS
1865 Charles Bie, Kirkcudbright.
1904-1909 Thomas Cullimore, Stonebridge, Wexford.
1910 John Brown, Green St., Wexford.
1911 7 April. Register closed. Vessel broken up.

In September 1903 the schooner **William Thompson** which had gone ashore at Ballygeary, near Rosslare, in the recent storm, was refloated but not without the loss of some of her cargo of bricks.
In January 1908, the **William Thompson** entered the Bay one Monday evening. She was loaded with coals from Newport. On Tuesday she began taking in water. Captain Kehoe signaled for assistance but the weather was so bad that the tugboat was unable to venture out to them. On New Year's Day, **Tom & Jenny**, the lifeboat from Rosslare, went out twice but were still unable to help. At the time of the report she was still riding at anchor in the Bay, waiting for fine weather.

WEXFORD PACKET
Reg. at Wexford 1835, 1837,

CREWS
1837
Master: Peter Clancy, 44;
Mates: James Cleary, 45; Michael Furlong, 25.
Sailors: Peter Monk, 35; Nicholas Cleary, 46; Laurence McGee, 17.

1838
Master: Ed Cleary, 45.
Mates: Nicholas Furlong, 26; Pat Moor, 35.
OS: Laurence McGee, 18.

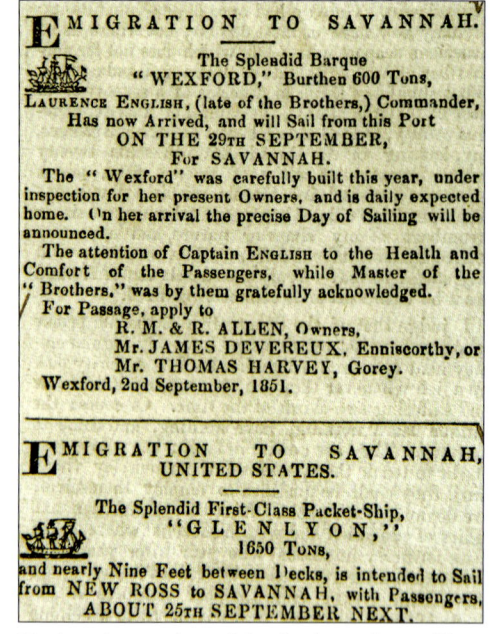

EMIGRATION TO SAVANNAH.

The Splendid Barque
"WEXFORD," Burthen 600 Tons,
LAURENCE ENGLISH, (late of the Brothers,) Commander,
Has now Arrived, and will Sail from this Port
ON THE 29TH SEPTEMBER,
For SAVANNAH.

The "Wexford" was carefully built this year, under inspection for her present Owners, and is daily expected home. On her arrival the precise Day of Sailing will be announced.

The attention of Captain ENGLISH to the Health and Comfort of the Passengers, while Master of the "Brothers," was by them gratefully acknowledged.

For Passage, apply to
R. M. & R. ALLEN, Owners,
Mr. JAMES DEVEREUX, Enniscorthy, or
Mr. THOMAS HARVEY, Gorey.
Wexford, 2nd September, 1851.

EMIGRATION TO SAVANNAH, UNITED STATES.

The Splendid First-Class Packet-Ship,
"GLENLYON,"
1650 Tons,
and nearly Nine Feet between Decks, is intended to Sail from NEW ROSS to SAVANNAH, with Passengers, ABOUT 25TH SEPTEMBER NEXT.

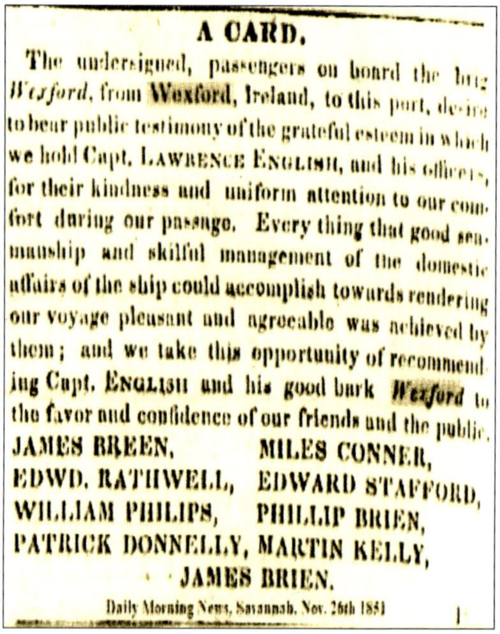

A CARD.

The undersigned, passengers on board the brig *Wexford*, from Wexford, Ireland, to this port, desire to bear public testimony of the grateful esteem in which we hold Capt. LAWRENCE ENGLISH, and his officers, for their kindness and uniform attention to our comfort during our passage. Every thing that good seamanship and skilful management of the domestic affairs of the ship could accomplish towards rendering our voyage pleasant and agreeable was achieved by them; and we take this opportunity of recommending Capt. ENGLISH and his good bark *Wexford* to the favor and confidence of our friends and the public.

JAMES BREEN,   MILES CONNER,
EDWD. RATHWELL,   EDWARD STAFFORD,
WILLIAM PHILIPS,   PHILLIP BRIEN,
PATRICK DONNELLY, MARTIN KELLY,
JAMES BRIEN.

Daily Morning News, Savannah, Nov. 26th 1851.

Emigration notice of the forthcoming sailing of the barque **Wexford** to Savannah, September 1851. *Co. Wexford Archives.*

Passenger testimony to Captain English of the barque **Wexford.** November 1851. *Courtesy, Peggy McHale and Kieran Cronin, Waterford Institute of Technology.*

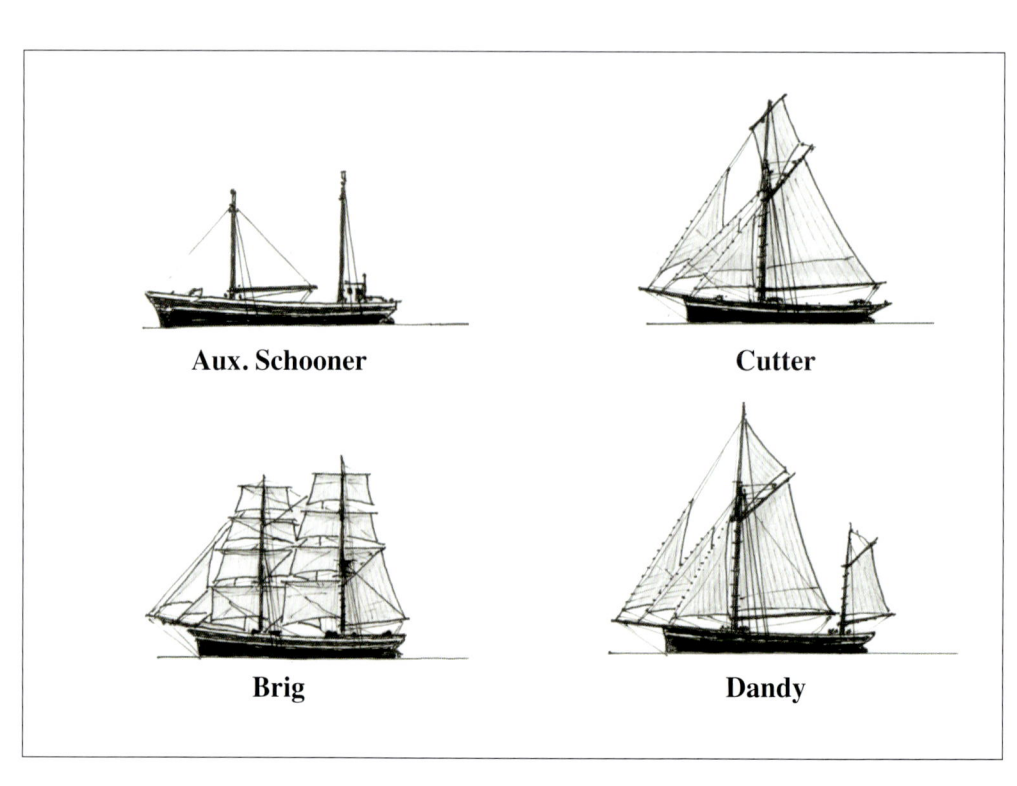

Aux. Schooner

Cutter

Brig

Dandy

294

Y

YARRA YARRA
No 45477

1870 Built at Douglas, Isle of Man, by William Qualtrought, 64 tons. Dimensions: 68x19x9ft.

OWNERS
1880 William Kelly, Douglas, Isle of Man.
1882 Michael Flanagan, Skerries, Co. Dublin.
1900 Mrs M. Flanagan;
1906, Patrick Byrne, Merchant, Wexford.
1908 J. J. Stafford, Patrick Byrne, both of Wexford.
1908 6 Jan. Sold to: Thomas Bridson, of Castletown, Isle of Man, labourer. James Claque, coal merchant; Charles Edward Watterson, Master carpenter. Register transferred to Isle of Man.
1915 Out of register.

The Skerries schooner, **Yarra Yarra**, came into Wexford ownership after she went ashore at Rosslare in March 1904. She had been moored at Rosslare by her small anchor due to a malfunctioning windlass that made it impossible to drop the main one. Once a gale blew up, her position was precarious and she eventually dragged her mooring and went up on the beach near the coastguard station. The coastguards went to her assistance immediately but were unable to utilise their rocket apparatus because of the schooner's distance from their position.

The Ballygeary (Rosslare Harbour) lifeboat, **Tom & Jenny**, came out and got the 5-man crew ashore safely. The **Yarra Yarra** afterwards shifted into deeper water and sank. However, she was later refloated and sold to Mr J.J. Stafford, Mayor of Wexford. He

Yarra Yarra at Waterford

appears to have sold it to Patrick Byrne of Wexford, described as a merchant. In 1908 he sold her to the Isle of Man. Wexford's well-known mariner Captain Thomas 'Lanigan' Walsh was master of **Yarra Yarra** for a time. On 11 February 1914, **Yarra Yarra** was en route from Point of Ayr to Castletown, with coal, when she became a total wreck at Port Erin, Isle of Man. Crew of three saved.

YOUNG DAN
No. 140470.

Built 1899 at Wick, Caithness by Harper. A ketch. Dimensions: 66.8x19.3x8.1ft. **Young Dan** was originally built as a fishing vessel but in 1920 she was registered in Dublin as auxiliary cargo vessel.

OWNERS: James Hagen, 13 shares; Thomas Biristee, 13 shares; Lawrence O'Toole, 13 shares; and Charles J. Louth, 12 shares, all from Arklow. Michael J. O'Connor, of Wexford, had the final 13 shares.

In January 1926, **Young Dan** struck the ground when trying to enter Arklow Harbour for shelter. She lost her rudder and was taken in tow by a motor vessel but the towrope parted and she went ashore about a mile north of Mizen Head, Co. Wicklow.

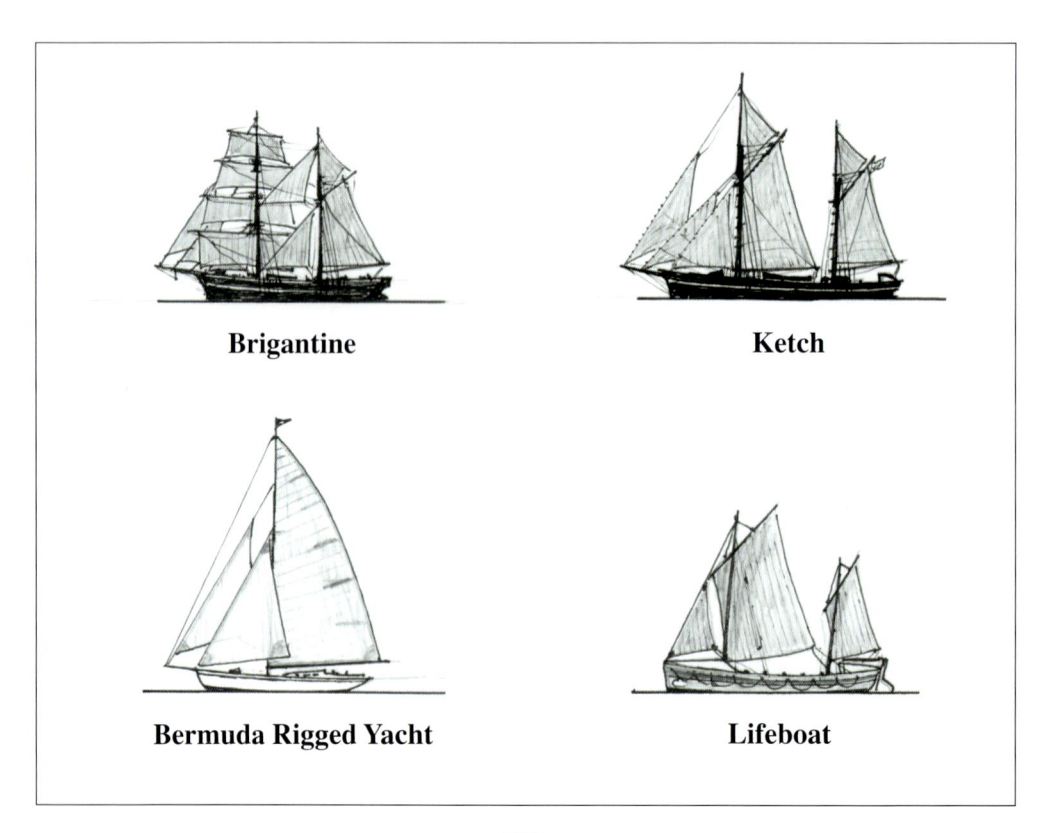

Brigantine

Ketch

Bermuda Rigged Yacht

Lifeboat

Z

ZION HILL
No. 55356.Code, KRVC.

Built 1866 at Llanealhaiarn, Caernarfon by Evans, a schooner of 79 tons. Dimensions: 76 x21.6 x11. 2ft.

OWNERS
1891 Stafford of Wexford;
1904 James Kinch of Arklow;
1913 Mrs Elizabeth Sherwood of 2 Lower Main St., Arklow;
1919 George Grounds of Runcorn, Cheshire;
1923 Out of register.

CREW 1891.
Master: Richard Smith, 21 William St, Wexford.
Mate: John Cahill, 57; William Connolly, 43.
ABs: Bernard Lacey, 20; William Smith, 17.
OS: Nicholas Hogan, 15 (Later signed on as OS and Cook).
Others: Walter Pender, 19; Laurence Cushie, 20 (First trip) Nicholas Marlow,15.

In June 1898, Patrick Byrne of Barntown, Wexford, Boy of the **Zion Hill**, was injured at Ayr. He was going aboard another Wexford schooner, **Jane Hughes**, owner Captain Morris, when he slipped and sustained serious injuries.

On 27 October 1913, **Zion Hill** left Wexford bound for Newport, Monmouthshire with a cargo of timber shipped by Billington of Wexford to Browning of Cardiff. They crossed Wexford Bar and proceeded to the South Bay where they went to anchor. About 2 am the wind freshened and came from the S.E. They let go the other anchor and put springs on both anchors to prevent them from slipping. The next day the ship was dragging her anchors so the captain slipped the cables and headed for the beach. In such circumstances this was the accepted method to try to save the vessel and the lives of the men. She came ashore about 2½ miles north of Ballygeary Coastguard Station. All hands were saved by lifesaving apparatus. On 17 July 1922, en route from Bideford to Glasgow with a cargo of clay she sprung a leak 7 miles S. by W. of Maughold Head, Isle of Man and, while under tow, she sank. All hands were saved.

Zion Hill, the two masted tops'l schooner of 79 tons. Built in 1866 at Llanealhaearn, Caernarfon. Original painting by Reuben Chappell.
Courtesy Arklow Maritime Mueseum.

Zion Hill, docked adjacent to Caernarfon Castle, North Wales.

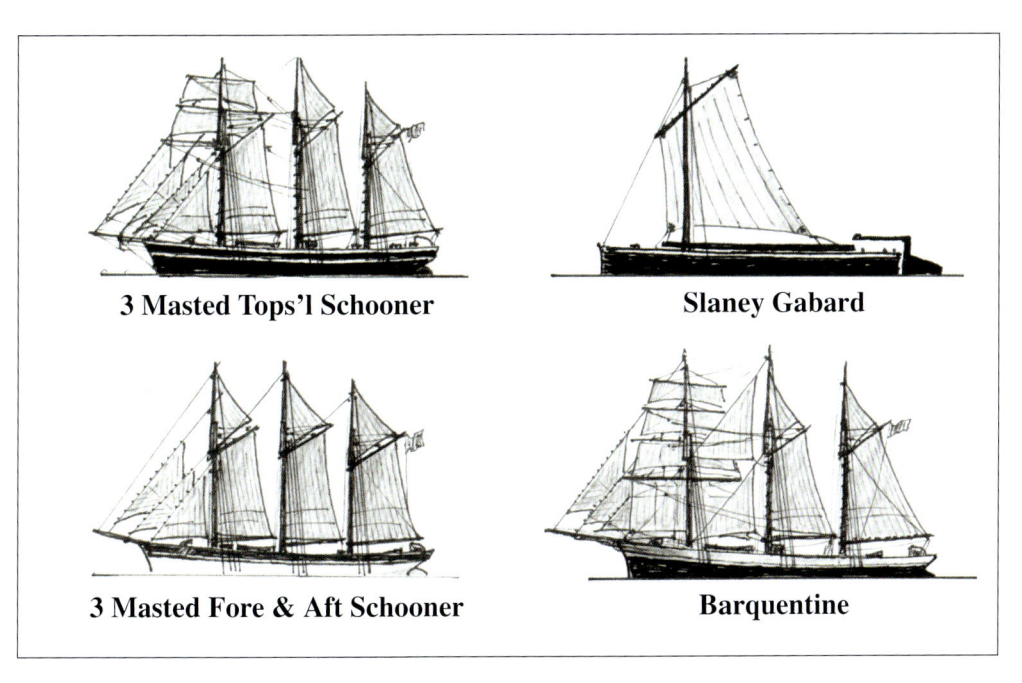

3 Masted Tops'l Schooner

Slaney Gabard

3 Masted Fore & Aft Schooner

Barquentine

Sail plans of a barque.

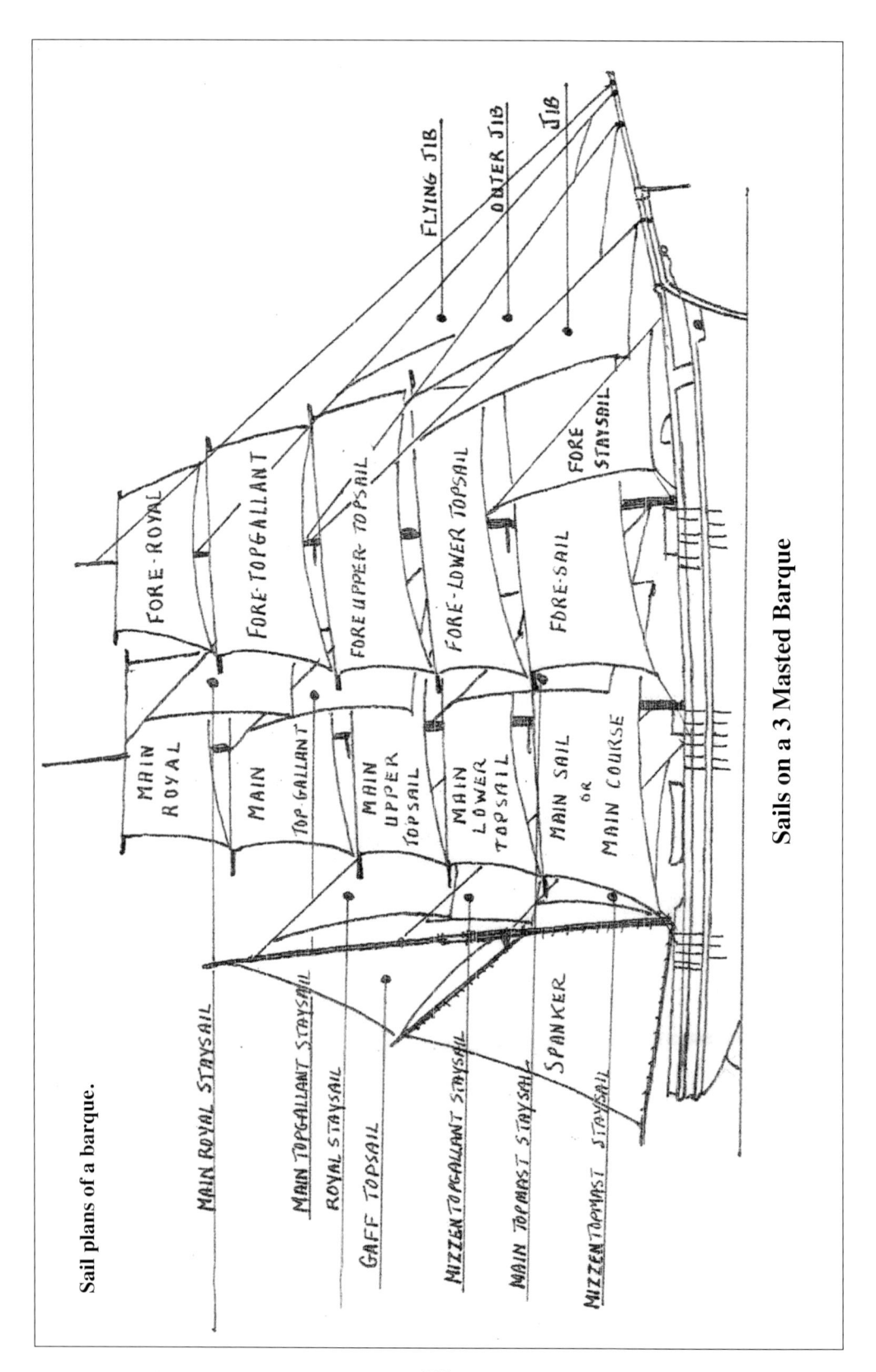

Sails on a 3 Masted Barque

Part 2:
Miscellaneous Other Wexford ships

A

ACTIVE: No.18234. Built 1829 at Bridport, Dorset. Registered at Wexford, 1834, 78 tons. Master: T Hawse

AGINORA: Built 1844 at St John, New Brunswick, a barque, 176 tons. Male figurehead. Registered at Wexford, 1845. Master: James Quinn.
OWNERS: Nicholas Sinnott of Enniscorthy, 32 shares; Coun ??, MM, of Wexford, 16 shares; James Quinn MM, of Wexford, 16 shares. Vessel wrecked off the coast of Cornwall.

AIMWELL: Registered, 1834. 90 tons. Master: J. English.

ALBINUS: No. 11537. Code KTCD. Built 1852 at Quebec. A barque of 500 tons. Dimensions: 137.6x28x 18.3 ft.
OWNERS
1855 Oxley of Liverpool.
1856 Payne of Liverpool.
1862 J. Galavan of New Ross.
1865 John Curran of New Ross.
1872 Galavan of New Ross.
1888 Out of Register.

ALBION: Registered 1834, 101 tons. Built at Chester, 1831.
OWNER: Devereux. Master: T. Connor.

ALERT: No. 39175. Code SNFP. Built 1857 at Prince Edward Island. A schooner 79 tons. Dimensions: 76.1 x 20.3 x 8.3 ft. Registered in Wexford 1858-1864.
OWNER: Barrington of Wexford. **1865** Out of Register.

ALMA: No. 37237. Code SDFL. Built 1855 at Digby, Nova Scotia. A schooner, 93 tons. Dimensions: 74x21.4x9.5ft.
OWNERS
1865 Thomas Brown, Waterford.
1872-1882 J. Cardiff, Wexford, registered as 74 tons.
In 1882, the **Alma** was in a collision with the **Rambler** off Cloughy Head. The **Alma** sank and the crew were taken into Donaghadee by the **Rambler**.

FIRE AT THE WEST DOCK, CARDIFF.

This morning, about two o'clock, the schooner Alma, of Wexford, Capt. Murphy, was discovered to be on fire in the West Dock, Cardiff, and before assistance could be obtained the fire had spread considerably in the fore part of the ship, where it originated. Major Bond, with the borough police force and fire brigade, was quickly on the spot; also Captains Frazer and Pengelley, and the dock police, through whose united efforts the fire was ultimately subdued.

Notice of the fire on the **Alma**.
Wexford Independent

Albinus, a 504 ton barque. Built in Quebec 1852.

ANN: Built 1827 at Quebec, 313 tons. Registered at Wexford, 1834.
OWNERS
Hartrick of Waterford, sailed from New Ross.
1843 Martin Howlett, James Commins, Joseph Jeffares.
Ann was one of the vessels detained in New Ross for tobacco smuggling in May, 1843.

ANN & KATE: No. 24426. Registered at Wexford, 20 Sept 1836. 46 tons.

ANNIE: No. 42170. Built 1861 at Prince Edward Island. A schooner, 106 tons. Dimensions: 76x21.8x9.4ft.
OWNERS
William Philpot of Arklow.
1872 William Tyrell of Arklow.
1883 John Cardiff of Wexford.
1888 Patrick Lambert of Wexford.
1897 Francis J. Walsh, Wexford Dockyard Co.
1897 K. Farrissy of Clonakilty, Co. Cork.
1903 August. The **Annie** was bound from Newport with coal for Bantry when she was wrecked near Brow Head, Co. Cork. All hands were rescued.

ANNIE: A fishing yawl.

ANTELOPE: No. 8663. Code VNBH. Built at Nantes, France. A schooner 42 tons. Registered in 1850.
OWNERS
Robert Sparrow, merchant, John Barrington, merchant, and Simon Lambert, MM.
1856 July. Sparrow sold his shares to the other two and the vessel was registered anew.
1865 John Barrington.
1887 Out of Register.
CREW 1852
Master: Simon Lambert, 60.
Walter Rossiter, 63; Matthew Bryan, 23; Joseph Breen, 17.
Later that same year Simon Lambert was still master and the crew were:
Mate: Walter Rossiter, 55.
Seaman: John Starling, 22.
Boy: James Williams, 21.

ARBITRATOR: No. 63406. Built 1864 at Wexford. A smack of 22 tons.
1875 OWNER: Matthew Dignam of Wexford. Tender to the Lucifer Light Vessel.
1885 Out of Register.

ARCTIC: Registered 1834. 53 tons. Master: J. Murphy.

ARTURO: Registered 1844, Wexford. At Wexford, 7 July 1849.
OWNERS
Nicholas Sinnott of Enniscorthy.
William James Lamport, of Liverpool.

Henry Jordan, of Liverpool, shipowner.
George Clifton, of Sunderland.
1856 Registration transferred to Sunderland. Vessel wrecked off the coast of Cornwall

AURORA: Built 1840 at Wexford Dockyard,
OWNERS: J O' Connor, Denis Kenselagh and Martin Walsh.

AUSPICIOUS. Registered 1834. Built at Bannow.
OWNER: C. Morris. Master: P. Meyler.

AVENELL: No. 105514. Code PHQC. Built 1895 at Poole. A yawl of 10 tons. Dimensions: 36.9 x 6ft.
OWNERS
1897 C.G. Hill of Torquay, Devon.
1898 W. E. Nicholson of Headingly, Yorks.
1899 Michael J. O'Connor of Glenville, Wexford.
1902 William Phillips, Southend, Essex.
1913 Col. D. M. Thompson, Peel, Isle of Man.
1917 Register closed.

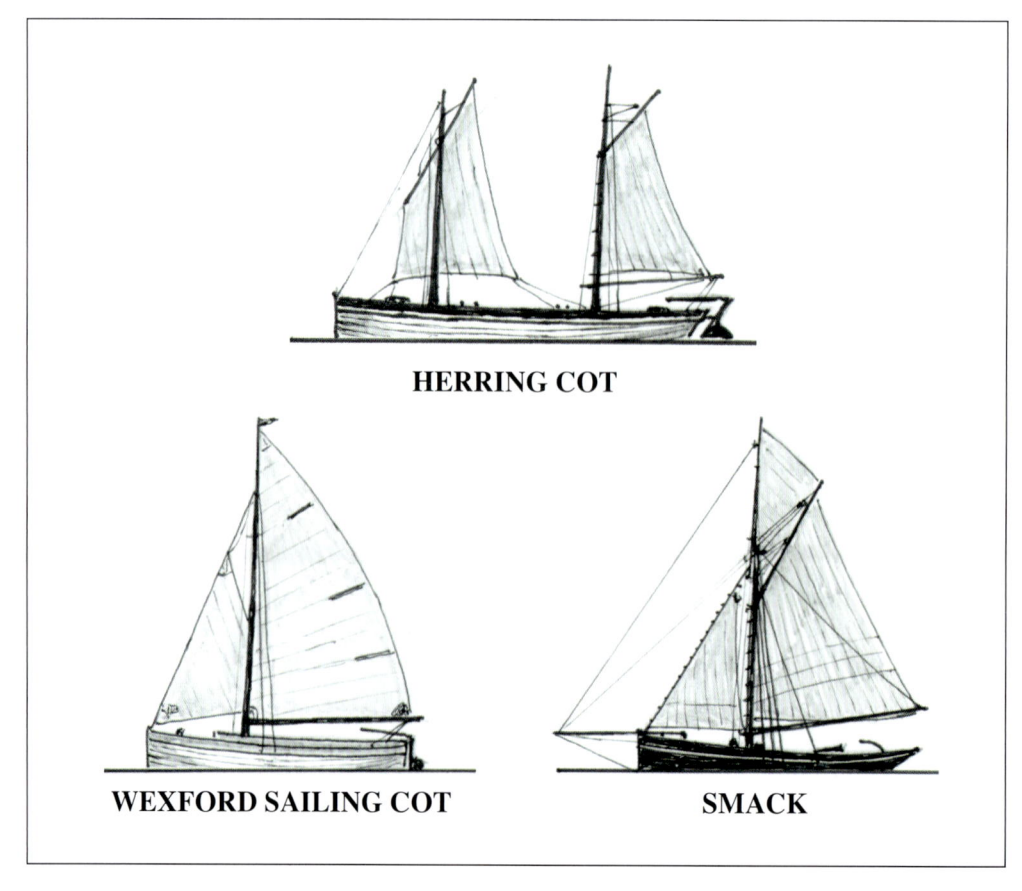

HERRING COT

WEXFORD SAILING COT

SMACK

B

BEE: No. 63405. Built at Wexford in 1862. A dandy, 17.65 tons.
OWNER
1875 Matthew Dignam of Wexford.
1878 Out of Register.

BERGMANN: No. 7939. Code JWCG. Built in 1846 at Bridgeport. A barque of 350 tons. **OWNER**: Galavan of New Ross.
1865 Out of Register.

BERTHOLLY: Built 1837 at Newport. A schooner of 58 tons.
OWNER: Graves of New Ross.

BESS: No. 1172. At Wexford, 1831. A sloop.
On 28 January 1831, the Wexford sloop**, Bess,** Captain George Hayes, was lost on the Horseshoe Bank near Wicklow. All hands were saved. She had left Wexford only two days previously.

BETSEY: No. 21446. Code NGJR. Registered at Wexford 1849. 17 tons.

BILLOW: No. 21422. Code NGHC. Built in 1836 at St. Martin's, New Brunswick. A schooner, 82 tons. Registered at Wexford 1855;
OWNER: A. Whitty of Wexford.
1855 6 May. Endorsed on articles: *I hereby certify that Laurence Butler whose certificate is 50312, has been appointed master of* **Billow** *in place of Greg. Devereux. Signed A. Watson, registrar.*
1861 8 February. Vessel abandoned. She was bound for Gloucester with a cargo of oats when she had to be abandoned near the Smalls. Six crew saved.

BREEZE: Official No. 8508. Code KCMF. Built in 1849 at St John, New Brunswick. 123 tons. Registered at Wexford in 1849.
OWNERS
Allen Bros. of Wexford.
1853 She was on the Galatz run when her master was Captain J. King.
1863 Allen Bros sold to James Farmer of Belfast, accountant and John McConnell of Bangor, MM. Registration transferred to Belfast.

BRIDGET: No. 23547. Code NSCR. Built in 1854. A barquentine.
OWNERS
1864 Edward Roche, Robert Browne, Liverpool; Thomas Hughes, Richard Walsh Liverpool.
1868 Henry Dixon, Workington.
1872 Out of Register

BRILLIANT: A schooner built in Bridgeport in 1787, 34 tons.
1853 OWNER: Francis Harper; Captain: J. Murphy.

BRITANNIA: No. 79369. Code JFPC. Built in 1883 at Stromness, Orkney, by Fred Stanger. A schooner, 73 tons.
OWNERS
1883 George Jamieson of Wicklow; in **1885** re-rigged as a ketch.
1888 T.J. O'Keefe of Paul Quay, Wexford, maltster, corn, and coal merchant.
1890 Claude William S. Gould of Barnstaple, Devon.
1890 Oliver William Jenkins of Beckenham, Kent and John J. Todd of North Walk, Barnstaple.
1899 Register closed.

BRITISH QUEEN: No. 8875. Code KDWP. Built in 1840 at Runcorn. A schooner of 77tons.
1882 registered as 67 tons.

OWNERS
1860 Thomas Kearns & Thomas Troy of Arklow.
1865 Thomas Troy of Wicklow;
1875 Mrs Nancy Troy of Wicklow;
1876 Captain Hutchinson of Wexford.
1882 25 March. Was driven ashore near Port Isaac on the coast of Cornwall. The crew were rescued by lifeboat but the ship was a total loss.

> **WRECK OF A WEXFORD VESSEL.**
> On Saturday last the schooner "British Queen" belonging to Captain Hutchinson, H.C., left here in ballast for the Bristol Channel. On Sunday she drove ashore during the storm at Port Isaac on the Cumberland coast. The crew were rescued by the lifeboat. The vessel soon afterwards became a total wreck.

Report of the wreck of the **British Queen,** 1882.
Wexford People.

BROTHERS: No. 21434. Registered 1846. **OWNER**: J.P. Devereux.

BROTHERS: No. 1259. Registered in 1846.
OWNERS: Richard, Robert and Maurice Allen.
1850 Maurice died January
1855 Sold to John Tyrell and Peter Kinch both MMs from Arklow.
1855 Register transferred to Dublin.

BULWARK. On 17 March 1832, the brigantine **Bulwark** of Wexford, Captain John Barry, with a cargo of grain for Glasgow, had to be taken into Port Patrick waterlogged. Captain and crew were all safe and the report stated that both the ship and the cargo were insured. However, it said that the **Bulwark** was left lying on her beam ends, wrecked.

C

CALUMET (ex **FAIR GERALDINE**): No. 70152. Built by Fairlie of Fife in 1864. A cutter, 1 mast. Registered at Wexford in 1886.
OWNERS: Simon Little, Cullentra, Co. Wexford, and John Perceval, Barntown, Co. Wexford. They sold to Norris Goddard.

CATHERINE: No. 28224. Code PVML. 72 tons.
OWNERS
1865 M.F. O'Connor, Wexford.
1870 Richard O'Connor, Wexford. 1875 out of reg.
1873 September. Llanelli to Wexford, struck the Crow Rocks at Milford Haven. Total loss. Crew saved.

CERES: Built in 1843 at Wexford. 118 tons. Dimensions: 76x19x10ft.

CHANCE: No 21415. Code NGFQ. Built in 1845 at Port Glasgow. A schooner, later re-rigged as a barquentine. 76 tons.
OWNERS
1865 Richard O'Connor of Wexford.
1876 Miss Anna O'Connor of Wexford.
1888 Out of Register.

CHARLOTTE: No. 1129. Code HGRF. Built in 1804 at Newport, Pembrokeshire. A schooner, 104 tons; in 1865 registered as 75 tons.
OWNERS
1865 James Hughes, Margaret Cullen, Michael Williams all of Wexford.
1867 James Sheil of William St., Wexford.
1868 James Hughes of Wexford.
1870 Richard Devereux, Wexford.
1879 J.T. Devereux of Wexford;
1885 Michael Dickenson of Arklow.
1890 Out of Register.

CHRISTINA DAVIS: No. 51975. Built in 1865 at Whitehaven, Cumbria. A schooner of 85 tons. Dimensions: 81.4x19.5x8.9ft.
OWNERS: Matthew Cassin of Waterford, Peter O'Shea of New Ross, and Kathleen Cassin of Notting Hill, London.
1918 29 April. Stopped by German submarine **U105** as she was en route from Newport to Duncannon, Co. Wexford. Sunk by gunfire. Crew saved.

CLAREEN: No. 86521. Built in 1884 at Plymouth. A ketch of 78 tons. Dimensions: 81.9x20.5x9.4ft.
1924 September. Wrecked and abandoned at Churchpoint, near Arthurstown, Co. Wexford. Wreck purchased by Bertie Downes of Duncannon, Co. Wexford. Repaired and sold to Catherine J. Griffiths of Aberystwyth.
1927 August. Registration closed. Vessel broken up.

COLLECTOR: No. 18332. Code MLJC. Built in 1852 at Prince Edward Island. A barquentine of 97 tons. Dimensions: 73x21. 2x9.7ft.
OWNERS
1865 William Parle, Waterford.
1880 William Parle of Bannow, Co. Wexford.
1885 Out of Register.

COMMERCE: No. 21433. NGHT. Registered at Wexford in **1853**.
OWNERS: J. T. Devereux. Sold to John Codd, Wexford, shipowner.
CREW 1888,
Master: James Murphy, 55.
Mate: Nicholas Bent, 36.
OS: John Hall, 19.
Boys: Charles Goran, 16; Laurence Furlong, 17.
Captain Cogley, Pilot Master, reported to the Harbour Commissioners that the schooner **Commerce** which had gone aground on the Swanton Bank on the 30 October 30 1891 was likely to become a wreck. She was in charge of Pilot Carley who said that he had mistook the buoys. The Chairman said *that was an error of judgement on his part, I suppose*, and there the matter ended.

COMPTON: of New Ross. Captain Houghton. Lost in the Atlantic. Bound from Dalhousie to Cardiff with timber. Four boys and the cook lost. Captain and twelve crew saved by British ship, **Correo** and the survivors were taken into New Orleans.

CONCORD. No. 20251. Code MWJB. Built 1859 at Wexford by Sparrow. A schooner. 77 tons. Dimensions, 80.0x20.7x9.5ft.
OWNERS
1870 J. Hamlet, Balbriggan, Co. Dublin.
1885 Thomas Ryan, Rush, Co. Dublin.
1887 John Fitzsimons, Baldoyle, Co. Dublin.
1909 John Ryan, Skerries, Co. Dublin.
1930 June. Registration closed; vessel broken up.

COUNTESS: No. 10152. Code KMGS. Built in 1848 at Gosport. A dandy, 18 tons. Registered at Wexford 11 March 1850.
OWNERS
1850 H. Knox Grogan of Johnstown Castle.
1854 Knox Grogan died. New owner was John Hatchell.
1856 13 June. Hatchell sold her to George Power Haughton of Kilmallock, Co. Wexford. Haughton then sold her to David Stewart Ker of County Down. Registration transferred to Strangford.
1861 19 June. Registration cancelled.

CRAYSHORT: Registered in 1834. 54 tons. Master: J. Kearon.

CRITERION. No. 11635. Code. KTLP. Built, 1834 at Yarmouth, a schooner, 86 tons. Registered 1854.
OWNERS
James Hughes MM, 16 shares; James Shile, MM, 10 shares; Mary Daloav, 16 shares; Edward Rouge, 11 shares; John Guilfoile, 11shares.
1860 Michael Williams; Thomas Laffan; Thomas Hughes; John Devereux.
1865 Margaret Cullen of Wexford.
1867 James Hughes, the Faythe, Wexford.
1876 Michael Williams, Wexford.
1885 Out of Register.

D

DANIEL O'CONNELL: No. 21432. Built in 1834 at New Brunswick. A schooner, carvel built. 73 tons.
OWNERS: J. T. Devereux.
1856 John Kearon of Arklow, registered at Dublin.

DART: No. 44128. Code RBTL. Built in 1862 at Garmouth. A schooner of 97 tons. Dimensions: 87x22.4x 9. 5ft. Registered at Wexford in 1863.
OWNERS
1863-1870 Richard Devereux.
1875 J.T. Devereux.
1885 John E. Barry, Crescent Quay, Wexford.
1890 Patrick Lambert, Wexford.
1897 Francis J. Walsh of Crescent Quay, Wexford.
1902 John McCarthy, Youghal, Co. Cork.
1909 George P. Francis, Pembroke Dock.
1910 March wrecked and registration closed, vessel broken up.
CREWS
1863
Master: William Neill of William St., Wexford, 58.
Mate: Thomas Neill, 35.
ABs: James Lambert, 24; James Corish, 25; Patrick Carty, 31.
Boy: William Neill, 17.
1864
Master: William Neill, William St., Wexford, 62.
Mate: Stephen Furlong 33.
AB: George Molloy, 30.
Others: William Neale, 18; James Cousins, 28.
Boy: Patrick Ennis, 16.

Captain Nicholas Dempsey of the **Dart** and his crew.
Courtesy of Mrs Kathleen Fitzpatrick. Trinity St. Wexford.

DARING: No. 20121. A cutter. New Ross, 1880.

DART: Registered in 1834. 54 tons. Master: E. Cullin.

DAZZLER: No. 63491. Built in 1865 at Wexford. A dandy of 24 tons.
1870 OWNER: Thomas Neill, Wexford.
1882 20 November. Vessel wrecked.

DINDEN: Registered at Wexford in 1835.

DOLPHIN: Registered at Wexford in 1845.
CREW 1845.
Master: James Codd, 31.
Mate: David Roche, 53.
Seaman: John Kelly, 24.
Apprentice: Michael McNamara, 18.
Boy: Laurence Walsh, 15.
Also that year: Seamen: John Breen, 40; John Tierney, 23.
Boys: Francis Parle, 15; James Byrne, 17.

DON JUAN: No. 20617. Code NBVK. Built in 1830 at Yarmouth, Nova Scotia. A schooner of 44 tons.
OWNERS
1865 D. Robertson, Ardrossan, Ayr.
1870 Robert Craig, Saltcoats, Ayr.
1875 David Mackay, Ardrossan, Ayr.
1876 James Clark, Ardrossan.
1876 Thomas Hutchinson, Wexford. Master: Thomas Newport, William St.
1878. **Don Juan** struck the rocks off Skokholm Island, West Wales and became a total loss. All crew were saved.

DOPSON: No. 14236. Code LMHB. Built in 1849 at Prince Edward Island. A schooner of 85 tons.
OWNERS
1865 Elizabeth Hearn, Dungarvan, Co. Waterford.
1867 Michael Whelan, Waterford.
1870 John Hanlon, Fisherstown, Co. Wexford.
1876 James Neill, Kilmannock, Co. Wexford.
1894 James O'Neill of Arthurstown, Mary O'Neill of Arthurstown, Co. Wexford.
1894 11 February. Ballyhack to Cardiff with hay went aground in a gale near Milford and became a complete wreck, crew saved. Captain Sweeney of Fethard-on-Sea was in command.
1894 Register closed.

DORDOGNE: No. 70146. Built in 1849 at Tressac, France. A schooner of 55tons.
1880
OWNER Simon Roche of Ballygow, Bannow, Co. Wexford.
1883 Out of Register.

DOVE: No. 21413. Code NGFM. Built in 1839 at Barnstaple. A schooner of 55 tons. Registered at Wexford 1845 to 1859.
CREW 1845
Master: John Hore, 30.

Mate: William Lawless, 53.
Seamen: Patrick Dowd, 24; John Codd, 19.
Boy: Patrick Devereux, 17.
The **Dove** was lost in a collision in the Severn during August 1859 when she was going down the river. She collided with a French ship going in the opposite direction. Afterwards she struck The Grogey and within an hour sank on the Shoots. All the crew got off safely with time to retrieve their belongings. As usual, her cargo of oats was insured but not so the ship itself.

DROVER: Registered at Wexford in 1841.
OWNERS: Breen & Devereux.
CREW 1841
Master: John Campbell, 40.
Seamen: Patrick Lambert, 40; Patrick Lynch, 26; Patrick Ray, 27; Martin Atkinson, 24.
Apprentices: Joseph Ray, 19; John Rowe, 18.

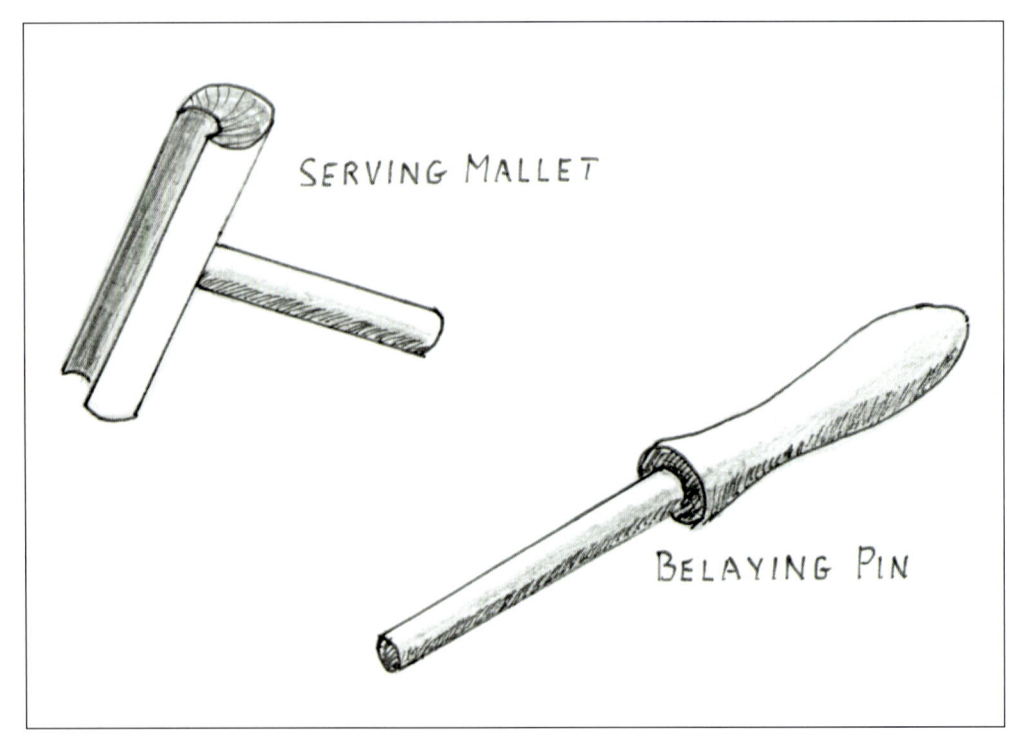

SERVING MALLET

BELAYING PIN

E

EDWARD: No. 70151. Built in 1863 at Penzance, Cornwall.
1882 Registered in Wexford. **OWNER**: Samuel Armstrong.
1893 08 May. Registration cancelled.

EDWARD
1872 Captain Lambert of the **Edward** donated his half share of the **Edward** towards the building of the wall of the new church at Bride St., Wexford.
1875 Registered at Wexford.
1875 November. Foundered near Carlingford Lough in heavy weather, when en route from Wexford to Ayr with a cargo of beans. A passing steamer took the crew off and brought them to Cardiff.

EFFORT
1843 OWNER: Mr Redmond of Lancaster Place, Wexford. Master: Captain Adams. There was great interest created in the port by the arrival of this barque. She arrived in mid-September after a trip from the African port of Magazan (?). Among her cargo were tortoises, chameleons, porcupines, African goats and other exotic species. Also she carried specimens of vegetable types from the tropics.

EGMONT: No. 50940. Built in 1867 at Prince Edward Island. A brig, 2 masts. 180 tons. Dimensions: 100.2x23.5x12.4ft.
OWNERS
1868 Abraham Sutton, Cork.
1879 William Collier, Newport, Monmouthshire.
1880 Mrs Sarah Lynch, Cork.
1885 Mrs Margaret Armstrong, Wexford.
1885 28 May. Broken up.
1888 Out of Register.

EILEEN: No. 63403. Code LVQN. Built in 1871 at Wexford. A schooner 20 tons.
OWNERS
1875 Laurence Devereux, Wexford.
1883 James P. Devereux, Wexford.
1940 Still registered in Wexford.

ELDORADO: No.70151. Built in1863 at Porthleven, Cornwall. A schooner, 2 masts. 15 tons. Registered at Wexford in 1882.
OWNERS
1883 Samuel Armstrong, Wexford; S. G. Armstrong.
1893 Vessel unseaworthy.
1894 Out of Register.

ELIZA LOUISE. 1843, Owner James Howlett, New Ross. Captain James Conway.

ELIZABETH JANE: No. 8825. Code KOSH. Built in 1855 at Arklow by John Tyrell. A ketch of 66tons.
1865-1889 John Doyle, Arklow.
1915 Registered in Wexford 1915.
1915 December. Lost off The Mumbles, Swansea with the loss of all three hands. Two boys walking the beach found a body that was thought to be a member of the crew of the ketch.

ELLEN HARRISON: No. 76891. Code HWKL. Built in 1878 at Ulverston.
A schooner of 103 tons. Dimensions: 83.5x21x9.6ft.
OWNERS
1878 William Postlethwaite of Barrow.
1913 Richard L. Birkin of Nottingham.
1917 February sold to Patrick Donovan of Wexford.
1917 29 April. While en route from Cardiff to Isigny, France with a cargo of coal, she was stopped and scuttled by U Boat **U32**, 7 miles north west of Cherbourg.

Ellen Harrison, two masted tops'l schooner of 103 tons. Built, 1878 at Ulverston. Owned in Wexford, 1917 by Patrick Donovan.

EMERALD: Built, 1849 at New Brunswick, a barque, 482 tons.
OWNER: Allen of Wexford;
1854 Out of Register.
CREW 1849.
Master: Laurence Murphy, 32.
Mates: J. Cullen, 52; James Cole, 17(?).

Seamen: Robert Scallan, 40; Ed. Cleary, 26; James Merlin(?) 22; Peter Walsh, 29; James Roche, 24; John Cousins, 22.
Apprentices: Thomas Brennan, 20; Patrick Cousins, 18; Thomas Breen, 22; Thomas Boland, 22.
Boy: Thomas Simpson, 19;

EMERALD ISLE: No. 15129. Code LRBN. Built in 1841 at Wexford. An iron schooner, 2-masted, 86 tons.
OWNERS
1841-1867 Walsh & Co. Wexford.
1868-1876 William Gafney of Wexford. Gafney sold her in 1876 due to bad health.
1878-1892 William Murphy of Carrig on Bannow, Co. Wexford.
1892 January. The **Emerald Isle** was at anchor at Caldy Roads near Tenby with a cargo of rock salt, when she parted her cables and went ashore at Tenby but it was hoped to salvage her. She was saved and returned to service.
1896 Broken up.
1897 Out of Register.

EMMA: No. 26024. Code PJKF. Built in 1837 at Lawrenny, Milford Haven.
A barquentine, 188 tons. Later re-rigged as a schooner.
OWNERS
1845 Hartrick of New Ross.
1855 William Thomas of Liverpool.
1869 Out of Register.

ENTERPRISE No. 20102. Code MVRC. Built in 1841 at Canada.
A schooner of 72 tons.
OWNER
1865-1872 James Gallivan of New Ross.
1883 Out of Registration.

EQUOIT: Built in 1864 at Prince Edward Island. A 2-masted brigantine.
OWNER: Mgt. Geraldine Ausling (?) (possibly Armstrong).
1885 Registered at Wexford.
1885 Broken up.

ERIN: No. 20104. Code MVRF. Built in 1840 at Nova Scotia. A brig of 187 tons.
OWNER: Brown, New Ross. Master: McDonald.
1865 out of register.

ERIN: No. 44126. Built in 1862 at Arbroath. A schooner of 89 tons.
OWNERS
1870 Richard Devereux, Wexford.
1874 J.T. Devereux, Wexford.
1883-1894 Mrs Clement Morris, 41 South Main St., Wexford.
1897 Out of Register.

ESPERIA: No. 63592. Built in1865 in Italy. A schooner 89 tons.
This is the only Wexford registered ship discovered that was built in Italy.
OWNERS
1865 John Hall of Newcastle. Registered in London.
1878 R. Allen of Wexford. Registered at Wexford as 79 tons.
1879 Out of Register.

ESSEX LASS: No. 63402. Built in 1869 at Winsford. A sloop of 39 tons.
1870 Registered at Wexford
OWNERS
1880 J.T. Devereux.
1885 Jasper W. Walsh, Wexford.
1895 Patrick Lambert. He died on Christmas day that year and his shares went to Margaret Lambert of Trinity St., Wexford.
1896 Margaret Lambert sold 16 shares to J.F. Walsh of Crescent Quay, Wexford, and 16 shares to F. J. Walsh, of Crescent Quay, Wexford, making them half owners;
1898 Vessel condemned.

EXCEL: No. 8593. Built in 1829 at Salcombe. A sloop of 23 tons.
1863 Registered in Waterford but owned in Saltmills, Co. Wexford and crewed from that area. Main trade Bannow to Llanelli and back.
Owner/Master William Caulfield, 42, of Saltmills.
Mate: William Clegg, 35, of Fethard.
Seaman: Peter Power, 20, of Dungulph.
1875: Out of Register.

EXPERT: No. 21417. Code NGFS. 48 tons.
1850 Registered at Wexford.
OWNERS
1850 Arthur Kavanagh, of Wexford, merchant.
1861 Bank of Ireland.
1863 William Jackson of Gloucester, MM.
1863 Registration transferred to Gloucester.
1870 Out of Register.

EXPRESS: No. 21411. Code NGFK. Built in 1839 at Barnstaple. A sloop, 41 tons.
OWNERS
1853 J.T. Devereux, James P. Devereux. Master: Captain N. Connors.
1867 Richard Devereux, merchant, Wexford.
1869-1882 John T. Devereux, merchant, Wexford.
1882 James Magee, Belfast.
1883 Registered as a smack.
1885 Out of Register.
CREW 1864
Master: Edward Clancy, 65.
Mate: Thomas Blanch, 60.
Seaman: John Clancy, 26.
Boy: Martin Gregory, 16.

F

FAIR GERALDINE: No. 70152. Code MRBS. Built in 1864 at Fairlie. A cutter, 20 tons.
OWNERS
Little of Cullentra, Wexford.
1900 N. Goddard, Dublin. Renamed **Calumet**.
1908 Register closed.

FAIRPLAY: Schooner. Built in Wexford.

FAIRY: No. 20500. Built in 1852 at Peel, Isle Of Man. A dandy of 25 tons.
OWNERS: Thomas Bell; Rudolphus Dugan, both of Wexford.
1882 Out of registration.

FAME: No. 70149. Built in Peel Isle of Man. 2 masts, dandy rigged. 17 tons.
OWNER: William Armstrong, South Main St., Wexford.
1897 4 October. Lost on Blackwater Bank.
CREW 1871.
Master: James Murphy; AB: David –? 21.

FOREIGNER. Schooner. 50 tons.
1852 Registered at Wexford.
CREW
Master: John Rowe, 36.
Mate: Patrick Terrill, 27.
Seaman: Patrick Marlowe, 24.
Boy: Francis Larkin, 17.

FRANCES: Built in 1838 at Wexford. **OWNER**: McCormack of New Ross.
Master: Captain Wilson.

FRANCES: No.55370. Built in 1867 at Caernarfon. 45 tons.
Dimensions: 64.2x18.6x8.1ft.
OWNERS
1916 Eliz. Roberts, Moelfre, Anglesey;
1917 June. Patrick Donovan, Wexford;
1917 August. Edmonde Bride, Cardiff;
1918 April. Sunk by a German submarine, 6 miles SE of the Lizard Point, Cornwall. Two crew saved, two lost.

FRIENDS: Built 1882. .17.65 tons. A dandy.
OWNER: Samuel G. Armstrong of Wexford, shipowner.
1892 19 December. Vessel broken up.

G

GAZELLE Official No. 11625. Code KTJW. A schooner, 48 tons.
1850 Registered.
OWNERS
Before 1855 Robert Sparrow, shipbuilder of, Wexford.
1855 2 October. Sparrow sold her to Patrick Breen of Castlebridge (Master: William Boggan).
1863 June. Sold to Joseph Fagen of Londonderry, MM.
1868 Peter Reilly, Co. Antrim.
1872 John Gordon, Glynn. Co. Antrim.
1879 Out of Register.

GEM: No. 1317. Code WJMS. Built in 1846 at Nova Scotia. A schooner, carvel built, 98 tons.
OWNERS
1846 Allen Bros., Wexford (Master: John Hayes)
1873 Kearns of Wexford.

GEM: No. 20711.
1863 Registered at 68 tons
OWNERS
c. 1863 Catherine Marlow (Master: James Sinnott).
c. 1873 Kehoe of Wexford.
1873 5 September. Lost at Dogger Bank.
CREW (OWNER Marlow)
Master: James Sinnott.
Mate: David Noonan, 52.
ABs: Christopher Williams, 22; John Redmond, 18.
Boy: Patrick Murphy, 16.
CREW 1873.
Master: Captain Doyle
Seamen: John Corish; John Furlong; James Hayes.
The **Gem** was from Ayr to Wexford when she struck the Dogger Bank outside Wexford Harbour on 5 September 1873 and became a complete loss.

GENERAL MOORE: Built at Wexford 1816. A brig, 140 tons. An emigrant ship.
OWNER: James Barry.

GEORGE PONSONBY: Built in 1803 at Dublin. A brig of 59 tons.
OWNER: Devereux of Wexford. Master: P. Quirk.

GEORGE RAMSEY: No. 6266. Code JNCR. Built in 1838 at Sunderland. A snow of 232 tons.
OWNERS
1850 Howlett, New Ross. Master: Joyce. Liverpool to Norfolk Virginia route.
1856 Whitfields, Stockton.
1869 Out of Register.

GLENDALOUGH:
OWNER: Graves & Co. New Ross.
During the Crimean War, the **Glendalough** was engaged in bringing supplies to the British and French forces, who, along with the Ottoman Empire and Sardinia, were in conflict with Russia. At the siege of Sebastopol, the **Glendalough** was anchored 30 miles from that port but nonetheless the captain reported to her owners that *the ship was kept in a continual tremor by the unceasing cannonade at Sebastopol*.

GLENLYON: No. 33042. Code RCPS. Built in 1842 at New Brunswick. A wooden ship of 908 tons.
OWNERS
1845 Boyson & Co. London.
1853-1861 A.R. Graves.
1861 6 January. Abandoned on a voyage from Savannah to Liverpool with cotton. All 25 crew saved.

GNAT: Built 1822. A brig, carvel built, 69 tons.
OWNERS: Timothy Gafney, Francis Augustus Codd, and J. Brennan (Last two from Dublin). Master J. Codd. Sold to Belfast.

GOOD TEMPLAR: No. 67835. Code WFLV. Built in 1881 at Goole. A ketch, 76 tons. Dimensions: 73.7x19.5x9.3ft.
OWNERS
1888 E.L. Burnette, Goole.
1891-1894 William J. O'Keefe of Wexford.
1896 George B. Sully, Bridgewater.
1909 John L. Harmon, Bridgewater.
1911 13 November. Foundered in heavy weather 15 miles off Aberystwyth while en route from Mersey to Bridgewater with coal. One man lost, remainder picked up by a trawler and landed at St. Tudwald's, Pembrokeshire.
1913 Out of Register.
CREW 1891
Master: Thos. Greene, 53.
Mate: Charles Byrne, 23.
AB: John David, 56;
OS: Matthew Lacey, 20.
Boy: James Gafney, 20 (First trip).

Glenlyon, report of her arrival at Savannah.
Courtesy, Peggy McHale & Kieron Cronin, Waterford Institute of Technology.

Glenlyon, Sailing advertisement.
Courtesy, Peggy McHale & Kieron Cronin, Waterford Institute of Technology.

H

HARMONY: Built in 1843 at Wexford. A schooner carvel built, female figurehead. 99 tons.
OWNERS
Before 1853 Nathanial Sparrow, and Robert Sparrow of Wexford (Master: William Gardner).
Sold to Robert Hughes of Ely Place, 16 shares; Thomas Fortune, 14 shares; Thomas Walsh, 21 shares.
1853 OWNER: A Whitty. Master: Captain N. Meany.
1858 Out of Registration

HAROLD: No. 59352. Built in 1873 at St. Patrick's, New Brunswick, by J. J. McMurray. A schooner, 189 tons. Dimensions: 105x28x10.5ft.
OWNERS
1873 St. Andrews, New Brunswick.
1880 G.F. Stickney, New Brunswick.
1885 Michael A. Ennis of Wexford, timber merchant.
1885 7 July. Sold to William Armstrong.
1887 Sold to William Wallace, Hugh Wallace, and Samuel Watson, all of Dublin.
1896 Out of Register.

HARP: Built at Quebec, a schooner of 71 tons, carvel built with a billet head.
OWNER J.J.Devereux of Wexford.

HARPER: Built in 1839 at Miramichi, New Brunswick. A barque, 345 tons, carvel built, female figurehead.
1842 Registered at Wexford
OWNER: Francis Harper of Wexford. Master: George. Murphy.

HARRIET:
1834 Registered at 97 tons. Master: G. Morgan.

HELEN: No. 21416. Code NGFR. Built in 1828 at Workington. A brigantine of 60 tons, carvel built. Billet Head.
1848 Registered at Wexford.
1860 Register transferred to Newport.
OWNERS
1848 Richard Devereux of Wexford. Master: John Redford.
1860 John Todd of Newport, Monmouth, carpenter.
1865-1872 John Allen, Watchett, Somerset;
1878 Out of Register.
CREW 1852
Master: Patrick Cogley, 42.
Seamen: Thomas Lambert, 32; Thomas Hughes, 54.

HENRIETTA: Built in 1841 at Milford. A smack, carvel built, 42 tons.
1841 Registered at Wexford.
OWNERS: William Clancy and Patrick Reck, both of Wexford.
CREW
Master: Laurence Furlong, 40.
Mate: John Laffan, 49.
Seaman: Thomas Bolger, 25.
Boy: George Lambert, 17.

HOPE: No. 20108.Code MVRK. Built,1835 at St. Martin's, New Brunswick ,71 tons.
1835,Registered at Wexford. Owners, J.W. Walsh & Patrick Lambert.
1865 June 11 broken up.

HOPEWELL: Registered 1839.
OWNER, Whitty of Wexford, Captain Hull.
1833, February, lost on the Bar at Wexford.

HULDAH:
1834, Registered 84 tons.
CREW 1845.
Masters; P. King; Peter Cleary
Mate; John Keane, 20;
Seamen, John Codd, 20 John Boland;
Boys; Thomas Cleary, 17; T McCarthy,15; Thomas Cahill, 17; Joseph Codd.

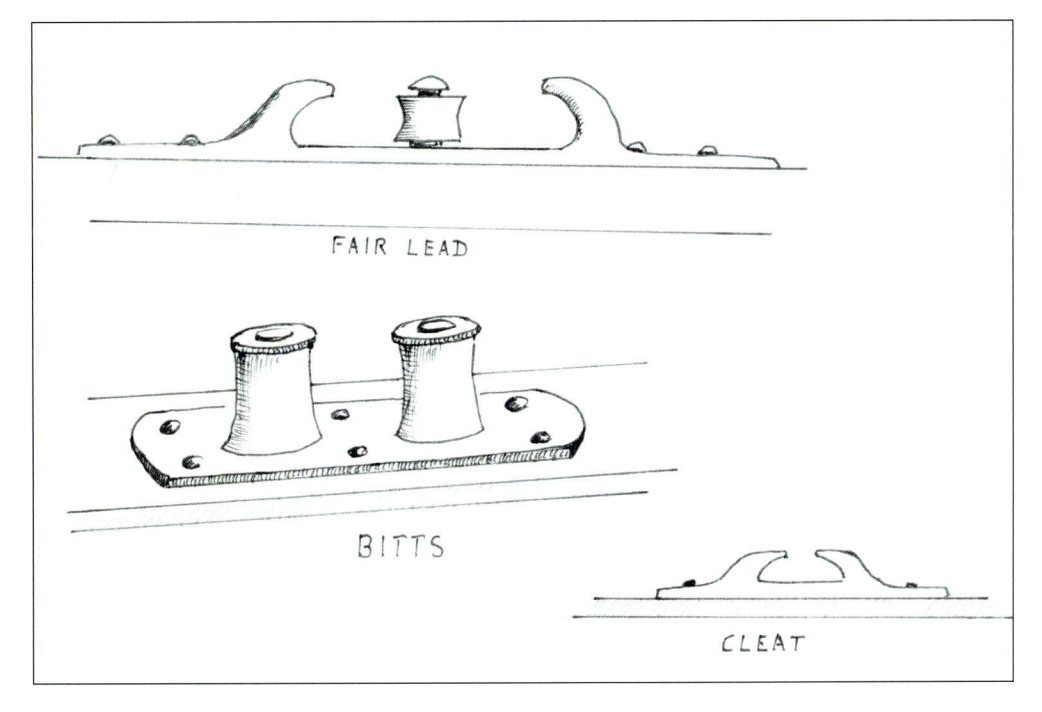

FAIR LEAD

BITTS

CLEAT

I

INTREPID: No. 27926. Code PTHQ. Built in 1856 at Wexford. A schooner, 71 tons.
OWNERS J.T. Devereux then Cecilia Gafney.
1876 Out of Registration.

INTREPID: Built in 1807 at Greenock. 74 tons.
1834 Registered Wexford
OWNER: Devereux. Master: H. Rowe.

ISABEL: No. 39204. Code EIGM. Built in 1857 at Murray Harbour, Prince Edward Island. A schooner of 74 tons. Dimensions: 88x21.4x9.7ft. Registered in Dublin.
OWNERS
William Kearon of Courtown, Co. Wexford.
1933: W.H. Weeks of Norwich

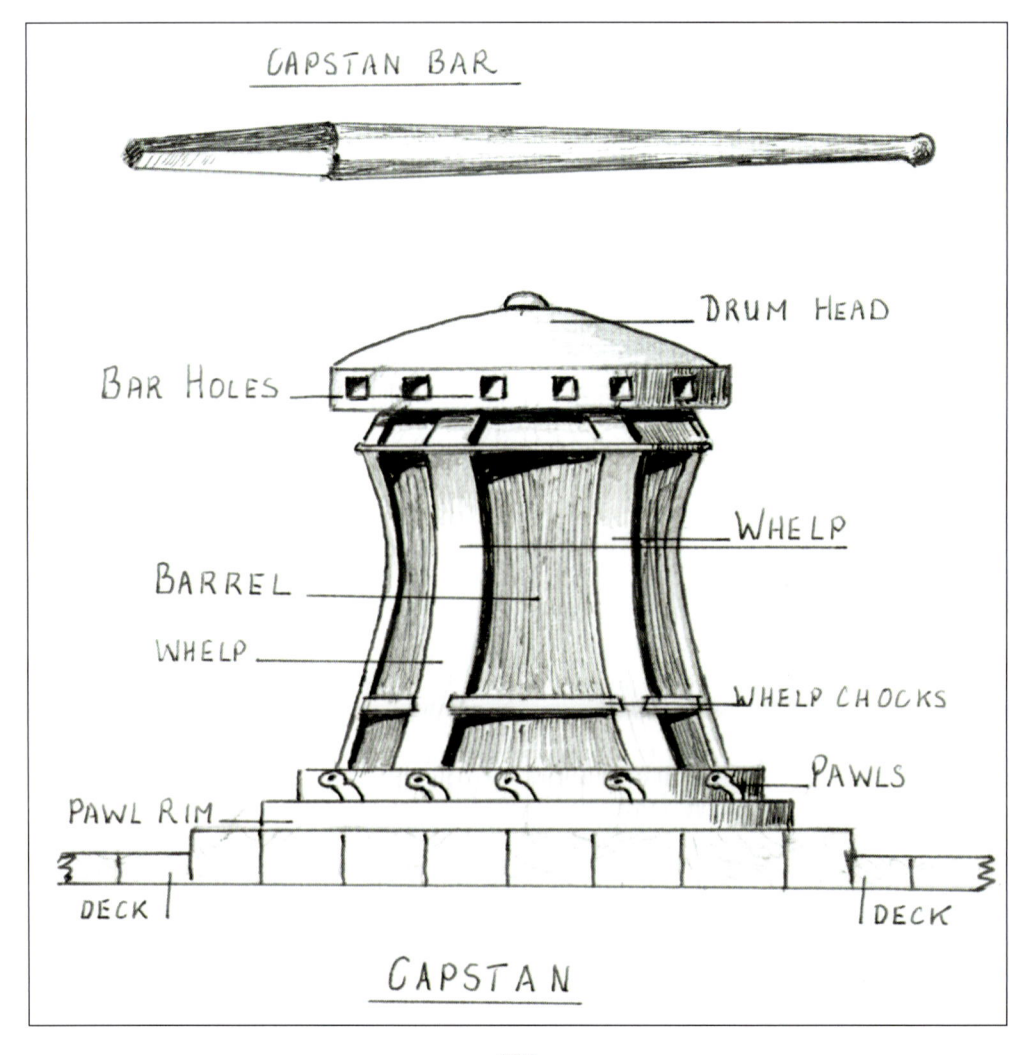

J

JAMES & MARY SINNOTT: Built in 1841 at Nova Scotia. A barque, carvel built. Male figurehead.
1845 Registered in Wexford.
1846 September. Wrecked off the coast of Newfoundland.
OWNERS: Thomas Brennan and Peter Connor, merchants. Master: Nicholas Sinnott.
CREW 1845. All Wexford unless otherwise indicated.
Master: Patrick Connors, 35.
Mate: Thomas Law, Mate, 25.
2nd Mate: George Walsh, 29.
Carpenter: John Codd, 25.
Steward: Thomas Moore, 24 (Bristol).
Seamen: Thomas Ryan, 38 (Passage East); George Harper, 21 (Edinburgh); Andrew Smith, 26 (Gothenburg); James Moore, 51 (Bristol); John Murphy, 22; Edward Rossiter, 21; Laurence Bent, 19; Patrick Keating, 22; James Evans, 27, (Glamorgan).
Sailmaker: Boyle, 30 (Waterford)
Apprentice: Charles Kersley, 27.

JANE: No. 21406. Code NGFB. Built in 1824 at Polperro. A schooner of 55 tons. Dimensions: 57.5x16x9ft.
OWNERS
1852-1864 Patrick Quirke, Wexford.
1865 John Acheson, Cork.
1876 John Penrose, Cork.
1885 Out of Register.
CREW 1852
Master/Owner: Patrick Quirke, 60
Mate: Stevens, 50.
Seamen: Patrick Murphy, 27; Peter Bryan, 21.

JANE FRANCES: Built in 1838 at Wexford. A schooner, carvel built, 48 tons
OWNERS
J. Barrington, merchant, 16 shares; Richard Allen merchant, 16 shares; Robert Sparrow, shipbuilder, 16 shares; Michael Jones, cabinetmaker, 16 shares.
1844 21 May. Ed. Watson of Lacken, Duncormick Co. Wexford.
1853 McCormack of New Ross. Master J. Wilson.
1856 Out of Register
CREWS
1844
Master Richard Cox.
Mate: Walter Bryan, 61.
Seaman: James –? 25.
Boy: Thomas Cox, 18.
1845.
Master: Michael Cox, Duncormick, Co. Wexford, 34.

Mate: Walter Bryan, 61.
Seaman: Thomas Cox, 18.

JANE HUGHES: No. 17367. Code MGJS. Built in 1857 at Port Dinorwic, Wales. A schooner of 76 tons. Dimensions: 72.5x19.7x10.2ft.
OWNERS
1898-1900: Captain Morris of Monck St., Wexford.
1904 George Scott of Newport, Monmouthshire.
1904 Register closed; vessel to be hulked.
1907 Out of Register.
In December 1903, **Jane Hughes** was badly damaged when lying in Newport, Wales; a Spanish steamer collided with her. At the time she was in the process of being sold and, despite the damage, the sale seems to have gone ahead. Under her new Welsh owners she was later lost on a trip from Lydney to St. Ives in Cornwall. While sheltering from gales, she stranded on Cardiff breakwater. Crew of four saved.

JEMIMA: No. 8703. Code KDHF. Built in 1840 at Wexford. Carvel built, 26 tons.
OWNERS
1842 April. Thomas Naylor. Naylor sold to J.T. Devereux of Paul Quay, MM.
1842 28 May. Sold to Richard & Robert Cuthbert of Bray.
1874 Out of Register.

JESSIE: Built in1845 at Prince Edward Island. A brigantine, 87 tons, carvel built. Billet head.
OWNER: Jos. Furlong of Ferrybank, Wexford. Master: Edwin Hore.
1850 March. Vessel lost.

JESSIE: No. 76576. Built in 1878 at Kingston on Spay, Morayshire, Scotland. A schooner, 91 tons. Dimensions: 85.8x21.4x10.6ft.
OWNER
1917 Patrick Donovan, Wexford.
1917 April. En route from Cardiff to Carpentan, France, with coal, the **Jessie** was sunk by a German submarine with scuttling charges, 7 miles WxS of Portland Bill, Dorset. Crew saved.

JESSIE ANN: No. 35053. Code RNBT. Built in 1854 at Prince Edward Island. A schooner, 81 tons.
OWNERS
1865 John McIwraith of Ayr.
1875 D. McEachran of Campbelltown.
1890 Peter McNab of Campbelltown.
1910 William Kearon of Ballintray, Courtown, Co. Wexford.
1913 October. From the Mersey to Cahore, Co. Wexford, she was wrecked on the Dogger Bank off Wexford. Crew saved.

JKL: Built in 1850 at Quebec. A barque of 672 tons. Emigrant ship.
OWNER: Howlett & Sons, New Ross.

1865 Out of Register.
Her master, Captain William Joyce, died in New Orleans in March 1851.

J M TIERNAN: No. 39101. Code SMVP. Built in 1856 at Prince Edward Island.
A schooner of 85 tons.
Dimensions: 72.7x21.6x9.6ft.
OWNERS
1876 Patrick Morris.
1879 J. E. Galavan, New Ross.
1883 Michael Ennis of Wexford.
1890 Out of Register.

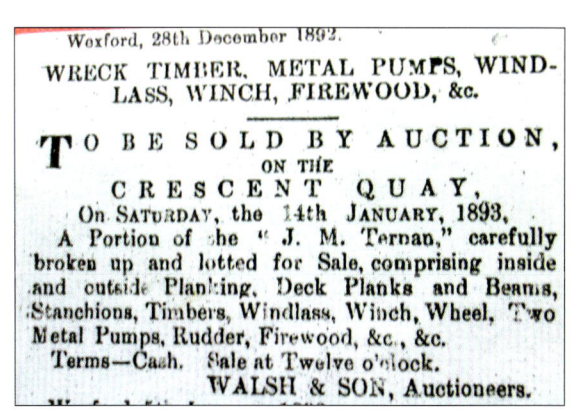

*Timber sale from the Wexford schooner **J.M. Tiernan**, January 1893.*

JOHN & JOHANNA: No. 63409. Built in 1859 at Port St. Mary, Isle of Man.
A dandy, 19 tons.
1873 29 November. Registered at Wexford.
1880 Owned in Dublin by Edward R. O'Connor.
1887 Out of Register.

JOHN BELL: Built in 1834 at Quebec.
A barque, 454 tons.
OWNER: Howlett of New Ross.
1843 Detained at New Ross in 1843 for tobacco smuggling.
1849 Her master was Captain William Joyce.
1850 September. Captain Clarke was her commander on a voyage to Quebec.
1855 Out of Register.
The **John Bell** was an emigrant ship carrying passengers outward to Canada and the US, and cotton homeward for Liverpool and the Lancashire mills.

JOHN BULL: No. 70161. Built in 1892 at Ardrosssan, Ayr, as the **Hugh Barclay**. A schooner, 91 tons. Dimensions: 88.2x21.3x10.2ft.
1915 OWNER: Thomas Kearns, New Ross, Co. Wexford.
1915 November. En route from Glasgow to New Ross with coal, **John Bull** was lost while trying to enter Rosslare Harbour.

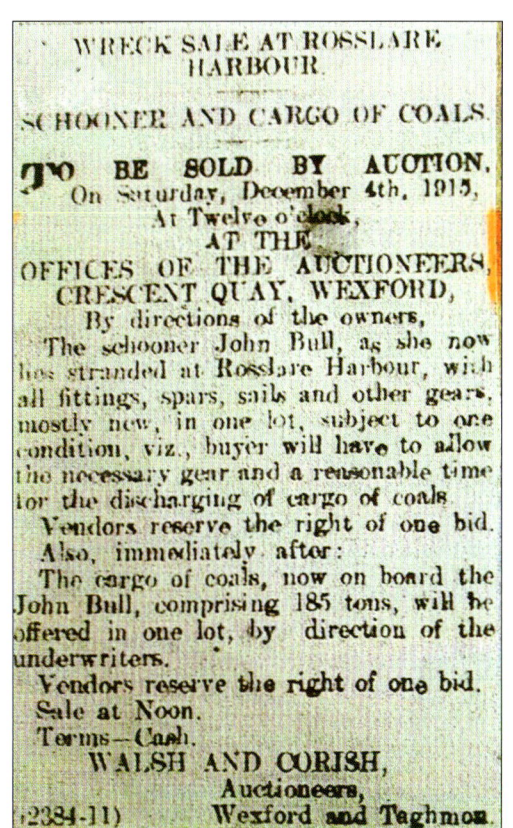

*Auction notice for the **John Bull**.*
Wexford People.

JONAH: No. 15902. Code LVGC. Built in 1838 at Preston, a schooner, 76 tons.
1870 Registered as 65 tons.
1880 9 March. The **Jonah** went aground on the Dogger Bank, Wexford. All crew were saved by the lifeboat **Ethel Eveleen.**
1883 Out of Register.
OWNERS
1865 George Lawson Jnr. of Lancaster.
1870 J.P. Devereux, of Rocklands, Wexford.
CREW
Master: John Murray, Faythe.
Mate: Joe Carberry.
AB: Murtha Whelan.
Boy: John Walsh.

JOSEPH: No. 25555. Code PGLQ. Built in 1812 at Whitehaven. A schooner, carvel built, 40 tons.
1848 Registered at Wexford.
1852 OWNERS: Martin Cullen & William Cullen, both of Bannow.
1879 Out of Register.
CREW 1852
Master: Martin Cullen, 33.
Mate: Patrick Shea, 41.
Seaman: Thomas Deavy, 37.

JOSEPH: No. 51912. Built in 1865 at Prince Edward Island. A barquentine, 107 tons. Dimensions: 82.9x22.8x9.9ft.
OWNERS
1870 James Codd of Wexford.
1872 John Cardiff of Wexford.
1875 John Morton of Drogheda.
1879 Robert Morton of Drogheda.
1882 John Simpson of Drogheda.
1884 Out of Register.

JOHN & MARY: No. 18357. Code MLKS. Built at Dungarvan in 1772. A smack, 19 tons. Registered at Wexford.
1865 OWNER Patrick Carew, Bannow, Co. Wexford.
CREW
Master: Patrick Kirwan, Bannow, 24.
Mate: Peter Brien, Fethard, 45.
Seaman: Michael Farrell, Bannow, 41.
1880 Out of Register.

JOSHUA: No.47126. Built in 1864, Knottingley, Yorkshire. A ketch, 60 tons. Dimensions: 62.3x17.9x8.3ft.
OWNERS
1917 Patrick Donovan, Wexford.
1917 June. Anglo French Coasting Company Limited.
1917 October. En route from Fowey to Dieppe with clay, the **Joshua** was sunk by a German submarine off the Isle of Wight. Crew of 3 killed.

JULIA
1839 Registered at Wexford.
CREW
Master: Edward Cleary, 40.
Mate: James Cleary, 48.
Sailor: Nicholas Cleary 45.
Others: Nicholas Devereux; Michael Devereux, 18.
Seaman: Laurence Magee, 19.
Boy: Patrick Morris, 15

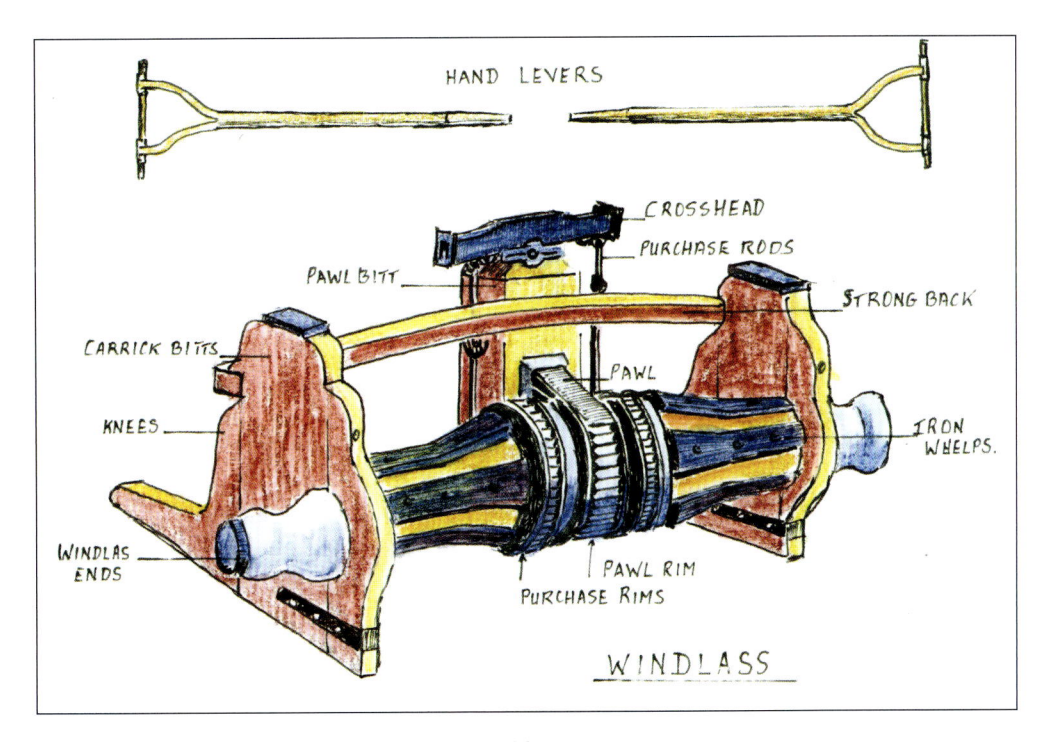

L

LADY DOUGLAS: Built in 1825 at New Brunswick. A brig, 120 tons. Registered 1834.
OWNERS Breen and Company. Master: J. Cullin. Trading Wexford to Glasgow.

LANDSHIPPING No. 21428. Code NGHM. Built at Landshipping, Lawrenny, Pembrokeshire. A schooner, carvel built, 63 tons. Registered at Wexford.
1843/'46/'52 OWNERS: Thomas Connor MM, 32 shares; John Hore, mariner, 32 shares.
1860 John Knight of Gloucester, and William Washbourne of Frampton-on-Severn, 32 shares.
1867 Out of Register.
CREW 1852
Master: John Hore.
Mate: John Devereux, 33.
Seamen: Nicholas Laffan, 22; –? Lambert, 40.

LARK: A smack, of Wexford.
1871 6 January. The **Lark** was wrecked in a storm. Two crew saved by the Wexford Lifeboat **Civil Service.**

LIBERATOR: No. 63404. Code NGHP. Built in 1863 at Wexford. A dandy, 26 tons.
OWNERS
1875 Thomas Bell.
1880 Samuel Armstrong.
1896 Out of Register.

LIBERTY: No. 21429. Code NGHP. 65 tons.
1834/1857 Registered at Wexford.
OWNERS
1850 Charles Ralph of Wicklow.
1850-57 Patrick Breen of Castlebridge, Wexford. Master: D. Roach.
1867-1870 George Newman of Wicklow.
1875 Out of Register.

LILY: No. 49505. Built in 1866 at Wexford. A schooner, 105 tons.
Dimensions: 88x21.7x10.2 ft.
OWNER: J.T. Devereux. Master: James Scallan.
1872 10 January. En route from Barrow to Cardiff with a cargo of pig iron, the **Lily** stranded and was wrecked on the Kish Bank off Dublin. Six crew saved.

LIVELY: No. 8710. Code KDHQ. Built in 1837 at Ayr. A smack, 25 tons.
1852/'53 Registered in Wexford
OWNERS: John Coady and John Cullen, both of Wexford.
1856 March. John Cullen died and his shares went to Mary Cullen (widow);
1856 Robert Williams of Caernarfon. Vessel wrecked 1888.
CREW 1852
Master: Nicholas Cousins, 34.
Mate: Patrick French, 35.
Seaman: Francis Wafer, 19.

LIVERPOOL: Registered 1834. 99 tons. Master: M. Scallan.

LUCIA: Registered at Wexford, 1852.
CREW 1852.
Master: James Morris, 30.
Mate: Francis Morris, 33.
Seamen: John Hayes, 21; William Cahill, 60.
Boy. Patrick Carty, 18.
Later that year:
Mate: Nicholas Murphy, 32.
Seamen: John Devereux, 32; John Hayes, 21.

LUCY: Captain Sam Wetherald.

LYNWOOD: No. 73993. Built in 1875 at Montague, Prince Edward Island.
A brigantine, 175 tons. Dimensions, 104.5x24.5x12.9ft.
1907 October. **OWNER** John McCullagh, Wexford.
1907 Thomas May, Liverpool, for use as a barge.
1928 December. Registration closed. Vessel broken up.

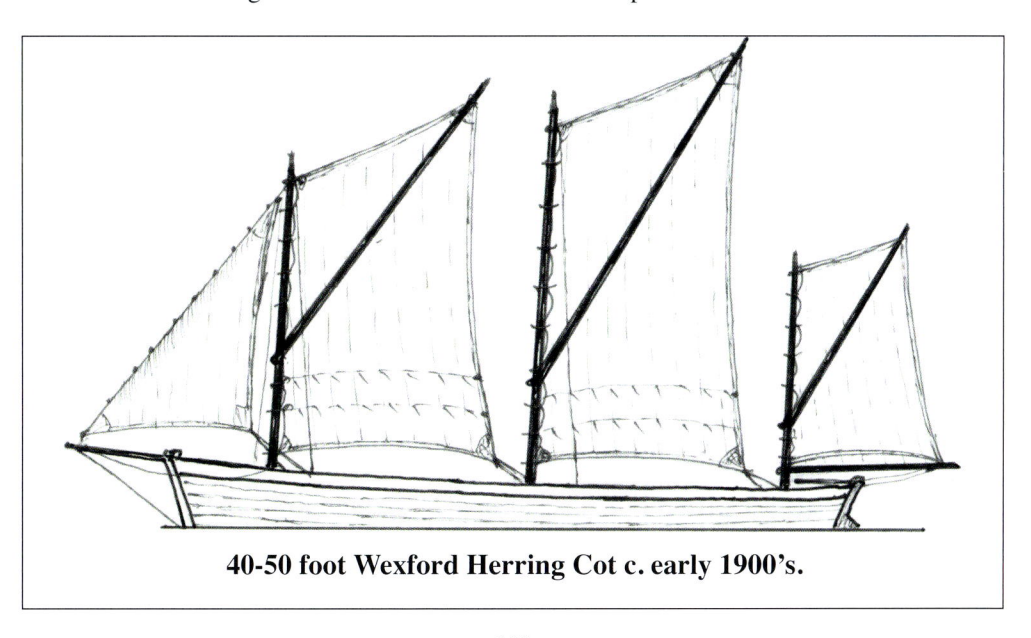

40-50 foot Wexford Herring Cot c. early 1900's.

M

MARGARET: No. 43867. Code TQRJ. Built in 1862 at Conway, North Wales. A ketch, 46 tons.
1909 Registered at Wexford.
OWNER Simon Roche, Ballygow, Bannow, Co. Wexford.
1922 26 June. Register closed.

MARIE LOUISE: No. 33107. Code RCWD. Built in 1865 at Quebec. 57 tons, registered at Beaumaris, Wales.
1858/1860 Registered at Wexford.
1870 Out of Register.

MARINER No. 15112. Code LQWJ. Built, 1838 at Barnstaple. A schooner, 50 tons.
OWNER Richard Devereux of Wexford.
1870 Out of Register.

MARQUIS OF ELY. No. 8667. Code KDCS. Built in 1804 at Aberystwyth. A schooner, 71 tons.
1852/1857/1863 Registered at Wexford.
1888 Out of Register.
OWNERS John Connors (snr), 64 shares; Mrs O'Connor; P.J. Doyle, all Wexford.
CREW 1863,
Masters: James Kean, 51; Richard Wafer, 27; Patrick Cullen, 35.
Mate: Nicholas Sinnott, 51.
Seaman: Martin Hayes, 20.
Boy: James Moran, 16.
CREW (undated)
Master: James Barry, 60.
Mate: John Murphy, 27.
Seaman: Michael Barry, 17.
Mariner: Philip Byrne, 22.

MARY: No. 8743. Code KDLT. 31 tons.
1851 Registered at Wexford
OWNERS
Peter Hewson, MM, & James Nolan, mariner, Wexford.
1863 11 May. John E. Pettitt, merchant, Wexford.
1867 11 September. Maurice Byrne of Wicklow.
CREW 1865
Master: Peter Hewson, 60.
Mate: James Nolan, 55.
Boy: John Murphy, 20.
1871 Broken up at Wicklow.

MARY: No. 25584. Code PGNM. Built in 1828 at Bannow, Co. Wexford. 31 tons.
1865 OWNER Michael Furlong, Bannow.
1887 Out of Register.

MARY:
1850 Registered at Wexford.
1850 OWNERS. James Ralph Crosbie, Wexford, James Carr, MM, Mary Murphy, shopkeeper, Wexford (16 shares).
1857 Mary Murphy sold 8 shares each to Crosbie and Carr, making them joint owners.

MARY ANN: Built in 1826 at Portmadog. Registered in Wexford in 1834. Lost off Nixon Sands, Wales.

MARY BLAIR: No. 8485. Code KCJQ. Built in 1854 at Nova Scotia. A barquentine, 146 tons. Dimensions: 89x20x10ft.
1854 Registered at Wexford
OWNERS: Richard Devereux and Richard Joseph Lawrence Devereux & Co.
1862 14 July. Sold to Hugh Jamieson of Leith (North) Scotland.
1862 17 July. Sold to John Bessey Hylton, of Great Yarmouth (shipowner).
1879 Out of Register.

MAVIS: Built in 1845 at Nova Scotia. A schooner, carvel built. 77 tons.
OWNER Richard Allen. Master: John Rossiter.
1850 Lost in St Brides Bay, Pembrokeshire, Wales.

MAYFLOWER:
1836/1845 Registered at Wexford.
CREWS
1836
Master: Francis Larkin, age 26.
Mate: Robert Scallan, 40.
Seaman: Laurence Doyle, 23.
Boy: Pat Myler, 19.
Sailor: John Myler, 21.
1845
Master: Nicholas Furlong, 42.
Mate: Michael Furlong, 46.
Seaman: Nicholas–?, 38.
Peter Cullen, 19.
Boy: James Furlong, 17.

MENAPIA: Built in 1841 at St John, New Brunswick. A barque, carvel built, 280 tons, female figurehead.
OWNERS R. Allen, M. Allen, J. Quinn (also the Master) Thos. White.
1852 16 February. Sold to John Hatchell Brennan, of London, shipowner.

MERMAID: Registered in 1834, 68 tons. Master: Doolittle.

MICHAEL WICKHAM: Built in 1833 at Wexford. 52 tons.
OWNER: Thomas Connick of Wexford.
1843 February. Master: Thomas Wickham.

MINERVA: No. 25365. Code PGMH. Built in 1842 at Cardigan. A cutter of 38 tons.
1842 OWNERS Patrick Rashford [sic], Kilmore, Co. Wexford MM, 28 shares; James Monaghan, Kilmore Quay, grocer, 28 shares; William Jones, St. Dogmaels, Cardigan, Wales, mariner, 28 shares.
1844 Lost on Blackwater Bank.

MITE: No. 6377. Code JNPC. Built in 1837 at Whitehaven. A schooner, two masts, scroll head, square stern, 55 tons. Dimensions: 61x17x8ft.
OWNERS
1841 Thomas Walsh of Wexford. Master: Nicholas Bourne.
1847 John Cousins of Wexford. Master: Evan Byrne.
1865 Ellen O'Connor of Wexford.
1879 J.P. Devereux of Wexford.
1885 John F. Yates of Enniscorthy, Co. Wexford.
1888 R.&R. Allen of Wexford.
1890 November. Sunk after a collision. Register closed.

MOODKEE: Built in 1846 at Quebec. A barque, carvel built, scroll head. 550 tons.
OWNERS
Devereux of Wexford (Captain John Howlin).
1870 T. Hutchinson of the Faythe, Wexford.
1870 12 February. Wrecked at Ballygeary. All hands saved by coastguard.

MORNING LIGHT: No. 45835. Built 1863 at Wexford by Robert Sparrow. A schooner, 78 tons.
OWNERS
1870 Richard Cuthbert, Bray, Co. Wicklow.
1874 John Doyle, Greystones.
1885 William Wallace, Dublin.
1888 William Armstrong, Wexford.
1890 24 November. Ship foundered after the steamer **Lady Mostyn** collided with her. An account of the collision appeared in the *Wexford People* on 5 November 1890:

*A report reached Wexford on Sunday, that the schooner **Morning Light** the property of Mr William Armstrong, had been run into and sunk by a steamer. No credence was at first attached to the story, but it afterwards appeared to be quite true. The **Morning Light** left Wexford on Friday morning, bound for Gloucester, with a cargo of oats and barley, belonging to Mr Yates, Enniscorthy. The crew consisted of four hands Captain Nicholas Murphy; mate Laurence Furlong; seaman Matthew Murphy, son of the Captain, and boy, John Wade. It appears that about 11.30, p.m., the same night, when some distance off the Helwick (sic) lightship, she was run into by the steamer, **Lady Mostyn**, of Liverpool, bound from Swansea to Rouen. The force of the collision was very great, the **Morning Light** being cut into the after-hatch, and sinking in about* seven or ten minutes afterward. The crew had barely time to scramble on board the steamer, without saving any of their effects.

THE CAPTAIN'S STATEMENT. The Captain of the **Morning Light** gives the following account of the collisions: "We left Wexford on Friday morning, October 31st, and at 11.30 p.m, steering E.S.E., wind about N.W. by W., Helwick lightship N.W. by W., saw a light on the port bow, and took it to be the Mumbles, after taking compass bearings. After four or five minutes, however, I made out the side lights through glasses, and knew that the light was from a steamer's masthead. I then went forward to see if my lights were all right, and found them burning brightly. A short time after, and as the steamer came nearer I took the helm, and kept the same course."

"The steamer continued to come on us, and I saw that a collision was inevitable. I called the watch below to come on deck, and we shouted to the steamer, but she didn't alter her course. She struck us on the port quarter, cutting the vessel into the after hatch. All hands climbed on board the steamer over the bows, and saw the schooner sinking within ten minutes after getting on the steamer's deck. The vessel that struck us was the **Lady Mostyn**, of Liverpool, from Swansea for Rouen. She had left the former port that night at six o'clock, and called at the Mumbles. After the collision she put about, and went for the Mumbles to land us. On arrival we were put on board the **City of Rotterdam**, which was waiting tide, and she landed us at Swansea."

The crew experienced great difficulty in getting on board the steamer, as no rope was thrown them, nor was any assistance given. The captain was the last to leave the schooner's deck, being dragged over the steamer's bows by his son and the mate. The mate gives a similar description of the collision. He says that when he climbed on board the steamer, there was no one on the forecastle head, and also states that he saw no one on the bridge. The chief officer was in charge of the steamer at the time, the captain being below.

The night was fine and clear, and the vessels were about a quarter of a mile apart when he and the captain first commenced to about. If the helm of the steamer had been put to port, the collision would have been avoided, but instead of this, it was put hard a-starboard. The mate of the steamer attributed the collision to the lights of the other vessels not being visible. The **Lady Mostyn** is described in Lloyd's Register as being owned by J. H. Lewis, Liverpool, and has a gross tonnage of 730 tons. The captain, however, gave her owners as living in Aberdovey. The cargo of the **Morning Light** was insured, but the vessel was uninsured.

N

NATIVE: Registered 1834. 119 tons. Built in Wexford 1834.
OWNER: C. Archer. Master: P. Codd.

NICHOLAS MICHAEL.
CREW 1845
Master: –? Ford, 42.
Mate: Patrick Lacey, 38.
Seaman: John Donlan, 23.
Boy: Peter Cullen, 19.
Other: C. Dooley, 18; Nicholas Gafney, 19.

NORRY KIRWAN: No. 8885. Code KFBJ. 97 tons. Built in 1844 at Waterford.
OWNERS
Pierce Kirwan of Dungarvan, Co. Waterford.
1867 John Davies of Sion Row, Waterford.
1868 Richard Coady of New Ross, Co. Wexford.
1870 Michael Doyle of New Ross.
1875 Out of Register.

NORTHUMBRIA: Built in 1847 at Pictou, Nova Scotia. A barque, 560 tons.
Dimensions: 98.1x24.2x9.7ft.
OWNER: Howlett and Co., New Ross, Co. Wexford.

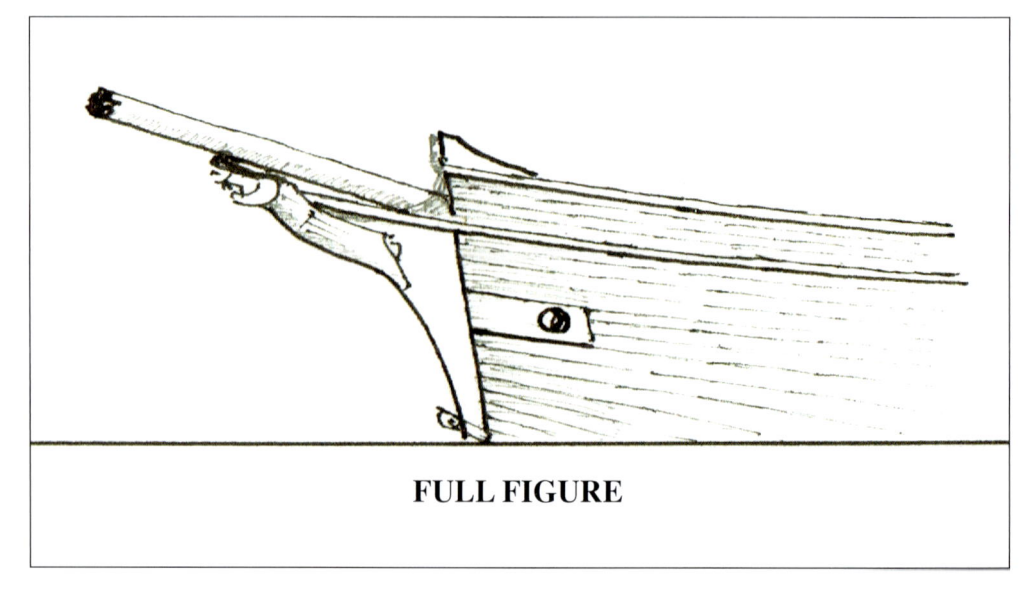

FULL FIGURE

O

OCEAN CHIEF: No. 128852. Built in 1866 at Arklow by Bernard Green. A dandy, 2 masts, 21 tons.
OWNERS
1910 Matt Hayes, James Hogan, Kilrane, Co. Wexford.
1912 Broken up.

OCEAN QUEEN: Built in 1845 at Wexford. A barque, carvel built, 359 tons, female figurehead.
OWNER: Robert Sparrow, of Wexford, shipbuilder. Master: John Redford.

OCEAN SPRAY: No. 42253. Built in 1860 at Miramichi Bay. A brig, 251 tons. Dimensions: 109x25x12.7ft.
OWNER: Devereux of Wexford.
1864 Out of Register.

ONWARD. No. 49524. Built in 1865 at Peterhead. A smack.
Dimensions: 62x18.7x8.1ft.
OWNERS
1870 M. Flanagan, Dublin; Mrs M.A. Flanagan, Dublin.
1910 Francis Flanagan, Dublin.
1911 Thomas Mansfield, Dublin.
1916 Patrick Donovan, Lamb House, Wexford, draper.
1918 H. Edmunds, MM, C. E. Trueman, MM, F. C. Morris, MM (All of Barry, South Wales).
1921-1924 W.J. Lamey, Appledore, Devon.
1928 5 December. En route from Newport to Courtmacsherry, Co. Cork, with coal, she struck wreckage off Co. Wexford and foundered. Crew rowed to Rosslare in their own boat.
1929 Out of Register.

ORION: Built in 1845 at Nova Scotia. A barque of 340 tons. Carvel built. Billet head. Registered at Wexford in 1847.
OWNERS
Nicholas Sinnott of Enniscorthy. Master: Peter Connor.
1847 Sinnott sold to William Thomas Lamport and George Holt of Liverpool.

ORLANDO: No. 42694. Built in 1849 at New Brunswick. A brigantine, 126 tons.
OWNERS: Michael Walsh of New Ross; Thomas Toole, Duncannon, Co. Wexford.
1875 Out of Register.

P

PANDORA: Built in 1846 at Prince Edward Island. A brigantine of 147 tons, carvel built, billet head. Registered at Wexford 1847.
OWNERS
1847 Richard Devereux.
1847 March. Patrick Chandler.
1847 September. Patrick Carroll.
1848 June. Nicholas Kearney; William Hardcastle.

PATRICK: 60 tons.
CREW
Master: William Carley.
Mate: William Murphy, 22.
Seamen: Patrick Devereux, 42; James Murphy, 18.

P.B. ROCHE: No. 70146. 20.9 tons. Registered at Wexford 30 Dec. 1876.

Petrel, a 15 ton cutter. Owned by Robinson's of Kilmore. Built Wexford 1857. Late 1800s, used as a tender to the lightships. *Jack O'Leary Collection.*

PETERBOROUGH: Registered at Wexford in 1842.
CREW 1842
Master: Captain John Campbell, 44.
Mariners: Patrick Grey, 28; Michael Atkinson, 30; John Hayes, 29.
Apprentices: Martin Kehoe, 18; Laurence Ray, 19.

PETREL: No. 11606. Code KTHQ. Built in 1839 at Wexford.
OWNERS
1865 Edward Smith, Dublin.
1872 Out of Register.

PETREL: No. 17572. Code MHFL. Built in 1857 at Wexford. A cutter, 15 tons.
OWNERS
1865 Edward Meadows, Ballyteigue Castle, Co. Wexford.
1879-1888 John A. Robinson, Kilmore Quay, Co. Wexford.
1940 Still owned by Robinson.

PEVERIL: Built in 1848 at Isle of Man. A smack of 35 tons.
OWNER Graves of New Ross.

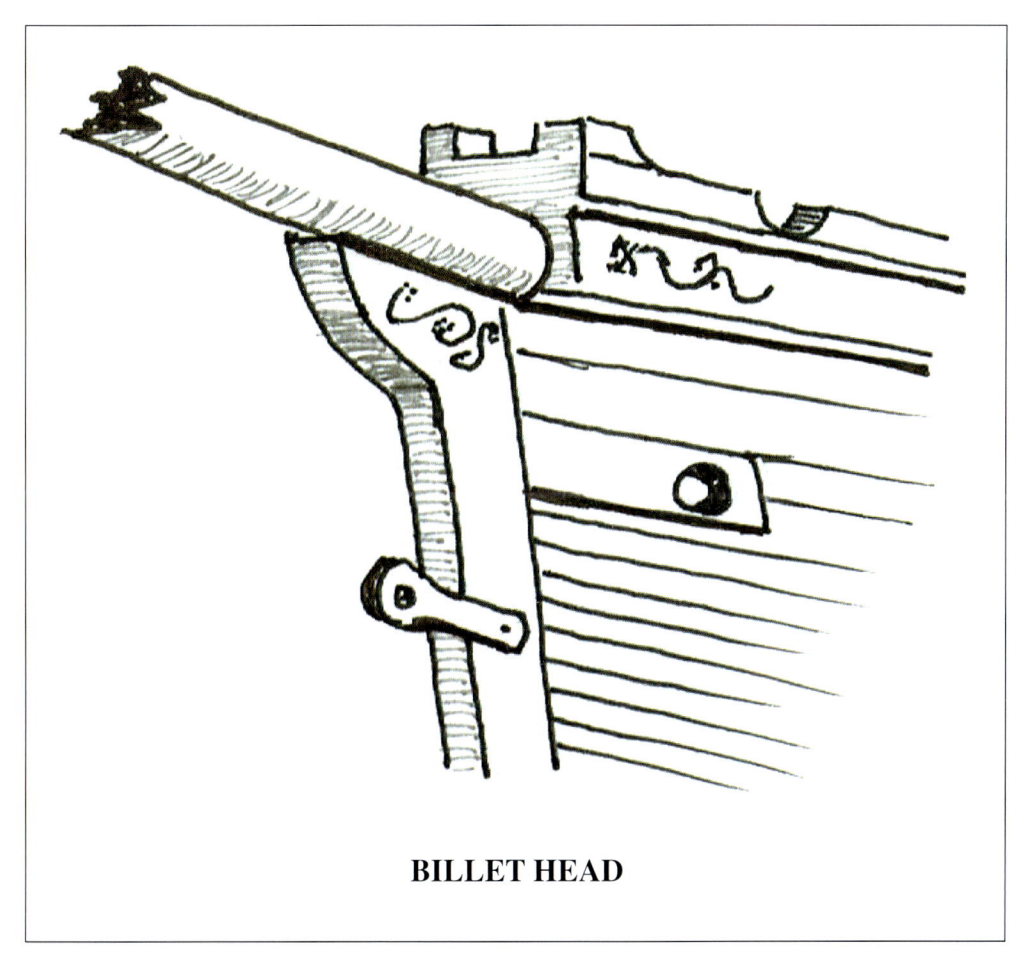

BILLET HEAD

PREVAIL: No. 119945. Built in 1895 at Bristol.
OWNERS
1931 June. Hughes of Ely House, Wexford. Sold to Martin Purcell.
1944 2 September. Broken up at Howth, Co. Dublin.

PRIMA DONNA: No. 49514. Built in 1864 at Peel, Isle of Man.
2 masts, dandy rigged, 27 tons.
OWNERS
1868 Rowland Rice of Dundalk Co. Louth.
1870 Thomas Devereux of Wexford.
1885.William Armstrong, Main St., Wexford.
1892 16 February. Total wreck off Blackwater, Co. Wexford.

PROVIDENCE: Wexford 1837. Master: Rowe.

PUFFIN: A yawl, of Wexford. Lost on 18 March 1906.

PURSUIT: No. 44244. Code TSHM. Built in 1862 at Nevin, Wales by Thomas.
A ketch.
OWNERS
1870 E. Jones, Port Dinorwic.
1890 L. Williams, Port Dinorwic.
1900 J. Phillips, Port Isaac, Cornwall.
1910 Mrs L. J. Gill, Port Isaac (re-rigged as a ketch).
1920 The Jersey Shipping Company, Jersey, Channel Islands.
1928 Bertie Downes, Duncannon, Co. Wexford. Broken up 1929.

The ketch **Pursuit**, was built 1862 at Nevin, Wales. In 1928, she was owned by Bertie Downes of Duncannon, Co. Wexford.

Q

QUERIDA: No. 17575. Code MHFQ. Built in 1857 at Fairlie, Ayr. A yacht, 23 tons.
1860 Registered in Wexford.
1861 Registered in Dublin.
1883 Re-registered as a cutter.
OWNERS
1865 John Gilmartin, Kinsale ,Co. Cork.
1870 Thomas Stawell Quin, Inishshannon.
1875 Richard Tonson Rye, Co. Cork.
1882 John Nicholls Court, Co. Cork.
1897 John Nicholls, Southampton.
1907 Register closed.

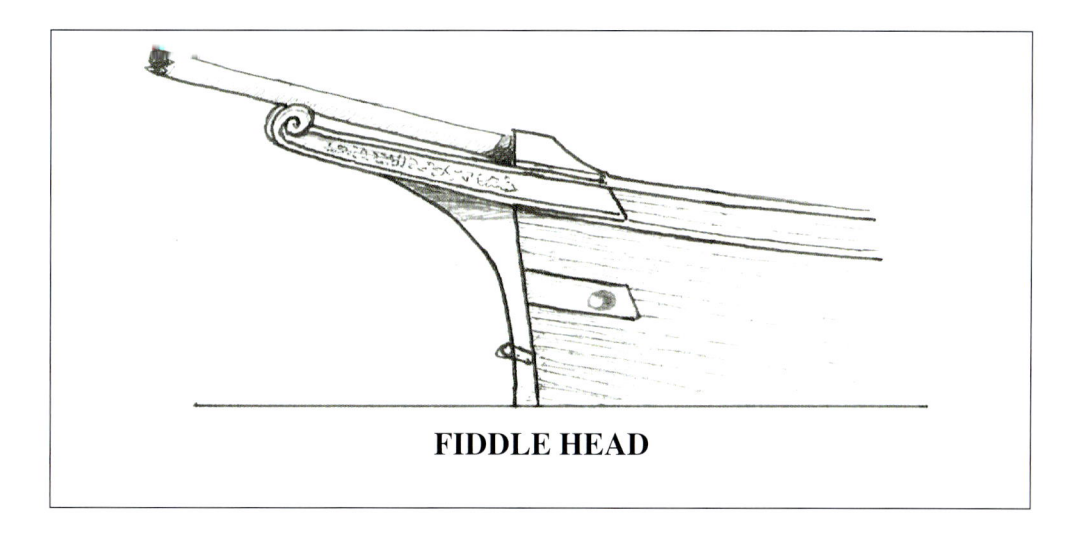

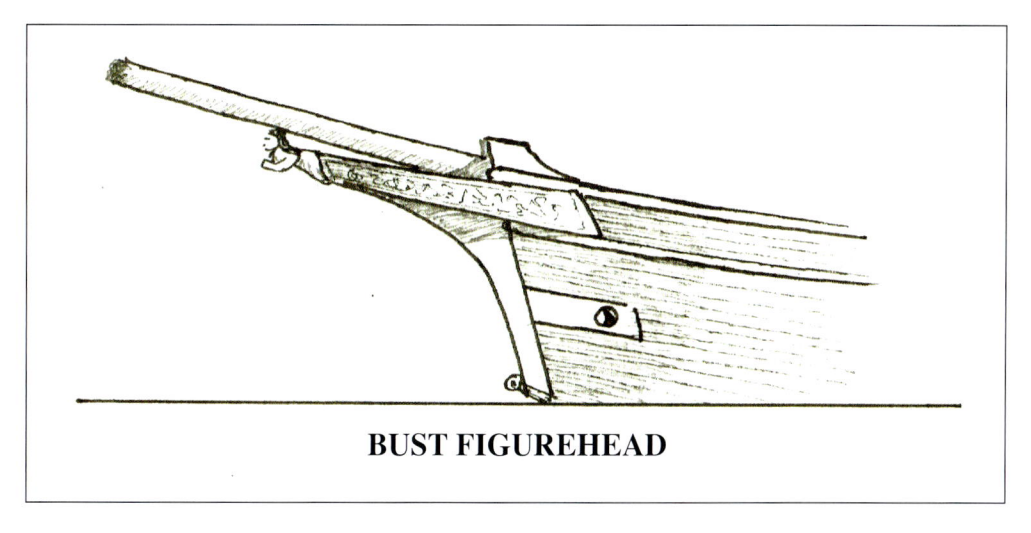

FIDDLE HEAD

BUST FIGUREHEAD

R

RAVEN: Registered at Wexford 1835.
CREWS
1835
Master: John Kehoe, 45.
Mate: Steven Larkin, 36.
Mariners: Laurence Furlong, 29; James Brien, 43; William Neil, 35.
Seaman: Bill Atkinson, 23.
Boys: Thomas Kehoe, 13; Edward Wickham, 19; Laurence Devereux, 20.
1837
Master: Thomas Wickham, 27.
Mate: James Keating, 40.
Seaman: John Rowe, 43.

REPEATER: No. 25845. Code PHQW. Built in 1849 at Nova Scotia.
A barque, 296 tons.
OWNERS
1853 Green & Co, Sligo. Master: J. Wilson.
1859 Harper and Co. of Wexford. Master: J. Hardcastle.
1870 Out of Register.

ROBERT: Built in 1831 at Waterford. A cutter, carvel built, 26 tons.
OWNER: James Donnelly of Bannow, Co. Wexford. He sold to Shudall of Duncormick.
1845/6 Master: John Parle.

ROCHFORD: No. 27925 Code PTHN. Built in 1858 at Nantes, France.
A schooner, 50 tons.
1856-1863 Registered in Wexford. **OWNER**: Rochford of Wexford.
1865 Out of Register.

S

SADIE R: She was owned by Captain George Ryder of Marsh Lane, New Ross, Co. Wexford, and named after his wife Sarah.

ST HELEN: No. 67617. Code VGTM. Built in 1874 at Wexford. A schooner of 22 tons.
OWNERS
1882 Henry Donovan, Tralee. Co. Kerry.
1890-1895 Philip Pierce, Rowe St., Wexford.
1897 Martin Pierce, Park House, Wexford.
1902 Benjamin A. W. Lett, Ballyvergan, Co. Wexford.
1907 St John H. Donovan, Tralee, Co. Kerry.
1912 Registration closed.

SARAH: Built in 1844 at Nova Scotia. A schooner, carvel built, 53 tons, female figurehead.
OWNERS Thomas Waters and Robert Pendergast, both of Enniscorthy, Co. Wexford.
1845 03 December. Master William Larkin.

SARAH: Built in 1826 at Dublin. A brigantine, carvel built, 63 tons, female figurehead.
OWNERS: Adam Loftus Lynn, of St. Kearns, Co. Wexford.
1841 7 May. Master: Daniel Rees.

SARAH A. BELL: No. 38031. Code SHIJ. Built in 1856 at Barrington, Nova Scotia. A brig, 183 tons.
1863 Registered at Wexford.
OWNERS
1870 William Barclay of Liverpool,
1874 Mrs L. Barclay, Rathgar, Co. Dublin,
1876 G. Inglis Jones, of Newport, Monmouthshire.
1878 Out of Register.

SARAH JANE: No. 49509. Built in 1864 at Wexford. A cutter of 24 tons.
OWNERS
1870 Matthew Dignam, Wexford.
1875-1878 George Wood, Milford.
1895 Out of Register.
CREW 1845
Master: Peter Devereux.
Mate: Patrick Sinnott.
Seamen: Michael Cody; Michael Murphy.

SARAH JANE: Built in 1829 at Nova Scotia. 48 tons
1841 January. Master: Patrick Meyler.
1852 13 February. Lost in Dalkey Sound.

SEA BIRD: No. 64488. Built in 1870 at Waterboro, New Brunswick. A schooner of 93 tons. Dimensions, 82x25x7ft.
OWNERS
1872 R. C. Elkin of Queens Co., New Brunswick.
1875 Hy. Weston Wilson of St. John, New Brunswick.
1879 Jasper W. Walsh of Wexford.
1890 December wrecked at the mouth of the River Clyde.
1891 Broken up.

SEAFARER:
1835/1837 Registered at Wexford.
CREW 1835
Master: Thomas Wickham, 25.
Mate: James Keating, 30.
ABs: Gerald Harding, 35; Pat Rowan, 30.
Boys: Nicholas Bawn (?); Michael Bent, 15.

SEA GULL: Built at Wexford in 1841. A smack, carvel built, 41 tons.
OWNER: R.&R. Sparrow, Wexford. Master: William Gardner.

SCEOLAN: No. 130063. Built in 1929. An auxiliary, schooner-rigged, 9 tons. Dimensions: 42.3x11.4x4.5 ft.
OWNER: Richard Walsh of Trinity St., Wexford.

SHELAH: No. 1934. Code HMBV. Built in 1845 at St. Mary's, Nova Scotia. A schooner, carvel built, 88 tons.
OWNERS
1865 Allen Bros, Wexford (Master: Jos. Fennell).
1870 John Tyrell MM and John Tyrell, shipwright, both of Arklow.
1888 Out of Registration.

SHELAH: Built in Wexford in 1841. 128 tons.
OWNERS
R.&R. Sparrow. Master: William Gardner.
1853 Dun & Hull Shipping Co., Dundee.

SHELMALIER: Built in 1835 at Nova Scotia. A barque, carvel built, male figurehead, 264 tons.
1842 Registered at Wexford.
OWNER: Nicholas Sinnott, merchant. Master: John Pierce.
1842 Sinnott to Thomas Brennan as security for £1,200.
It was said that the **SHELMALIER** was built specifically for Nicholas Sinnott and caused a sensation on her first arrival in Wexford as her figurehead depicted Esmonde Kyan one of the leaders of the 1798 rebellion.

SIMON:
1861-1872 Registered at Wexford. Master: Captain Patrick Chandler.
CREW 1861.
Master: Evan Byrne, 50, of William St., Wexford.
Mate: William Codd, 40.
AB: Nicholas Doyle, 30.
OS: Patrick Doyle, 17; James Codd, 17.
Boy: James Walsh, 16 (first trip).

SIMOON: No. 47582. Code VPGC. Built in 1853 at New York.
A full rigged ship, 1162 tons.
OWNERS
1865 Lamport & Holt, Liverpool.
1872 Nicholas Sinnott, Enniscorthy, Co. Wexford.
1874 Out of Register (Ship registered at Liverpool).

SIMOON: No. 25970. Code PJFH. Built in 1851 at Wexford. A barque, 466 tons.
1853-1869 OWNER: Bates of Liverpool.
1870 Out of Register.

SINAI: No. 29069. Code QDCV. Built in 1861 at Plymouth, 98 tons.
1865 OWNER: Ellen O'Connor of Richmond Terrace, Wexford.
1874 Out of Register.

SLANEY: No. 63410. Built in 1863 at Wexford. A smack, 21 tons.
OWNER: William Armstrong of Wexford.
1882 Out of Register.

SMALL LARK:
1840 Registered at Wexford.
CREW 1840
Master: John Delaney, 25.
Mate: James –?.
Seaman: Nicholas Rogers, 40.

SPEED: No. 1471. Code KHDB. Built in 1846 at Nova Scotia. A schooner, 99 tons, carvel built.
OWNERS
1846-1870 Allen of Wexford;
1870 E. Purfield, Balbriggan, Co. Dublin;
1878 Out of Register

SPY: No. 8752. Code KDML. Built in 1845 at Nova Scotia. A schooner, carvel built, 78 tons.
1845 Registered at Wexford.
OWNERS
1845 R. Allen, Wexford Master: John Hayes.
1870 William Jackson, Larne; Patrick Mooney, Belfast.
1875 Out of Register.
CREW 1845 (Three men signed on as Mate during the year)
Master: John Campbell, 47.
Mate: John Hayes, 24.
Apprentice: George Codd, 18.
Sailor: Nicholas English, 28.
Boy: Frank Rowe, 15.
Other crew: Thomas Keogh, 25; John Murphy, 23; David Roche, 40; Michael Furlong, 26; John Clancy, 28; Owen Mason, 17; Michael Dillon, 35; Thomas Campbell, 44.

ST CECILE: Built in 1841 at Wexford. A schooner of 55 tons.
OWNER: John McIntire.
1870 20 November. Stranded at Cahore Point on a voyage from Ayr to Wexford with coal.

STAR OF THE SEA: No. 10157. Code KMHC. Built in 1856 at St John, New Brunswick. A barquentine, 111tons. Dimensions 84. 7x21.2x11ft.
OWNERS
1856 John Walsh, Nth. Main St., Wexford.
1865 Richard S. Dillon of Liverpool.
1867 Francis Allen Christie of Ipswich.
1900 Converted to a lighter.
CREW 1856.
Master: Laurence English, 35 of Keyser St., Wexford.
Mate: Nicholas Cullen, 51.
ABs: Edward Walsh, 33; James Ennis, 21; Andrew Kehoe, 25.
OS: Patrick Murphy, 20.
Boy: George Kelly, 18.

SUCCESS: Built in 1817 at Prince Edward Island. A schooner, 67 tons.
1837/38 Registered at Wexford.
OWNER: Codd & Co. Master: Captain Shannon.
CREW 1837
Master: John Delaney, 25.
Mate: James Furlong.
AB: Nicholas Rogers, 40.

SULTANA: **1837** Wrecked in Wexford Bay. Master: Captain Hill.

SWIFT: No.17574. Code MHFP. Built in 1857 at St. John, New Brunswick. A brig of 210 tons.
1858-1861 Registered at Wexford.
OWNER: Devereux, Wexford.
1864 Out of Register.

SWIFT: No. 21443. Code NGJM. Built in 1846 at Prince Edward Island. A schooner of 60 tons. Dimensions: 61x16x9ft.
1865-1872 OWNER: Mary Carr.
1872 20 December. En route from Wexford to Glasgow with a cargo of beans, she stranded in Dundrum Bay. All hands saved.

SYLPH: No.15722. Code LRBD. Built in 1839 at St. Martin's, New Brunswick. 58 tons. The **Sylph** arrived at Wexford in November 1839 on her maiden voyage and was immediately put up for sale.
1839: Registered at Wexford .
OWNERS
S. Kavanagh of Wexford became her managing owner. Master: J. Mansfield.
1865 William S. Lang of Newport, Monmouthshire.
1867 Fredrick Wathen of Gloucestershire.
1868 W. H. Beach of Gloucestershire.
1872 Ben Williams of Pembroke Dock.
1875 Out of Register.
CREW 1863
Master: J. Mansfield.
Mate: William Moore, 56.
ABs: Michael Darby, 26; Peter Mansfield, 17.
Boy: Patrick Kelly, 16.

SHANNON: Built in 1814 at Lyme Regis. A cutter, carvel built.
1843 Registered at Wexford.
OWNER: Thomas Brennan. Master: Daniel Doyle.
CREW
Master: Nicholas Fanning, 29.
Mate: John Ormsby, 40.
Seamen: John Bolger, 25; Martin Greene, 35; James Scallan, 30.
Apprentice: James McGrath, 18.
Crew: Mathew Sinnott, 33.

T

TANGO:
1835 Registered at Wexford.
CREW
Master: Patrick Turner, 21.
Mate: Brian Bruen (?).
Sailors: James Hughes; Pat. Campbell; John Shields; John English; Edward Murphy; John Breen; Bartle Kinsella.

TAYLOR & NAYLOR: Built 1839 at Wexford, a cutter, carvel built, 34 tons.
OWNERS
J.T. Devereux, Master: Ed. Cleary.
1868 Evan John, Newport, Pembrokeshire.

THOMAS:
1837/1845 Registered at Wexford.
CREW
Master: James Murphy, 45.
Mate: Patrick Hayes, 36.
Sailor: Oliver Hyland, 20.
Seaman: John Dempsey, 36.
Other: Patrick Dillon.

THOMAS: Built in 1839 at Barnstaple. A schooner of 128 tons.
OWNER: T. Brennan of Wexford.
CREW 1845
Master: Christopher Hayes, 45.
Mate: Miles Connors.
Seamen: Patrick Ryan; Patrick Cole.
Boys: William Murphy; Bartholomew Carthy.

TIGER: Built in 1821 at Nova Scotia. A schooner of 69 tons.
1845 Registered at Wexford.
OWNER: Thomas Brennan of Wexford.
CREW 1845
Master: Christopher Lambert, 25.
Mate: Peter Murphy, 41.
Seamen: James Cousins, 21; Nicholas Lambert, 19.
Lost on the Blackwater Bank.

VESSELS FOR SALE.

JOHN WALSH, AUCTIONEER,

HAS been instructed, by the Trustees of THOMAS BRENNAN, Esq., Wexford, to SELL BY PUBLIC AUCTION, on FRIDAY, the 25th instant, at the OFFICE, WIGRAM-QUAY, the following First-class Trading VESSELS, all well found, and in good sea-going order :—
The Schooner THOMAS, 93 Tons, N.M., carries about 150 Tons; the Schooner TIGER, 70 Tons, do, do 112 Tons; the Schooner EDWARD, 53 Tons, do, do 85 Tons; the Sloop SHANNON, 49 Tons, do, do 75 Tons ; Three-fourths of the Schooner MARIA, 74 Tons, do, do 115 Tons.
Sale to commence at One o'clock, when the Terms will be announced.
The above Vessels are moored in the River, and can be viewed at any time previous to the day of Sale. An inventory of the Stores can be had on application to the Auctioneer.
Wexford, October 11, 1850.

Advertisement for the **Thomas**.

TORRANCE: No. 21439. Code NGJF. Built in 1846 at Quebec. A brig, carvel built, 175 tons, female figurehead.
OWNERS
1858-1862 Richard Devereux of Wexford.
1863 William Patrick, New Quay, Troon, Ayr.
1870 John Neil Marr, Glasgow.
1872 James Neil Marr, Glasgow.
1876 Out of Register.

TOWN OF WEXFORD: Built in 1837 at Wexford. A schooner of 228 tons. Launched at Wexford Dockyard on 19 January 1836. Afterwards converted to steam. The only coastal steamer built in Wexford.
OWNERS: John Edward Redmond (Also Master in 1842).
1842 June. D. Williams appointed master at Liverpool.
1845 4 July. James Carr appointed master at Wexford.
1847 Sold to Glasgow.
1852 3 January. Ship lost near Holyhead.

TRIO: A brig owned by Devereux. In November 1845, Captain Rowe of the brig **Trio** was lauded in the local press for carrying out two trips to North America in the fast time of 5 months and 2 days. The first was to Miramichi and the second to Quebec. The **Trio** was lost on Splaugh Rock near Ballygeary on 28 January 1849. She was homeward bound from Galatz.

TRITON: No. 20120. Code MVSG. Built in 1844 at Gosport. A cutter, 24 tons. Owned in New Ross up to 1860.
OWNERS
1865 Fitzroy Clayton of Kent.
1870 C. R. Conybeare ,Hants.
1890 J. W. Dyer of Gosport.
1900 R.J. Passby of Gillingham.
1913 Register closed.

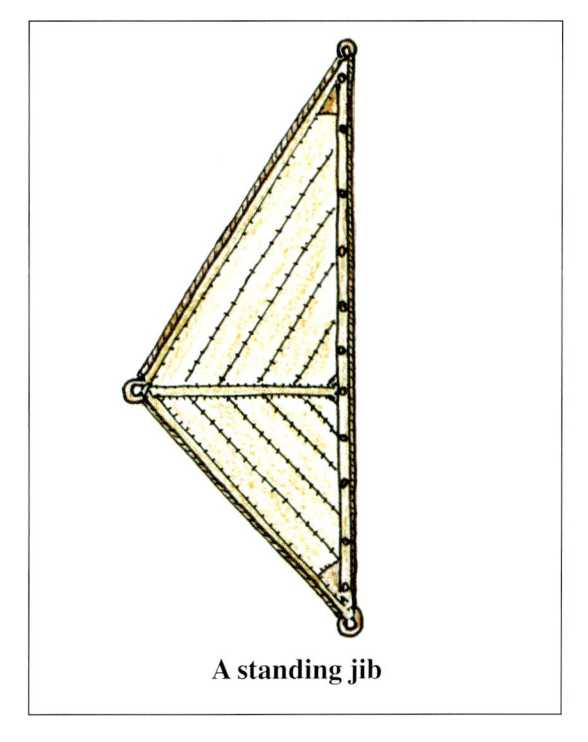

A standing jib

U

UNION: **1836/1837** Registered at Wexford.

V

VALIANT: 34 tons.
1852 Registered at Wexford.
CREW 1852.
Master: John Murphy, 40.
Mate: Nicholas Murphy, 42.
Seaman: Nicholas Wadding, 25.

VARNA. No. 26210. Code PJHW. Built in 1854 at New Brunswick. A brig of 157 tons.
OWNERS
1858 1861 Devereux of Wexford. Master: Captain J. Sheil.
1861/1863/1864 Richard Page and G. C. Smith of Barnstaple, Devon.
1865 Out of Register.

VENN: Schooner, built at Wexford in 1854.

VENUS: No. 21442 Code NGJL. Built in 1854 at Wexford. A schooner, 96 tons.
OWNERS
1858 A. Whitty, Wexford.
1858 N. Whitty, Wexford.
1858 James Howlett, New Ross, Co. Wexford.
1859 25 November. William Parle of Christendom, Waterford.
1869 22 October. Lost in the Bristol Channel.

VICTORIA: No. 21444. Built in 1845 at Wexford. A cutter, carvel built, 19 tons.
1845 Master: John Cahill.
1865 OWNERS: John and Edmund Roach.
1872 Out of Register.

VICTORIA:
OWNER: J.T.Devereux.
On 12 January 1841, John Pearce, aged 17, was drowned when he fell overboard from the Wexford schooner **Victoria** at Glasson Dock Basin, Lancaster.
  On 7 January 1854, the *Downpatrick Reporter* reported that:
  *The schooner **Victoria**, which ran on shore on the bar of sand outside Portrane, on Thursday morning last before daybreak, has become a total wreck. The spot where this unhappy vessel struck is a well-known and dangerous reef of small rocks, nearly covered*

with sand, lying about quarter of a mile from the shore nearly opposite the Donabate coast-guard station. She proves to have been the **Victoria** of Wexford, a schooner rigged craft, of 80 tons burden, bound from Liverpool to Dublin, with a cargo of coals. She was commanded Thomas Roe, master, assisted by O'Dowd, mate, and four men, with a cabin boy.

This luckless vessel was the property of John Thomas Devereux, Esq., of Wexford. All on board have perished. The bodies of the captain and his mate were washed on shore on Thursday, and subsequently the body of one of the crew. The bodies of the captain and mate were found clothed in a manner indicating that they must have been suffering great hardship from cold previous to the wreck. Both bodies were found clothed with double pairs flannel drawers and vests, and with oilcloth trousers and storm jackets outside of their regular clothes.

The schooner, it would appear, had made tolerable good weather of it, running before the easterly gale, although deeply laden, until she was caught by the squall of Wednesday afternoon and driven on this formidable coast. In the pockets of the captain's clothes were found three sovereigns, three and six pence in silver, and a silver watch, which was partly wound up, and, as it would appear, had been going up to the time when the unfortunate owner lost his life. The papers etc. in the pockets of the mate, O'Dowd, proved so far the identity his body. He was a native of Wexford. A sum of five shillings in silver and some copper coins were found in his pockets. A tea chest was washed ashore by the tide on Saturday on the strand. Fragments of timber, planks, and broken spars, and quantities of coal have been thrown upon the waves from the wreck, which lies sunk on the outside the bar, and is rapidly going pieces.

VISION: No.25788. Code PHLD. Built in 1846 at Sunderland. A schooner, 136 tons.
OWNERS
1853 Devereux, Wexford. Master: O'Connor.
1865 Francis Haselman, Co. Durham.
1870 Out of Register.

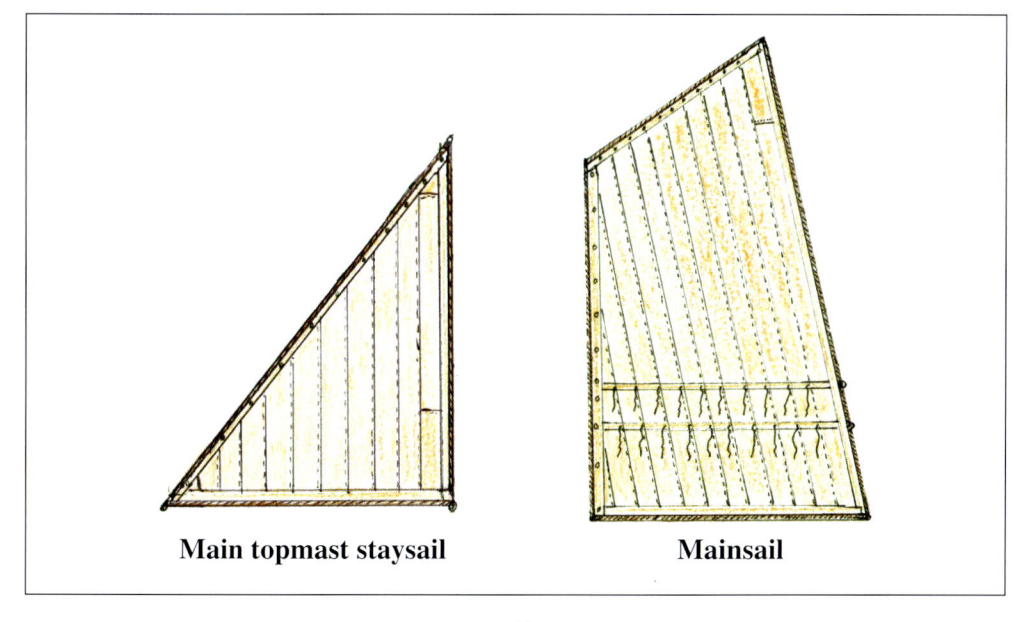

Main topmast staysail   **Mainsail**

W

WASP: No. 37297. Built in 1856 at Grainville, Nova Scotia. Wooden schooner, 2 masts. Registered in Dublin in 1857.
1884 Registered in Wexford.
OWNERS
James Marlow, Wexford.
1895 Marlow died and his shares went to Catherine Kearns of Paul Quay.
1896 Sold to Francis J. Walsh.
1898 February. Converted to a lighter.

WESTERN STAR: No. 18364. Code MLNF. Built in 1822 at Wexford. A schooner of 61 tons.
1853 OWNER: P. Power of New Ross. Master: Condon.

WEXFORD: No. 16021. Code LVRB. Built in 1851 at New Brunswick. A barque of 307 tons. Dimensions: 105x26x16ft.
1851-1868 OWNER: R.&R. Allen of Wexford. Wexford to Savannah, Georgia route.
1872 Out of Register.

WEXFORD PACKET: Registered at Wexford 1835, 1837.
CREWS
1837
Master: Peter Clancy, 44.
Mate: James Cleary, 45; Michael Furlong, 25.
Sailors: Peter Monk, 35; Nicholas Cleary, 46; Laurence McGee, 17.
1838
Master: Edward Cleary, 45.
Mate: Nicholas Furlong, 26; Pat Moor, 35.
OS: Laurence McGee, 18.

WILD FLOWER: No. 27927. Code PTHR, later EIFZ. Built in 1860 at Fairlie, Ayr.
OWNERS
1870 Simon Little of Cullentra, Co. Wexford.
1878 Lord Muskerry of Springfield Castle, Co. Limerick.
1900-1934 (now named **Wildflower**, one word) E. Hadlow Suggate of London.
1940 Herbert J. Finch of Stanstead, Essex. Throughout all this time she was registered in Wexford.

WILLIAM: A sloop. On March 8, 1876, six of her crew were saved by the lifeboat **Ethel Eveleen**.

WILLIAM WHITTY:
1836 Registered at Wexford.
CREW 1836,
Master: Michael Sheil, 40.
Mate: Patrick Codd, 43.
Sailor: James Murphy, 29; Nicholas Hayes, 20.
Seaman: Peter Dunphy, 37.
Nicholas Hayes, 20; John Cahill, 17; John Sheil, 22.
1837 February. Lost on the Bar of Wexford.

WIND: No. 20112. Code MVRQ. Built in New Brunswick in 1857.
A brig of 133 tons.
OWNER: R.&R. Allen of Wexford. Master: Howlin.
1871 Out of Register.

WOODMAN: No. 12029. Code KWCT. Built in 1841 at Palnakie, Scotland.
A schooner of 58 tons.
OWNERS
1865 Dan McSweeney of Cork.
1866 Richard Cox of Bannow, Co. Wexford.
1870 Philip Murphy of Waterford.
1871 William Murphy of Carrig on Bannow, Wexford.
1883 12 December. Wrecked

WOODSTOCK: No. 26815. Code PMRN. Built in 1850 at Quebec.
A ship of 967 tons. Dimensions: 151.7x31.5x21.8ft.
OWNERS
1855 Graves & Sons. Master: John Williams.
1865 Samuel Graves of Liverpool.
1867 George Wigglesworth of Kingston-Upon-Hull. Registered Liverpool.
1870 Out of Register.

Z

ZOUAVE: No. 1142. Built in 1855 at Salcombe, Devon, by Bonker. A schooner, 3 masts, 116 tons. Dimensions: 97.5x20.5x10.7ft.
OWNERS
William Hartland, Tranmere, Merseyside, and Morgan Merdith, Aberystwyth.
1902 November. Francis J. Walsh of the Wexford Dockyard.
1904 24 March. Registration closed. Vessel converted to a lighter.

Port *of* Waterford

3rd Floor, Marine Point, Belview Port,
Waterford X91 W0XW, Ireland.

Tel: +353 51 874907
Email: info@portofwaterford.com

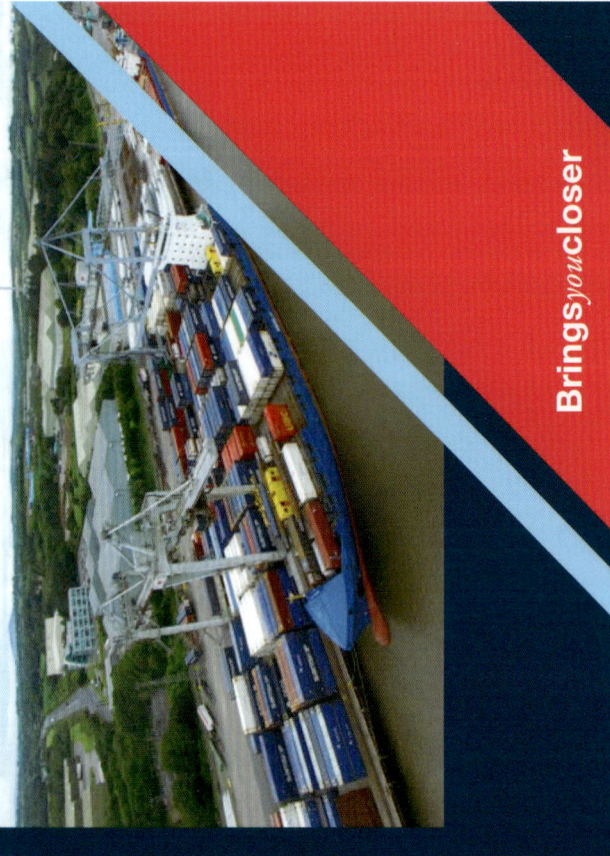

Web: www.portofwaterford.com

Brings *you* **closer**

Port *of* Waterford

Part 3:
Visitors to the Ports

The vessels listed here did not belong to Wexford but were, nonetheless, very familiar to local people due to their frequent visits to the main Wexford ports.

Agnes Craig, three masted tops'l schooner. Built in 1884 by Ferguson & Baird, Connah's Quay.

Another view of the **Agnes Craig** at Waterford.
Photo Robert Shortall, Andrew Kelly Collection.

BROOKLANDS. No. 27753. Code PSND. Built 1859 at Sandquay, Dartmouth, Devon by Kelly as a two-masted, double top, gallant schooner of 106 tons. Dimensions: 100.6x 21.4x 12.1 ft.

Built for Vitterys of Brixham and named **Susan Vittery**. She was said to be a typical Brixham fruiter, a long flat vessel with sharp ends. Her first voyages were in the fruit trade to the Azores and she operated in this trade for many years. She was also said to have been a very fast clipper, and she created and held the record for the fastest trips, under sail, between London and St Michael's in the Azores. In 1860 she was bound for St Michaels when she rescued the crew of barque **Island Queen** in the North Atlantic. The **Island Queen** was sinking with 7ft of water in her holds. Captain Kendrick of the **Susan Vittery** ordered a boat launched to go to the aid of the sinking vessel. This was done and after taking two trips to the **Island Queen,** with no small risk to their own lives, the crew of the lifeboat saved the 16-man crew of the barque. The six men who manned the rescue boat were later awarded the sum of ten pounds between them and Captain Kendrick was awarded a telescope. Then came the decline in sail in the fruit trade and she was sent further afield to Newfoundland, bringing salt out and salted cod back.

In 1879, Vitterys sold her to another Brixham owner, H.A. Hawkey. Shortly after he bought her she damaged her bows and, during the repairs, Hawkey had a figure head made and fitted, using his wife as the model. Hawkey's sold her to Newquay in 1884 and she went into the coasting trade. In 1918 she was sold to Parker and Mengel of Grimsby. Shortly after that she suffered some serious damage in running ashore on the east coast of England and had to be taken to the Acorn shipyard at Rochester for survey. There it was discovered that her keel was broken in three places along with many of her flooring timbers. Due to there being no spare slipway at Rochester she had to be towed to Whitstable where she was practically rebuilt and had an extra mast fitted.

In 1923 Parkers sold her to Captain John Creenan of Ballinacurra Co. Cork who renamed her **Brooklands**. From then, he successfully operated her around the Irish coast and one of her regular runs was between New Ross and the Bristol Channel. The *Daily Telegraph* carried a report in early December 1928 that the **Brooklands** had gone down with all hands. This, fortunately, was incorrect. The **Brooklands** was on a voyage from Glasgow to New Ross with a cargo of coal for the New Ross Gas Co. and arrived at her destination. In 1937 she was lying wind-bound when she was run into by a steamer off The Mumbles and had to put into Swansea with damaged bows and minus a bowsprit.

In the 20s and 30s most of the coastal schooners and ketches had auxiliary engines installed but Captain Creenan refused to take this course and **Brooklands** depended completely on wind power for propulsion. He was also noted for the pristine condition in which he kept the vessel, and was said to have a real pride in the old ship. Captain Creenan's continuing refusal to have an engine installed on his vessel, making her the last Irish schooner to depend totally on sail, and gained him and his ship a lot of attention. Around March of 1940 the local Enniscorthy, Co. Wexford, paper the **Echo** carried a report that had appeared in the *Irish Times* telling of the wonderment of the people having an afternoon stroll on Dublin's North and South Wall at the sight of an 83-year-old schooner coming in, every inch of her canvas stretched for the dying wind. It was the **Brooklands** of Cork. The report continues: *She sailed right up to her berth on the South Wall without the aid of any tug and as she neared the dockside her crew of five ran spider wise up the rigging and out on her topmost spars to furl her sails.*

Tops'l schooner **Brooklands** at New Ross. September 9th 1939.
Photo Robert Shortall, Andrew Kelly Collection.

On board the **Brooklands,** New Ross to Lydney c1939
Original photo by D. Bennett.

In 1941, in a desperate attempt to keep the supply routes open during the War and to replace lost vessels and augment the few left, the Irish Government called up the last of the Irish coastal schooners, among them **Brooklands**. She survived the war years without mishap. Captain Creenan retired handing over command of the **Brooklands** to his son Christy who had served as Mate for many years. In September 1946 **Brooklands** took her last trip under sail from Ballinacurra to Western Point with salt. She was then laid up until a deal was struck to charter her. Unfortunately, the intended charterer, Mr A.A. Harris, died when the **Isallt** was wrecked, the charter fell through, and the **Brooklands** remained laid up in the Mersey.

Captain P.G. Ashworth of Courtown, Co. Wexford purchased her in June of 1948 and after some more re-fitting had her towed to the open sea where sails were set and she sailed for Arklow to have engines installed. (At this period she was said to have been owned by the exotically named San Antonio Shipping Company Ltd. of Courtown Co. Wexford. This seems to indicate that Captain Ashworth was the owner of this company.) She also had her topmasts and yards removed and changed her name back to **Susan Vittery**. This was said by Captain Ashworth to be in deference to a seafaring tradition that it was bad luck to change a ship's name. In August of 1949 **Susan Vittery**, a shadow of her former self, left Arklow bound for Garston. There she loaded her first cargo in three years. On 18 September, she cleared for Youghal and ran into a southeast gale which carried away her mainsail. Her engines were also giving trouble but she made Wexford Bay and went to anchor. Rosslare Harbour lifeboat, the **Mabel Marion Thompson**, took the crew off but they later went back on board and eventually brought her into Youghal. She then sailed for Wicklow where she was laid up again, this time for two years. In 1952 she was sold yet again, this time to a Dublin group who had her re-fitted and had two new 140 horse power engines installed.

Brooklands at New Ross, July 14th 1938. "Slightly down by the head".
Photo Robert Shortall, Andrew Kelly Collection.

In 1953 she took on a cargo of phosphate for Dungarvan and had another mishap when she went aground near the quay at Dungarvan. On her last voyage, the **Susan Vittery** left Dungarvan for Dublin to have repairs carried out. In command was Captain Arne Drensgrud, a Norwegian resident in Dublin, and a crew of three: the mate, Stephen Doolin, age 21 of Ballyvaughan, Co. Clare; John Larkin age 29, A.B. of Dun Laoghaire and the cook, Thomas Parle aged 30 of Manchester. They left Dungarvan on Sunday evening and that night were off the Saltee Islands. About then someone discovered that she was taking water. Unfortunately, there were no pumps fitted in the ship and very soon her engine room reported 5 feet of water.

About 5 am on 5 April, the holds were full of water and the engine was rendered useless. The ship's boat was launched and tied astern. Soon afterwards the captain ordered the crew into the boat. By this time, they were only about two miles from Rosslare Harbour. The captain was still in the wheelhouse when someone shouted to him that she was sinking. He had barely time to jump into the lifeboat and cut her free before she went down. They were adrift in choppy seas and, as the wind was taking them out to sea, they decided to make for the Welsh coast. Steamers were spotted and flares sent up to attract them but all to no avail as the choppy seas hampered visibility. After some hours the tide changed and blew them back towards the Irish coast again. Around eight hours later they made Tuskar Rock. With the assistance of the keepers they landed on the rock where their saturated clothes were dried and they were provided with hot food.

The Tuskar sent a radio message to the shore where it was picked up by Miss Rita Whelan, of the Faythe, Wexford (All Irish Lights' families had domestic radios with Marine Bands capable of receiving broadcasts from lighthouses and lightships), sister of keeper Vincent Whelan, stationed on the Tuskar but at the time on shore leave. They relayed it to the Rosslare Lifeboat Station and the RNLIs **Douglas Hyde**, under Cox Richard Walsh, picked the shipwrecked sailors up and brought them ashore at Rosslare Harbour.

CYMRIC

No. 101751. Code NBFI. Built 1893 at Amlwch in North Wales in the yard of Captain William Thomas. A steel hulled schooner, 224 tons. Dimensions: 123 x 24 . 6x 10.8 ft.

Operated as a 'Q' ship in World War 1 under the alias **Olive**, among others.

Cymric was not a Wexford-owned ship and was never registered in Wexford which is the reason she is in this section of the book. Many people assume that she was but this is probably due to the fact that she is commemorated on the plaques on Wexford quays dedicated to Wexford sailing ships, and by the fact that at the time she disappeared there were six Wexford Town men among her crew.

In April 1893, her maiden voyage, under Amlwch man Captain Robert Jones, took her to Rio Grande do Sul and Porto Alegre in Brazil and home to Runcorn in April 1894. This was to be a regular run for the next six years under Captain Jones; UK to South America with coal and general cargo and back to Europe with hides. All these runs were interspersed with trips to Scandinavia for timber. In 1899 J. & S. Holt of Liverpool bought her for the sum of 2, 650 pounds, a good price at the time. Then in 1906 Holts sold her to Captain Richard Hall of Arklow, the port where she was to spend the rest of her career.

Hall put her into the wine trade to Spain until World War 1 broke out when she was

Cymric alongside at Waterford.

converted to be a decoy or 'Q' ship. As a ' Q' ship **Cymric** was armed with 1x4-inch gun, 2 twelve pounders and 1x7.5-inch howitzer. The effectiveness of the 'Q' ships was brought into question after the end of the War, but it has to be said some of them were successful in drawing German submarines into range and sinking them. However, the **Cymric**'s only target turned out to be a Royal Navy submarine that she sank by mistake, thinking it was an enemy vessel. It happened on the 15 October 1918 off Blythe, Northumberland where the **Cymric** was on her regular patrol of the South Western Approaches. **Cymric** observed a submarine on the surface and, thinking it was a German vessel attacked and sank it, with all of her 14-man crew going down with her. It transpired that **Cymric** had mistaken her number **J6**, that of a 'J' Class British submarine, for **U6**, the German designation.

After the war ended, the **Cymric** was back with Hall's of Arklow and trading mainly on the Ireland to Bristol Channel ports. She was a frequent visitor to the Port of Wexford and other ports in the county. In August 1922, she went up on the Brandies Rocks off Kilmore and was beached. It took two days before she could be re-floated. In January 1924 she was aground again, this time at Rosslare when, laden with bricks, she was driven ashore. The task of lightening her in the hope that she would float off was given to P. Donovan of Wexford, but due to the bad weather it was a slow tedious job. It was thought that she could be towed off at the next spring tides but it was decided not to attempt that because of her leaking condition.

She was eventually got off and went about her normal business until February 1928 when she appeared in the newspapers as the ship that speared a tram! It appears that the **Cymric** was waiting to pass through the McMahon Bridge, a drawbridge, at Ringsend Basin, Dublin, when a sudden gust of wind drove her forward and driving her bowsprit through the window of a passing tram. Fortunately, no one was injured. Christmas Eve,

1933 she grounded on the treacherous Bar of Wexford Harbour after her propeller became fouled in some rope that had been left in the water after another ship was refloated the previous day. She was there for 5 days and could only be floated off by lightening her of cargo and with the aid of a diver.

When World War 2 broke out the **Cymric**'s trading pattern changed. Like many other Irish motor schooners, she began running to Spain, Portugal etc., bringing coal out and vital supplies back to Ireland. In October 1943, after a re-fit at Ringsend Dock, the **Cymric** sailed for Port Talbot to load coal for Lisbon. Her master was Captain Michael Cardiff of Wexford. Bad weather held her up in the channel and then Captain Cardiff became ill and the Mate, James Sydney Kerr had to take her into Rosslare to get medical attention for him. Captain Cardiff paid off sick and his place was taken by Captain Christopher Cassidy. A few days before Christmas 1943 she left Rosslare Harbour for Lisbon with a cargo of Welsh coal, arriving on New Year's Day 1944.

The passage back home was a rough one. The main fore sail and main gaff top sail were blown to pieces in the Bay of Biscay, but she did get home. She was again put into Ringsend Dock in Dublin for a re-fit to get her ready for sea again. On 23 February she sailed from Ardrossan, Scotland with a cargo of coal for Lisbon and apart from a sighting off Dublin the next day she was never seen again. There was great consternation in Wexford Town when she was posted missing, as there would be in any tight-knit, seafaring community when news of a ship missing or lost became known. But this time it was different as no less than six of the **Cymric**'s crew were from Wexford Town.

Lost on the **Cymric** were:

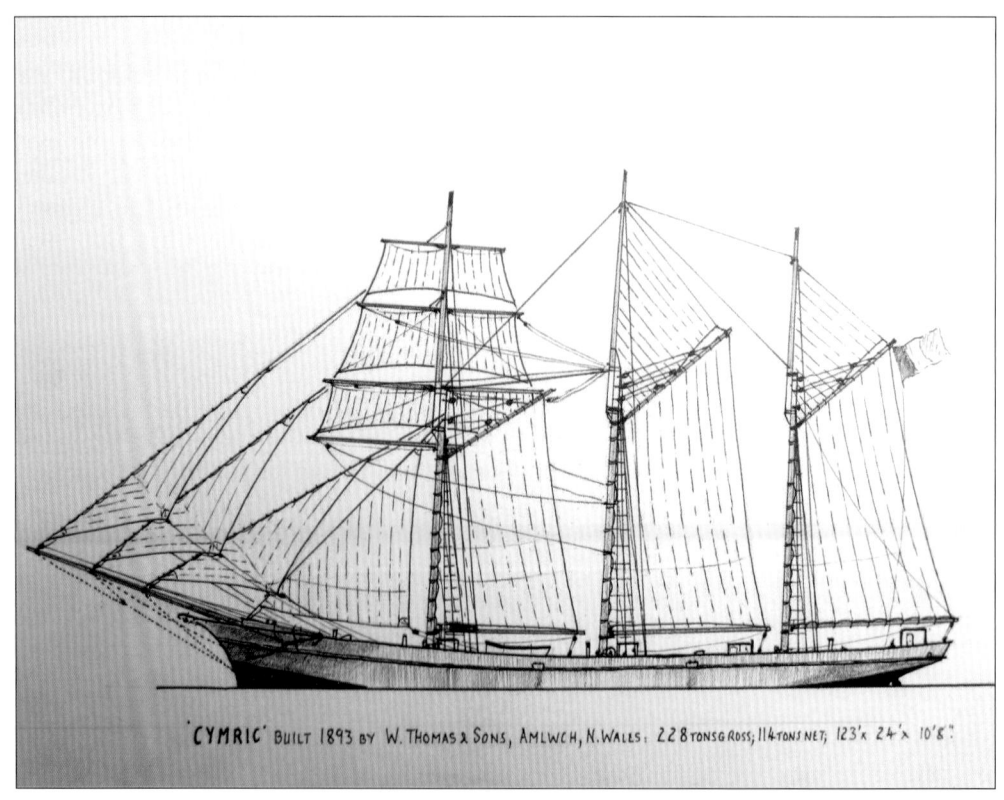

Cymric's sail plan when rigged as a three masted t'gallant schooner.

Cymric, Alongside at Wexford, June 6th 1941, during World War II. Note the neutral markings on her hull.
Photo Robert Shortall, Andrew Kelly Collection.

Cymric, an auxiliary schooner of 224 tons. Built, 1893 at Amlwch, North Wales. Seen here passing the Coningbeg Lightship.

Master: Christopher Cassidy, 59, of Monkstown Road, Dublin;
1st Officer: B Kiernan, 41, of Roden Place, Dundalk;
Bosun: Peter Seaver, 35, of Quay Street, Skerries, Dublin;
1st Engineer: Michael Tierney, 42, of 14 White Rock View, Wexford;
2nd Engineer: Kevin Furlong, 32, of Emmett Place, Wexford;
William O'Rourke, 67, of 36 Parnell St., Wexford;
ABs: James Brennan, 59, of Trinity Place, Wexford; James Crosbie, 66, of 3 The Faythe, Wexford;
Seaman: C. F. McConnell, 22, of 'The Grawn', Clonskeagh, Dublin;
Cook: M.C. Ryan, 45, of Dungarvan, Co. Waterford;
OS: Philip Bergin, 18, of Peter Street, Wexford.

The three Wexford ABs were veteran sailors and well experienced in sail but young Bergin was just on his second trip to sea.

Mike Williams, a Byrne's Lane man and latterly from St Bernadette's Place, Wexford, 'worked by' i.e., worked on her in dock, but fortunately for him, didn't sail with her. James Sydney Kerr from Enniscorthy who was Mate, and had taken her into Rosslare when Captain Cardiff got sick, also worked by her in dock but left her and joined the **Irish Larch**. Other fortunate Wexford sailors were Billy Maher of Maudlintown, who also left the **Cymric** and joined the **Irish Cedar**, and Peter Quirke of William Street, who left to join the **Menapia**. As nothing is shown in U Boats files on the sinking of the **Cymric**, it is widely believed that she struck a mine, possibly in the Bay of Biscay.

DE WADDEN

No. 144980. Code EIKF. Built in 1917 in the Netherlands by Gebr Van Diepan for N.V Scheepvoart Maatschappy de Wadden. Steel hull, 239 tons. Dimensions: 116 .8 x 24. 4 x 10. 3ft

De Wadden was also a 'Q' ship in World War1. In 1922 she was bought by Captain Richard Hall of Arklow and she was to remain in Arklow hands for the next 40 years, trading between Ireland and Great Britain. During the economic slump in the 1930s, she was laid up but fortunately for her owners the lay-up didn't last long and after 4 months she was back running on the cross channel trade. Then, after the outbreak of WW2, **De Wadden**, like the **Cymric** and other Irish auxiliary schooners, she made several trips to Portugal. In 1941 she had a new engine fitted and 10 years

De Wadden at sea with a deck cargo of logs, possibly pit props.

De Wadden, a steel auxiliary schooner of 224 tons. Built in 1917. Berthed at Waterford. Pre 1928.

later had major repairs, including a new main deck, fitted at Manchester.

De Wadden's career was fairly uneventful for the next 5 years until she was in collision with a Belfast steamer in the Mersey. Then, in 1959, on a trip from Liverpool to Crosshaven, she suffered engine trouble and had to make for Waterford to carry out repairs. In 1961, she left Arklow hands when her then owner, Capt. Victor Hall, son of her original Irish owner, sold her to Scottish owners. On her first trip under her new owners, **De Wadden** arrived on the Clyde with a cargo of motor cars which she discharged at Greenock. She was then laid up at Loch Long, pending a re-fit. The intention was to convert her to a passenger-carrying vessel but this plan never materialized and **De Wadden** was put up for sale once again.

In 1970, Mr Kenneth Kennedy of Dunoon became her new owner. He set to work and enlarged the accommodation, mounted a crane on deck and, after months of toil, got the engine working again. Using family and friends as crew, he set off down the Clyde to dredge for sand. Later in the '70s **De Wadden** entered the film business when she became one of the vessels featured in the very successful BBC TV series ' The Onedin Line', starring Peter Gilmore and Anne Stallybrass. Later she was used for fishing trips, taking anglers off for day or weekend trips.

As time went on, the cost of her upkeep became prohibitive and in 1983 she was put up for sale. Her purchasers were the Merseyside Maritime Museum and in August of the following year she arrived in the Mersey. Restoration began and the saloon that had been built over the No. 2 hatch was removed. Work is still ongoing and **De Wadden**, one of the last of the Irish owned schooners, can be seen today in dry dock at the Merseyside Maritime Museum, Liverpool.

De Wadden at New Ross, June 23rd, 1951.
Photo, Robert Shortall, Andrew Kelly Collection.

JT&S and **De Wadden** at New Ross, April 10th 1952.
Photo Robert Shortall, Andrew Kelly Collection.

ELLIE PARK

No 76894. Code JGNB (1940 EIDK). Built in 1879 at Barrow, by the Furness Shipbuilding Company. An auxiliary schooner 70 tons. Dimensions: 85.1x20.9x8.9ft. During her time in New Ross ownership, the **Ellie Park** was registered in Cork. Launched in May 1879, she was the last ship to be built by The Furness Shipbuilding Company at Barrow in Furness.

OWNERS
1880 Barrow Shipbuilding Co.
1888, John Fisher of Barrow.
1902 James Fisher of Barrow;
1917 William Sinclair of Barrow.
1918 John Fisher of Barrow.
1923 William McBurney of Annalong, Co. Down.
1933 L. Ryan, Strokestown, New Ross, Co. Wexford.
1947 Capt Ambersboll of Denmark.

On Friday 9 April 1923, distress signals were seen coming from two vessels anchored in Wexford's South Bay. There was a fierce gale blowing with heavy rain squalls. Both vessels, the **Ellie Park** and the **Mabel** were inbound with coal for Nunn's of Wexford.

Wooden schooner **Ellie Park.** Built 1879. Arriving at New Ross, August 23rd 1939.
Photo Robert Shortall, Andrew Kelly Collection.

Ellie Park in the River Mersey, early in her career, still carrying her fore tops'l yards and sails.

The Fort lifeboat, **William Evans**, immediately answered the call and were about two miles from Rosslare Point when signals were sent up recalling her. Apparently the signalman ashore had received news that both schooners had reached Rosslare. The lifeboat turned for home and just as she reached her berth another distress signal was seen coming from the direction of the South Bay.

The lifeboat again put out towards the direction of the signals and found that the **Ellie Park** had grounded, whereas the **Mabel** had reached the harbour safely. In the teeth of the heavy wind the lifeboat was manoeuvred close enough to the **Ellie Park** to enable the crew to jump aboard safely. It was 4 am on Saturday before the lifeboat returned to her station with her exhausted crew and equally exhausted survivors. Later, in a letter to the R.N.L.I., Captain M. McVeigh of the **Ellie Park** complimented Cox. Wickham and his crew saying that: *During my 37 years' experience of the sea, I never saw a boat handled so well in such a heavy sea. Having been landed at Rosslare Point, we were treated with the utmost kindness and consideration by Mr Wickham and his wife.*

During the rescue operation two members of the lifeboat crew were injured. One of them, William Duggan, was leaning forward trying to prevent one of the **Ellie Park's** crew from slipping into the sea when he was thrown forward onto a sharp object which

Ellie Park passing through the Barrow Bridge, bound for New Ross, August 8th 1940.
Note the neutral markings on her hull.
Photo by Robert Shortall, Andrew Kelly Collection.

injured him severely. About two weeks later she was re-floated and after a check at the Pier she was taken in tow by a tug and left in a north-easterly direction.

On the evening of Monday, 10 November 1947, the **Ellie Park** left Douglas, Isle of Man with a cargo of scrap iron bound for Connah's Quay. She was under the command of Captain Ambersboll, her new owner, and had three crew. At about 5 am a heavy gale blowing SW came up and the old ship began leaking badly. All hands manned the pumps and they managed to stay ahead of the incoming water for about 90 minutes when the **Ellie Park** suddenly capsized. All on board were thrown into the water. The captain and the mate clung on to a piece of the wheelhouse. The AB, Noel Burns, from Bangor, Co. Down, also held on to some floating wreckage. The mate on the wreckage of the wheelhouse soon succumbed and slipped under the waves. John Quinn, the cook, had not been seen since the ship capsized.

The Isle of Man Steam Packet Company's steamer, **King Orry** was on passage to Liverpool when, at about 10.50 am her Chief Officer spotted wreckage and a waving arm. The **King Orry** immediately hove to and a boat was sent off to look for the source of the waving arm. Battling through heavy seas they first came up on Noel Burns, barely alive. They got him on board and shortly afterwards they found Captain Ambersboll, still clinging to the wreckage of the wheelhouse. Both men were hospitalised in Liverpool.

Garlandstone was a ketch that traded regularly between the Bristol Channel and the south coast of Ireland. Built in 1909 at Calstock. Seen here at New Ross, June 1940.
Photo Robert Shortall, Andrew Kelly Collection.

A stern view of the **Gaelic.**

GAELIC
No. 101760. Code QBHR. Built in 1898 at Amlwch by Thomas & Son. A barquentine of 224 tons. Dimensions: 126.8x24x10.8ft.

Registered at Beaumaris for William and Lewis Thomas of Amlwch. Built of iron, she was a sister ship of the **Cymric**, and, like her sister, she too was a 'Q' ship in WW1, designated Q22. She was armed with two eight hundredweight 12 pounders and two twelve hundredweight 12 pounders, plus two Maxims. About this time an auxiliary

The **Gaelic**, was a three masted, iron built schooner of 224 tons. Built in 1898 she was a sister ship of the **Cymric.**

engine was fitted and her rigging reduced. Her final owners were George Kearon (Manager), Anna M.O 'Toole, and Muriel E. Hall of Arklow. Registered at Dublin.
On 7 February 1939, the **Gaelic** was in the Mersey when she was in collision with the dredger **Burbo** and sank south-east of Rock Ferry Pier. However, she was raised on 26 February and moved to Tranmere beach. After repairs were carried out, she was back in service in August 1940. On 25 February 1952, en route from Ards, Co. Donegal to the River Mersey with a cargo of silica sand, **Gaelic** was wrecked on Frenchman's Reef, Mulroy, Co. Donegal.

HAPPY HARRY
No 102462 Code EIMZ. Built in 1894 at Duddon, near Barrow on Furness by the Duddon Shipbuilding Company. She was a three-masted, tops'l schooner of 142 tons. Dimensions, 101.2x23.10x10.3ft. Registered at Whitehaven. Managed by Robert Johnson of Millom, Cumberland.

Said to be named for a local Duddon man of pleasant disposition, **Happy Harry** came into Arklow hands in 1921 when she was purchased by Captain Job Tyrell. A report in the *Liverpool Mercury* on 5 January 5 1907 told of the death of her master, Captain John Williams, in Ramsey Harbour, Isle of Man. The **Happy Harry** had been bound from Greenock to her home port of Duddon when she put into Ramsey for shelter. Captain Williams went ashore and returned about 4 pm. At 5.30 the mate went below and found the captain on his knees. A doctor was summoned and he pronounced the 72-year-old captain dead.

From her time in Arklow ownership until her eventual demise in 1950, **Happy Harry** made the newspapers on a few occasions. In September 1923 **Happy Harry** arrived at

Happy Harry, a tops'l schooner. Built at Duddon, near Barrow-in-Furness in 1894.

Happy Harry under sail in a light breeze.

Happy Harry, now fitted with her auxiliary engine.

Wexford with malting coal for Messrs Nunn & Co., straight into the local dockworkers' strike. She remained tied up at Wexford Quays for six weeks due to the Dockers' Union demanding written guarantee be given that the old rate of pay would be paid until a settlement of the port's strike. Nunn's agreed to the old rate of pay but would not provide the written guarantee. This resulted in a deadlock that was not resolved until the Union agreed to allow the men to discharge the ship without the guarantee and at the old rates.

In 1943, in an incident similar to that of the **Cymric** fifteen years earlier, **Happy Harry** made headlines after jamming her bowsprit into the Victoria Bridge, Dublin and holding up traffic for half an hour before she was cut free. In October 1945 she ran aground in dense fog off Rosslare. The coastguard unit were soon on the scene but, due to the thickness of the fog, they were unable to see the vessel. The Rosslare Harbour lifeboat, **Mabel Marion Thompson**, and several other local craft came out to the aid of **Happy Harry** and, with the help of her crew, transferred some of her cargo of coal to their boats and managed to re-float her and get her into Rosslare Harbour.

On 29 September 1946, **Happy Harry** was on passage to Youghal with a cargo of salt when her engine caught fire. The crew worked to extinguish it but, as they worked, the vessel was drifting towards the rocky shore at Ardmore, Co. Waterford. The local lifeboat came along and after two attempts managed to get a rope on board and towed **Happy Harry** clear of the rocks. The crew successfully extinguished the fire, using the salt to smother the flames. Four years later, in September 1950 **Happy Harry** was not so lucky. Bound for Garston for coal, her engine failed off the South Stack Light. The

Happy Harry, wrecked at Southport Pier in September 1950. Note only two masts and her reduced rigging.

crew hoisted the sails and sailed her to her destination. However, sometime later she grounded on Taylor's Bank in the Mersey. Stuck fast, they sent up flares that came to the attention of the New Brighton lifeboat which came out and took the crew ashore. On the next high tide **Happy Harry** re floated, the crew boarded her and sailed her into Southport.

On arrival they dropped anchor but it dragged and **Happy Harry** crashed into the famous Southport Pier. The pier was slightly damaged but the unfortunate **Happy Harry** suffered major damage. Time after time, and despite all efforts to prevent it, she crashed into the pier. Her bowsprit was gone as was her mizzen mast and her deck housing. After this continuous battering the **Happy Harry** was eventually declared a total loss. The Liverpool firm of dismantlers Routledge and Sons were given the task of breaking her up on the nearby beach. With this in mind, three land anchors were attached to the ship and she was winched away from the pier. Once safely away from the pier anything of value was removed and the hull was set alight. A sad end to a gallant little schooner.

SCHOONER ASHORE.

For the second time in four days Rosslare Harbour lifeboat was called to the assistance of another victim of the fog. This time it was the three-masted auxiliary schooner, Happy Harry, of Dublin, carrying coal for Cork, which ran ashore on the coast, one mile south-west of Rosslare Lighthouse, during the dense fog last Sunday. Rosslare coast life-saving crew took the breeches buoy to the cliff top, but the schooner was invisible owing to fog, and a lifeboat then went out, and succeeded in locating the schooner among the rocks. The captain, James Hagan, and the crew of four remained in the ship, which was making water, but pumps kept it under control. Later two Rosslare motor boats, the Liberty and the Onward, went to her assistance, and removed some of her cargo, with the result that she was successfully refloated at high tide and escorted to Rosslare Harbour.

Report of the grounding of **Happy Harry** in fog near Rosslare Harbour, October 1945.
John Power Collection.

Harvest King, seen here at New Ross, a three masted wooden tops'l schooner. Built 1879 at Runcorn. 119 tons. 1901 owned by G. Kearon of Arklow,1924, 70hp motor fitted .1942, sold to Arklow Pottery Ltd. Laid up, 1952. 1954 used at Youghal when filming Moby Dick.1955, returned to Arklow and broken up.
Photo Robert Shortall, Andrew Kelly Collection.

Harvest King, arriving at Waterford.
The World Ship Society Collection.

Another view of the **Harvest King,** date and location unknown.

HELGOLAND

No. 124584. Built in 1895 in the Netherlands. A brigantine registered at 310 tons. Dimensions: 122.9x23.3x9.8ft. **Owner/master** Captain Arthur Fielding of Southport in Lancashire.

Early in World War1, **Helgoland** was commissioned by the Admiralty and converted for use as a 'Q' ship. She operated as such under the aliases of Q17, Brig 10, Hoogezand 11 and Horley. Her armaments were four 12 pounder guns and one Maxim gun. In the beginning she was based at Milford Haven but, later in the war, was transferred to the Mediterranean where she was responsible for the sinking of 7 submarines. After the war ended she went back to her trade as a merchant vessel.

On 11 January 1927, only two weeks after she had come into Captain Fielding's hands, and on her first trip under his command, the **Helgoland** was on a voyage from Wexford to Port Ellen on the Isle of Islay with a cargo of barley for a local distillery. They had bad weather all the way up the channel and, that night when they were in Cloughey Bay on the County Down coast, it began to blow even harder. The **Helgoland** was tossed about like a cork and gradually all of the rigging on her after mast was torn away and the sails on the main mast were torn to shreds. Both anchors were let go but refused to take hold and the ship began to drift towards the rocks at Tara Point. At that point they sent up a series of 12 distress rockets in the hope of attracting attention from the shore.

The signals were seen and answered by the Tara Point Signalling Station who also informed the Cloughey Coastguard, who in turn notified the local lifeboat. As all this was happening, the position of the men on the **Helgoland** was becoming more precarious. Massive waves were breaking over them and all hands had to take to what remained of the rigging in order to have something to cling on to and prevent the waves from washing them over the side. The lifeboat came within hailing distance but the wind and seas were so fierce that there was no hope getting in close enough to take the men off the stricken brigantine. They stood by the **Helgoland** all night but apart from firing lifelines to the ship there was nothing they could do. They fired off 10 lines but only 2 passed over the ship near enough to the men in the rigging but by this stage the men were soaked by the waves and frozen by the cold and were unable to reach out to grab the lines.

By now the **Helgoland** had settled on a sandbank a few yards from the dangerous rocks but, even so, the position of the crew was still precarious. The lifeboat had maintained its position as near to the wreck as possible and kept shouting out words of encouragement to the men still clinging on for dear life in the rigging. About 7 o'clock in the morning the weather abated and the lifeboat was able to manoeuvre around to the lee side, between the rocks and the sandbank, and take the men off. The men were taken to the coastguard station where they were fed and made as comfortable as possible before being brought to the Belfast Seaman's Home.

Later, in an interview, Captain Fielding said he hoped that his ship could be refloated. However, the **Helgoland** never was re floated and remains to this day near the rocks of Tara Point. Apart from Captain Fielding, the crew were all from Wexford town. They were: Bob Higginbotham and Jim Delaney, both Ordinary Seamen and both from Parnell Street, and Larry O' Reilly, Able Seaman, from Clifford Street. The Cox of the Cloughy RNLI lifeboat was awarded the Bronze Medal for Gallantry for saving the crew of the **Helgoland**.

The brigantine **Helgoland**, 310 tons. Built in the Netherlands. Under sail in a good quartering breeze.

Invermore and **JT&S** at New Ross,
April 10th, 1952.
Photo Robert Shortall, Andrew Kelly Collection.

Invermore, a wooden auxiliary fore and aft rigged schooner. Built in 1921 at Tyrell's Boatyard, Arklow. 146 tons. Dimensions, 92.0x22.04x11ft. The last trading schooner to be built in Ireland. In 1960 she was sold to Dartmouth, England. Following a failed venture to sail to Australia she was laid up in the River Dart and became derelict.

JAMES POSTLETHWAITE
No. 83976. Code KFRP. Built in 1881 at Barrow by Ashburner shipbuilders. A three masted tops'l schooner of 134 tons. Dimensions: 99.7x23x10ft.

James Postlethwaite was operated by Ashburner on the coastal trade until 1909 when their fleet was sold off. The sale was held at Connah's Quay and the **James Postlethwaite** was purchased by Arklow ship-owner, Captain Ned Hall, for the sum of 995 pounds. Hall operated her around the coast and to continental ports until the outbreak of World War 1 when the ship was unfortunate enough to be berthed in the port of Hamburg. She was seized immediately and her crew were interned. Her masts were removed and she spent the war years as an ammunition barge on the Elbe.

In 1919 the year after hostilities ceased she was towed to South Shields for a refit and was returned to Captain Hall. Her first trip after her refit was from South Shields to St. Valery, France. In 1926 her top masts were lowered and Captain Hall had an engine fitted. Three years later, in May 1929, she was at anchor in Carlingford Lough under the command of Captain Hagen when she was run down by the steamer **J.J. Monks** and sank. Fortunately, all hands were saved and the ship was later re-floated.

The next notable occurrence was in 1938 when she lost her mainsail in a gale and was run ashore near Holyhead. However, once again she was salvaged and put to sea. She remained in service throughout WW2. In 1945 she had a larger engine installed and had her masts reduced yet again. The **James Postlethwaite** made her last trip to Barrow,

Auxiliary schooner **James Postlethwaite.** Built, 1881 in Barrow at Ashburner's yard.

her original port of registry, in 1952 and due to the lack of trade for sailing ships was shortly afterwards laid up at Arklow.

However, the **James Postlethwaite**'s days were not yet over. In June 1954, she was towed to Youghal to be used as a quayside prop in John Huston's classic film 'Moby Dick' and re named **Devil Dan**. In late November that year filming was completed and the **James Postlethwaite** was still tied up at Youghal when a strong south-east gale blew into the harbour and caused the old timer to break her moorings. Her owners went down with the intention of having her towed back to her home port but found that she was so extensively damaged the operation was not practical. In the end she was sold to Patrick Connor of Ballinvarrig, Youghal, a local merchant, and was beached and broken up.

Bow of the **James Postlethwaite.**

The **James Postlethwaite**, now with a much reduced rig. Seen here, from the Pink Rock, motoring down the River Barrow, outbound from New Ross, July 16th 1952.
Photo Robert Shortall, Andrew Kelly Collection.

James Postlethwaite, at anchor.

Auxiliary schooner **J T & S**. Built at Arklow, 1919 by John Tyrell & Sons for Captain Michael Tyrell.120 tons. Dimensions. 95.0 x 22.0x10 ft. Sold in 1960, she sank of Start Point in Devon, following a fire on board. Seen here moored at New Ross, April 10th, 1952.
Photo, Robert Shortall, Andrew Kelly Collection.

JT &S and **Kathleen & May** at Waterford, May 19th 1952.
Photo Robert Shortall, Andrew Kelly Collection.

KATHLEEN & MAY

No. 104473. Code, QHGB. Built 1900 at Connah's Quay, Wales, by Ferguson & Baird for Captain John Coppack. A double tops'l schooner of 136 tons. Dimensions: 98.4 x 23.2 x 10.1 ft.

Originally named **Lizzie May** after Captain Coppack's two daughters, she was renamed **Kathleen & May** in 1908 when she came into the hands of Youghal, Co. Cork, shipowner, M.J. Fleming. Following tradition, she was renamed after Mr Fleming's two daughters. Prior to coming into Fleming's hands **Kathleen & May** had traded around the UK, with the occasional trip to Irish ports. It appears that she was in Rochester in September 1908, discharging a cargo of Welsh fire bricks when Fleming acquired her. Shortly afterwards she loaded 209 tons of cement at London for the Bristol Channel. Unfortunately, she went aground on the Goodwin Sands, but she was re floated and taken into Dover, where her cargo was discharged.

She was being towed to Appledore, for repairs, when she broke away from the tow near the Longships and from there she sailed to Cardiff Roads. At the end of November, under tow again, she reached Appledore. She was to remain in Appledore undergoing repairs until late January 1909. Then she went into what was to be her normal run, from Youghal to the Bristol Channel for coal. Throughout the period 1908 to 1931, **Kathleen & May** also carried other cargoes, such as, oats, manure, bricks, timber, etc., but her main cargo was definitely coal. During that time, she brought 31,730 tons of coal into Ireland. Her next biggest cargo was oats, with a total of 7,574 tons carried. April 1931 was her final trip to Youghal, with coal from Cardiff. Shortly afterwards she was bought by two men from Appledore, Captain Tommy Jewell and his brother William.

Kathleen & May, an auxiliary schooner of 136 tons. Built, 1900 at Connah's Quay. Seen heading up the River Suir, off Ballyhack, bound for Waterford, September 2001.

In June she sailed for the river Torridge in Devon where she had an auxiliary engine installed. She then resumed her trade of coal to Youghal. In February 1936, en route from Lydney in Gloucestershire to Youghal, she ran into a south-easterly gale and heavy seas that forced them to return and go to anchor at Angle, Milford Haven. The gales increased and held them at Angle for another two days. In fact, they seem to have been very lucky to have made it to Angle. Another of Mr Fleming's ships, the **Nellie Fleming,** left Lydney around the same time, also bound for Youghal, and was never heard of again. By the time the winds abated, and the **Kathleen & May** resumed her voyage, it had taken her 4 weeks to reach Youghal.

The next year, 1937, she went ashore near the lighthouse at Youghal but was re floated again when the schooner **Happy Harry** towed her off on the next tide. She came through the War unscathed. Then, in July 1947, she collided with the trawler **Tenby Castle** at Swansea. Her bow was badly damaged but nonetheless she made it to Appledore for repairs. During the 1950s she frequently traded to Irish ports, including in 1954, the port of Wexford. A year later she made the history books by being the first vessel to take a cargo of coal from Ireland to England.

Kathleen & May was still owned by the Jewell's when, in February 1961, she came into the hands of the Maritime Trust and underwent refurbishment. The **Kathleen & May** can be seen today cruising around our coasts, one of the last examples of a coastal schooner.

M.E. JOHNSON

No. 76895. Code EINB. Built in 1879 at Barrow, by Ashburner, shipbuilders. A schooner of 131 tons. Dimensions: 98.3x23x9.9ft.

She was named after her first master, Captain Johnson. Like the **James Postlethwaite**, the **M.E. Johnson** traded around the British coast, and also to

Three masted tops'l schooner **M.E. Johnson**. Built in Barrow, 1879, 131 tons. Depicted here as built, under full sail. *Artist unknown.*

Continental ports. When Ashburner decided to sell off its fleet, the **M.E. Johnson** was put up for sale in the same auction as her sister ship. A group of Arklow owners attended the auction, as did some other owners from the UK. Among the English prospective buyers was the Appledore shipbuilder, Philip Kelly Harris. Harris was apparently intent on procuring the **M.E. Johnson**, as were the Arklow men, and bidding was intense. Finally, the ship was sold to an Arklow consortium of Captains Frank Tyrell, Thomas Price, and members of the Kearon family, for the sum of 1,110 pounds, a higher price than her newer and bigger sisters. (There were eight ships in that auction and five of them went to the Arklow bidders).

Once in Arklow ownership the **M.E. Johnson** went about her business, trading to British and Irish ports, still under her original rigging

M.E. Johnson, post 1920, after her auxiliary engine was fitted.

and still totally dependent on the wind for her propulsion. Then, in 1920, she was fitted with an auxiliary engine but still retained most of her original sail plan. In 1934 her new master and part owner was Captain Jack Kinch of Arklow and around that time she had a wheelhouse built. Until then the wheel was open to the elements. Around 1937 a new engine was fitted and her rigging was considerably reduced.

In 1938 **M.E. Johnson** got into serious trouble when she was on a trip from Cornwall to Runcorn with a cargo of china clay. She ran into a fierce storm and was dismasted and had to be abandoned by her crew. However, they returned to her the following day, jury-rigged her and sailed her to port. In December that same year she was yet again bound for Runcorn, out of Plymouth, when she ran into trouble again. On this occasion they were off Fishguard when she lost her propeller in a severe snowstorm and began to drift. For three days they battled against the weather until they went aground on Carnsore Point.

The Rosslare lifeboat, **J.B. Proudfoot**, went out to her assistance and took off Mrs Kinch, the captain's new wife, but the captain and crew stayed on board until the lightship tender **Willie Wag**, and an Arklow fishing boat, came down and towed her home. Temporary repairs were carried out in Arklow and the **M. E. Johnson** then continued on her voyage. Proper repairs were then carried out in Stubbs yard. Nothing of a serious nature seemed to happen until March 1942 when she ran ashore at Skerries, Co. Dublin. The crew were taken off by breeches buoy, but they returned a few days later day and re-floated her. Then she was taken back to Arklow, slipped and repaired.

Captain Jack Kinch died in October 1951 and another Arklow man, Captain Jack

Rezin took over command. Her final voyage began in November 1953 when she arrived in Barrow-in-Furness from Dublin via Holyhead. Approaching Barrow she grounded on a sandbank at Piel Island and had to be pulled off it by tug. She remained in Barrow for five days and then set sail for the Clyde. She returned to Arklow early in December, arriving at her home port in a fierce northerly gale. As they were attempting to enter the harbour, heavy seas caught her and forced her to the wrong side of the pier where she grounded and was battered by the winds and sea. Luckily for the crew, the Arklow lifeboat, **Inbhear Mór**, was entering the harbour after rescuing the **Pride of Leinster**, a local fishing boat that had also got in trouble in the storm. The lifeboat towed the fishing boat to safety and immediately turned around and went to the aid of the **M. E. Johnson**. After two attempts to get alongside the stricken vessel, and suffering a severe battering, the lifeboat got everyone safely off the **M.E. Johnson**. Sadly, within a day the gallant little coaster had disintegrated under the force of the fierce winds and seas.

MARY B. MITCHELL.
No. 97575.Code MPHV. Built in 1892 at Carrickfergus by Paul Rodgers. A steel. Three masted top'sl schooner of 227tons. Dimensions, 129.7x24.4x10.8ft.

She was built for a Beaumaris, Wales shipowner named William Preston, who put her into the Welsh slate trade to Germany. In 1896, on 27 December, she went aground on a passage to Hamburg. It was a severe grounding and all of her crew were taken off. By 18 January 1897, half of her cargo had been discharged and she was re-floated, but still in a sinking condition. Under tow she made the outer harbour of Nieuwe Diep, Amsterdam where she sank. Two days later she was pumped out, floated and moved to

The auxiliary steel schooner **Mary B. Mitchell,** shown here as a "Q" ship during World War 1.

Mary B. Mitchell. Built at Carrickfergus in 1892 by Paul Rodgers. Seen here at Charleston in 1927 to load china clay.

Another photo of the **Mary B. Mitchell,** seen here at Padstow c1934. Occupying the opposite berth is the Wexford Steamship Company's Elsie Annie.

the inner harbour where she was found to be damaged along her keel and bottom plating.

Seven years later in January 1903 she was at anchor at Weymouth Roads on a voyage from London to Bristol with cement when she was run into by **HMS Hogue**. Her bowsprit carried away and she also suffered some damage to her stem. In September 1908, on another cement run, this time to Bangor, North Wales she ran into a gale and sustained some damage, losing a topsail and a gaff. Also, the master was injured and had to be landed at Deal with a broken leg. After about twenty years in that trade she underwent a complete transformation when, in 1912, she was purchased by Lord Penrhyn and converted into his personal yacht. However, this change didn't last too long and she was soon back operating as a merchant vessel in the china clay trade.

In 1916 she was lying at Falmouth when the Admiralty requisitioned her and she was converted yet again, this time into a 'Q' ship. Her regular civilian crew were paid off and replaced by Royal Navy personnel. During her conversion she was armed with one twelve pounder, two six pounders, two Lewis guns, plus Mills Bombs and small arms. She also was given no less than ten aliases, one of them being an abbreviation of her own name, **Mitchell**. Her first engagement as a 'Q' ship was south of the Lizard on 2 December 1916 when she took on a surfaced U boat. She fired 9 shells and had two strikes before the U boat dived.

Then another U boat attempted to torpedo the **Mary B** but she managed to evade it and got clear away. About a month later she was off Torbay when she ran into a westerly gale and was hove to. During that time, she was hove to for twenty four hours, and she was dismasted in the dark. Both the fore and main masts collapsed. She had never had an auxiliary engine fitted so was still dependant solely on her sails. This left her in a very perilous position. The crew succeeded in setting a reefed headsail and she was driven to the south all day. A steamer in the vicinity was signalled for assistance but due to the fierce weather conditions her attempts to get a line onto the schooner failed. Darkness fell again and the schooner sent up flares in the hope of being seen from the land. This time a Norwegian steamer, **Sardinia**, saw them and came along and stood by until daylight. Then the Norwegian got a line aboard and took them under tow. Soon afterwards a French naval vessel came along and took the **Mary B Mitchell** into Brest for repairs.

Two months later the **Mary B** came out of the French dockyard completely re-rigged and with a newly fitted auxiliary engine. Her next engagement with the enemy was the next June when she exchanged rounds with a German submarine. She claimed several hits on the sub but it dived and none

Wreck of the **Mary B. Mitchell** at Senwick Wood, Kircudbrightshire Bay, Scotland, December 1944. *Kircudbright Historical Society.*

of the hits could be verified. She was in action again in August when she appears to have got the worst of the engagement. She took on a submarine about 20 miles off Start Point and suffered damage to her rails, rigging and deck gear and two of her crew were wounded. However, three hits were confirmed on the submarine before it withdrew.

After the war ended the **Mary B Mitchell** came into Arklow hands when she was purchased for 6,500 pounds by a consortium consisting of eight people from that port with Captain Job Tyrrell as managing owner. She was towed to Arklow for a re-fit, which cost another 1,373 pounds. It also resulted in having her net tonnage reduced to 153 tons. There was no reason given for the reduction in tonnage but it should be noted that lesser tonnage led to a corresponding reduction in harbour dues. In October 1919 the **Mary B Mitchell** was ready to go into service again. Her first trip was under the command of Captain George Kearon and was to Newport, Monmouthshire with pit props. From there she loaded coal for Granville in Brittany. On the return trip she was off the Lizard in a gale that forced her to run for Falmouth for shelter. Later on the same trip she had to shelter off the French coast for over 24 hours after being caught in another gale.

In 1923 Captain Kearon left the **Mary B** to take command of another Arklow schooner, the **Julia**, and Captain Tyrell himself took over on the **Mary B**. By now her upper tops'l and t'gallant had been removed and a large single top'l was fitted on the foremast. Other renovations resulted in her net tonnage being reduced to 133 tons. Captain Tyrell retired in 1933 and his son Captain Jim succeeded him. Despite all this time in Arklow ownership, her registration was still in Beaumaris and it wasn't until 1933 that it was changed to Dublin. During her time in Arklow ownership, the **Mary B** traded mainly to the Mersey and to Bristol Channel ports or to Cornwall to load china clay. In 1934 she gave up her trading career for a while to take part in the film, 'McClusky the Sea Rover', starring the boxer, Jack Doyle. Then the following year she was used in another film, 'The Mystery of the **Mary Celeste**' (US title, 'Phantom Ship') starring Bela Lugosi. For filming purposes her wheel house was removed and some alterations were carried out to the configuration of her sails. Between filming, she also managed to carry out the odd run to Cornwall for china clay.

After the outbreak of war in 1939, the **Mary B Mitchell** was, like all other Irish schooners and coastal steamers, called upon to aid in the effort to keep Ireland stocked with vital supplies. In 1943, after a complete re-fit and under the command of Captain Arthur Dowds, former principal of the Irish Nautical College, the **Mary B Mitchell** sailed for Lisbon. The regular procedure was to load coal, often from the Bristol Channel ports or from Ardrossan in Scotland, and head directly to Lisbon or to Huelva in Spain and then to Lisbon where a cargo of supplies for Ireland was shipped. On the return trip all vessels had to call to Fishguard in Wales for examination to ensure that no prohibited goods were being carried. Once clearance was granted, they then set out for their final destination. The **Mary B** made five return trips on this run safely, unlike Tyrell's other schooner, the tragic **Cymric**. In May 1944 the Lisbon run came to an end when the Admiralty withdrew the navicerts that gave permission for Irish ships to sail this route. This was as a precaution to prevent any possible leaks of information regarding the planned D-Day landings.

By this time the coal supplies in Éire were running low, so the 14 surviving schooners were sent to Cumberland and the Bristol Channel to boost the lagging stocks. The **Mary B Mitchell** loaded a cargo of burnt ore at Dublin on Wednesday 13 December 1944 for Silloth in Cumbria and sailed that night. The next day she was off the Isle of Man in a fresh southerly breeze that soon increased into a gale. She had just one engine, the other was ashore for repair, and her sails blew out so she was making little progress and was drifting towards the Scottish coast. On Friday morning she was close to Kirkcudbright Bay and about 6 o'clock that evening in driving rain and wind she grounded on mud near Torrs Point.

The **Mary B.** sent out distress signals and at about 8.30 that evening the Kirkcudbright lifeboat **Marion Morrison** came out and took the crew off. The next morning it was discovered that the **Mary B.** had re-floated herself and had driven across the bay and had gone ashore on rocks at Senwick Wood. Her rudder and stern frame were smashed and a long gash extended from the stern. Due to her position it was thought not to be viable to salvage her, so the **Mary B. Mitchell** was left where she had grounded. She remained there for 12 months until, in 1945, a fierce south east gale smashed up what remained of her.

Uncle Ned a three masted wooden auxiliary schooner of 130 tons. Built at Ipswich in 1867. In later years she was owned by George Kearon of Arklow. She ceased trading in in the early 1900s..Seen here, c1931, heading up the River Suir, off Ballyhack, en route to Waterford.
Photo by J. Hartery of Waterford.

At New Ross, October,1952, the **Venturer**, a steel auxiliary schooner .Built in 1920 at Scheveningen ,The Netherlands .Owned by Cecil Gregory of Arklow.
Photo Robert Shortall, Andrew Kelly Collection.

Three schooners at New Ross, June 23rd 1951. They are the **Harvest King, Venturer** and **De Wadden** with a deck load of pit props and more on the dockside ready to be loaded. Note on the left the location of Graves' timber and coalyard.
Photo Robert Shortall, Andrew Kelly Collection.

This is the **William Ashburner,** a frequent visitor to New Ross. Built in 1876 at Barrow for Ashburners of Barrow. She was a three masted tops'l schooner of 205 tons. She was sold to Richard Kearon of Arklow in 1909 and traded mainly between Irish ports and the Bristol Channel. She had an auxiliary engine fitted in 1925. On the 1st of February 1950 when under the ownership of Captain N. Sinnott of Limerick she was en route from Swansea to Sharpness she grounded in a fog in the River Severn and was severely damaged. She was later re-floated, then beached and became a total loss. She is seen here under sail in the early 1930s.Note her heavily patched sails.

The bow of the **William Ashburner.**

William Ashburner at New Ross, April 1941.
Photo Robert Shortall, Andrew Kelly Collection.

WILLIAM ASHBURNER As Built 1876.

WILLIAM ASHBURNER c. 1930's.

WILLIAM ASHBURNER c. Late 1940's.

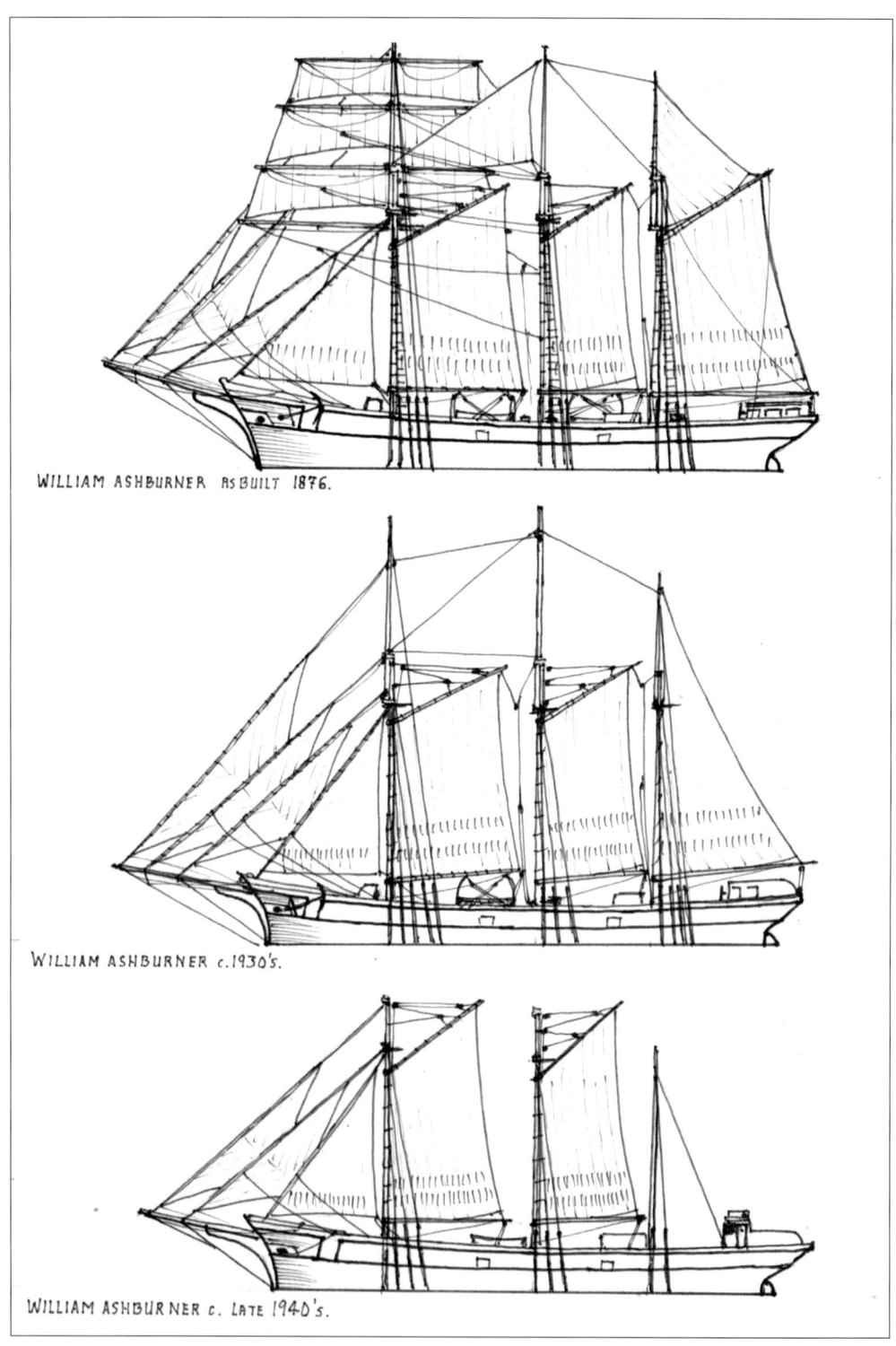

Some of the changes to the rigging of the **William Ashburner** during her long career. These changes would be typical of the alterations made to many three masted schooners when an engine/motor is installed.

WINDERMERE

No. 93420. Code LVWT. Built 1890 at Connah's Quay by Ferguson and Baird for Mr W. Reney of Chester. Dimensions: 104.2x24.3x11.3ft.

By 1914 **Windermere** had come into Arklow hands when she was bought by Tyrells and continued in the coasting trade, calling to ports in the Bristol Channel and up to the Clyde. It wasn't until 1929 that her registration was changed to Dublin and she had an 80 horse power engine installed. This had the effect of reducing her net tonnage from 147 to 127 tons and increasing her gross tonnage from 174 tons to 179 tons. At the same time her upper and lower topsail yards were removed.

She had a few mishaps in her career. **Windermere's** first was as an auxiliary schooner in 1931 when she collided with the Dublin trawler **Father O' Flynn**, necessitating extensive repairs including a new bowsprit. After the outbreak of World War 2, **Windermere**, along with every other vessel flying the Irish flag, was involved in bringing vital supplies into home ports. In 1945 she ran aground off Carnsore Point but the crew managed to re-float her by jettisoning 30 tons of her cargo of coal. It was said that that winter fires burned very brightly in the Carne area after that! In 1947 **Windermere** underwent further alterations including having a more powerful engine fitted, having her topmasts shortened and a wheelhouse installed. Previously her wheel had been open to the elements.

On 24 October 1949 **Windermere** left Whitehaven for Wicklow with a cargo of coal when she ran into a fierce south-westerly gale. As the weather worsened, she changed course and ran for shelter behind the Rockabill Islands off Skerries. Oil drums that had been stowed on deck broke loose and began hurtling around the deck, threatening to damage the bulwarks and making it hazardous for the sailors – who were already waist deep in water – trying to work the pumps and attend to the sails. Then the main boom smashed and the jib and main sail carried away.

Captain Tyrell sent up distress flares at about 5.30 that evening. They were seen from the land and shortly afterwards the Howth lifeboat was launched. By this time the winds

Windermere at Waterford, July 1943.
Photo Robert Shortall, Andrew Kelly Collection.

Windermere, a three masted wooden auxiliary schooner. Built in 1890 at Connah's Quay. Shown here in Waterford. July 1943.Showing her WWII neutral markings on her hull.

Windermere, being loaded via gangway, at New Ross, c1950.
Photo Robert Shortall, Andrew Kelly Collection.

Windermere, heading down the River Barrow, to sea from New Ross, July 19th, 1951.
Photo Robert Shortall, Andrew Kelly Collection.

were at their fiercest and the lifeboat had a gruelling battle through the mighty seas, but in the end had to turn back. Meanwhile the **Windermere** was in further trouble. She had made the Rockabill and gone to anchor but then the wind changed to the northerly direction and she began to drag her anchor. In fear of being driven ashore onto the rocks, Captain Tyrell decided to try to get around Howth Head. After a fierce battle they succeeded in rounding the head that evening, sails gone, doors missing and in a generally battered condition. However, she was taken into dock had all repairs carried out and she was soon back at sea.

In October 1953, the late Aiden Roche, from Park, Wexford, latterly of Talbot Green, Wexford, and then a young 'first tripper', joined the **Windermere** as a deck hand and about 4 months later in February 1954, she had another near disaster in the Mersey. As Aiden told it, the **Windermere** was bound for Garston in thick fog when she collided with an anchored dredger, the **Hilbre Island**. She struck the main and the mizzen rigging and, had it not been for the prompt action of the dredger's crew, **Windermere** would likely have capsized. They hauled her in close and lashed her to their own vessel thus preventing her likely capsizing. A local salvage ship came out and put pumps aboard and kept her afloat until she reached Birkenhead. Upon inspection severe damage to her planking was discovered that took two months to repair.

Two years later, on 5 April 1956, the **Windermere** was sailing light for Swansea when she stranded near the Tusker Rock, Porthcawl. After sending out distress signals she soon had two merchant ships, the **ss Dunkerton** and the **mv Cato,** standing by along with the Mumbles lifeboat. But the crew refused to be taken off and later that night she was re-floated and towed into Swansea, where she was inspected and considered fit for a passage back to Arklow. As a precaution she loaded just half a cargo of coal and sailed home. In Arklow a more detailed survey was carried out and it was decided that it would not be economically feasible to carry out the repairs required and so **Windermere** was laid up. Six months later she was sold to a French master mariner Captain Locassio and towed to Appledore, Devon by the Arklow coaster **George Emilie**, for a major refit. In June 1957 she set sail for the Mediterranean, under the command of Captain Locassio, flying the Costa Rican flag. Sadly, her career in the Mediterranean was not a long one, for on 13 January 1958 she was caught in a gale in the Gulf of Lyon, sprang a leak and sank. All hands were rescued by a passing ship the **mv Montana.**

Deck scene aboard the **Windermere** at Arklow, c1956.

The bow of the **Windermere,** moored at Arklow. *Courtesy, Arklow Maritime Museum.*

On a fine day c1895, the paddle tug **Wexford** towed no fewer than 17 sailing vessels, in one tow, out of the Port of Wexford.

Appendix 1:
Extracts from Ships' Logs

Summary of the Log of the Alert, from 12 June 1866 to 14 November 1866;
Captain: Paddy Cogley; Mate (who kept the log): Laurence Murphy.

They arrived at Cardiff on 16 June 1866 and went into a berth to discharge her ballast. This took two days and everything went smoothly, apart from three of the crew who 'went adrift', deserting the ship. The log notes, *Brady, Greene and Clancy off duty onshore without liberty*. This was not deemed unusual for a merchant ship, although it might have been considered so in this case as the vessel was only two or three days away from home. It is likely that the captain 'logged' (fined) them a day's pay. Brady was also mentioned in the log as being off duty on 2 and 3 July. Then the **Alert** loaded coal for the steamer coaling station at Malta.

On 6 July they were towed out of the docks and put to sea. From then until arrival at Malta, all that is shown in the daily log entries are remarks on the weather, the course taken, their position and whatever work the crew were undertaking, such as scraping, painting and working on sails.

On Tuesday 17 July the log notes *People imployed* [sic] *picking the bread, the small from the large*. The only log not concerning daily work and general weather conditions was entered on 2 August noting that they had passed the **Thomas English** with her foremast gone. At 6 pm on Saturday 11 August, the Malta pilot came alongside and ordered them into the quarantine harbour. This was a regular procedure. They remained there for two days and on 13 August they were moved to a regular berth.

On 16 August they began to unload the cargo and on the first day discharged 80 tons. Two hands went adrift here at Malta as well but for a more serious reason than the three who went adrift at Cardiff. The two men, Clancy and Duggan had got into a row with some foreign sailors, which resulted in Clancy being stabbed in the side and Duggan in the arm. Clancy was in hospital and Duggan incapacitated on board the ship. They were still unable to work on 18 August.

On 19 August Brady and Green came on board, drunk, after being ashore without permission. They went aft and *gave abusive language*. Duggan returned to work on 20 August. However, Brady was unable to 'turn to' as the result of a beating he had taken from some American sailors the previous night. Fighting ashore was not an uncommon occurrence. The resulting injuries often meant hospitalisation, with the injured sailor being left behind, to be replaced by another. Despite the fairly regular reports of violence in foreign ports, only one fatality was recorded and that was a report of the September 1856 murder in Galatz of a Wexford sailor, John Butler. There was no mention of the ship he was on and it is possible, though unlikely, that it was not one of the Wexford vessels.

On Wednesday 22 August, all 360 tons coal had been discharged and the ship was made ready for sea. Clancy appears to have still been in hospital, so his belongings were sent ashore and a man was shipped in his place. However, the new man didn't report that day. The next day the ship was ballasted. Brady returned to work and the **Alert** was ready for the next stage of her voyage to Sulina at the mouth of the Danube, in the Black Sea. The log also noted that *The strange man left his clothes aboard tonight*. The 'strange man' was never named but he was obviously the man signed on to replace Clancy. The next day, Friday 24 August, for some reason, they took on more ballast The pilot then came on board and took them out to sea.

Once they were out to sea and the course set, the normal daily work of maintaining the ship commenced. Watches would have already been set and, apart from bad weather when all hands were required to man the sails, they were rigidly adhered to. By Wednesday 29 August they were north of the island of Cerigo, off Crete, and the next day under the island of Milo. They hove to and men were employed cleaning the bulwarks, ready for painting.

On 2 September all hands were required to 'work' the ship through the Dora Passage towards Constantinople (Istanbul). On 5 September they were 25 miles North East by North of the Turkish island of Tenados. A steam tug came alongside at 9 am on Saturday 8 September and towed them around Point Niagra. It let them go that afternoon at 2 pm. Noon the next day found them off Gallipoli and in the Sea of Marmora. At 1 am the following day the **Alert** hove to and dropped anchor at the back of Seraglio Point, near Constantinople. Her sails were stowed and she waited for the steamer to come along to tow them into the Black Sea. Once they were in the Black Sea, their steamer let them go *in a fresh breeze and clear weather*. On Thursday 20 September at 8.30 pm the Sulina Light was seen bearing North West and at 8 am the next day, they tacked in for the pier and took a pilot on board. The pilot had them alongside at 11 am. With little delay they commenced unloading the ballast at 12 noon. By 4.30 pm the next day, Friday 20 September, all the ballast was off and the ship was ready to take on her cargo. By Monday the cargo was stowed and the crew were trimming it, making ready for sea.

The next day some hands were sent to obtain fresh water, as apparently the water near where they were docked was salty. They were ready to sail but the weather turned bad and a heavy sea was running on the bar. The pilot refused to take them out. On Saturday 29 September the weather improved and the steamboat towed them out into the Black Sea, where they made all sail and set the port topmost studding sail.

At midnight on Thursday 4 October they were in the Sea of Marmora and by noon the next day they were off Cape Hellas on the southernmost tip of the Gallipoli Peninsula. On Monday the 22 October they were in *a great fleet of ships* and 25 miles North by West of Cape St. Vincent. Still sailing in company, on 2 November they passed the Hartlepool brig **Fred H. Parker** dismasted and waterlogged. At 2 pm on Monday 12 November they were 12 miles NNE of the Metal Man off Tramore. At 6 pm they spoke the Coningbeg Lightship and at 2 am they passed the Tuskar light.

Extract from Log of the Dispatch of Wexford

The Log starts with the **Dispatch** in Cardiff Dock. Each daily entry ends with the words *Pumps carefully attended to*. Many entries told of uneventful days with details such as weather conditions and wind direction. There are both misspelling and archaic spelling in the log, e.g. Gloster instead of Gloucester. The remarkable difference in handwriting indicates that more than one man kept the log, but that is not surprising as the log here covers three years and crews could change every 6 months. It was normally the duty of the First Officer or Chief Mate to do this daily task.

It commences on October 24 1877, and records that it was good weather and that the steam tug took them in tow and brought them out to Penarth Roads where they went to anchor. There she lay until Friday 2 November. During that time each entry noted that a strict anchor watch was kept and, of course, pumps were carefully attended to. Throughout the log the vessel taking them in tow is referred to as the steam boat. This is obviously a steam tug.

November 1877

On Friday 2: a light breeze was recorded and the vessel *hove up anchor and made all sail, at 6 am. Passed the Bank Light Vessel. Tacked at 7 am, tacked ship frequently until midnight.*

Saturday 3: *Moderate breeze, Hartland Point bore west. Tacked at 2 pm, Lundy Island in sight. Wind increasing, tacked at 9.30. Wind veers N by W. Jib Pennant gave way, foresail gave way and split sail. Midnight, fresh breeze and squally.*

Sunday 4: *Light breeze, clear weather, Longships bore S. by E. 4 pm. Passed Wolf Rock at 8 pm. Passed Lizards at midnight. Made Eddystone at 6 am. Made French Land, moderate breeze clear weather.*

Monday 5: *Moderate clear weather, all sails set at 4 pm, made the Caskets, at 10 pm made Cape Barfluer at midnight. At 4 pm made Cape La Hague Pilot on board, steam boat took in tow to port. This ends Sea Log.*

In Honfleur

Tuesday 6: *Dock 7 am, tied up, fresh day. Ship ready to discharge.*
Wednesday 7: *Heavy weather.*
Thursday 8: *Fresh breeze, started work on cargo. Finished for day at 7.30.*
Friday 9: *Still on cargo, finish for day at 5.30.*
Saturday 10: *Crew employed on cargo, 5.30 finish for day.*

On Sunday there was traditionally no work in port, the weather was noted as were the pumps. Normal gangway watches would also have been kept. For the next 5 days all that was noted was the weather, which was showery, and of course, the pumps were attended to. On Saturday 17 it was noted that they had finished cargo. Sunday no work.

Monday 19: *Strong winds. Cleaning hold for cargo.* Tuesday, Wednesday, Thursday, Friday and Saturday all contained the same entry: showers and rain. Sunday no work. They started to load cargo on Monday 26 and loaded 620 bags, finishing at 5.30 pm. The next day they began work at 7 am and loaded 441 bags by 5.00. On Wednesday 487 bags came on board by 5.30, and on Thursday a further 370 were loaded. Friday, 621 bags. Saturday December 1: 264 bags. That was the full cargo loaded. Throughout all of this the pumps were attended to. Sunday no work. Thus far, there is no indication of just what the cargo was.

December 1877

Monday 3 December: *Fresh weather, 8 am, moved out ship, could not get a steam boat. Got ship all ready for sea.*

Tuesday 4: *Rain, 9 am Pilot on board, steam boat in tow to sea. This ends Harbour Log.*

To Gloucester

Wednesday 5: *Light breeze, Cape La Hague passed.*

Thursday 6: *Passed Cape Barfluer, 7 miles distance.*
Friday 7: *Strong winds violent squalls, high seas, at 1 pm made English Land.*
Saturday 8: *Strong winds, 6 pm Start Point N.E, 18 miles distance.*
Sunday 9: *Light breeze, clear weather. At 7.30 pm passed Wolf Rock. 8 pm the Longships bore ENE. At noon passed Ilfracombe, strong winds violent squalls.*
Monday 10: *Strong winds, 6 pm passed the Nash Light, WNW. 7.30 passed Grassholm Br Light vessel. Came to anchor at 10 pm.*
Tuesday 11: *Moderate light weather, 7.30 am, steam boat and Pilot came at 8am. Hove and towed ship to dock, at noon came to dock. Hove ship up ready for towing ship. Got all ready for canal.*

In Gloucester

Wednesday 12: *Fresh weather, could not get steam boat to tow ship up.*
Thursday 13: *Moderate wind, at 8 am ship in tow, for Gloucester at 1 pm got foul of the barque,* **Day Star**, *carried away lanyards up mizzen. Righting and starting steamer. At 4 pm got ship in discharge berth.*

They began discharging her cargo on Friday, unloading 1625 bags. The carpenter was also on board, working at the damaged quarter. Saturday they unloaded a further 1241 bags and the carpenter was still working at the quarter. As usual there was no work on Sunday. Monday and Tuesday, just a moderate breeze recorded.

On Wednesday 19: *Got ship ready for sea.*

Thursday 20: *Moderate, calm, fog. At 9 am steam boat took in tow down channel. Pilot, two track men employed. At 2 pm ship locked through into Sharpness, moored ship ready for morning.*

The next morning, Friday 21, the steam tug came along and took them in tow to Cardiff. At 2 am they came to anchor in Cardiff Roads. At 7.30 hove ship.

At Cardiff

On Saturday 22, two men were paid off but their names were not given. From Sunday 23 to Sunday 30 only *moderate breezes* are recorded. No mention was made of the Christmas holiday or New Year's Eve. It was noted that three men came on board: only two were named but by their first names only, James and Martin. Were these men who had deserted and gone on a spree over the Christmas period? Or were two of them the men who were paid off and came back and signed on again?

Monday 31: *6 am started loading cargo. One man came on board.*

January 1878

Tuesday 1: *Started cargo at 9 am. 6 pm finished for the day. James – came on board.*
Wednesday 2: *Hauled ship down dock. Martin – came on board. Got ship ready for sea.*
Thursday 3: *Moderate weather, at 7 am commenced work getting ship down to the gates. Getting ship ready for sea. Light breeze, heavy rain.*
Friday 4: *Ship in basin, ready for morning tide.*
Saturday 5: *Moderate calm weather, at 8 am, steam boat took ship in tow, out of dock. Came to anchor in Penarth Roads at 9 am, righted out jibboom. Got ready for sea.*
Sunday 6: *This day heavy weather from the NW; 8.30 am made the schooner* **Spray** *and sent boat with four hands to get foresail. Light breeze.*
Monday 7: *This day violent squalls and showers of rain. Bent foresail.*

Cardiff towards Honfleur

The next day the weather was clear and they made sail at 8 am, passing Barry Island at 11. On Wednesday 9 they passed Lundy Island, then the Longships and on Thursday 10 they tacked to Gucrnscy Island. On Friday at 8 am Alderney Island bore SW and later that day Cape Lahague (Cap de la Hague) bore SSW. On Sunday 13 they were 12 miles S.W. of Cape Lahague. On Monday 14 the pilot came on board and at 5 pm they docked *laying on ground*. That ended the Sea Log. The next day, Tuesday 15, the log read: *This day commenced with a fresh breeze, heavy weather. Work rig in jibboom. Heaved ship in berth. Moored ship, got ready to discharge cargo.*

Honfleur

The next day, Wednesday 16, they started discharging cargo. They commenced at noon and finished for the day at 5pm, and unloaded 315 baskets. Thursday they discharged 700 baskets; Friday, 125 baskets; Saturday, 540 baskets. Sunday no work. Monday, discharged 520 baskets and 1 waggon; Tuesday, 620 baskets; Wednesday, 615 baskets; Thursday, 610 baskets; and Friday 435. Discharging was complete and there is still no indication as to what the baskets contained. Saturday no work, Sunday, no work.

There was no work noted for the next three days, until Thursday 31 January when the ship was got ready for sea. From the commencement of discharging up to the days when there was no work the pumps were looked at and logged. On Thursday 31, as part of getting ready for sea, the ship was painted outside and they bent on a new main topmast sail.

February 1878

Friday 1 February the ship was *painted outside, unbent fore topmast, staysail and flying jibboom, repairs*. From that day until Monday 11 February, the only entries concerned the weather. Then they started to load cargo.

Monday 11: *3 pm commenced loading cargo .5 30 pm finished for the day received 142 bags.*
Tuesday 12: *Commenced work 7.30 am, finished 5.30 pm, received 226 bags.*
Wednesday, 13: *Commenced work 7 am finished 6 pm, received 806 bags.*
There was no work on Thursday, no reason given, but log notes the weather conditions and the pumps. On Friday 15, work started again, loaded 510 bags; Saturday, 239 bags. No work on Sunday. Monday, 715 bags; Tuesday, finished loading when the last 246 bags were taken on board. There was still no indication of what the bags contained.

Towards Gloucester.

Wednesday 20: *Got ship ready for sea, steam boat took ship in tow to sea. This ends harbour log.*

Thursday they passed Cape Lahague (Cap de la Hague) and on Saturday they made 'English Land'. All went well, the weather was fair. Then on Thursday, February 28 at 2.15 am, they came to anchor at King Road. All sail was stowed and the pilot came on board. At 7am the ship was got ready for harbour and at 2 pm the steam boat took them in tow for Sharpness. That was the end of the sea log.

March 1878

On Friday, the steam boat took them through the canal and brought them to moor 6 miles from Sharpness, in a strong gale and heavy rain. At 7 am the following day, Saturday 12 March, they started the tow to Gloucester and at 11 am they made the berth. By 1 o'clock they began unloading, delivering 400 bags. As usual in port, there was no work on Sunday but on Monday they discharged 2,250 bags and on Tuesday they completed discharging, unloading 863 bags.

On Wednesday 6 March it blew a gale and one man was paid off. There was no mention of who he was. The following day another man was paid off, his name wasn't mentioned either. On Friday they began loading salt, for Limerick. From Friday 8 to Friday 15, they loaded 298 tons of salt with the help of 2 labourers who were employed on the Monday to help the crew. On Thursday it was noted that James came on board, once again no mention of a surname. Then the log recommences.

Saturday 16: *Ship hauled down behind brig, ready for steam boat. Brought down canal, locked down in basin, moored for the night. One man came on board.*

Sunday 17: *Moderate breeze, steam boat took ship in tow at Sharpness Point. Pilot came on board, towed ship to Cardiff Roads. Came to anchor. Righted our jibboom, got ship all ready for sea.*

Monday 18: *Came to anchor Sharpness Light Vessel. This ends harbour log.*

Gloucester towards Limerick.
Tuesday 19: *4 pm hove anchor, made sail, wind increasing from North, Midnight Helvick Light Vessel bore, distance 6 miles. Noon made St Govan's.*
Wednesday 20: *Moderate breeze 4 pm made St Ann's Light. Smalls bore North distance 6 miles. Calm weather.*
Thursday 21: *Light and calm.*
Friday 22: *Noon passed the Old Head of Kinsale, moderate breeze, clear weather.*
Saturday 23: *Passed the Fastnet Rock. Mid Night, the Bull Light, 5 am the Fore Rock Light. Violent squalls with showers. Making sail.*
Sunday 24: *Fresh breeze, clear weather with violent squalls. Lower top sail gave way at 8 am. Frequent tacking in sail, tacked ship.*
Monday 25: *Violent squalls, 4 pm bent lower top sail, tacked to West, 8 pm took in foresail gib, reefed mainsail.*
Tuesday 26: *Moderate breeze, light squall, tacking. Fore Rock bore East.*
Wednesday 27: *Passed Loop Head, 1.30 pilot came on board. At 6 am passed Scattery Light.* This ends the sea log.
Thursday 28: *Moderate light breeze, at 8 am hove up anchor, made sail. Wind from NE. At 5pm came to anchor at Grass Island, stowed all sails. Pilot went on shore.*
Friday 29: *Weather clear.*
Saturday 30: *Light breeze, at 1 pm hove up anchor, made sail. At 3 pm made fast in berth at Limerick Quay.* No work on Sunday.

April 1878

On Monday 1 April they commenced unloading cargo and by Friday 5 they had finished 'Lump Salt' and had begun unloading 'Coarse'. On Saturday, 26 tons was delivered; Monday 39 tons; Tuesday another 39 tons; That completed the unloading. On Wednesday 10 they were hauled down to a loading berth, made the ship fast and the crew went ashore. No reason given as to why they went ashore. The next day they began loading 'pitwood' for Liverpool. With the exception of Sunday, they loaded the pit wood for 12 hours a day until Thursday 18 when loading was completed. On Saturday the log noted *Harey and Eberham came on board*. Yet again, no complete names were given. Monday 22: *9.30 unmoored the ship. Pilot came on board, made sail, at 2 pm pilot went on shore. Moderate breeze. This ends Harbour Log. Two men came on board*. No mention of names or of what their function was.

LIMERICK TO LIVERPOOL

Tuesday 23: *All sail set. At 3 pm passed Scattery Island, at 4 pm passed Loop Head. At 8 pm the Fore Rock bore WSW distance 15 miles. At 10.30 passed Fore Rock. Took in all light sails, at 4 pm passed Skelligs, at 7.30 pm passed Bull, Cow and Calf. Moderate breeze and squalls.*
Wednesday 24: *Squalls, Lost Light bore NE. At 10 pm, distance 10 miles. Took in topgallant sail and flying gib. Squalls with rain.*
Thursday 25: *Moderate weather.*
Friday 26: *Fresh breeze, clear weather, at 8 pm Roche's Point bore NE.*
Saturday 27: *pm, light breeze. All sails set. 8 pm Mine Head bore NE.*
Sunday 28: *At 10 pm made Tower of Hook, at 11pm made Saltees light, at 5 pm passed Light Ship. At 9 am passed Tuskar. Moderate breeze, clear weather.*
Monday 29: *8 pm Bardsey Island, 2.30 passed Cardigan light ship (?), at 4 pm passed Holyhead. At 7 pm tacked ship to the South.*
Tuesday 30: *Passed Point Linas, heavy weather, frequently tacking. 7 am passed Nore light vessel. At 11 am came to anchor at the Bar light vessel, thick fog. Pilot came on board.*

May 1878

LIVERPOOL

Wednesday 1 May: *Thick fog with rain, at 4 pm hove up anchor, steam boat tooch* [took] *ship in tow, at 5pm came to back of the Canada Dock, at 8 pm heaved ship to dock at 10.30 pm made fast for night. This ends sea log. Day commenced with moderate calm weather, at noon hove ship into Carrier Dock made fast, got ship ready for discharge.*
Thursday 2: *Calm weather, moderate rain. Commenced discharging cargo 7 am, finished 5 pm.*
This continued until Wednesday 8 May when, at 11 am, they finished unloading cargo. Here the log ceased.

There were no further entries until Tuesday 6 August 1878. There is no explanation given as to what happened to the **Dispatch** in the intervening period. Was she in Dry Dock, or was she tied up for that time? Even then, a log would, or should, have been kept, but for some reason that did not happen. There are two entries for 6 and 7 of August. They don't say where the ship is bound, the only heading is *from Cardiff*.

August 1878

Tuesday 6 August: *Finished the thing in the morning, hove the ship into the basin at 11 am took steam boat and towed the ship to sea. Havre tug boat let go of us and made all possible sail and proceeded down channel with a light breeze from the south, pm got the head gear set up 8 am pumped ship and set the wach* [watch].
Wednesday 7: *Noon tacked ship abreast of Ilfracombe. Noon, Lundy Island, distance 5*

miles. Men employed putting up the head gear and other gibs,3 pm pumped her out and set the watch.
Thursday 8: *11.30 pm Milford lights bore, distance 15 miles.1 am Lundy SE 8 miles. Men employed setting up rigging.*
Friday 9: *Fore Head bore 12 miles,1 am Godsey distance 15 miles. St Agnes bore WS distance 11 miles. Men employed mending rigging.*
Saturday 10: *St Agnes light house, distance 8 miles. 8 am tacked ship, heavy gale causing ship to pitch and filling decks with water. Ship labouring heavy.*
Sunday 11: *PM, weather and seas moderating, 4 pm set the upper topsail, 8 pm weather fine again made all necessary sail.*
Monday 12: *More gales, reefed topsail and double reefed the mizzen, shipping large quantities of water, 4 pm ditto.*
Tuesday 13: *Unbent cables and put them below.*
Wednesday 14: *Gales.*
Thursday 15: *Weather fine, men employed taking in the slack of the sea fore rigging and back stays.*
Friday 16: *Gales heavy weather.*
Saturday 17: *Weather moderate, men employed aloft repairing chafes and necessary jobs.*
Sunday 18: *Moderate breeze and fine.*
Monday 19: *Moderate weather, men employed making F? And pump coats*
Tuesday 20: *Moderate and clear, strong weather, westerly, swell causing ship to roll heavy.*

Cardiff to Galatz
Wednesday 21: *fresh light breeze, fine weather. Men employed scraping mast, strong breeze throughout.*

From then until Sunday, the men were painting the mast and other parts of the ship. On Sunday they passed Spartel light off Morocco, still in fine weather. At 10 pm they passed the Europa light off Gibraltar. Monday, Tuesday, Wednesday and Thursday, the men were still working at painting and then setting up rigging and squaring rattling.

September 1878
And so it went on, until Monday September 2 when they 'showed their colours' to the brig **Industry**. Between 3 and 5 September, the weather was still fine and all hands were still painting and doing whatever jobs were required about the ship. On Friday 6, William Byrnes, AB, was sick and off duty. On 8 September the Island of Galita bore NE. The men were still painting. Then on 11 September, Byrnes was back on duty. All this time they had remarkably fine weather thus giving the master the opportunity to get all painting and rigging work done. The log commences again at this point.

Monday 16: *Noon weather moderate, Cape Matapan bore north, men employed.*
Tuesday 17: *Light breeze, Cape Spathi (Spada) bore south of ship about 6 miles. Mid Night cold, abreast of Island of Keravi* (?)
Wednesday 18: *Belapola Island bore SWxS. Distance 8 miles* (?) *out the log, Anti Mile Island* [Antimilos?]
Thursday 19: *Fresh gales and squalls from North and Eastward throughout, short head*

sea working ship to the best advantage of the winds through the Grecian Archipeligo. All light sail filled. Serpho [Serifos] *Island bore NexN, distance 8 miles.*

Friday 20: *PM, fresh gales, 4 pm, tacked ship to the Island of H Georgia (?) in strong gale, heavy squall, dangerous to carry much sail.*

Saturday 21: *Winds moderate, noon got up under land to the westward of Dora Passage. Several ships in company.*

Sunday 22: *PM, dodging under the land, waiting for fair wind to get through the passage. 8 pm Cape Fossa (?) light bore ENE, distance about 15 miles. Made sail and steered for Dora Passage.*

Monday 23: *Cape Fossa Light House bore S, distance 6 miles. 9 pm Ligri (?). Light House bore SExE about 4 miles.*

Tuesday 24: *Weather calm, Gaduro Light House bore WSW, passed between it and the Ocean Rocks.*

Wednesday 25: *2 pm passed Basheka Bay, 6 pm abreast of Cape Elles and passed the Fort, 2 pm wind cleared to the North Eastward, came to anchor with a warp and ridge. 7 am winds easterly, took a Tug Boat, noon passed the Castles.*

Thursday 26: *PM calm, came to anchor at Bashri Bay. Discharged the Tug Boat. 3 pm breeze sprung up from the South, got under way to run up to Galata and came to anchor off shore about three quarters of a mile.*

Friday 27: *Laying at anchor all day. Wind light from the NE. Men employed setting up rigging for most of the day.*

Saturday 28: *PM, got under way, 4 pm passed Gallipoli, 8 pm saw Pheros Light, noon abreast of Pheros Light.*

Sunday 29: *AM, Pheros Light bore W½N distance about 6 miles. moderate wind, hold to NW, fresh breeze, all light sails. 4 am, the Koullen Island Light bore SxE½E, distance about 12 miles, just, out the log. Remains fresh.*

Monday 30: *PM fresh and cloudy, 4 pm came to anchor off the town of Constantinople in 15 fathoms of water, furled all sails and 6 pm set the anchor watch. Midnight light and cloudy with rain, noon varying wind light and from the North and Westward. Men employed variously. M. Byrnes AB went on shore this day, sick.*

October 1878

Tuesday 1 October (written on side of log for that day): *This day sent on shore M. Byrne's clothes and shipped another man in his place. Still laying at anchor, 4 am hove up and proceeded on tow through the Bosphorus. Noon entered the Black Sea. Made all sail and discharged the tug, with fine light breeze from E.*

Wednesday 2: *made European Tower Light breeze, SW distance, 2 miles. Mid Night light airs and cloudy. 4 pm, ditto weather. Noon fine, men employed painting ship outside.*

Thursday and Friday were much the same. Then on Saturday they took on a pilot and at 4 am saw the Sulina Harbour Light and at 10 am came to anchor in the harbour. The rest of the day was spent hauling her into her berth and folding sails and clearing up the decks. The next day being Sunday, very little work was done, except the decks were washed and the pumps checked and watches set. Monday and Tuesday they were still laying at anchor at the South side of Sulina Harbour, in fine weather. The men were taking down the topsail yards and side stitching sails. Then on Wednesday at 5 pm the pilot came on board. They hove up the anchor and proceeded in tow up the river Danube. The trip up the river was uneventful and on Friday they dropped anchor off Galatz. This ended the sea log. Pumps were checked as always and the watches were set.

GALATZ

Saturday 12 October: *Laying at anchor, men employed getting ready for discharge, first part of the day. Latter part, cleared decks and washed her down.* Sunday 13: *Light and fine throughout. First thing in the morning hauled ship to her berth and moored her. Remainder of the day, all necessary work done.*
Monday 14: *First thing in the morning rigged up a stage. Remainder men working about the decks, unbending sails.*
Tuesday 15: *Moderate breeze, discharging cargo all day.*
On Wednesday, Thursday and Friday they continued discharging cargo. On Saturday the weather changed for the worse but they continued discharging and finished at 5 pm. Then the stage was shipped. Sunday no work as was usual.
Monday 21: *Discharged all day but was hindered for the want of carts to take the coal away.*
Tuesday 22: *Discharged all day, one man employed to fill coals in the hold.*
Wednesday 23: *Discharging all day, one man employed to fill coals in the hold.*
Thursday 24: *First thing unmoored and dropped down to the loading berth, noon moored, pm men employed in the hold about the dunnage* (usually material or loose timber to keep cargo in place).
Friday 25: *Fine weather, laying dunnage.*
Saturday 26: *Part of the day breaking out tar. Remainder laying mats.*
Sunday 27: *Fine weather, no work done.*
Monday 28: *Taking in Corn all day. Men in the hold putting up mats and trimming.*
Tuesday 29: *Fine weather, 11 am finished loading. Afterward clean up decks, tried the pumps. Midnight unmoored and proceeded down the river in tow.*
Wednesday 30: *Fresh breeze and cloudy, 5 am passed Sulch, came to anchor in Selina, weather as above. Pumped hip, set the wach* [watch].
Thursday 31: *Light breeze, men employed bending the sails and getting ship ready for sea.*

November 1878

Sulina
Friday 1 November: *Down the river to sea.*
Saturday 2: *Sulina Harbour Light bore Nx W, put out the log. Midnight, St. Georgia Light bore NxN½W, distance 9 miles. Set the log and took a departure.*
Sunday 3: *Fine breeze. Peter Corish AB off duty, sick.*

Galatz towards Wexford
Monday 4 November: *Peter Corish, off duty again.*
Tuesday 5: *10 am, entered the Bosphorus, 5 pm came to anchor above Constantinople in The Man O' War ground. Furled the sails, at 8 pm pumped her out and set the watch. Antony AB off duty, sick* (Antony was most likely the man brought on in Byrne's place). *This log contains 36 hours and ends at Midnight.*
Wednesday 6: *Laying at anchor all day, men employed repairing sails. Wind fresh*

throughout day. Antony AB sick and off duty.
Thursday 7: *Strong gales and cloudy. Men employed mending sails.*
Friday 8: *Heavy rain, men employed various jobs.*
Saturday 9: *Fresh breeze at times. Wind increased to all parts of the compass. Ends wind calm and rain. Antony AB, sick and off duty.*
Sunday 10: *Proceed to sea. Antony still off sick.*
Tuesday 12: *Abreast of Gallipoli, noon. Antony back on duty.*
Wednesday 13: *Came to anchor below Gallipoli. 5 am got under way.*
Thursday 14: *Came to anchor off Niagara Point, 6 am.*

There they lay until Monday 18 November when at 7 am, they weighed anchor and proceeded on their voyage. Next day they were off Cape Gallipoli. On the 20 November the Lyeri Light bore SxN, at a distance of about 12 miles. On Friday 22 they were off Georgia Island Light ship and on Sunday 24, at noon, they made Cape St Angels. The weather gods were certainly smiling on them thus far, but on Sunday 1 December that was all to change.

December 1878

Sunday 1 December: *10 pm squalls. 3 am fresh gales.*
Monday 2: *PM brisk gale with rain and squalls, stowed up upper top sail and jib. 1 pm hands on the fore sail. Gales on the increase with a heavy sea causing the ship to labour and strain, taking large quantities of water on deck. 8 am made all necessary sail to keep her stead. Noon strong breeze, sea going down.*
Tuesday 3: *Fresh gales throughout and heavy seas with rain and squalls, lightening. Ship rolling heavy and shipping large quantities of water. MN saw Cape Passina Light bearing SW, noon tacked ship in under the land.*
Wednesday 4: *Dodging in under the land under easy sail. Fresh gales and cloudy with rain and lightning. Midnight, calm, 4 am, ditto weather. Noon, Passara Lighthouse bore WSW, distance about 5 miles.*
Thursday 5: *PM moderate and fine, made all necessary sail and stood to the South and Westward till midnight, then tacked and shaped a course for the Maltese Channel. 8 am, calm strong current, tacking to the South and Eastward of Malta Island.*
Friday 6: *Strong gale from Westward. 3 pm Valetta Light bore SW1/2W distance about 12 miles. Midnight, heavy seas and squalls, ship labouring heavy, shifted the cargo 4 am Gozo Lighthouse WSW, distance about 8 miles. 8 am, wind and sea increasing, kept away for Malta. Noon, came to anchor, remainder of the day moored ship. This log contains 26 hours, ends midnight.*

For the next few days they lay off Malta, the hands were employed doing various jobs about the ship, not least trimming the cargo that had shifted in the gale. Throughout this time, they were also experiencing bad weather, with winds sometimes blowing at gale force. On Tuesday 10, at 5 in the morning, they began to get ready for sea. At 8 am they made all sail and headed out in fine weather. The fine weather didn't last too long, though.

Thursday 12 December: *Strong breeze with a nasty head sea, meeting the Southerly sea, causing the ship and labour throwing quantities of grain from the pumps. Middle part*

raining. 8 am moderate, made all necessary sail. Noon, ditto weather, sea gone down, the Isle of Pantalluri [Pantalleria off Sicily?] bore NE distance about 14 miles.
Friday 13: *PM light breeze and cloudy. 11 pm, calm. Midnight, light breeze Pantalurri now NEx E. 4 am, strong and increasing breeze, sea getting up very fast. 5 am, carried away the main top mast backstay. Ship at the time making a very heavy sudden roll. 7 am, Cape Bon bore distance 4 miles. For gales and heavy squalls, hauled to West and double reefed topsail and jibboom.*
Saturday 14: *Fresh the middle part, strong gales with heavy rain squalls and a dangerous heavy cross sea. Ending this day with a moderate breeze from the NE. I found this day a large increase of water at the pumps and grain coming up.*

The next day, Sunday 15 December, was recorded as *looking very threatening* and Galita Island bearing WxS at a distance of 20 miles. From 8 am until noon there was a fresh and varying breeze and a cloudy sky. On Monday the day was fresh with an increasing gale. At 6 pm Galita bore WSW, at a distance of 8 miles. The gale was increasing in force. It was blowing from the NW with a dangerous sea. They hove to and lowered the topsail and double reefed the mainsail.

By now the ship was labouring heavily with water filling the decks. Once again it was logged that large amounts of grain were coming up through the pumps. At 4 pm the weather hadn't changed and at 9 am a heavy sea struck her *in the mast*. At the same time a heavy body of water fell onto the ship, making her stagger as if she had struck a rock. The mate checked the pumps regularly and noticed that there was more grain coming up. Tuesday 17 was moderate and they made all necessary sail to keep her steady. The wind was backing to the SW and falling. The pumps were still pumping up grain and the crew had to clear them occasionally. Then the weather changed again.

Wednesday 18 December: *PM, strong breeze and hard squalls and rain. Tacked ship to the SW. Sparlivento Light bore WxN. 8 pm fresh gale with a terrible head sea, was forced to head reach under very short canvas. Up to 4 am ship pitching and rowling about, shipping heavy water all over her, it being a very heavy sea, giving her no chance to use to it. Noon, moderate. The foresail, let a reef out of the mainsail.*

Thursday the weather was moderate and on Friday the weather was both moderate and dull and they spoke the barque **Rosslare**. No indication was given as to her direction, but it is likely she was outward bound. The weather continued to be moderate for the next few weeks and the hands were employed at various jobs around the ship, such as cleaning the decks, scraping the mast and repairing sails. They also opened the hatches to help air the cargo. Cape Andorra was passed on Christmas Day. As was usual, no reference was made to the day and, on St. Stephen's Day, all hands were busy repairing sails. The normal working day on a sailing ship carried on.

January 1879

On New Year's Day they were 12 miles off the Spanish Coast, near Cartagena, and the weather was still moderate and remained so until 8 January.

Wednesday 8 January: *Fresh gales, ship pitching and straddling. Large quota of corn coming up pumps.*

Thursday 9: *PM strong gales and a high sea. Ship labouring heavy and shipping large quantities of water. 4 pm, hordes the foresail and the topsail, head reached under the above, Reefed mainsail, fore and main top sail. Winds and sea terrible. 4 am, ditto weather and increase of grain coming up so much was obliged to draw the box every spell. Noon, wind same sea dangerous.*

Friday 10: *Heavy gales and dangerous sea. 4 pm, bent the storm mainsail, wore ship and hove her to under it. 10 pm, weather various and fluffy. Midnight, ship labouring terrible and falling off in the truff* [trough] *of the sea. Whore* [wore] *her round on the other tack to keep her head onto the sea. When in the act of whoring a heavy sea struck her under the counter and a large body of water falling on the deck. 4 am, weather the same. 8 am, a little more moderate sea. Set the fore and main topsail. Noticed more grain coming up through the pumps this day and also on discharge of water. Winds increased again hauled down the stay sails.*

Saturday 11: *PM gales moderate, 8 pm set the topsail, foresail and double reefed the mizzen. Whore the ship, Cape de Galt bore eastward about 8 miles. Stood to the Southward till midnight. Whore ship again, wind and sea moderating fast, 4 am, Cape de Galt bore ExN. Distance about 8 miles. Remain of day working short tacks to get up under the highlands of Albermaria but towards noon winds increased too much, drifted more to the Eastward on each tack.*

Sunday 12: *Fresh gales and cloudy. 4 pm stowed the topsail. 8 pm, gales increased, handed the topsail and hove her to under the L mainsail. Very heavy sea, ship labouring heavy. Cape de Galt now bore ENE, 10 miles. Midnight, gale broke, wore ship. 8 am, calm, ship falling off in the trough of the sea and rolling rails under. Noon, ditto weather.*

Monday 13: *Calm. Men employed drying sails and repairing running gear.*

For the next eleven days, the weather was calm and the men were employed repairing sails and doing other jobs about the decks. On Wednesday 22 the Rock of Gibraltar was sighted WxS, at a distance of 15 miles. At 8 am there was a moderate breeze from the North West. Noon they hauled to the SE and Europa Point bore to the North. On Friday 24 January, the winds had changed to from the South East and 4 pm found them working the ship to the best advantage of the winds.

Friday 24 January: *Sky dull, got in collision with a barque, name unknown. Carried away bowsprit and jibboom. When two ships cleared, one hand went down the pumps but there was no more water than usual. Bore up for Gibraltar, during the time she was running. All hands to work getting the anchors and chains ready. 3 am, came to anchor at Gibraltar with the port anchor in 31 fathoms of water, furled the sails, tried the pumps and set the watch. Remainder of the day, raining. 8 am clearing away the wrecks and other necessary jobs. Pm, securing the foremast, rain very heavy. This log contains 36 hours ends at Midnight.*

Saturday 25: *Stiff squall with heavy rain, hove short and waited for steam boat up to 10 am but did not come. Remainder of the day clearing decks and washing her down. Day ends as above.*

Sunday 26: *First thing in the morning hove up the anchor and towed further in shore and came to again.*

Monday 27: *Loosed sails to dry, first thing after rigged a derrick to lift out the bowsprit. Pm, showers with fresh squalls.*

Tuesday 28: *Lifted out bowsprit, sent it ashore. Remainder of day two hands scrubbing ship outside, rest repairing the headgear.*
Wednesday 29: *Gales and rain.*
Thursday 30: *Bowsprit came alongside and got it shipped. Remainder setting it up, carpenter bolting it.*
Friday 31: *Moderate winds, the carpenter finished the bowsprit. Ship's hands set up the stay and bent the jibs. 6 pm finished.*

February 1879

The weather stayed fine for the next 9 days and the men were employed painting, bending sails and generally cleaning the ship. On Monday 10 February, the wind freshened somewhat and they let go the second anchor and let out 20 fathoms of chain. For most of the day men were down below 'turning' the cargo. Still at anchor, for the next few days all hands were working at cleaning out lockers, stowing gear and painting. On Monday 17 the other anchor was hove up and the men were put to chipping the rust off and then blacking the anchor and chain gear.

Nothing of account was recorded for the next five days. On Monday 24 February Peter Corish, an AB, reported sick. At 6 pm on Wednesday 26 they got under way and proceeded on their voyage. At 10 pm they made all sail and steered a course down along the North shore at a safe distance from the land. The ship was pumped and the watch was set. From then on the weather was fair and the hatches were lifted to air the cargo.

March 1879

On Monday 3 the weather changed to a fresh gale. The main topgallant sail, the main topsail and the flying sail were stowed. However, the stormy weather didn't last long and, on Friday 7, the hands were employed turning the grain in the main hatchway. It must have remained calm, for on Friday 14 the crew were over the side scraping what they called the grass – probably algae and barnacles – off her sides, and the hatches were opened fore and aft.

Saturday 15: *Smooth sea, saw several ships in company bound North. Wind fresh and drizzly.*
Sunday 16: *Wind baffling about, squally looking sky.*
Monday 17: *4 am, slight NW swell throughout, ship constantly rolling and chaffing with the sails very much.*

Nothing of note happened until Sunday 23 March when Cape Clear came into sight. On Monday at 8 pm Kinsale Light bore NE, about 6 miles distance. Then on Tuesday they were in a fresh gale. Surprisingly, this is where the log ends, without comment. It does however, give another glimpse of the voyages of a Wexford ship in the 1870s. We do know, from the registration and ownership details, that the **Dispatch** carried on for some years afterwards.

Extract from Log of the Fame of Wexford

It commences on Saturday 25 June 1870, and was kept by the Mate of the ship, John Murphy. It was an uneventful trip but the log provides a good example of the day to day running of a sailing ship. The first entry every day was the weather, the wind strength and direction. The final daily entry at sea was always 'pumps attended to'.

The log begins as the vessel left Wexford with *Moderate breeze. The tug* **Erin** *brought the ship in tow at 4 pm. Made all possible sail and proceeded to sea.* The next day, Sunday 26 June, they are off the coast of Wales, with a moderate breeze to the WNW and The Nash to the berth a distance of 3 miles. At 3 pm they anchored at Penarth Roads. The day ended with a moderate breeze and clear.
Monday 27 June: *Light breeze and clear, got in the jib boom and peaked the yards and got all ready for docking. At 5 pm hove short at the tug boat, took the ship in tow at 6 pm. Dock ship at 8 pm. Moored ship. People variously employed.*
Tuesday 28: *This day light breeze and cloudy at noon. Got in the discharge berth at 4.30, finished the ballast. This day ends with a moderate breeze and people employed clearing the holds.*
Wednesday 29: *Moderate breeze and clear weather, people variously employed.*
Thursday 30: *Light breeze and cloudy ending moderate breeze and showers. People employed setting up the top fore gallant mast and yard.*
Friday 1 July: *Day commenced with moderate breeze and cloudy ending with a strong breeze and showers. People employed stowing away the dunnage and mats.*
Saturday 2 July: *Strong breeze and showers. People employed repairing sails.*
Sunday 3: *Breezy and clear.*
Monday 4: *This day strong breeze and showers, at 4 pm moored the ship and dropped down to the loading berth at 8 pm and commenced loading. At 5 am finished loading. The ships draft is 13ft 8ins aft and 13ft 2ins forward.*
Tuesday 5: *Strong breeze and showers. People employed washing ship and setting up the mast for rigging.*
Wednesday 6: *Light breeze ending in moderate. People employed getting out the jib boom and getting up the royal yards.*
Thursday 7: *People employed setting up the fore and main rigging. At 1 am the pilot came on board and took ship. At 1.30 the tug came and took the ship in tow. At 3.00 made all possible sail with a light breeze from the north. Tug boat let ship go at 8 am. The Nash bore NE by N distance of 3 miles with a light breeze from ESE.*

Log of Fame from Cardiff to Galatz

Saturday 9 July; *pm, Commenced with light breeze and variable winds at 11.30 calm. Am; Late part of the day calm at 2.30 pm, hove up anchor with a light breeze from the south. This day ends cloudy with thunder and lightning. Pumps attended to.*
Sunday 10: *pm, Light breeze from the north and rain and heavy. At 5 pm clear and moderate breeze from west, tacking when required. Several sail in sight. Am, ends, Pumps attended to.*

And so it went, sails were taken in, and were set again, winds were moderate and pumps were attended to, all a normal day's work on a sailing brig at sea. On 17 July, Cape St Vincent was seen 10 miles off NE by E and several sails were noted bound towards the East. Wednesday found them 10 miles NE by E of Cape Trafalgar. Nothing more of note was logged until Friday 11 August, when it was noted that they were 15 miles E by N of Cape Matapan. The next day, 12 August, they sighted Cape Anglow, 12 miles distance. The next land sighted was on the next day Sunday 13 August when it was noted that the island of Anta Mila bore SSW at a distance of 15 miles. On the following Tuesday, a large fleet was seen sailing in company towards the East. Then on Friday 18 August. they made the Dardenelles. The log starts again from this point.

Friday 18 August: *Anchored in the Dardenelles, on the port side, with Capbra Point bearing SSE, distance 6 miles. Furled the sails and set the watch. At 7 am the tugboat took ship in tow. At 10 am let the ship go. Made sail and proceeded towards Constantinople.*
Saturday 19: *pm moderate breeze at 7.30, anchored at Fisherman's Point in 7 fathoms of water, sails furled and watches set. Am. calm and variable winds. At 6 am hove short and made sail, hove up anchor and proceeded toward Constantinople.*
Sunday 20: *pm moderate breeze, 3 pm Marmora light bore NNE.*
Monday 21: *am at anchor with Seraglio Point bearing NE distance 2 miles.*

On Wednesday 23 August, the tug took them in tow at 6.30 pm and let them go at 8 pm. All sail was set and there was nothing else of note until Saturday 26 August when they sighted the Sulina Light. At 8 am they anchored at Sulina. People (the crew) were employed getting out the longboat. At 6 pm on Sunday 27 August, the tug came along and took them and two other vessels in tow. They anchored in the Delta as the river was blocked by a dredger barge at work. The next morning, they were under tow again towards Galatz. At this stage the people were employed cleaning out the fore hold ready for cargo. Apparently they had only discharged part cargo at Sulina. The next day they docked at the discharging berth at Galatz.

On the morning of 31 August, they commenced discharging the remaining cargo. This operation took 9 days including a break on Sunday and on Saturday 10 September, the log states *Hove out made sail and proceeded towards Ibrail. At noon anchored 1 mile off. At 7 took steamer, moored ship in loading berth.* Once again there was no work done on Sunday but on Saturday it states *People variously employed getting hold ready for cargo.* On 15 September, they finished loading at 11am. They then 'hove out' and anchored 1 mile from Ibrail, where the crew were set to trimming the cargo. At 6 pm they got under way and two hours later they anchored 5 miles off Galatz.

It is somewhat confusing at this juncture, for the next entry for Saturday 16 September states, *Light breeze. At 9 am <u>finished loading</u>. At 11 am, hove out. At 1 pm anchored 1 mile from Ibrail in a moderate breeze from WSW and cloudy. At 6pm got under way with a light breeze. At 8 pm anchored 5 miles from Galatz with a strong breeze from ENE and cloudy.* It appears that they returned to Galatz for the rest of their cargo. They got under way the next day, Sunday 17 September and at 10 am anchored 2 miles from Georgy mouth. The next morning, they sailed again and anchored at Sulina at 8 pm. At Sulina the crew got the ship ready for sea and on Wednesday 20, at 2 pm, the tugboat came along, took them in tow and at 5 pm they made sail in a light breeze.

On 22 September they reached the Bosphorus. Thunder, lightning and rain was encountered a few days later and sails had to be taken in. They sighted the lighthouse at Cape Matapan. Nothing else of note was recorded, sails were taken in, sails were set and winds were moderate. Then, on Sunday 1 October, the lighthouse of Gozo was seen to the SW at 10 miles distance. By 16 October they were plying to windward along the coast of Spain and noted that Malaga lighthouse, bore NE 11miles away. At 11.30 on the morning of Thursday 18, they passed the Rock of Gibraltar Lighthouses and their positions to them were logged throughout but apart from logging a 'strong breeze' on the odd occasion, nothing else of note occurred.

On 31 October at 8 in the evening the Tuskar light was sighted, bearing NE by E at a distance of 12 miles. Here the log continues:

Tuesday 1 November: *pm, moderate breeze and fog, at noon clearing. Made sail and tacked the ship towards North at 11 pm. Hoist colours and stood close in with log hands in to 7 fathoms. Tacked the ship towards the E and W various. At 5 pm the tugboat took ship in tow. At 7 pm anchored in South Bay in 4 fathoms of water. At 9 am the lighter came alongside. Day ends in a light breeze and variable winds.*
Wednesday November 2: *pm, light breeze at 5 pm finished the lightening. At 5.30 the* **Charlotte** *came alongside First part of the day ends with moderate breeze and cloudy. Am. moderate breeze and cloudy. At 4 am finished loading the* **Charlotte**. *Day ends moderate breeze and cloudy. People variously employed. Pumps attended to*. Lighters, were usually older schooners or vessels not currently at sea. They were used to take some of a ship's cargo out to lighten her, otherwise she would never get in over the Bar. The next day, 3 November, the log stated; pm, *moderate breeze and cloudy. Ship's draft 10ft 3ins forward and 9 ft 8ins aft. Am. light and various winds. At 11 am the tugboat took ship in tow and towed up to the outer buoy of the Hantoon. Anchored in a light wind from NNE. At 2.30 took ship in tow. At 4 pm anchored in the river and moored the ship with the two hawsers. This log contains 36 hours.*

The log finishes there. Usually the log was closed when the vessel was tied up in the port, but for some reason that didn't happen here. It was a very lucky voyage for the captain and crew; there was no bad weather, no one lost over the side, no crewmen going sick or ending up in jail for fighting ashore, or in hospital after being stabbed or badly beaten in fights with foreign crews. A most remarkable voyage.

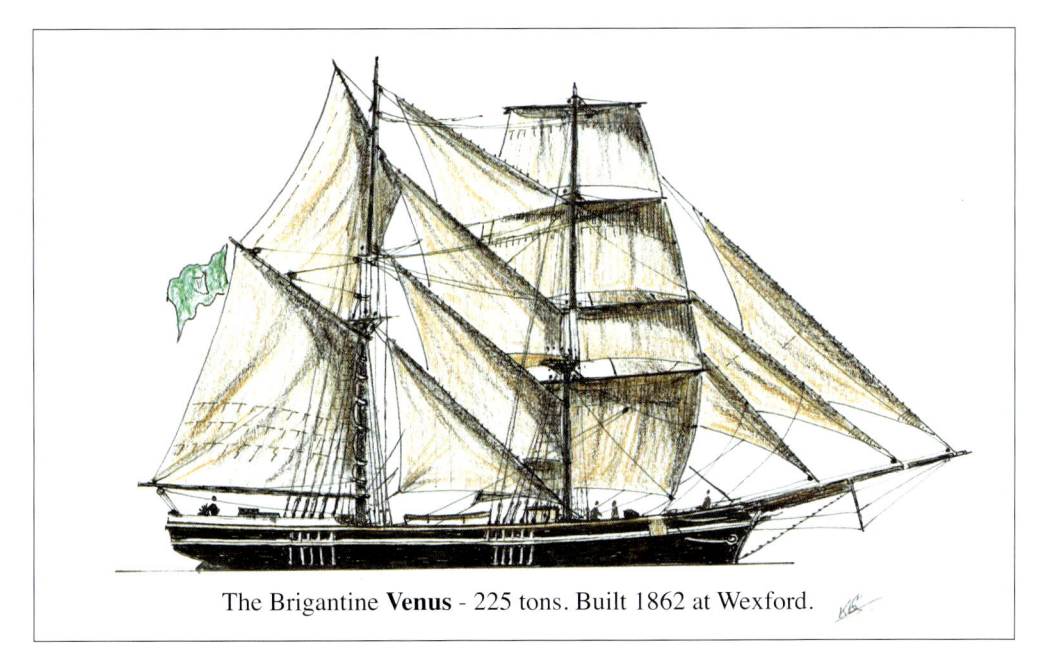

The Brigantine **Venus** - 225 tons. Built 1862 at Wexford.

Appendix 2:
Traditional Local Craft

When writing any history of Wexford's maritime past it would be remiss not to mention the vessels that worked mainly in the confines of Wexford Harbour and out in the Bay. These are the Cots and Gabards, peculiar to Rosslare and Wexford. Locally, Gabards were also known as Cots and, as a result, some confusion still exists as to which was which.

THE WEXFORD SAILING COT
The word 'Cot' is derived from *Coite*, the old Irish for a log boat. In his study, 'The Cots of Rosslare and Wexford', published in *The Mariners Mirror*, February, 1985, Owain T. P. Roberts posits the likelihood that cots, as log boats, were built up to the eighteenth century and that the loss of our forests was the major cause of their demise. These craft, due to their shallow draft, would have been totally unsuitable for the open sea but entirely suited to harbours and rivers. Over the years the planked, clinker-built sea-going cot that we know today, with some modern modifications, was developed. Originally the Wexford cot was double ended, i.e., sharp at both ends, but the invention of the outboard engine made that design impractical. Initially, a transom was built to facilitate the outboard but in time the pointed stern was succeeded by the square stern we know today. These developments happened mainly, if not wholly, in the Rosslare Harbour area.

For generations the principle builders in the Rosslare area, both on the Fort and Rosslare Harbour, were the Wickham family. Until the early years of the twentieth century, the Rosslare cots that were used in the fishing industry were up to 40ft. long. The late Mike Williams of Byrne's Lane, also known as Fisher's Row, an old Wexford Deep Sea sailor, told of his first job afloat fishing for herrings in a Wickham built, 40ft. cot, the **Irish Leader**, at the time owned by George Murphy of Byrne's Lane.

The modern cot is still being built today in Rosslare Harbour by Fergus Wickham and Ron O'Rourke. In the Burrow of Rosslare, the foremost cot builder for many years was the late Mr Larry Duggan, latterly of Carcur, Wexford, where he carried on cot building to an advanced age. Today in the Burrow, Billy Doyle still builds cots, and the craft is flourishing in the Maudlintown area of Wexford Town where there are numerous cot builders and a thriving cot sailing club. In season their regular Sunday races attract appreciative audiences.

THE SLANEY GABARD
The name Gabard derives from the French word *Gabare*, a shallow wooden vessel. The word has frequently been written with two 'b's, but Dr George Hadden, the eminent local historian, spelled it with one 'b' and his spelling of the word will be used here. Apart from a small working foredeck of 11ft between the bow and the forward bulkhead, the gabard was an undecked craft of shallow draft and up to 55ft. in length. It was double-ended with a small f'o'csle that contained two bunks, one each side, a small stove and just enough height for the two-man crew to sit or lie in. Entry was gained by

an 18-inch hatchway in the deck above. There was a 'walkway' of two feet in width on each side of the boat and, when there was little wind, she was propelled by being 'walked' or poled. She carried one mast, that was 'stepped' so that it could be lowered to get under bridges, and therefore had just one sail.

For over a hundred years, the Gabard was a familiar sight in the harbour and up the Slaney to Castlebridge and Enniscorthy, and all inlets in between. In 1794 when the new Wexford bridge was built at Ferrybank, almost where the present bridge is, there was a toll to anyone who used it. Naturally this wasn't popular with local business men and farmers and one enterprising Castlebridge maltster/businessman named Dixon used the Gabards to sail under the bridge to deliver his malt to town and then load up general goods for the return journey. In the early 1800s there was a boom in the shipping trade to and from Wexford Port and it was then that the Gabard came into its own. Wexford Port saw large cargoes of maize, Canadian wheat and other grains imported from Liverpool and further afield such as Galatz in Romania. Much of it was bound for the mills up the River Slaney at Enniscorthy. Fully-laden Gabards could make four return trips to Enniscorthy in a week. They returned with Pollard (wheat bran), wheat maize or general cargo. If there were no return cargoes, or during slack periods, the Gabard would load sand from the pit just above Ferrycarrig to be used as ballast for outbound sailing vessels.

They also plied to the south side of the harbour, delivering goods to places such as Ballybrennan, and up the small Assaly river, both near Killinick. In his first draft of his article in the *Journal of the Old Wexford Society*, Dr Hadden states that, around 1730, when Wexford Castle was being demolished, the surplus stone was brought to Killinick via Gabard for the building of St. Enoch's Church, Killinick. Gabards were also utilised to carry sand and gravel from the gravel pit above Ferrycarrig up the Assaly River to near where the old Killinick Railway Station was, for the construction of the Waterford-Rosslare railway line. The huge scar left by the withdrawal of gravel from that pit can still be seen to this day. Gabards, with slight variations in design, were built in various sites along the river, at Castlebridge, Carcur, Killurin, Polehore, Enniscorthy, in fact anywhere near where a boat builder lived. However, the principal builder, and the most popular design, was the Wexford Dockyard Co. at Trinity St.

With improvements to the road system and the invention of motorised transport, the popularity of the Slaney Gabard declined. Yet it wasn't until 1949, when the last Gabard to ply the Slaney and Wexford Harbour (the **Hope**, owned by Mr Paddy Ryan of Castlebridge), was sold to an Enniscorthy man and met her demise in a flood there shortly afterwards.

A Slaney Gabard at Enniscorthy.
The National Library of Ireland.

Gabards at Enniscorthy.
The National Library of Ireland.

Gabards at Enniscorthy.
The National Library of Ireland.

Up river from Killurin Bridge on the River Slaney, Gabards bound for Enniscorthy.

A Gabard at work at Killurin Bridge, 1905.
Courtesy, Barntown Heritage Group.

A double ended traditional herring cot.
Courtesy, Fergus Wickham, Rosslare Harbour.

At Ballineskar, shaking out the herrings from a big herring cot. The man in the centre with the black moustache is Simon Donahoe, owner.
Courtesy, Des Peare, Rosslare Strand.

SMALLER SAILING VESSELS, CUTTERS, YACHTS, FISHING BOATS, GABARDS ETC.

AURORA: A Gabard, 22 tons. **OWNER 1869**: William Armstrong.
CRUISKEEN LAWN: A yacht, 1875.
DAZZLER: A fishing yawl. Lost on the Bar, November 1882. Crew of six saved by the lifeboat, **Ethel Eveleen**.
DOLPHIN: A fishing lugger, 1879.
FAIRY: A fishing vessel. **OWNER**: John Bell of Wexford, 1869.
FAME: Fishing lugger. Lost on Blackwater Bank, September 1887. **OWNER**: William Armstrong, Wexford.
FAVOURITE: A fishing lugger, 1879.
GANNETT: Fishing vessel. **OWNER**: Gannett Fishing Co. Wexford.
GEISHA: Fishing vessel, 1925.
JOSEPH PATRICK: of Courtown. Ran ashore and lost at Rosslare, February 1892.
MAURA: A yawl, 1925.
MOUNTAIN HARE: A lugger, 1877.
PEEP O' DAY: An oyster lugger. **OWNER**: William White of Wexford, 1865.
PRIMA DONNA: A fishing smack. Sunk February 1892.
SILVER BELLE: A yawl, 1925.
ST. QUINTON: A cutter, Doyle owner and master.
ZEPHYR: Belonging to Ballinoulart, Co. Wexford. On 12 January 1850, under her master Philip Mitten, she was involved in the rescue of passengers and crew of the 1050 ton **Hottingeur** off Blackwater Bank.

A Gabard alongside an unknown schooner at Wexford.

The Crescent Quay with a steam train arriving from Rosslare, early 1900s.
Courtesy, Liam Gaul Collection.

Kaat's Boatyard, just above present day Dunne's Stores, Wexford.

Appendix 3
'The Mariners' and Wexford's Twin Churches

After Wexford's twin churches were opened in 1858, the campaign to raise funds to help pay off the massive loans incurred by their building continued for many years. The yearly collections were published in the local press until comparatively recently. It is said that Father James Roche, the man credited with the building of the churches, visited each and every local vessel on their arrival at the Quays to collect contributions from the masters and crew. It is more likely however, that he attended the shipping company office, where, on the day after a vessel arrived, the crew would be collecting any money due to them after the voyage. Both the local newspapers, *The People* and *Wexford Independent* published a regular list of contributors and the one below is from 29 October 1870. This particular collection was said to help defray the cost of 'the great wall' around the church perimeter. Each section is headed by profession, such as Wexford Union Officers or Local Constabulary but by far the largest portion of these is headed, 'The Mariners'.

Antelope: Capt. Busher, 5s; Mr James Devereux, William Street, 10s
Brothers: Capt. Rowe, 5s; the crew, 3s
Brothers: Capt. Clem Morris, 10s
Charles Walker: Capt. Busher, 5s; the crew 2s
Charlotte: Capt. English, 5s
Clara & Jessie: Capt. James Morris, 5s; Capt. Francis Morris, 10s; Capt. James Hughes, 10s
Criterion: Capt. Codd, 5s; the crew, 3s
Commerce: Capt. Redmond, 5s
Dart: Capt. Neill, 5s; the crew, 3s
Dispatch: Capt. Furlong, 10s, the Mate, Cooney, 5s the crew, 4s
Emerald Isle: The crew, 3s
Enterprise: Capt. Smith, 10s; Mate Smith, 5s; the crew, 7s
Erin (tugboat): Capt. Blake, 5s; the crew, 4s
Erin: Capt. Bent 5; the crew, 4s
Essex Lass: Capt. Neill, 2s
Express: Capt. Barlow, 5s
Fame: Capt. Murphy, 10s; Mate Murphy, 5s; the crew 5s
Forth: Capt. Lambert, 5s; the crew, 3s
Handy: Capt. Carty, 5s; the crew, 2s
Hantoon: Capt. King, 10s
Henry: Capt. Busher, 5s; the crew, 2s
Hope: Capt. Meany, 5s; the crew 3s

I'll Try: Capt. Murphy, 5s; the crew, 2s.5d
Industry: Capt. Murphy. 10s; Mate, Rossiter, 5s; the crew 5s
Joseph: Capt. James Codd, 5s; the crew, 3s
Kate: Capt. Bell, 10s
The Lightship: Capt. James Murphy, Michael Street, 2s
Maude Annie: Capt. Neville, 7s; the crew, 3s
Mary Agnes: Capt. Butler, 5s; the crew 3s
May Queen: Capt. Ryan, 10s, Mate Carr, 5s; the crew 5s
Mermaid: Capt. Murphy, 5s; the crew 3s
Mite: Capt. Moran, 5s; the crew, 3s
Portia: Capt. Devereux, 10s; Michael Murphy, 5s; the crew, 5s
Princess: Capt. Neill, 5s; the crew, 2s
Pilot: Capt. Williams, 5s; the crew, 3s
Ranger: Capt. Lambert, 5s; the crew, 3s
Rapid: Capt. Kelly, 10s
Reliance: Capt. Codd, 5s; the crew, 3s
Rosslare: Capt. English, 10s; the crew, 5s
Rover: Capt. Roche, 5s; the crew 3s
Ruby (tugboat): Capt. John Smith, 5s; Mr. Peter Cunningham, 2s; the crew, 2s
Intrepid: Capt. Roche, 5s; the crew, 3s
Saltee: Capt. Codd, 10s; Mate Smith, 5s; the crew,5s
Seaflower: Capt. Hutchinson, 7s; the crew, 2s
Shamrock: Capt. Hayes, 5s; the crew 2s
Slaney: Capt. Bolger, 5s; the crew,3s
Swift: Capt. Cousins, 2s; the crew 1s
Star: Capt. Walsh, 5s; the crew 3s
Topaz: Capt. Murphy, 10s; the crew, 4s; Mr Patrick Reigh, 10s
Wave: Capt. Neill, 5s; the crew, 4s

It should be noted that, in 1870, 5 shillings was approximately what a skilled tradesman would earn per day. In today's £ sterling, it is the equivalent of £15.

Appendix 4

IRISH EMIGRATION

(from the Waterford Mail)

In our review of the work recently published by Mr Pliny Miles, we had occasion to refer particularly to emigration. We showed that out of 10,324 passengers who sailed from Liverpool in 21 ships, no less than 811 died on the voyage; and we said that the mortality of our Irish vessels had not been anything like this. We have, through the kindness of the eminent firm of Messrs W Graves & Son, been furnished with a statement of the mortality on board their vessels during a period of twelve years, in which nearly 20,000 embarked from New Ross for America; and during that period the entire number of deaths on board their vessels was 86; and it will be seen that but for the occurrence of cholera in their vessel, the *Jane*, in 1849, which carried off 33 persons, the deaths on passage would only have been 53. The disproportion between the deaths on board the New Ross vessels and the Liverpool ships is very striking. On the average of the twelve years, including the vessel in which the cholera occurred, the mortality was one in 250 persons; excluding the *Jane*, in which the cholera occurred, it is one in 860. On board the Liverpool vessels the mortality was one in every 11 passengers, or 23 in 250. The following is the return of the names of the vessels, the places of their destination, the number of passengers and deaths on board: -

Date	Ship	Destination	Number of Passengers	Deaths on Voyage
1847	Dunbrody	Quebec	297	4
	Standard	Quebec	342	0
	Progress	Quebec	535	0
	Agent	Quebec	373	0
	Solway	Quebec	166	0
	Lady Bagot	St John's N.B.	320	4
1848	Aberfoyle	Quebec	342	0
	Star	St Andrews	383	9
	Jessie	Quebec	316	0
	Swan	Quebec	317	0
1849	Lady Constable	New York	211	0
	Aberfoyle	Quebec	287	0
	Jane	Quebec	392	33
	Dunbrody	New York	177	0
	Bridgetown	Quebec	322	0
	Swan	Quebec	415	0
1850	India	Quebec	405	5
	Aberfoyle	Quebec	277	1
	Juno	Quebec	367	0
	Triton	Quebec	353	0
	Jenny Lind	Quebec	51	0
1851	India	Quebec	430	0
	Glenlyon	Quebec	469	5
	Pilgrim	Quebec	482	1
	Milicete	Quebec	369	0
	Lord Elgin	Quebec	292	0
	Orinoco	Quebec	49	0
	Glenlyon	Savannah	227	0
	Jorea	New Orleans	322	0
1852	India	Quebec	408	3
	Dunbrody	Quebec	253	0
	Confiance	Quebec	482	9
	Lord Ashburton	Quebec	420	0

Year	Ship	Port	Number	Deaths
	Huron	Quebec	198	0
	Glenlyon	Quebec	341	0
	Dunbrody	Quebec	226	0
	Glenlyon	Savannah	250	0
1853	India	Quebec	400	1
	Glenlyon	Quebec	439	0
	Star	Quebec	401	1
	Harmony	Quebec	455	1
	Petrel	Quebec	429	2
	Dunbrody	Quebec	275	1
	Marion	Quebec	64	0
	Glenlyon	Quebec	316	0
	India	Quebec	295	3
	Dunbrody	Savannah	164	1
1854	India	Quebec	397	2
	Dunbrody	Quebec	242	0
	Ward Chipman	Quebec	384	0
	Glenlyon	Quebec	452	1
	Albatross	Quebec	207	1
	Delta	Quebec	546	0
	Dunbrody	Quebec	209	0
	India	Quebec	28	0
	Glenlyon	Savannah	82	0
1855	Dunbrody	Quebec	140	0
	India	Quebec	315	3
	Favourite	Quebec	216	0
	Dunbrody	Quebec	126	0
	India	Quebec	33	0
1856	Dunbrody	Quebec	212	0
	Woodstock	Quebec	310	1
	Dunbrody	Quebec	80	3
1857	Dunbrody	Quebec	209	0
	Carnatie	Quebec	270	1
	Dunbrody	Quebec	87	0
1858	Dunbrody	Quebec	150	0
	Star	Quebec	112	0
	Dunbrody	Quebec	36	0
	TOTAL		19,913	86

Appendix 5
Wexford: Masters and Mates Certificates

Name	YOB	Resident	Certificate Issued	Certificate Number
John Allen	1810	Wexford	25 Mar 1851	50.156
Alexander Allen	1853	Wexford	28 Jul 1884	4524
Alexander Allen	1853	Wexford	16 Mar 1881	4524
Alexander Allen	1853	Wexford	21 Jan 1878	4524
John Percival Angrove	1838	Wexford	22 Mar 1875	99322
Robert Armstrong	1823	Wexford, Wexford	27 Jun 1877	79.513
William Atkinson	7 Nov 1807	Wexford, Wexford	25 Aug 1851	55.339
Thomas Barron	1839	Wexford, Wexford	09 Feb 1860	21.772
Thomas Barron	1839	Wexford, Wexford	29 Jul 1862	21.772
Edward Bell	1840	Wexford, Wexford	02 Dec 1859	21.304
Edward John Bell	1840	Wexford, Wexford	23 Jun 1863	21.304
Richard Alexander	1850	Wexford, Wexford	15 Oct 1869	91251
William Bent	2 Jan 1816	Wexford, Wexford	16 Jan 1851	56.326
Walter Bent	17 Aug 1821	Wexford, Wexford	04 Sep 1851	57.729
Richard Bent	1843	Wexford, Wexford	20 Aug 1867	86012
Patrick Walter	1832	Wexford, Wexford	22 Sep 1852	6934
Patrick Walter	1832	Wexford, Wexford	02 Aug 1862	6934
Robert Blake	14 Nov 1820	Wexford, Wexford	30 Dec 1852	57.71
Robert Blake	1820	Wexford, Wexford	07 Feb 1855	79.092
John Blake	1847	Wexford	27 Oct 1875	898
Patrick Boggan	1814	Wexford, Wexford	15 Aug 1873	76050
Patrick Boggan	1814	Wexford, Wexford	20 Mar 1851	50.593
Mathew Boggan	1865	Wexford	15 May 1893	26483
Mathew Boggan	1865	Wexford	16 Jul 1894	26483
Mathew Boggan	1865	Wexford, Ireland	14 Sep 1895	26483
Mathew Boggan	1865	Wexford	19 Apr 00	26483
Edward Bolger	1827	Wexford, Wexford	03 Dec 1861	100628
William Bolger	1844	Wexford, Wexford	07 Jun 1866	82.809
Patrick Boyle	1839	Wexford, Wexford	15 Jul 1869	83118
John Boyle	1856	Wexford	18 Sep 1878	5566
John Boyle	1856	Wexford	19 Jul 1880	5566
John Boyle	1856	Wexford	06 Mar 1883	5566
Peter Boyle	1860	Wexford	03 Oct 1883	13397
Peter Boyle	1860	Wexford	17 Mar 1885	13397
Peter Boyle	1860	Wexford	17 Oct 1887	16528
Peter Boyle	1860	Wexford	25 Jan 1886	16528
John Breen	1820	Wexford, Wexford	25 Sep 1873	79.457
John Breen	1840	Wexford, Wexford	21 Mar 1866	82319
Edward Edmond Brett	1840	Wexford, Wexford	09 Oct 1860	23.087
Edward Edmond Brett	1840	Wexford, Wexford	31 Dec 1861	24840
Edward Edmond Brett	1840	Wexford, Wexford	31 Jan 1862	24840

Edward Edmond Brett	1840	Wexford, Wexford	06 Sep 1862	24840
Edward Edmond Brett	1840	Wexford, Wexford	30 Sep 1865	24840
Charles Campbell Brett	1851	Wexford	04 Nov 1875	935
Peter Bronn	1811	Wexford, Wexford	22 Apr 1851	1652
Edward Brown	1792	Wexford, Wexford	13 Mar 1851	50.59
Robert Henry Brown	15 Jan 1824	Wexford, Wexford	22 Apr 1851	36.013
Robert Brown	1825	Wexford, Wexford	13 May 1851	4933
Samuel Brown	1830	Wexford, Wexford	07 Feb 1855	11791
John Bryne	1825	Wexford, Wexford	28 Jul 1853	8.822
Patrick Bunphy	1848	Wexford, Ireland	23 Apr 1872	95937
Lawrence Butler	1796	Wexford, Wexford	18 Mar 1851	50.312
Clement Butler	1872	Wexford	09 Apr 1898	33009
Clement Butler	1872	Wexford	26 Sep 02	33009
Clement Butler	1872	Wexford	09 Nov 04	33009
John Butter	1834	Wexford	08 Mar 1865	25.53
Bran Byrne	24 Dec 1817	Wexford, Wexford	22 Jul 1851	49.926
Evan Byrne	1817	Wexford, Wexford	04 Mar 1878	76.352
Evan Byrne	1817	Wexford, Wexford	04 Mar 1878	76.352
Michael Joseph Byrne	1837	Wexford, Wexford	09 May 1860	22337
Michael Joseph Byrne	1837	Wexford, Wexford	13 Aug 1862	22337
William Byrne	1838	Wexford, Wexford	31 Mar 1868	101.262
William Byrne	1838	Wexford, Wexford	08 Feb 1865	33.202
Martin Byrne	1843	Wexford	08 Oct 1874	92933
Martin Byrne	1843	Wexford, Wexford	25 Jun 1870	92933
John Byrne	1858	Wexford	23 Sep 1889	11438
John Byrne	1858	Wexford	07 Feb 1901	11438
Edward Byrnes	1841	Wexford	09 Jul 1881	10290
John Cahill	24 Dec 1790	Wexford, Wexford	26 Mar 1851	37.461
Christopher Cahill	1802	Wexford, Wexford	20 Mar 1851	70.431
Nicholas Cahill	21 Nov 1817	Wexford, Wexford	15 Sep 1853	57.412
Lawrence Cahill	24 Jan 1824	Wexford, Wexford	04 Sep 1851	57.246
Lawrence Cahill	4 Jul 1828	Wexford, Wexford	13 Feb 1852	57.33
Timothy Caine	24 Jul 1821	Wexford, Wexford	27 Nov 1851	57.18
John Campbell	7 May 1793	Wexford, Wexford	20 May 1851	37.279
Charles Campbell	1810	Wexford, Wexford	13 Jun 1851	70.625
Michael Cardiff	1875	Wexford	04 Oct 1904	38611
John Gregory Carhill	4 Jun 1823	Wexford, Wexford	04 Jan 1851	36.835
John Gregory Carhill	4 Jun 1823	Wexford, Wexford	04 Jan 1851	36.835
John Gregory Carhill	4 Jan 1823	Wexford, Wexford	04 Jan 1851	36.835
William Carley	1834	Wexford, Wexford	15 Sep 1855	71.056
James Carr	3 May 1799	Wexford, Wexford	26 Jan 1851	37.42
John Carr	1804	Wexford, Wexford	13 Jun 1851	70.621
John Carr	22 Aug 1805	Wexford, Wexford	25 Jan 1851	37.463
John Carr	27 Apr 1830	Wexford, Wexford	31 Aug 1857	58.658
Thomas Carr	1843	Wexford, Wexford	02 Jul 1866	83.018

Thomas Carr	1843	Wexford, Wexford	10 Jul 1869	83.018
John Carr	1846	Wexford	21 Sep 1875	760
John Carr	1846	Wexford, Wexford	29 Jan 1869	83117
John Carr	1846	Wexford, Wexford	11 Jul 1866	83117
John Carr	1846	Wexford	06-Jul-05	760
Patrick Carroll	20 Mar 1806	Wexford, Wexford	10 Mar 1851	37.672
John Casey	28 Feb 1830	Wexford, Wexford	09 Feb 1853	57.328
John Casey	1830	Wexford	09 Mar 1876	1496
John Casey	1830	Wexford, Wexford	12 Jan 1856	15255
John Casey	1830	Wexford, Wexford	22 Jul 1856	15255
Michael Cassidy	1820	Wexford, Wexford	08 Mar 1851	70.423
John Chambers	1833	Wexford, Wexford	17 Sep 1864	32.043
John Chambers	1833	Wexford, Wexford	06 Jul 1869	32.043
Patrick Chandler	1812	Wexford, Wexford	14 Aug 1851	70.672
Patrick Chandler	21 May 1814	Wexford, Wexford	27 Jan 1851	56.842
Thomas Chapman	1809	Wexford, Wexford	25 Feb 1852	70.768
Michael Chary	15 Feb 1793	Wexford, Wexford	03 Mar 1851	37.283
Edward Clancy	1843	Wexford	07 Apr 1875	85315
Edward Clancy	1843	Wexford, Wexford	08 May 1867	85315
James Clancy	1848	Wexford	20 Oct 1875	863
Patrick Clancy	1848	Wexford, Wexford	29 Jan 1874	30344
Peter Clancy	1851	Wexford	20 Oct 1875	864
Richard Patrick Clancy	1881	Wexford	27-May-05	39052
Richard Patrick Clancy	1881	Wexford	19-Dec-08	39.052
Richard Patrick Clancy	1881	Wexford	08-Oct-10	39.052
Michael Claney	1814	Wexford, Wexford	06 Aug 1851	57.111
Edward Cleary	1795	Wexford, Wexford	26 Feb 1851	37.285
John Codd	1799	Wexford, Wexford	18 Feb 1851	37.667
Patrick Codd	1812	Wexford, Wexford	23 May 1851	70.425
James Codd	20 Dec 1813	Wexford, Wexford	03 Mar 1851	37.669
Christopher Codd	23 Nov 1814	Wexford, Wexford	31 Mar 1851	37.682
John Codd	1823	Wexford, Wexford	10 Mar 1851	70.456
Thomas Codd	14 Jun 1826	Wexford, Wexford	01 Aug 1851	57.147
Thomas Codd	1826	Wexford, Wexford	12 Aug 1858	19.135
Joseph Codd	23 May 1828	Wexford, Wexford	15 Feb 1851	37.626
Joseph Codd	1846	Wexford, Wexford	10 Jul 1867	85770
Nicholas Codd	1847	Wexford, Wexford	15 Feb 1870	92063
William Codd	1847	Wexford, Wexford	06 Jan 1873	92062
William Codd	1847	Wexford, Wexford	11 Feb 1870	92062
James Codd	1848	Wexford	08 Oct 1874	90679
James Codd	1848	Wexford, Wexford	19 Jul 1869	90679
James Codd	1848	Wexford	03 Jul 1882	90679
Joseph Codd	1848	Wexford, Wexford	17 Oct 1868	88846
Joseph Codd	1848	Wexford, Wexford	16 Dec 1871	88846
Joseph Codd	1850	Wexford	26 Apr 1879	1649

Name	Year	Place	Date	Number
Joseph Codd	1850	Wexford	12 Apr 1876	1649
Stephen Codd	1855	Wexford	04 Jun 1878	1207
Stephen Codd	1855	Wexford	08 Jan 1876	1207
John Francis Codd	1893	Wexford	19-Feb-17	10.597
John Francis Codd	1893	Wexford	25-Jan-19	10597
John Francis Codd	1893	Wexford		10597
William Code	1829	Wexford, Wexford	05 Jun 1852	3157
William Code	1829	Wexford, Wexford	14 Mar 1854	3157
Nicholas Coghlan	1819	Wexford, Wexford	16 Sep 1858	42.016
Nicholas Coghlan	17 Mar 1819	Wexford, Wexford	22 Jan 1851	37.181
Nicholas Coghlan	1819	Wexford, Wexford	06 Jan 1875	76.155
James Coghlan	1827	Wexford, Wexford	26 Feb 1852	3708
James Coglan	26 Jan 1827	Wexford, Wexford	29 Mar 1851	57.044
Patrick Cogley	1821	Wexford, Wexfordrd	12 May 1851	70.579
Aiden Cogley	1859	Wexford	01 Feb 1882	8658
Aiden Cogley	1859	Wexford	31 Jul 1880	8658
Aiden Cogley	1859	Wexford	17 Mar 1884	8658
Aiden Cogley	1859	Wexford	21-Oct-1902	37235
Christopher Cogley	1868	Wexford	17 Jun 1890	20411
Christopher Cogley	1868	Wexford	6 Dec 1888	20411
James Colford	1848	Wexford	6 Apr 1878	98842
James Colford	1848	Wexford	14 Oct 1876	98842
James Colford	1848	Wexford	28 Nov 1874	98842
Patrick Connolly	Jul 1800	Wexford, Wexford	10 Feb 1851	37.304
Alexander Connolly	1883	Wexford	14-May-09	41.376
Alexander Connolly	1883	Wexford	18-May-15	41376
Thomas Connor	7 Jul 1797	Wexford, Wexford	22 Feb 1857	37.671
Michael Connor	4 Jun 1799	Wexford, Wexford	03 Mar 1851	37.306
Peter Connor	29 Jun 1810	Wexford, Wexford	23 Jan 1851	37.363
Thomas Conway	1839	Wexford, Wexford	12 Apr 1865	21.772
Thomas Cooney	1828	Wexford, Wexford	15 Jun 1855	12562
Thomas Cooney	1828	Wexford, Wexford	24 Jan 1861	12562
Thomas Corcoran	1826	Wexford, Wexford	26 Jan 1852	57.323
John Corish	1810	Wexford, Wexford	14 Feb 1855	71.004
Barnaby Corish	1811	Wexford, Wexford	20 Apr 1851	70.401
Raymond Corish	1 Nov 1823	Wexford, Wexford	24 Jan 1851	37.341
Nicholas Cousins	18 Nov 1818	Wexford, Wexford	08 Mar 1851	37.567
John Cousins	1824	Wexford, Wexford	04 Oct 1851	57.103
William Coussins	1843	Wexford	18 Apr 1888	102953
Christopher Patrick	1868	Wexford	08 Jul 1892	20411
Nicholas Crellin	1812	Wexford, Wexford	15 May 1851	70.44
James Ralph Crosbie	10 Nov 1804	Wexford, Wexford	15 Jan 1851	37.217
Michael Crowley	1838	Wexford, Wexford	26 Feb 1870	89551
Michael Crowley	1838	Wexford, Wexford	29 Jan 1869	89551
Michael Crowley	1838	Wexford, Wexford	24 Apr 1863	28196

Name	Born	Place	Date	Number
Nicholas Cullen	1812	Wexford, Wexford	11 Apr 1867	75.319
Daniel Nicholas Cullcn	1824	Wexford, Wexford	15 Aug 1856	15489
Daniel Nicholas Cullen	1824	Wexford, Wexford	11 Mar 1858	15489
Daniel Nicholas Cullen	2 May 1824	Wexford, Wexford	21 Jun 1851	57.161
Nicholas Cullin	1812	Wexford, Wexford	24 Dec 1861	54.399
Partrick Culliton	1816	Wexford, Wexford	10 Jul 1851	1340
Thomas Davies	1892	Wexford		12506
Richard Delaney	1874	Wexford	29-Sep-00	35541
Richard Delaney	1874	Wexford, Ireland	31-May-02	35541
Richard Delaney	1874	Wexford	18-Mar-05	35541
John Delany	23 Dec 1814	Wexford, Wexford	04 Mar 1851	38.359
Lawrence Dempsey	1825	Wexford, Wexford	11 Dec 1861	24.704
Lawrence Dempsy	10 Aug 1825	Wexford, Wexford	29 Mar 1851	58.256
Thomas Deveraux	21 Dec 1820	Wexford, Wexford	14 Nov 1854	58.561
James Devereaux	24 Aug 1807	Wexford, Wexford	11 Feb 1851	38.42
Peter Deverence	28 Jun 1796	Wexford, Wexford	27 Mar 1851	38.689
Mark Devereux	1800	Wexford, Wexford	05 Jun 1871	75844
Patrick Devereux	24 Aug 1810	Wexford, Wexford	20 Mar 1851	58.231
Lawrence Devereux	20 Aug 1815	Wexford, Wexford	21 Mar 1857	59.516
Gregory Devereux	1834	Wexford, Wexford	02 Apr 1871	15353
Gregory Devereux	1834	Wexford, Wexford	11 Jul 1856	15353
Gregory Devereux	1834	Wexford, Wexford	13 Oct 1858	15353
Martin Devereux	1839	Wexford, Wexford	24 Mar 1865	6739
Martin Devereux	1839	Wexford, Wexford	13 Mar 1861	6739
Mathew Devereux	1843	Wexford, Wexford	23 Oct 1869	82169
Mathew Devereux	1843	Wexford, Wexford	7 Mar 1866	82169
James Devereux	1846	Wexford, Wexford	29 Jul 1872	96068
John Joseph Devereux	1882	Wexford	23-Dec-10	6085
John Joseph Devereux	1882	Wexford	11-May-12	6.085
John Joseph Devereux	1882	Wexford	23-Feb-14	6085
James Doyle	13 Mar 1814	Wexford, Wexford	22 Jan 1851	38.382
Patrick Joseph Doyle	23 Nov 1814	Wexford, Wexford	05 Mar 1851	38.532
Patrick Joseph Doyle	1814	Wexford, Wexford	27 Feb 1856	14288
Henry Doyle	1831	Wexford, Wexford	23 Mar 1854	10020
Patrick Doyle	1839	Wexford, Wexford	11 Jul 1866	83118
Patrick Joseph Doyle	1867	Wexford	22 Aug 1889	21402
Patrick Joseph Doyle	1867	Wexford	20 Feb 1891	21402
Patrick Joseph Doyle	1867	Wexford	8 Oct 1894	21402
John Joseph Doyle	1870	Wexford	27 Dec 1893	24070
John Joseph Doyle	1870	Wexford	1 Jul 1892	24070
John Joseph Doyle	1870	Wexford	8 Jul 1891	24070
John Joseph Doyle	1870	Wexford	19 Jul 1890	22746
John Duffey	1812	Wexford, Wexford	7 Nov 1851	72.124
Thomas Edwards	9 Jan 1809	Wexford, Wexford	3 Feb 1855	59
Thomas Edwards	1809	Wexford, Wexford	17 Apr 1855	59.006

Patrick Egan	1818	Wexford, Wexford	19 Nov 1861	74.202
Edward English	1791	Wexford, Wexford	27 Sep 1851	70.021
James English	24 Jun 1805	Wexford, Wexford	3 Feb 1851	39.01
William English	25 Aug 1805	Wexford, Wexford	14 Mar 1851	38.968
William English	1810	Wexford, Wexford	19 Mar 1860	44.251
Lawrence English	1822	Wexford, Wexford	12 Dec 1864	74.934
Lawrence English	1822	Wexford, Wexford	11 Apr 1851	70.065
Edward English	1863	Wexford	20 Aug 1886	17306
Edward English	1863	Wexford	20 Apr 1885	13113
Edward English	1863	Wexford	16 Jul 1883	13113
Edward Joseph English	1863	Wexford	31 Aug 1886	17306
Edward Joseph English	1865	Wexford	9 Aug 1898	17306
James Ennis	1879	Wexford		38701
Patrick Farady	1847	Wexford	15 Mar 1881	9686
Patrick Farady	1847	Wexford	14 Aug 1885	9686
George Feeney	1866	Wexford	22 Mar 1889	252
George Feeney	1866	Wexford	7 Dec 1891	252
Andrew Fennell	1815	Wexford, Wexford	26 May 1851	59.39
Patrick Fielding	1828	Wexford, Wexford	12 Jun 1851	59.306
Howard Fleetwood	1876	Wexford	4 Apr 1896	30293
Howard Fleetwood	1876	Wexford	18 Dec 1897	30293
Howard Fleetwood	1876	Wexford	8-Jun-00	30293
John Joseph Flaherty	1871	Wexford	4 Jan 1894	103596
Thomas Foley	1851	Wexford	30 Jun 1881	7688
Thomas Foley	1851	Wexford	17 Jan 1880	7688
Thomas Foley	1851	Wexford	16 Aug 1886	7688
Thomas Foley	1851	Wexford	9 Jan 1883	7688
Charles Fortune	20 May 1812	Wexford, Wexford	24 Feb 1851	39.499
William Fortune	1820	Wexford, Wexford	21 May 1851	59.374
Matthew Fraine	31 Mar 1819	Wexford, Wexford	27 Jan 1853	59.5
Patrick French	12 May 1817	Wexford, Wexford	13 Jun 1851	59.38
Gregory French	1842	Wexford, Wexford	23 Jan 1866	81.737
Gregory French	1842	Wexford, Wexford	15 Oct 1868	81.737
Edward Furlong	23 Nov 1811	Wexford, Wexford	3 Jan 1851	59.081
Stephen Furlong	1811	Wexford, Wexford	30 Oct 1867	75.383
Michael Furlong	1832	Wexford, Wexford	28 Feb 1856	14302
Michael Furlong	1832	Wexford, Wexford	25 Aug 1860	14302
John Furlong	1842	Wexford, Wexford	22 Jan 1863	27.433
Patrick James Furlong	1896	Wexford	6-Oct-19	43795
William James Furniss	1839	Wexford, Wexford	4 Jul 1865	34.339
William Gaul	1839	Wexford, Wexford	25 Sep 1869	91098
William Gaul	1839	Wexford	13 Apr 1875	91098
James Edward Gaul	1852	Wexford	7 Sep 1876	2019
James Edward Gaul	1852	Wexford	6 Nov 1884	14885
John Wheaton Goff	1833	Wexford, Wexford	11 Jun 1859	9427

Name	Date	Place	Date 2	Number
John Goodall	1852	Wexford	8-Oct-00	7746
John Goodall	1852	Wexford	1 Dec 1882	7746
John Goodall	1852	Wexford	4 Feb 1880	7746
John Goodall	1853	Wexford	28-Jan-02	36450
James William Grant	1865	Wexford	5 Apr 1890	22276
Robert Guynn	1838	Wexford, Wexford	31 Dec 1862	27.3
Robert Guynn	1838	Wexford, Wexford	5 Nov 1864	27.3
Robert Guynn	1838	Wexford, Wexford	26 Oct 1869	27.3
James Hanrahan	1863	Wexford	7 May 1892	25135
Richard Hardy	19 Jul 1828	Wexford, Wexford	24 Dec 1850	60.715
Richard Hardy	1828	Wexford, Wexford	26 Dec 1851	3189
James Hart	4 Jun 1802	Wexford, Wexford	29 Mar 1851	41.471
George Hatchell	1834	Wexford, Wexford	17 Feb 1871	2896
George Hatchell	1834	Wexford, Ireland	3 Feb 1872	2896
Willam Hawkins	1838	Wexford, Wexford	23 Jul 1862	26.351
Michael Hayes	1842	Wexford, Wexford	13 Mar 1867	84868
James Hays	1835	Wexford, Wexford	23 Aug 1859	20.898
James Hays	1835	Wexford, Wexford	29 May 1862	20.898
James Hays	1836	Wexford, Wexford	3 Oct 1863	20.898
Bernard Henson	1838	Wexford, Wexford	13 Mar 1863	19.136
Thomas Heron	1858	Wexford	25-Aug-06	39834
Thomas Heron	1858	Wexford	30 Apr 1883	12793
Thomas Heron	1858	Wexford	31 May 1887	12793
Bernard Hewson	1838	Wexford, Hewson	30 Nov 1894	28419
Peter Hewson	19-Mar	Wexford, Wexford	12 Aug 1851	61.423
John Holbrook	1830	Wexford, Wexford	12 Feb 1857	16225
John Holbrook	1830	Wexford, Wexford	12 Sep 1860	16225
John Hore	1819	Wexford, Wexford	17 Jul 1869	75.609
Edwin James Hore	1825	Wexford, Wexford	29 Aug 1856	50.882
Edwin James Hore	1825	Wexford, Wexford	8 May 1851	54.854
Edwin James Hore	1825	Wexford, Wexford	8 Apr 1863	28.07
James Edwin Hore	1836	Wexford, Wexford	10 Mar 1859	20.099
John Hove	1819	Wexford, Wexford	3 Mar 1851	54.613
Patrick Howlin	17 Mar 1802	Wexford, Wexford	13 Dec 1850	41.247
James William Howlin	1817	Wexford, Wexford	14 Jul 1851	54.903
Thomas Francis Howlin	Apr 1820	Wexford, Wexford	25 Mar 1851	61.253
Martin Howlin	13 Mar 1823	Wexford, Wexford	12 May 1856	62.439
Martin Howlin	1823	Wexford, Wexford	20 Jun 1861	23.642
John Howlin	1825	Wexford, Wexford	12 Mar 1852	3837
Thomas Howlin	1831	Wexford, Wexford	13 May 1857	16.844
Robert Howlin	1862	Wexford	16 Jul 1888	19894
Robert Howlin	1862	Wexford	17 Aug 1894	813
Patrick Hughes	1798	Wexford, Wexford	18 Feb 1851	54.738
John Hughes	4 May 1823	Wexford, Wexford	25 Jul 1851	61.414
Algernon George Stewart	1904	Wexford	3-Apr-25	18864

Name	Born	Place	Date	Number
Thomas Hull	1817	Wexford, Wexford	11 Mar 1851	54.741
William Hull	1824	Wexford, Wexford	25 Feb 1860	42.739
William Hull	25 Mar 1824	Wexford, Wexford	19 Feb 1851	41.534
William Hull	1824	Wexford, Wexford	24 Sep 1858	73.897
William Hull	1824	Wexford, Wexford	13 Jan 1853	72.691
Bernard Huson	1838	Wexford, Wexford	12 Aug 1858	19.136
John Huson	1840	Wexford, Wexford	12 Jun 1862	26.063
John Irveeny	6 Jun 1823	Wexford, Wexford	5 Feb 1851	66.853
Richard Clifford Jeffares	1810	Wexford, Wexford	30 Mar 1861	23.573
Samuel Jeffares	1829	Wexford, Wexford	25 Jul 1861	23.922
Samuel Jeffares	1829	Wexford, Wexford	24 Jun 1864	23.922
Mathew Kavanagh	1844	Wexford, Wexford	31 Mar 1868	87596
Mathew Kavanagh	1844	Wexford	25 May 1875	101837
Mathew Kavanagh	1844	Wexford	31 Mar 1881	101837
Charles William	1892	Wexford	29-May-16	8593
Charles William	1892	Wexford	23-Aug-18	8593
Charles William	1895	Wexford	24-Jul-14	8593
Thomas Kehoe	1830	Wexford, Wexford	16 Nov 1858	19.512
James Kean	30 May 1815	Wexford, Wexford	23 Jan 1851	42.605
John Kehoe	10 Apr 1827	Wexford, Wexford	5 Apr 1851	62.736
John Kehoe	1827	Wexford, Wexford	27 Jan 1853	7662
Lawrance Kehoe	9 Mar 1829	Wexford, Wexford	3 Jun 1853	62.845
Lawrence Kehoe	1829	Wexford, Wexford	10 May 1854	59.645
John Kehoe	1848	Wexford	11 Dec 1875	1066
Arthur Kellett	1846	Wexford, Wexford	1 May 1873	82503
Arthur Kellett	1846	Wexford, Wexford	3 Feb 1869	82503
John Kelly	17 Jul 1820	Wexford, Wexford	25 Apr 1851	62.708
John Kelly	1820	Wexford, Wexford	10 Nov 1876	79.502
James Kelly	1826	Wexford, Wexford	18 Jul 1855	12771
James Kelly	1826	Wexford, Wexford	27 Aug 1857	12771
Patrick Kelly	1 May 1829	Wexford, Wexford	11 Feb 1853	62.842
Patrick Kelly	1829	Wexford, Wexford	28 Jun 1859	20.621
Michael Kelly	1844	Wexford, Wexford	5 Jun 1867	85.521
Michael Kelly	1844	Wexford, Wexford	31 Aug 1878	85521
Patrick Francis Kelly	1867	Wexford	22 Feb 1893	20903
Patrick Francis Kelly	1867	Wexford	16 Apr 1889	20903
William Kelly	1877	Wexford	8 Oct 1898	33580
William Kelly	1877	Wexford	21-May-00	33580
William Joseph Kelly	1877	Wexford	17-Nov-02	33580
Pierce Kendrick	1841	Wexford, Wexford	10 Feb 1874	30341
Peter King	4 May 1794	Wexford, Wexford	21 Jan 1851	42.686
John King	11 Oct 1823	Wexford, Wexford	12 Apr 1851	62.643
John King	1823	Wexford, Wexford	25 Aug 1851	5488
Joseph King	1 Jan 1831	Wexford, Wexford	2 Aug 1852	62.832
Joseph King	1831	Wexford, Wexford	24 May 1856	14953

Peter King	1836	Wexford, Wexford	13 Mar 1857	16477
Peter King	1836	Wexford, Wexford	11 Sep 1861	16477
George Leigh King	1854	Wexford	6 Apr 1883	3505
John Joseph Kirwan	1877	Wexford	27-May-05	39053
John Joseph Kirwan	1877	Wexford	21-Aug-09	39.053
John Joseph Kirwan	1877	Wexford	19-Apr-16	39.053
John James Lacey	1840	Wexford, Wexford	10 Apr 1861	10.096
John James Lacey	1840	Wexford, Wexford	23 Sep 1862	10.096
William Richard Lacy	1830	Wexford, Wexford	18 Oct 1852	7050
Simon Lambert	25 Mar 1790	Wexford, Wexford	7 Feb 1851	43.446
John Lambert	7 Mar 1814	Wexford, Wexford	23 Jan 1851	43.333
Thomas Lambert	15 Jun 1816	Wexford, Wexford	18 Feb 1851	43.096
Thomas Lambert	4 Mar 1820	Wexford, Wexford	19 Jul 1851	63.268
John Lambert	1823	Wexford, Wexford	12 Feb 1851	50.829
Thomas Lambert	1860	Wexford	9 Jun 1881	10112
Thomas Lambert	1860	Wexford	30 Jun 1890	10112
George Lambert	1865	Wexford	3-Apr-00	25447
George Lambert	1865	Wexford	2 Jul 1892	25447
Francis Larkin	1811	Wexford, Wexford	24 Feb 1851	50.89
Thomas Larkin	1837	Wexford, Wexford	11 Jan 1860	21.558
William Lodd	1847	Wexford	14 Aug 1880	8639
John Luinn	4 Nov 1818	Wexford, Wexford	26 Feb 1851	45.677
Patrick Luirk	15 Mar 1790	Wexford, Wexford	21 Feb 1851	45.681
John Maddock	1873	Wexford	30 Sep 1895	29609
John Maddock	1873	Wexford	23 Jan 1895	29609
John Maddock	1873	Wexford	5-Aug-02	29609
John James Malone	1826	Wexford, Wexford	9 Apr 1856	13521
John James Malone	1826	Wexford, Wexford	15 Nov 1859	13521
John James Malone	1826	Wexford, Wexford	7 Feb 1862	13521
James Mansfield	1805	Wexford, Wexford	26 Apr 1852	64.404
Patrick Marley	24 Dec 1818	Wexford, Wexford	1 Mar 1851	44.176
Patrick Marlow	1866	Wexford	21 Jun 1890	22639
Patrick Marlow	1866	Wexford	4 Feb 1893	22639
Patrick Marlow	1866	Wexford	29 Aug 1896	22639
Nicholas Marshall	1833	Wexford, Wexford	12 Jun 1862	26.062
John Marshall	1836	Wexford, Wexford	24 Dec 1862	27.262
Thomas Martin	1821	Wexford, Wexford	8 Jul 1863	62.143
Thomas Martin	8 Jun 1821	Wexford, Wexford	24 Jun 1851	64.226
Patrick Mc Cann	25 Apr 1825	Wexford, Wexford	8 Mar 1851	36.655
James Mc Namara	1844	Wexford	18 May 1881	102342
Charles McDonald	1830	Wexford, Wexford	30 Dec 1856	15.852
Michael McGrath	1847	Wexford, Wexford	13 May 1870	92625
Nicholas McGrath	1888	Wexford	21-Jul-13	7845
Nicholas McGrath	1888	Wexford	9-Mar-15	7845
Nicholas McGrath	1889	Wexford	12-Oct-17	7845

Name	Year	Place	Date	Number
Peter Joseph McGrath	1897	Wexford	3-Jun-21	14871
Peter Joseph McGrath	1897	Wexford	2-Jun-23	14871
Hugh McGuire	1832	Wexford, Wexford	21 Oct 1864	25636
Hugh McGuire	1832	Wexford, Wexford	26 Jul 1862	25636
James McNamara	1844	Wexford, Wexford	11 Nov 1871	94853
Nicholas Meaney	12 Mar 1799	Wexford, Wexford	4 Mar 1851	44.365
John Meaney	1 Nov 1821	Wexford, Wexford	7 Apr 1851	44.448
Walter Meyler	1833	Wexford, Wexford	7 Oct 1857	17.481
Walter Meyler	1833	Wexford, Wexford	30 Dec 1859	17.481
John Meylor	24 Jun 1811	Wexford, Wexford	17 Dec 1850	43.76
Thomas Molloy	1836	Wexford, Wexford	11 Oct 1858	1811
Willam Molloy	1863	Wexford	19 Feb 1896	22239
William Molloy	1863	Wexford, Wexford	5 Apr 1890	22239
William Molloy	1863	Wexford	15 Feb 1887	17968
John Moore	15 Jan 1817	Wexford, Wexford	3 Mar 1851	63.992
William Moore	10 Jul 1822	Wexford, Wexford	7 Oct 1853	64.453
John Moore	4 Mar 1824	Wexford, Wexford	27 Nov 1857	64.332
John Moore	1824	Wexford, Wexford	24 Apr 1856	59.684
James Moran	1862	Wexford	5 Oct 1883	13398
James Moran	1862	Wexford	23 Jan 1890	13398
Michael Joseph Moran	1888	Wexford	12-Apr-15	9043
Mathew Moran	1890	Wexford	18-Jul-18	42758
Matthew Moran	1890	Wexford	14-Sep-15	42758
Matthews Moran	1890	Wexford	9-Jul-13	42758
James Morris	22 Mar 1822	Wexford, Wexford	May 1851	44.517
Francis Morris	24 Sep 1824	Wexford, Wexford	4 Aug 1851	64.301
Francis Morris	1824	Wexford, Wexford	4 Feb 1854	9505
Patrick Morris	1830	Wexford, Wexford	11 Apr 1861	9913
Patrick Morris	21 Mar 1830	Wexford, Wexford	18 Feb 1856	64.512
Patrick Morris	1830	Wexford, Wexford	18 Nov 1856	64.525
Thomas Morris	1835	Wexford, Wexford	23 Feb 1866	82038
Thomas Morris	1835	Wexford, Wexford	20 Feb 1869	82038
Clement Morris	1837	Wexford, Wexford	1 Sep 1858	19.21
Clement Morris	1837	Wexford, Wexford	11 Jul 1868	19.21
John Morris	1847	Wexford, Wexford	31 Mar 1868	87619
John Morris	1847	Wexford, Wexford	6 May 1871	87619
Patrick Joseph Morris	1867	Wexford	29 Mar 1890	22249
Patrick Joseph Morris	1867	Wexford	11 Aug 1891	22249
Patrick Joseph Morris	1869	Wexford	3 Jan 1893	22249
Henry Mullen	1840	Wexford, Wexford	19 Aug 1862	26.505
John Murphy	1789	Wexford, Wexford	8 Jan 1858	44.487
Nicholas Murphy	6 Dec 1798	Wexford, Wexford	19 Feb 1851	44.225
Moses Murphy	3 Feb 1803	Wexford, Wexford	10 Feb 1851	44.51
John Murphy	24 Jun 1806	Wexford, Wexford	3 Mar 1851	44.44
John Murphy	9 Jun 1806	Wexford, Wexford	1 Apr 1851	63.623

Name	Date	Place	Date	Number
William Murphy	12 May 1811	Wexford, Wexford	15 Jan 1851	44.164
William Murphy	1811	Wexford, Wexford	16 Feb 1858	72.586
Robert Murphy	1818	Wexford, Wexford	8 Jul 1851	51.33
Robert Murphy	1818	Wexford, Wexford	17 Oct 1857	72.582
Robert Murphy	1818	Wexford, Wexford	14 Sep 1861	74.164
John Murphy	17 Dec 1820	Wexford, Wexford	21 Jun 1851	64.234
William Murphy	1820	Wexford, Wexford	12 Dec 1854	51.531
Thomas Murphy	6 Jan 1822	Wexford, Wexford	11 Feb 1852	64.38
John Murphy	1 Feb 1823	Wexford, Wexford	4 Aug 1851	51.38
John Murphy	3 Feb 1825	Wexford, Wexford	1 Apr 1857	64.183
Michael Murphy	1827	Wexford, Wexford	8 Nov 1852	7143
Micheal Murphy	1827	Wexford, Wexford	18 Feb 1854	9.767
John Murphy	16 Dec 1828	Wexford, Wexford	19 Nov 1852	64.39
Michael Murphy	1828	Wexford, Wexford	7 Feb 1851	63.926
William Murphy	1830	Wexford, Wexford	23 Mar 1852	69.757
William Murphy	16 Nov 1830	Wexford, Wexford	28 Jan 1851	64.046
William Murphy	1832	Wexford, Wexford	4 Oct 1860	16.223
William Murphy	1832	Wexford, Wexford	11 Feb 1857	16.223
John Murphy	1835	Wexford	12 May 1883	12539
John Murphy	1835	Wexford, Wexford	20 Nov 1868	89102
John Murphy	1838	Wexford, Wexford	24 Jun 1858	18.911
John Murphy	1838	Wexford, Wexford	27 Feb 1861	18.911
John Murphy	1839	Wexford	10 Sep 1877	102.053
Michael Murphy	1841	Wexford, Wexford	22 Jan 1863	27.435
Michael Murphy	1841	Wexford, Wexford	30 Oct 1867	27.435
James Murphy	1842	Wexford, Wexford	13 Mar 1867	31.792
James Murphy	1842	Wexford, Wexford	10 Aug 1864	31792
Lawrence Murphy	1843	Wexford, Wexford	20 Mar 1867	31.991
Lawrence Murphy	1843	Wexford, Wexford	30 Jan 1867	31.991
Lawrence Murphy	1843	Wexford, Wexford	6 Sep 1864	31.991
John Murphy	1844	Wexford, Wexford	23 Aug 1870	93.222
Francis Murphy	1846	Wexford	31 Dec 1874	98372
Francis Murphy	1846	Wexford, Wexford	6 Aug 1874	98372
Francis Murphy	1846	Wexford	11 Oct 1876	98372
William Murphy	1847	Wexford, Wexford	15 Feb 1870	92061
William Murphy	1847	Wexford	24 Mar 1875	92061
Michael William Murphy	1858	Wexford	4 Nov 1882	11979
Michael William Murphy	1858	Wexford	11 Jan 1886	11979
Nicholas Murphy	1865	Wexford	20 May 1887	18285
John Murphy	1873	Wexford	11 Oct 1895	29640
Patrick Murphy	1899	Wexford	20-Dec-17	11438
Patrick Murphy	1899	Wexford	8-Oct-18	11438
Patrick Parle Murphy	1899	Wexford	18-Dec-20	11438
Patrick Parle Murphy	1899	Wexford	8-Aug-23	11438
Joseph Neil	1835	Wexford, Wexford	12 Jul 1861	23.83

Name	Birth	Place	Date	Number
Joseph Neil	1835	Wexford, Wexford	12 May 1864	23.83
William Neill	25 Jun 1805	Wexford, Wexford	3 Mar 1851	44.796
John Joseph Neill	1836	Wexford, Wexford	26 Feb 1862	25.286
John Neill	1838	Wexford, Wexford	12 Jun 1863	26.061
John Neill	1838	Wexford, Wexford	22 Apr 1865	26.061
Matthew Neill	1846	Wexford	29 Mar 1870	89694
Matthew Neill	1846	Wexford, Wexford	13 Feb 1869	89694
Joseph Neils	1835	Wexford, Wexford	6 Feb 1873	97350
William Neville	25 Jan 1802	Wexford, Wexford	4 Jan 1851	44.661
Nicholas Neville	1832	Wexford, Wexford	21 Apr 1856	14652
Nicholas Joseph Neville	1832	Wexford, Wexford	13 Mar 1861	14652
Nicholas Joseph Neville	1832	Wexford	9 Jul 1885	14652
Michael Neville	1836	Wexford, Wexford	22 Jan 1857	16009
Michael Neville	1836	Wexford, Wexford	27 Aug 1862	16009
John North	22 Jun 1822	Wexford, Wexford	4 Aug 1851	64.796
Patrick Nowlan	1834	Wexford, Wexford	21 Sep 1867	34496
Patrick Nowlan	1834	Wexford, Wexford	29 Jul 1865	34496
Patrick Nowlan	1834	Wexford, Wexford	9 Nov 1869	34496
Owen O Brien	1804	Wexford, Wexford	20 Jan 1851	44.916
Owen O Brien	Jun 1804	Wexford, Wexford	20 Jan 1851	44.916
Edward O' Brien	1846	Wexford, Wexford	19 Jun 1868	88143
John O Connor	15 Dec 1822	Wexford, Wexford	22 Feb 1851	44.985
Mark Doyle O' Connor	1846	Wexford, Wexford	23 Sep 1872	88463
Mark Doyle O' Connor	1846	Wexford, Wexford	29 Sep 1868	88463
Mark Doyle O' Connor	1846	Wexford, Wexford	28 Aug 1868	88463
William O Connor	1874	Wexford	17 Nov 1898	33691
William O Connor	1874	Wexford	21-Nov-01	33691
John O'Brien	1832	Wexford, Wexford	5 May 1873	101688
John O'Brien	1832	Wexford, Wexford	12 Apr 1864	30.921
Thomas O'Connor	6 Jun 1808	Wexford, Wexford	11 Dec 1851	44.997
Mark Doyle O'Connor	1846	Wexford, Wexford	23 Feb 1867	84711
William O'Flaherty	1861	Wexford	19 Mar 1886	102764
Mathew O'Neil	1901	Wexford	6-Dec-23	17437
John O'Neill	1890	Wexford	7-Jul-13	42751
John O'Neill	1890	Wexford	21-Oct-15	42751
John O'Neill	1890	Wexford		42751
John Pender	1834	Wexford, Wexford	8 Oct 1862	26.765
John Pender	1834	Wexford, Wexford	14 Jan 1868	26765
John Penston	1835	Wexford	14 Nov 1876	101975
Thomas Pitt	1842	Wexford, Wexford	23 Jan 1867	84479
Thomas Pitt	1842	Wexford	9 Sep 1879	84479
George Thomas Pollard	1825	Wexford, Wexford	29 Aug 1852	6829
George Thomas Pollard	1825	Wexford, Wexford	7 Sep 1852	6829
John Power	1833	Wexford, Wexford	8 Apr 1856	14.611
John Power	1834	Wexford, Wexford	25 Jun 1858	14611

John Power	1834	Wexford, Wexford	9 Jun 1860	14611
Thomas Power	1849	Wexford, Wexford	2 Apr 1870	92356
James Rackard	1828	Wexford, Wexford	22 Nov 1851	52.337
John Radford	24 Jun 1816	Wexford, Wexford	17 Jan 1851	46.281
Michael Redmond	7 Nov 1811	Wexford, Wexford	4 Apr 1851	66.206
Michael James Redmond	1811	Wexford, Wexford	9 May 1854	10.297
William Redmond	1837	Wexford, Wexford	9 Apr 1873	83119
William Redmond	1837	Wexford, Wexford	11 Jul 1866	83119
David Redmond	1841	Wexford	8 Jul 1887	9314
David Redmond	1841	Wexford	28 Mar 1881	9314
William Redmond	1844	Wexford, Wexford	26 Jul 1865	34490
William Redmond	1844	Wexford, Wexford	27 Nov 1867	34490
Michael Redmond	1851	Wexford	21 Jun 1899	102893
Patrick Reigh	1813	Wexford, Wexford	25 Mar 1857	71.168
John Reigh	26 May 1818	Wexford, Wexford	6 Jan 1851	46.119
Walter Reigh	14 May 1819	Wexford, Wexford	18 Feb 1851	65.998
Patrick Reigh		Wexford, Wexford	1 Feb 1851	49.894
Joseph Reilly	14 Jan 1816	Wexford, Wexford	23 Jan 1852	69.31
Joseph Reilly	14 Jan 1816	Wexford, Wexford	23 Jan 1852	69.31
James Reilly	1823	Wexford, Wexford	30 Mar 1861	51.934
James Reilly	1823	Wexford, Wexford	28 Feb 1855	52.691
George Reilly	1839	Wexford, Wexford	26 Jun 1867	85675
James Reily	1823	Wexford, Wexford	2 Apr 1851	52.323
James Richards	1809	Wexford, Wexford	18 Jun 1859	71.199
James Richards	1809	Wexford, Wexford	30 Dec 1852	72.684
James Richards	11 Apr 1809	Wexford, Wexford	12 Mar 1851	46.045
Samuel Vicary	1836	Wexford	3 Sep 1880	8817
David Riches	1794	Wexford, Wexford	19 Apr 1851	52.314
Edmond Roach	1815	Wexford, Wexford	4 Sep 1858	100.356
Edmond Roach	10 Jun 1815	Wexford, Wexford	26 Apr 1851	46.347
James Roche	1796	Wexford, Wexford	31 Dec 1853	70.904
James Roche	29 Jun 1796	Wexford, Wexford	15 May 1851	46.104
Garret Roche	2 Jan 1809	Wexford, Wexford	13 Feb 1851	66.084
Nicholas Roche	1826	Wexford, Wexford	14 Nov 1855	13478
Nicholas Roche	1826	Wexford, Wexford	15 Mar 1860	21.94
Nicholas Roche	26 Feb 1826	Wexford, Wexford	11 Oct 1855	60.531
Michael Roche	1841	Wexford, Wexford	27 Jun 1862	26.149
Michael Roche	1841	Wexford, Wexford	27 Dec 1865	26.149
Patrick Roche	1873	Wexford	26-Nov-00	31510
Patrick Roche	1873	Wexford	11 Jul 1898	31510
Patrick Roche	1873	Wexford	1 Mar 1897	31510
Patrick Rone	1811	Wexford, Wexford	10 Feb 1851	52.319
John Ronie	16 Jun 1814	Wexford, Wexford	23 Jun 1851	46.342
Joseph Rooney	1839	Wexford, Wexford	24 Dec 1862	27.263
Joseph Rooney	1839	Wexford, Wexford	15 Nov 1865	27.263

Name	Birth	Place	Date	Number
James Ropiler	20 Mar 1814	Wexford, Wexford	22 Feb 1851	49.813
Jasper Rossiter	11 Jun 1819	Wexford, Wexford	10 Mar 1851	66.067
Walter Rossiter	1794	Wexford, Wexford	3 Mar 1851	52.408
John Rossiter	8 Jun 1810	Wexford, Wexford	9 Jan 1851	46.225
John Rossiter	14 Jan 1816	Wexford, Wexford	18 Feb 1851	46.348
Jasper Rossiter	1819	Wexford, Wexford	23 Mar 1854	59.603
Andrew George Rossiter	12 May 1823	Wexford, Wexford	23 Jan 1851	65.988
Joseph Rossiter	1831	Wexford, Wexford	25 Jul 1857	16354
Joseph Rossiter	1 Jun 1831	Wexford, Wexford	14 Sep 1852	69.349
Richard Rossiter	1835	Wexford, Wexford	20 Aug 1867	86009
James Rossiter	1840	Wexford, Wexford	20 Aug 1867	86010
Patrick Rossiter	1846	Wexford, Wexford	20 Dec 1866	84.242
Patrick Rossiter	1846	Wexford, Wexford	11 Jun 1867	85.588
Mark Rossiter	1850	Wexford, Wexford	22 Jan 1872	95151
James Rossiter	1862	Wexford	15 Dec 1891	103325
Thomas Rowe	15 Aug 1804	Wexford, Rowe	3 Jan 1851	46.15
Henry Rowe	18 Oct 1809	Wexford, Wexford	1 May 1851	46.155
Edward Rowe	4 Nov 1812	Wexford, Wexford	15 Jan 1851	46.227
Thomas Rowe	1820	Wexford, Wexford	30 Jan 1851	52.207
Edward Rowe	5 May 1825	Wexford, Wexford	30 Jun 1852	69.339
Thomas Rowe	1826	Wexford, Wexford	10 Oct 1864	60.486
Thomas Rowe	7 Jul 1826	Wexford, Wexford	16 Jul 1853	69.373
Patrick Ryan	1821	Wexford, Wexford	9 Aug 1855	12937
Patrick Ryan	21 Jul 1821	Wexford, Wexford	15 Mar 1857	66.189
Patrick Ryan	1821	Wexford, Wexford	21 Aug 1851	52.582
William Sarkin	1804	Wexford, Wexford	12 Sep 1856	71.702
Frederick Saunders	1889	Wexford	7-Nov-13	8050
John Scallan	20 Jan 1828	Wexford, Wexford	20 Aug 1851	66.776
Richard Scallan	1833	Wexford, Wexford	21 Jan 1863	27.434
Richard Scallan	1833	Wexford, Wexford	15 Nov 1865	27.434
George Scallan	1836	Wexford, Wexford	24 Oct 1861	24.517
George Scallan	1836	Wexford, Wexford	10 Aug 1864	24517
James Scallan	1838	Wexford	19 Jan 1885	14973
James Scallan	1838	Wexford, Wexford	14 Mar 1867	29.268
James Scallan	1838	Wexford, Wexford	14 Oct 1863	29.268
James Scallan	1838	Wexford, Wexford	14 Oct 1863	29.268
Nicholas Scallan	1839	Wexford, Wexford	2 Mar 1861	4821
Richard Clifford Seffares	1810	Wexford, Wexford	19 Sep 1852	1855
Michael Shannon	1811	Wexford, Wexford	28 Feb 1851	52.821
John Shea	1836	Wexford, Wexford	24 Oct 1864	16.796
John Shea	1836	Wexford, Wexford	11 May 1857	16.796
John Shea	1836	Wexford	28 Feb 1887	16796
Luke Sheil	1794	Wexford, Wexford	12 Feb 1851	52.776
Michael Sheil	1828	Wexford, Wexford	8 Mar 1851	53.022
Luke Sheil	10 Mar 1830	Wexford, Wexford	1 Jun 1851	67.062

Name	Birth	Place	Date	Number
Luke Sheil	1830	Wexford, Wexford	26 Sep 1860	23.039
James Shiel	1807	Wexford, Wexford	7 Apr 1851	52.835
Phillip Cullin Shipley	1815	Wexford, Wexford	27 Oct 1852	53.281
Nicholas Sinnet	22 Mar 1820	Wexford, Wexford	5 May 1852	67.375
James Sinnott	27 May 1807	Wexford, Wexford	3 Feb 1851	46.994
John Sinnott	10 Jan 1813	Wexford, Wexford	16 May 1851	46.367
Nicholas Sinnott	1820	Wexford, Wexford	30 Mar 1853	69.597
Nicholas Sinnott	1821	Wexford, Wexford	28 Jul 1857	17.177
Nicholas Sinnott	1821	Wexford, Wexford	22 May 1854	59.643
Nicholas Sinnott	15 Dec 1821	Wexford, Wexford	21 Nov 1850	66.405
Robert Smith	1806	Wexford, Wexford	24 Feb 1851	52.83
John Smith	1831	Wexford, Wexford	20 Jan 1868	87025
John Smith	1839	Wexford, Wexford	10 Apr 1867	32237
John Smith	1839	Wexford, Wexford	12 Oct 1864	32.237
James Smith	1840	Wexford, Wexford	27 Jun 1866	32.556
James Smith	1840	Wexford, Wexford	23 Nov 1864	32.556
John Smith	1868	Wexford	21 Jun 1897	1305
Richard Smith	1870	Wexford	7 Oct 1892	25065
Richard Smith	1870	Wexford	11 Apr 1892	25065
Richard Smith	1870	Wexford	15 Feb 1895	25065
Richard Smith	1870	Wexford	3 Apr 1895	25065
John Anselm Smith	1874	Wexford	16 Apr 1898	33030
John Anselm Smith	1874	Wexford	22 Sep 1899	33030
John Anselm Smith	1874	Wexford	17-Mar-02	33030
Eugene Squirl	1837	Wexford, Wexford	9 Dec 1858	19.615
Patrick Stafford	1843	Wexford, Wexford	17 Apr 1874	82921
Patrick Stafford	1843	Wexford, Wexford	9 Jun 1866	82.921
Patrick Stafford	1843	Wexford, Wexford	31 Dec 1869	82921
Francis Stone	1845	Wexford, Wexford	21 Apr 1874	91198
Francis Stone	1845	Wexford, Wexford	8 Oct 1869	91198
Francis Stone	1845	Wexford, Wexford	15 Nov 1872	91198
John Stone	1871	Wexford	7 Sep 1894	28260
James Storey	1842	Wexford, Wexford	5 Jun 1867	85.522
John Sweeny	1823	Wexford, Wexford	5 Jan 1857	17.921
John Sweeny	1823	Wexford, Wexford	3 Aug 1857	57.533
Edward Butler Tanner	1865	Wexford	22 Jan 1891	18934
Edward Butler Tanner	1865	Wexford	30 Sep 1889	18934
Edward Butler Tanner	1865	Wexford	9 Nov 1887	18934
James Walsh	20 Jul 1814	Wexford, Wexford	2 Feb 1851	48.831
John Walsh	21 Jun 1819	Wexford, Wexford	13 Jun 1851	48.977
Richen Walsh	1821	Wexford, Wexford	3 Jan 1852	54.176
John Walsh	1836	Wexford, Wexford	8 Mar 1866	82168
Patrick Walsh	1841	Wexford, Wexford	24 Jun 1863	28.582
Patrick Walsh	1841	Wexford	15 Jun 1897	31926
Patrick Walsh	1844	Wexford, Wexford	24 Jun 1863	28.582

Patrick Walsh	1849	Wexford	14 Sep 1885	7163
Patrick Walsh	1849	Wexford	23 Dec 1882	7163
Patrick Walsh	1849	Wexford	5 Sep 1879	7163
John Walsh	1859	Wexford	17 Sep 1883	13354
John Walsh	1859	Wexford	27 Oct 1890	13354
John Walsh	1859	Wexford	27 Dec 1892	13354
Thomas White	21 Dec 1813	Wexford, Wexford	25 Jul 1851	68.937
Matthew White	1838	Wexford, Wexford	16 Oct 1866	83773
William Whitmore	1812	Wexford, Wexford	10 Feb 1852	69.106
William Whitmore	1812	Wexford, Wexford	27 Aug 1852	6802
George Whitmore	1888	Wexford	8-Oct-20	10670
George Stanislaus	1892	Wexford	2-Mar-17	10670
George Stanislaus	1892	Wexford	22-Nov-18	10670
John Whitty	1808	Wexford, Wexford	28 Jan 1854	70.926
John Whitty	26 May 1808	Wexford, Wexford	11 Feb 1851	49.351
Robert Whitty	1839	Wexford, Wexford	21 Dec 1863	29.884
John Wickham	1814	Wexford, Wexford	19 Mar 1851	53.922
James Williams	25 Dec 1810	Wexford, Wexford	25 Mar 1851	68.81
Joseph Williams	1838	Wexford, Wexford	23 Jul 1862	26.35
Joseph Williams	1838	Wexford, Wexford	9 Aug 1865	26.35
Michael Williams	1838	Wexford	12 May 1875	101832
Martin Williams	1842	Wexford, Wexford	12 Sep 1866	83491
Martin Williams	1842	Wexford	29 Dec 1877	4340
Martin Williams	1842	Wexford	10 Dec 1877	4340
Martin Williams	1842	Wexford, Wexford	23 Aug 1865	34677
James Williams	1843	Wexford, Wexford	14 Jun 1866	82950
James Williams	1844	Wexford, Wexford	2 Jul 1866	83017
David Williams	1848	Wexford	10 Sep 1873	24.278
David Williams	1848	Wexford	30-Nov-04	16081
David Williams	1848	Wexford	21 Sep 1885	16081
James Williams	1848	Wexford	11-Nov-01	36522
Robert Joseph Wills	1902	Wexford	Sep-25	19259
John Percival Angrove	1838	New Ross, Wexford	1 Jun 1867	85473
John Percival Angrove	1838	New Ross, Wexford	9 Nov 1869	85473
Robert Armstrong	1843	New Ross, Wexford	7 Aug 1875	517
Thomas Aspel	1843	Fethard, Wexford	18 Mar 1870	92219
Thomas Aspel	1843	Fethard, Wexford	13 Apr 1874	92219
George Bardo	1827	Blackwater, Wexford	24 Dec 1852	7471
George Bardo	1827	Blackwater, Wexford	31 Jan 1853	7471
Richard Barren	25 Aug 1822	Shielbaygan, Wexford	18 Jan 1851	55.883
Robert Clifford Bassett	1832	New Ross, Wexford	16 Jun 1857	3799
Robert Clifford Bassett	1832	New Ross, Wexford	16 Nov 1855	3799
Robert Clifford Bassett	1832	New Ross, Wexford	6 Mar 1852	3799
Patrick Bent	1847	Faythe, Wexford	2 Apr 1870	92355

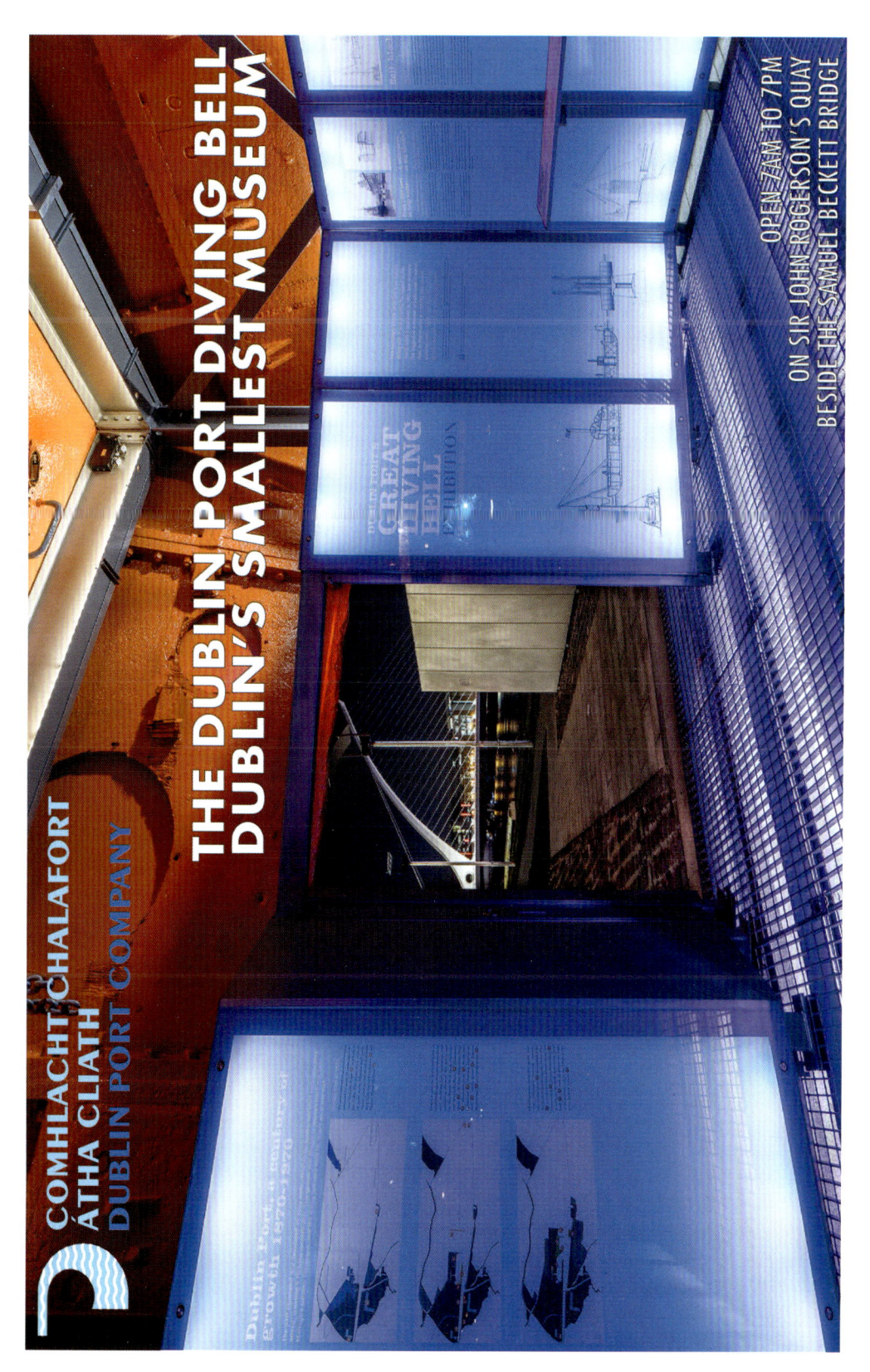

COMHLACHT CHALAFORT
ÁTHA CLIATH
DUBLIN PORT COMPANY

THE DUBLIN PORT DIVING BELL
DUBLIN'S SMALLEST MUSEUM

OPEN 7AM TO 7PM
ON SIR JOHN ROGERSON'S QUAY
BESIDE THE SAMUEL BECKETT BRIDGE

Appendix 6
Prominent Nineteenth-Century County Wexford Shipowners

Allen of Wexford
The Allen family of ship owners originated in Latimerstown, near Rathaspeck, County Wexford. In early directories the family are referred to as either merchants or maltsters. The first reference found to any of the Allens as ship owners was in 1820 when they were registered as owners of the **Mary & Betty**. Their ship-owning interests appear to have developed from that point and the Allen Brothers, Richard, William and Maurice, became owners of many famous Wexford sailing vessels. When the last of the family, Robert J. Allen, died on 24 November 1891, and was buried in the family burial ground at Rathaspeck, the firm of Allen ceased to trade.

Devereux of Wexford
The Devereux ship-owning company began when Richard Devereux of Ballyminane settled in Wexford town. He later married Christina Herron, a member of an old Wexford merchant and ship-owning family and it is through this connection that his interest in shipping may have been ignited. This marriage produced five children: four boys, Richard, John Thomas, Nicholas, James, and a girl whose name is unknown. James became a very successful grain merchant in Dublin, Nicholas established the Bishopswater Distillery and Richard and John Thomas became Devereux Brothers, the successful Wexford shipping company.

J T. Devereux, Wexford ship owner and philanthropist.
Courtesy, Presentation Convent, Wexford.

Of the four brothers, Richard was said to be the keenest business man and, apart from the shipping interests, he employed many in his maltings in Enniscorthy, New Ross and Wexford and built many of the malt houses that can still be seen in Wexford today. He amassed a great fortune that he used to promote Catholic education and gave vast amounts to charities and to the Catholic Church. For this, he was honoured as a Knight of St Gregory. John Thomas, the other 'shipping brother' became an M.P. and represented the county in Parliament for a considerable time.

Richard Devereux died 6 March 1883, leaving all of his fortune to local charities. John Thomas died 31 December 1885. He had married three times, but only had two children, a son and a daughter, with his first wife. His son, the Rev. John Thomas was an Oblate Father based in Bath, Somerset and his daughter became Mrs Hodgins. His fortune was bequeathed to her children.

Graves of New Ross
The Graves family originated in Thomastown, Co. Kilkenny. Anthony Graves, a banker from that town moved his family to New Ross in 1805 and established himself as a

merchant. His son, William carried on the family business and by 1815 was engaged in the emigrant trade from New Ross to Quebec, in partnership with his brother in law a Mr Elly. By 1825 the company owned four ships on that run. That company ceased trading in 1827 and Mr Graves founded another company with a Mr Watson. Graves moved their headquarters to Waterford in 1851.

William had four sons, Anthony Elly Graves, Samuel Robert Graves, William Cameron Graves and James Palmer Graves. James Palmer went to Savannah, Georgia, where the company already had business interests. Samuel Robert expanded the business to Liverpool, building a successful shipping fleet of over forty sailing vessels. He was Mayor of Liverpool in 1861 and was elected as M.P. for Liverpool in the 1865 General Election. He remained in that position until his death in 1873. He was a director of the London & North Western Railways and of the Pacific Steam Navigation Co. and looked after the Graves Company fleet of over 50 ships sailing out of Liverpool. Anthony Elly Graves looked after the family's business in New Ross.

Gafney of Wexford
The Gafney family ship-owning interests appear to have been established by William J. Gafney, who was Postmaster in Wexford Town in the mid-1800s. He was also a member of Wexford Harbour Commissioners and, at the time of his death in February 1884, was chairman of that organization. His wife, Cecilia died the following year in October 1885. The Gafney holdings were then passed to their three daughters, Mary, Margaret, and Angela. Angela Gafney died 3 November 1897, followed by Mary on 23 May 1900. Margaret married Thomas O'Reilly, a draper, of Main St. Wexford. All died without issue. In 1896 the company sold off its last three ships: **Glynn** and **Caledonia** were purchased by John E. Barry, and the **Charles Walker** by Captain Hutchinson, Harbour Commissioner. The company was taken over by William Hutchinson, formerly manager of the Gafney Company.

Schooner **Dispatch** of Gloucester off Ballyhack, Co. Wexford, early 1900s.

A sailing cot at Wexford Woodenworks.
Capuchin Archives, Ireland.

Glossary of Nautical Terms

A

AB: Able bodied seaman. A qualified seaman.
Aback: The position of the sails when the wind is on the forward side of them.
Abaft: Behind, generally used of things that are in the ship.
Abeam: When an object is about right angles to the ship.
A'lee: The helm is pressed down to the lee side of the ship.
Amidships: The middle section of a ship.
Athwart: Across the ship.

B

Backing wind: A wind that changes course against the sun.
Backstays: The aftermost stays of a mast to the side of the ship, to resist the pressure of the wind from astern.
Barque: A sailing ship with three or more masts, with the after mast rigged fore and aft.
Barquentine: A sailing vessel with three or more masts, with a square-rigged foremast and fore and aft rigged main-mizzen or any other masts.
Battens: Longs strips of wood or metal used for fastening hatch covers.
Beam: The width of a vessel.
Beating to windward: Sailing against the wind by tacking.
Belay: To make fast any running rope.
Belly of a sail: The inside of the curve of a sail when filled with wind.
Bend: To fasten.
Bight: The middle part of a rope.
Binnacle: The case for the ship's compass.
Block: A wooden pulley with sheaves to increase the purchase power of a rope.
Board: Each tack when a sailing ship is beating against the wind.
Bollards: Small stanchions for making ropes fast to.
Boom: The spar at the foot of a fore and aft sail or studding sail.
Bowline: A knot to form a fixed eye on a rope to hold the leach of a square sail well forward.
Bowsprit: The spar projecting out over the bow.
Braces: The ropes used for trimming the yards to the wind.
Brig: A two-masted square-rigged ship with a fore and aft sail on the gaff and a boom to the main mast.
Brigantine: A two masted vessel with a fully square rigged foremast and at least two sails on the main mast, a square topsail and a gaff sail mainsail behind the mast. The main mast is the second and the taller of the two masts.
Bulkhead: The internal walls of a ship.
Bulwarks: The walls, when solid, around the outside of a ship.
Bunkers: The spaces in a ship where fuel is stowed, or the fuel itself.

C

Cable: A strong rope or a chain, attached to the anchor. Also a measurement, a cable is 100 fathoms or 600 feet.
Capstan: A vertical devise for hauling in the anchor chain.
Carry away: To break something, especially aloft.
Carvel: When the planking on a ships side is laid edge to edge as opposed to being clinker built.
Clew line: The rope for lifting the corners of a square sail to the yards.
Clinker: Clinker built is when the ship's planking is over lapped.
Close hauled: Sailing as close to the wind as possible.
Counter: The overhanging stern of a ship.
Cringle: An eye in the bolt rope of a sail.
Cutter: A single mast sailing ship.

D

Dandy: A small sailing vessel with two masts, a small mizzen is aft of the rudder post.
Davits: Cranes used for lowering ship's boats into the water.
Dead eye: Circular blocks for securing the lower rigging of a sail.
Derrick: A spar used for lifting weights.
Driver (or **Spanker**): The aftermost, fore and aft sail on a square rigged vessel.
Dunnage: Material used to pack a cargo into a hold so that it is not damaged.

F

Fall: Part of a tackle on which the men haul.
Fetch: To reach.
Flotsam: Floating articles, thrown over the side.
Fluke: The point of an anchor.
Flying Jib: A headsail set outside the jib.
Fore and Aft: Lengthways in a ship.
Forecastle: Crew accommodation at the front end of the ship. Also the forward end of the upper deck.
Foremast: Where a ship has more than one mast, the foremast is the first mast from the bow.
Forepeak: The space at the bottom of the bow.
Foresail: The lowest square sail on the foremast of a schooner or the triangular sail set on the forestay of a cutter, yawl or ketch.
Freeboard: The height of a ship's deck above the waterline.

G

Gaff: A spar to take the head of a fore and aft sail.
Gaff topsail: A sail set over the gaff.
Gangway: A means of communication over the deck or on to the ship from the shore.
Gimbals: Concentric rings used to keep compasses or lamps upright independent of the motion of the ship.

Ground swell: A heavy rolling sea in shallow water.
Gunwale: The edge or rim of a boat's side.
Guy: A rope fixed to steady something.

H

Half deck: The living place of the apprentices on a sailing ship.
Halyards: Ropes for hoisting yards or gaffs.
Hawse-pipes. The holes in a ship's bow that the anchor chain passes through.
Hobbler: Boatmen who rowed out to incoming vessels to guide them into port.
Hulk: A ship, generally dismantled and used for harbour work only.
Hull: The body of the ship, without upperworks or rigging.

I

Irons, **In**: The condition of a ship in tacking when she heads into the wind and will not fall off any either way.

J

Jetsam: Articles from a ship which are sunk in the water.
Jib: A triangular headsail.
Jib-boom: An extension of the bowsprit to take the headsails.
Jury: Anything makeshift that is made up on a ship. i.e.jury rigged.

K

Ketch: The name is derived from 'Catch' and is a small two-masted sailing ship, rigged fore and aft, whose main mast is taller than the mizzen or aft mast.
Keel: The backbone of a ship.
Keelson: An internal keel above the timbers, bolted down to the keel itself to add strength.
Knight-head: Two stout timbers, each side of the stem to which the bowsprit is fixed.
Knot: A nautical mile per hour.

L

Landfall: The first sight of land from a ship, from the sea.
Leach: The side edge of a sail.
Leeward: The ground lost by a sailing vessel drifting to leeward of her course.
Life-line: Line running along the deck of a ship when men were liable to be washed overboard in bad weather.
Lighter: A barge without sails.
List: The inclination of a ship.

M

Mainmast: The principal mast on a ship, generally the second.
Manifest: A complete list of a ship's cargo.
Marlin-spike: A small short pointed spike used in splicing ropes and wires.

Martingale: Also known as a Dolphin Striker it is a perpendicular bar under the bowsprit to prevent upward strain.
Missing stays: Failing to come right round across the wind when a ship is tacking.
Mizzen. The third mast in a vessel or the second in a two masted vessel in which it is much shorter than the main mast.

N

Nautical mile: 6082.66 feet (about 1.2 land miles).

O

Oakum: Old rope untwisted and used for caulking and other similar tasks.
Offing: The distance from the land.

P

Painter: The rope used for securing a boat.
Pawls: Hinged pieces of metal to prevent a capstan from running backwards.
Pay out: To slacken a rope.
Peak: The outer end of a gaff.
Pendant: A long narrow flag, pronounced and often incorrectly spelt 'Pennant'.

Q

Quarter: The after end of a ship's side.
Quartermaster: Rating in charge of the steering of a vessel.

R

Ratlines: Short lines between the shrouds to make a ladder for going aloft.
Reef: To reduce the area of a sail by rolling up one part of it.
Ribs: The timber frames of a ship.
Rig, to: To fix anything up.
Roads: An anchorage outside of port e.g. Tenby Roads.

S

Schooner: A fore and aft rigged vessel with two or more masts of approximately equal height.
Scud: To run right before the wind.
Sextant: An instrument to determine the sun's angle with the horizon to ascertain position.
Sheepshank: A hitch used to shorten a rope temporarily.
Ship: A sailing vessel with three or more masts, square rigged on all of them.
Shrouds: The rope running from the mast head to the ship's sides to support the masts.
Sloop: A single masted ship with a short bowsprit or none at all and fewer headsails than a cutter.
Snow: A two masted square rigged vessel similar to a brig but with her spanker on an auxiliary trysail mast.

Splice: To join two ropes by intertwining their strands.
Spanker: see **Driver**
Spoke: Communicating with a passing ship or a signal station either by loud hailer or semaphore.
Stays: Ropes used for supporting masts.
Steerage: Part of the tween decks before the cabin. The part of a ship providing the cheapest accommodation for passengers.
Stem: The principal timber in a ship's bow.
Step, to: To erect a mast.
Strake: A continuous line of planking from stem to stern.
Studding sail: A light quadrilateral sail set outside a square sail.

T

Tack: To put a ship across the direction of the wind.
Tonnage or tons burden: A measurement to indicate the cargo carrying capacity of a ship on which dues have been paid.
Tonnage gross: A method used by shipbuilders to calculate the cost of building a ship per ton
Tonnage registered: A measurement used to charge dues.
Taffrail: The rail across the stern of a ship.
Truck: The extreme top of a mast.

W

Windlass. A rotating machine at the forward part of a ship, used mainly for raising and lowering the anchor, often worked by the capstan.

Y

Yardarm. The end of a yard.
Yards. The horizontal spars on which the square sails are set.

The schooner 'Wave' of Wexford

Bibliography

Publications

Anderson, Ernest B. *Sailing Ships of Ireland*. Dublin: Morris, 1951.

Anderson, John. *Coastwise Sail*. Percival Marshall & Company Ltd. 1948.

Bartlet, John. *Ships of North Cornwall*. Tabb House, 1995.

Benn, Martin W. *Closing Down Sail*. Preston 2011.

Bennett, Douglas. *Schooner Sunset: The Last British Sailing Coasters*. Chatham, 2003.

Bouquet, Michael. *Westcountry Sail: Merchant Shipping, 1840-1960*. David and Charles, 1971.

Bourke, Edward J. *Shipwrecks of the Irish Coast*. 3 vols (1994-2000).

Campbell-Jones, Susan. *Welsh Sail: A Pictorial History*. Gomer Press, 1976.

Eames, Aled. *The Twilight of Welsh Sail*. Univerity of Wales, 1984.

Forde, Frank. *Maritime Arklow*. Glendale Press, 1988.

Greenhill, Basil. *The Merchant Schooners* 2 vols. Percival Marshall, 1951-57.

Greenhill Basil and Ann Giffard. *The Merchant Sailing Ship: A Photographic History*. Praeger, 1970.

Greenhill, Manning, and Samuel F. Manning. *The evolution of the Wooden Ship*. London: Batsford, 1988.

Griffiths, George. *Chronicles of the County Wexford*. Printed at the *Watchman* Office, Enniscorthy, 1877.

Harland, John and Mark Myers. *Seamanship in the Age of Sail: An Account of Shiphandling of the Sailing Man-O-War, 1600-1860*. Conway, 2012.

Hughes, Emrys and Aled Eames. *Portmadog Ships*. Gwynedd Archive Services 1975.

Hughes, Henry. *Immortal sails: A story of a Welsh port and some of its ships*. T. Stephenson, 1969.

Irish, Bill and Andrew Kelly. *Two Centuries of Tall Ships in Waterford*. Rectory Press, 2011.

Jones, Robert. *Reuben Chappell - Pierhead Painter*. Halsgrove, 2006.

Jones, Tristan. *A steady trade: a boyhood at sea*. The Bodley Head, 1982.

Laxton, Edward. *The Famine Ships: The Irish exodus to America, 1846-51*. Bloomsbury, 1996.

McCaughan, Michael. *Sailing the Seaways: Historic Maritime Photographs from the Ulster Folk and Transport Museum, 1864-1939*. Friars Bush Press, 1991.

MacGregor, David R. *The Schooner: Its Design and Development from 1600 to the Present*. Naval Institute Press, 2001.

Mahon, John. *Kate Tyrrell: ''Lady Mariner': the story of the extraordinary woman who sailed the Denbighshire Lass*. Basement Press, 1995.

Nurse, James. *The Nurse Family of Bridgewater and Their Ships*. Carmania Press, 1999.

O'Leary, Jack and Nicky Rossiter (author). *Maritime Wexford: the life of an Irish port town*. History Press, 2014.

Power, John. *A Maritime History of County Wexford* 3 vols. Olinda Publications, Kilmore Quay.

Rees, Jim and Liam Charlton. *Arklow, last stronghold of sail: Arklow ships 1850-1985*. Arklow Historical Society, 1986.

Ritchie, Carson. *Q Ships*. Terence Dalton, 1985.
Roche, Richard and Tom Williams. *Tales of the Wexford Coast*, with a list of shipwrecks and groundings. Duffry Press, 1993.
Rossiter, Nicholas. *Wexford Port: a history*. Wexford Council of Trade Unions, 1989.
Scott, Richard J. *Irish Sea Schooner Twilight: The Last Years of the Western Seas Traders*. Black Dwarf Publications, 2012.
Simper, Robert. *British Sail*. David & Charles, 1977
Simper, Robert. *East Coast Sail: Working Sail, 1850-1970*. David & Charles, 1972.
Simper, Robert. *North East Sail*. David and Charles, 1976.
Simper, Robert. *Scottish Sail*. David and Charles, 1974.
Slade, William James, and Basil Greenhill. *West Country Coasting Ketches*. Harper Collins, 1974.
Starkey, H.F. *Schooner Port: Two Centuries of Upper Mersey Sail*. Hesketh, 1983.
Underhill, Harold A. *Deep-Water Sail*. Brown, Son & Ferguson, 1988.
Underhill, Harold A. *Masting and Rigging: the Clipper Ship and Ocean Carrier, with authentic plans*. Brown Son and Ferguson, 1965.
Underhill, Harold A. *Sailing Ships Rigs and Rigging*. Brown, Son & Ferguson Ltd, Glasgow, 1948.
Williams, David. *Tall Ships on Camera. Photographs of David E. Smith*. 1992.

Other printed sources:

Newspapers
Wexford Constitution (April 1877).
County Wexford Free Press 'Mariner Column', 2000-2017.
Free Press, Wexford. 'At the Crossroads' column, 1930-1950s. Reminiscences of Captain James Murphy and Captain Nicholas Saunders, both of whom served on the **Saltee** and other Wexford ships as ABs in their early seafaring careers.
Wexford People, various issues.

Perodicals
Sea Breezes, the Ship Lovers' Digest. Various editions, 1950s-1980s.
Ships Monthly, 1967: Vol. 1, No. 11 and Vol. 2, No. 6 Articles by Richard J. Scott.

Unpublished and manuscript sources
Log of the **Alert**. Courtesy of Eamon Doyle, Athlone.
Logs of the **Alert** and the **Fame**. Courtesy of Wexford County Archives.
Log of the **Dispatch** of Wexford (in private keeping).
Ships' Articles, National Archives, Bishop St. Dublin.
Shipping Registers, Wexford County Archives.
Shipping Registers, Customs and Excise, Rosslare Harbour.

Online sources
Ancestry.com
Books Boxes and Boats: Maritime and Historical Research Service (for Lloyd's Shipping Registers, 1764 to 1899) www.maritimearchives.co.uk
CLIP Crew Lists Index Project: www.crewlist.org.uk/
Irish Shipwrecks Database: www.irishshipwrecks.com/
Lloyd's Register of Ships online: https://hec.lrfoundation.org.uk/archive-library/lloyds-register-of-ships-online
New Ross Street Focus: https://visitnewross.ie/listings/new-ross-street-focus-new-ross/
Through Mighty Seas website: www.mightyseas.co.uk/
Welsh Newspapers Online: newspapers.library. wales/

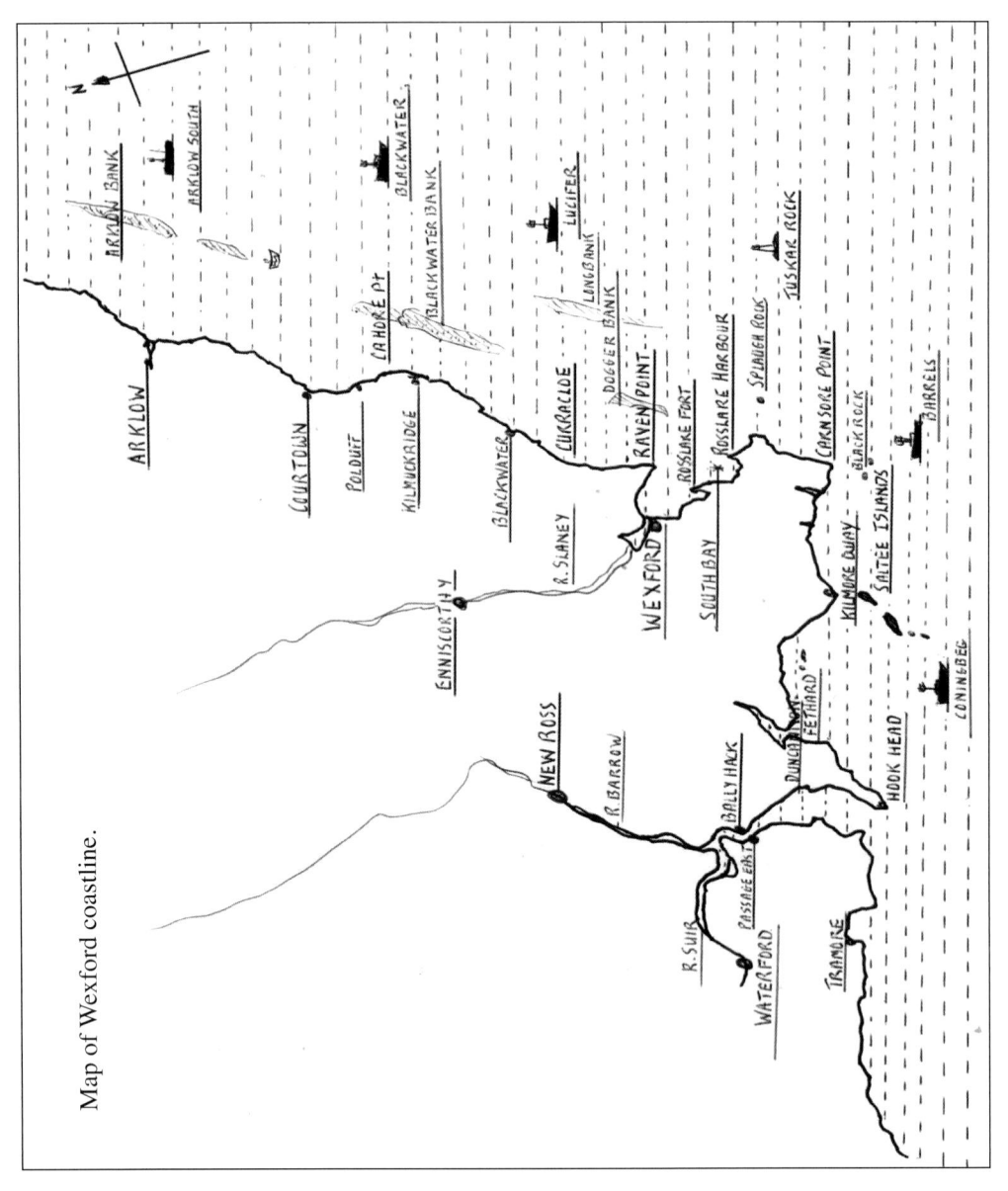

Map of Wexford coastline.

- SKIFF
- SLANEY GABBARD
- OLD WEXFORD COT
- WEXFORD SAILING COT
- SNOW
- BERMUDA KETCH
- FISHING SMACK
- 3 MASTED FORE & AFT SCHOONER
- SAILING LIFEBOAT
- 3 MASTED TOPS'L SCHOONER